CUBA: FROM CONQUISTADOR TO CASTRO

Cuba

From Conquistador to Castro

Geoff Simons

St. Martin's Press
New York

St. Martin's Press, Scholarly and Reference Division,
175 Fifth Avenue, New York, N.Y. 10010

First published in the United States of America in 1996

Printed in Great Britain

ISBN 0–312–12822–3

Library of Congress Cataloging-in-Publication Data
Simons, G. L. (Geoffrey Leslie), 1939–
Cuba : from conquistador to Castro / Geoff Simons.
p. cm.
Includes bibliographical references and index.
ISBN 0–312–12822–3
1. Cuba—History. 2. Spaniards—Cuba—History. 3. Cuba–
–Relations—United States. 4. United States—Relations—Cuba.
5. Cuba—History—Revolution, 1959—Social Aspects. 6. Political
atrocities—Cuba—History. I. Title.
F1776.S55   1996
972.91'00461—dc20   95–14918
                                                         CIP

To Jasmine

We are an army of light, and nothing shall prevail against us. It remains for us to do what we know we have to do, and it will be done, because everything that must pass will pass, and in those places where the sun is darkened, it will overcome.

José Martí

Contents

Contents

Appendices

List of Figures

List of Tables

Preface

The United States is today committing crimes against humanity. This is quite literally true, whether one considers the traditional crime category of acts *mala in se* (wrong in themselves), or the manifest violation of international law.

In the cases of both Cuba and Iraq the US government is denying civilian populations access to food and medicine – to the point that the incidence of disease and malnutrition is substantially increasing in Cuba, and that hundreds of thousands of people (100,000 children per annum) are being starved to death in Iraq.

The cases are different. The United States strives to deny Cuba food and medicine via the mechanism of domestic legislation, most recently the Cuban Democracy Act of 1992. It denies Iraq food and medicine via the mechanisms of freezing Iraqi assets and prohibiting Iraqi oil sales, so denying Iraq the essential revenues to purchase the foodstuffs and medicines that are nominally exempted from UN sanctions resolutions.

The results are the same in the two cases. The United States is in violation of the Geneva Convention (Protocol I, Article 54(3)(b)) in using starvation as a political weapon against civilian populations. Thus Ramsey Clark, former US Attorney-General, recently declared in interview (February 1995):

As a lawyer . . . I see the blockade as a crime against humanity, in the Nüremburg sense, as a weapon of mass destruction. The blockade is a weapon for the destruction of the masses, and it attacks those segments of society that are the most vulnerable . . . infants and children, the chronically ill, the elderly and emergency medical cases.

This is the stark fact, the moral bankruptcy, behind all US talk of democracy and human rights.

GEOFF SIMONS

Acknowledgements

When my daughter Colette went on a study tour of Cuba in 1992, an old man invited her into his tiny home. As she was leaving, this man, who owned virtually nothing, gave her a precious item from off his wall: a small and faded picture of Che Guevara. I am grateful to Colette for her testimony and for her research: and again to Christine for her unstinting support.

Thanks are due to Alexandra McLeod at the United Nations Information Centre (18 Buckingham Gate, London SW1E 6LB) for providing UN resolutions, speeches and reports that are relevant to the Cuba Question.

I am grateful also for permission to reproduce copyright material: an extract (my page 79) from John Cummins' translation of the Columbus journal (*The Voyage of Christopher Columbus*, Weidenfeld & Nicolson, 1992, pp. 108–9); the map 'Archaeological Exploration in Cuba, to July 1919' (my Figure 2.1) from M. R. Harrington, *Cuba Before Columbus*, Museum of the American Indian, Heye Foundation, New York, 1921; and an extract (my Appendix 6) from Fidel Castro's reconstruction of his courtroom speech (16 October 1953), 'History Will Absolve Me', as translated and published as an appendix in Marta Harnecker, *Fidel Castro's Political Strategy*, Pathfinder Press, New York, 1987, pp. 77–152.

GEOFF SIMONS

Introduction

In January 1959 Fidel Castro's Cuban Rebel Army succeeded in overthrowing the hated dictator General Fulgencio Batista. A frantic exodus then ensued: police chiefs, torturers, corrupt officials and gangsters – carrying what loot they could – rushed to leave the country; while former Cuban exiles began returning to begin the task of building a new society. For a brief time the United States appeared uncertain how to react. In the closing phase of the Batista tyranny Washington had pragmatically withdrawn its support from the doomed dictator – after sustaining him with weapons, funds and ideological support over many years. But the American dilemma did not last long. It soon became clear what sort of society the new Cuban government intended to create. Cuba would no longer be a milch cow, brothel and gambling den for the rich and powerful: for the first time Cuba would emerge as a sovereign nation in which the Cuban people would take control over their own lives. It did not take Washington long to conclude that such an alarming development – a possible model for the wider world – was completely intolerable. In 1959 there were already plans afoot for the violent overthrow of the Castro regime.

The Cuban Revolution brought an unprecedented economic and social transformation. In the teeth of sustained and virulent US hostility, a revolutionary programme of change was accomplished:

- the rich land-owning classes (including many absentee landlords and foreign companies) were expropriated, with the land then distributed to the poor peasants and agricultural labourers;

- a massive programme of public works brought new roads, hospitals, clinics, schools and electrification to the rural areas. An ambitious literacy campaign was launched which quickly brought illiteracy levels down to those of the developed world. Care was taken to end the traditional divides between urban and rural life;

- the formalised system of racial apartheid was instantly abolished;

- for the first time comprehensive measures were introduced to guarantee the equality of women. The new provisions included free contraception, 6–9 months' maternity leave on full pay and a rapidly expanding network of childcare centres;

- a free health care system was introduced, superior to any in the Third World and rivalling many of those in developed countries. A 24-hour family doctor system was developed, specialist clinics were established, and support was given to basic biomedical research that today, in some particulars, leads the world;

- a universal system of free education, from primary schools to universities, was developed – producing teachers, doctors, engineers and scientists in numbers that were unprecedented for the Third World and even comparable *per capita* with most of the developed countries.

From its earliest days the Cuban Revolution succeeded in demonstrating that a progressive social philosophy could bring immense social and economic benefits to the broad mass of the people, once a nation's resources had been prised out of the grip of exploiters and profiteers interested only in the financial enrichment of socially irresponsible élites. This simple fact had a potent and vital relevance to a modern world in which the governments of the richest countries remain eternally incapable of meeting the basic needs of their peoples; and in which the bulk of poor countries continue to suffer under the financial and economic conditions stipulated by global finance capitalism.

In such circumstances it was inevitable that the United States, as the principal protector of world financial privilege, would remain bitterly hostile to what the Cuban Revolution represented and what it continues to represent today. Chapter 1 profiles the main tool that Washington has continuously used against the Cuban people: the 35-year-long economic embargo (or, more properly, 'blockade') designed to destroy the Cuban economy and so undermine the Castro regime. Some indication is given of the character of the society that Washington – heartened by the collapse of the Socialist bloc – is so intent upon destroying. The response of Cuba, under conditions of virtual siege, to what Fidel Castro had dubbed 'the special period in peacetime' is profiled, with attention also to the 'migration problem' that has so confused the Clinton administration. *The US government – in gross violation of international law – does all it can to plunge the Cuban people yet deeper into destitution, to the point that it struggles to deny them food and medical supplies, and then incarcerates in razor-wire concentration camps those Cubans who flee from the US-imposed privations.*

The scale of the international response to the US economic blockade of Cuba is also indicated: from the protests of non-governmental groups, through the unwillingness of other capitalist governments to agree the terms of Washington's Cuban Democracy Act, to the resounding United Nations condemnations of US policy. The United States has remained indifferent to the mounting international rejection of the trade embargo, even to the point that the White House chief of staff Leon Panetta can suggest that a total military blockade of Cuba is an option to consider (*The Daily Telegraph*, London, 22 August 1994); and to the point that Jesse Helms, chairman of the US Senate Foreign Relations Committee, can propose (February 1995) fresh legislation* designed to cripple yet further the Cuban economy, at the same time declaring: 'Let me be clear. Whether Castro leaves Cuba in a vertical or horizontal position is up to him and the Cuban people. But he must and will leave Cuba. It's time to tighten the screws, not loosen them.'

In this context of New World oppression it is important to appreciate the background to the modern Cuba Question, to remember that Cuba suffered four centuries of slavery under Spanish colonialism before falling under the lengthening shadow of US imperialism. Chapters 2–4 profile the imperial impact of Spain on Cuba – from the early genocide perpetrated by the Christian conquistadores to the Cuban struggles for independence. Chapter 5 charts the final expulsion of the Spanish colonialists, evicted from Cuba as much by Cubans struggling for independence as by invading US forces intent upon ensuring that the island remained subservient to the capitalist interest.

The American domination of Cuba began in 1898 and ended in 1959, an abrupt termination that Washington refused to tolerate. The US control over the island had been sustained by an unholy mix of military invasion, military occupation, economic pressure, propaganda, and support for successive business-oriented tyrants. Something of this dismal catalogue of *realpolitik* machination and brutality is conveyed in Chapter 6. It is useful to remember what this period meant in terms of profiteering, gangsters consorting with corrupt politicians, US support for military 'butchers', American legislation (for example, the notorious Platt Amendment) designed to subvert Cuban independence, and the destitution and miseries of a wretched Cuban people exploited by homegrown and foreign (mainly American) profiteers. Chapter 6 profiles also the emergence of Fidel Castro, a vigorous and imaginative young lawyer who entertained the alarming notion that the Cuban people had more right to control their own

---

*The Cuban Liberty and Democratic Solidarity (Libertad) Act.

destinies and have access to their island's resources than did American gangsters, domestic élites and US capitalists.

The Batista dictatorship had failed Washington. The corrupt officials, the police torturers, the suppression of popular opinion – none of this had troubled the US strategists, until it had become clear that the dictator, once fêted and bemedalled in Washington, was losing his grip. Batista had served the United States but had then been tossed into history (though perhaps his final looting of the Cuban treasury smoothed his later years). Now it was necessary for the United States to reassert its hegemony in the Caribbean – which it attempted to do by (Chapter 7) sponsoring economic embargo, propaganda, a fresh military invasion, assassination attempts (and some successful assassinations), and various other terrorist plans. Such initiatives, inclining the Cuban government to suspect US hostility, pushed Cuba further into the embrace of the Socialist bloc – which in turn led to what has become known as the Cuban Missile Crisis.*

Over the years and decades that followed, Cuba succeeded in consolidating many of its social gains, though circumstance – mainly US hostility – had rendered the island heavily dependent on aid deals and favourable trade arrangements with the Socialist bloc. The progressive collapse (late 1980s/early 1990s) of this substantial source of support plunged Cuba into the unprecedented ideological and trade isolation of the Special Period. Washington had contrived, through the usual combination of terrorism and military means (Chapter 7), to secure a clutch of sympathetic Latin American governments. Cuba, at the heart of the Caribbean, has remained defiant. It remains to be seen whether the policy changes being forced upon Cuba by superpower malevolence, illegality and capitalist greed will finally expunge the vision of the Cuban Revolution.

---

*To the Cubans, who refer to this 1962 event as the October Crisis, there was much more at issue than missiles. The Cubans were suffering from economic embargo, black propaganda and terrorist attacks; and there was evidence of a fresh US-sponsored invasion in preparation.

Part I
New World Oppression

1 The Special Period

This action [cancelling US imports of Cuban sugar] amounts to economic sanctions against Cuba. Now we must look ahead to other moves – economic, diplomatic and strategic.

President Dwight D. Eisenhower, 6 July 1960

No State may use or encourage the use of economic, political, or any other type of measures to coerce another State in order to obtain from it the subordination of the exercise of its sovereign rights...

Charter (Article 16) of the Organisation of American States, adopted 1948

No State may use or encourage the use of economic, political, or any other type of measures to coerce another State in order to obtain from it the subordination of the exercise of its sovereign rights...

Declaration of the United Nations, adopted in 1970 without dissent

Whether Castro leaves Cuba in a vertical or horizontal position is up to him and the Cuban people. But he must and will leave Cuba.

Senator Jesse Helms, Chairman of US Senate Foreign Relations Committee, 12 February 1995

For three and a half decades the United States (today's population 240 million) has striven to overthrow the Castro regime in Cuba (population 11 million). Many different tactics have been used: industrial sabotage, agricultural arson, assassination, threat of assassination, military invasion, manipulation of regional bodies, intimidation of domestic and foreign companies, black propaganda, threats to trading nations, economic embargo – all have been deployed in the attempt to subvert, pressure and terrorise a small sovereign state into subservience to Washington. The various measures – violations of both international law and natural justice – signal at one level a psychopathic mind-set, an obsessional disorder born of megalomania; at another, the clear perception that Cuba stands as an alarming demonstration that human society need not be rooted in money-grubbing exploitation.

The strategic exigencies of the Cold War seemingly provided adequate reason for traditional US malevolence towards Cuba; but, with the Cold War over, the obvious malevolence remains. Why should this be so? Washington, we find, gives virtuous reasons: its commitment to 'democracy', its support for 'human rights', its interest in economic 'reform'. Such professed concerns, deemed useful in propaganda, are specious. The United States has always found Third World tyrannies more congenial than genuine movements for democracy; devotion to human rights has never been best exemplified by such US darlings as Somoza, Pinochet, Marcos, Mobutu, Batista, Diem, Rhee, Duvalier, Suharto *et al.*; and US applause for democracy sits badly with the timely (mid-1995) reminder that only American citizens able to raise $30 million can expect to campaign for office in the United States. It is clear that Washington remains hostile to the Cuban regime, not for any professed reasons of virtue or humanity, but because – for 35 years – a national people in Uncle Sam's 'backyard' has refused to be forced into the insatiable maw of American capitalism; and continues to advertise an alternative political model to that of materialistic greed and economic exploitation.

The sovereignty of the Cuban people is enshrined in international law, not least in the Charter (Article 2(1)) of the United Nations; but a principal objective of Washington remains the destruction of this sovereignty in the interest of US capitalism. It is useful in this context to note aspects of the US-sustained economic embargo, a policy almost universally condemned but one with no end in sight.

THE LONG EMBARGO

On 1 January 1959 the popular Cuban revolutionary forces overthrew the military dictatorship of General Fulgencio Batista. Within weeks Washington strategists, despite US recognition of the new Cuban government on 7 January, were devising a range of measures for the subversion of the Castro regime. Soon restrictions were placed on US exports to Cuba (Figure 1.1); and the Central Intelligence Agency (CIA) began to develop plans, using Cuban exiles and other subversive assets, for a terrorist campaign against Cuba (see Chapter 7). On 5 June Senator George Smathers, a Florida Democrat, proposed legislation for a reduction in the Cuban sugar quota purchased by the United States; and early in 1960, after planes flying from US territory had bombed Havana and sugar cane fields in Camagüey and Oriente, President Eisenhower began pressing for authority to block all imports of Cuban sugar.[1] On 3 July 1960 the US Congress enacted a newly-amended Sugar Act authorising the president to cancel all Cuban sugar imports. A few days later (6 July), President Eisenhower moved to cancel the entire sugar quota (including the remaining 700,000 tons in the formerly agreed 1960 quota), at the same time declaring that

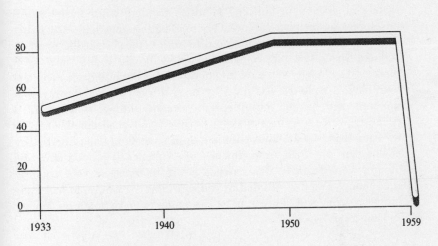

Figure 1.1   Percentage of Cuban imports supplied by the US

SOURCE: *The Guardian*, London, 6 September 1994

other measures ('economic, diplomatic and strategic') against the Cuban government must now be considered. In October Washington announced a partial embargo on other categories of trade with Cuba, prohibiting all exports to the island except for foodstuffs, medical supplies and a few products requiring special licences. Vice-President Richard Nixon, then the Republican presidential candidate, later described the new policy as an 'all-out "quarantine" – economically, politically and diplomatically – of the Castro regime'. At the same time John F. Kennedy, the Democratic presidential candidate, began urging support for the 'fighters for freedom' against the Cuban government, a freeze on all Cuban assets held in the United States, and collective action against the Castro regime by the United States, the Organisation of American States (OAS), and Washington's European allies.

Fidel Castro himself had been quick to comment on such developments. On 8 July 1960, speaking on Cuba's Televisión-Revolución, he analysed the purpose of the economic blockade:

This action is aimed against the Revolution's achievement and savings . . . it is an attack on the people, an attempt to keep us from having more schools, teachers, roads, houses and universities. It is an attempt to obstruct our work of training our young people and giving them scholarships, of building factories so there will be jobs and of developing agriculture.... Now, they're planning something else, thinking that, if they cause economic difficulties, they'll get the people's support. That's how they think the people will react to their tactic of 'I make you go hungry and have a hard time; and, because I'm not content with having exploited you for 50 years, with having taken away your minerals and having multiplied my wealth through your work – because, with those investments, I tripled and quadrupled what I'd invested there – with having limited your sovereignty and imposed an amendment [the Platt Amendment – see Chapter 5] on you after you thought you were free that enabled me to intervene in your country; even though I've done all that to you and I don't want you to make any progress, I can count on you now; I'm going to make you grow hungry so I can count on you.'[2]

Now began the long struggle of revolutionary Cuba (Castro: 'The people of Cuba will have to love their Revolution more, because every new obstacle that's placed in our path will mean that we'll have to fight harder and make more sacrifices for it'[3]). In 1960 few observers imagined that Castro's words would continue to be as relevant as late as the second half of the 1990s.

In October 1960 Washington moved to develop another anti-Cuban tactic that was to have increased significance in the decades that followed: that of pressuring other sovereign states to reduce their trade with Cuba. For example, on 22 October US officials discussed with their Canadian counterparts ways of preventing US exports from reaching Cuba via Canada. A few weeks later (16 December), President Eisenhower set the Cuban sugar quota at zero for the first quarter of 1961, so encouraging the Cuban government to become increasingly dependent on Socialist-bloc sugar purchases. Now it was clear that the anti-Cuban policies introduced by the Eisenhower/Nixon administration would survive any change of US government: on 31 March 1961 President John F. Kennedy announced that the quota of Cuban sugar would be maintained at zero for the rest of the year; and three weeks later (22 April) he held discussions with the National Security Council on whether to introduce a total embargo on US trade with Cuba.

On 3 February 1962 the US government (via decree no. 3447 signed by Kennedy) declared that a total embargo of trade with Cuba, excepting some foodstuffs and medical supplies, would take effect from 7 February. A few weeks later, on 23 March, the embargo was extended to imports of all goods manufactured from Cuban materials or containing any Cuban materials, even if produced in other countries. Now the evidence was mounting that the US block on trade with Cuba was being developed to impact on the commercial practices of sovereign states not nominally involved in the US–Cuban confrontation. On 8 September, in furtherance of this widening policy, Washington succeeded in securing agreement from the other members of the North Atlantic Treaty Organisation (NATO) that they would stop all financial credits to Cuba. At the same time various other options were being explored as ways of extending the scope of the trade embargo.

New US government regulations were introduced on 2 October: US ports would be closed to any country allowing its ships to transport arms to Cuba; any vessel that docked in a Socialist-bloc country (for example, Cuba) would not be allowed to dock in any US port during that voyage; any country allowing planes or ships under its registry to carry materials to Cuba would not be eligible for US aid; companies trading with Cuba would be banned from transporting US aid shipments; and no US ships would be allowed to participate in trade with Cuba. Early in 1963 (6 February), President Kennedy ruled that no US government-funded shipments were to be transported on foreign vessels which had docked at a Cuban port on or after 1 January of that year.

On 8 July the US Treasury Department, using its authority under the war-time Trading with the Enemy Act (1917),* revoked the Cuban Import Regulations and replaced them with the more draconian Cuban Assets Control Regulations, designed to tighten the operation of the trade embargo. The new regulations prohibited all unlicensed commercial or financial transactions between US citizens and Cuba, prohibited US citizens from the unlicensed importing of or dealing abroad in Cuban products, and prohibited the importing of any goods manufactured abroad out of Cuban materials. In addition, all Cuban assets (including $33 million in US banks) in the United States were frozen, with US citizens prohibited from using US dollars in unlicensed commercial transactions with Cuba (principal targets here were the spending of dollars in Cuba and the purchase of Cuban airline tickets).

In early 1964 the Johnson administration, continuing the policy of its predecessors, was working both to tighten the terms of the US-sustained embargo and to encourage other states to join the anti-Cuban campaign. Thus Secretary of State Dean Rusk commented (10 January): 'Those

---

*Legislation allowing the president to prohibit economic transactions between the US and foreign countries during war or national emergency. The Act was later exploited in the Cuban Democracy Act 1992 – see below and Appendix 1.

countries which, for commercial reasons, supply Cuba, especially with goods critical to the Cuban economy, are prejudicing the efforts of the countries of this hemisphere to reduce the threat from Cuba.' Two months later (13 March), Rusk made a statement to the Senate Foreign Relations Committee to indicate the specific objectives of the trade embargo:

1. To reduce Castro's will and ability to export subversion and violence to other American states;

2. To make it plain to the people of Cuba that Castro's regime cannot serve their interests;

3. To demonstrate to the peoples of the American Republics that communism has no future in the Western Hemisphere;

4. To increase the cost to the Soviet Union of maintaining a communist outpost in the Western Hemisphere.

And again he indicated his concern that Washington's allies were not fully supportive of US policy: 'We are disturbed when other free world countries supply products that cannot help but increase Castro's capacity for mischief.' The planned British sale of buses to Cuba – a deal subsequently sabotaged by the CIA – was apparently seen as contributing to such mischief (Rusk noted that the buses 'would almost double the public transport of Havana').

On 14 May 1964 the US government announced that foodstuffs and medical supplies would no longer be exempted from the embargo. *The New York Times* (15 May) reflected widespread opinion in its comment that this was hardly the best way to win the Cold War against Cuba or to present the United States to the world as a humanitarian country. The *Times* editorial, flashed around the world by Associated Press (AP), observed that Washington would gain nothing by making the Cubans hungrier, and would win no friends in Cuba by making people suffer for lack of medicine.

In subsequent years the economic embargo, varying in intensity from one US administration to another, was held in place; though what would have been its direst effects were largely avoided by aid and favourable trade deals negotiated with Socialist-bloc countries and other states prepared to continue trading despite US pressure. By the 1970s the Cuban Revolution had consolidated its position and could demonstrate substantial social gains. The Castro regime had withstood CIA-orchestrated terrorism (which still continued), military invasion and the endless stream of black propaganda. The intended effects of the economic embargo had been largely avoided – to the point that on 26 July 1974 Prime Minister Castro chose to observe that 'the isolation of Cuba is slowly withering away'. And he commented also, in the context of the current Watergate scandal in Washington: 'Mercenaries trained by the CIA to carry out such acts of sabotage, subversion and aggression against Cuba were later used to spy on and steal documents from the Democratic Party headquarters.' The CIA and its trained subversives had been 'much more effective in destroying the presidency of the United States than in overthrowing the Cuban Revolution'.

Now there seemed scope for an improvement in relations between Havana and Washington. In November 1974 Cuban and American officials began a series of secret talks with a view to moving away from the seemingly endless confrontation between the two countries. On 4 March 1975 Senator Edward Kennedy, then as now a Massachusetts Democrat, introduced a bill to remove the economic embargo against Cuba – a move that provoked an instant reaction from the Cuban exile community. Thus Juan José Peruyero, the former president of the Bay of Pigs Veterans Association, declared in Miami that his organisation was under pressure 'to undertake some direct action to prevent any rapprochement with Castro since it was Senator Kennedy's brother who bungled our invasion plans'; the Kennedy bill was 'an act of extreme villainy' and 'the reaction that Cuban exile groups . . . are planning is violent'. On 29 July the OAS voted (16 to 3, with two abstentions) to terminate the collective sanctions against diplomatic and consular relations with Cuba. The meeting had been called by Mexico and nine other states in protest against US pressure designed to curtail the sovereign rights of trading nations. Now, despite the opposition of Chile, Paraguay and Uruguay (Brazil and Nicaragua abstaining), each OAS state would be 'free to normalise or carry on relations with the Republic of Cuba at the level and in the form that each state deems convenient'. William S. Maillard, the Ford Administration's delegate, recognising the progressive collapse of sanctions, voted with the majority. Three weeks later (21 August), the Ford administration brought to an end the prohibition of exports to Cuba by foreign subsidiaries of US companies. Despite the continuing ban on direct US–Cuba trade, it now appeared that Castro was right in proclaiming the gradual 'withering away' of Cuba's isolation.

On 8 October 1975 the US Treasury Department revoked the specific regulation making it illegal for US subsidiaries in other countries to trade with Cuba. A new regulation lifted restrictions on vessels docking in

Cuban ports, while at the same time various travel restrictions were lifted. In the same spirit the Secretary of State designate Cyrus R. Vance, testifying in January 1977 at confirmation hearings before the Senate Foreign Relations Committee, declared that it was time to remove obstacles to the normalising of relations with Cuba. In March President Carter declined to renew the ban on travel by US citizens to Cuba, Vietnam, Cambodia and North Korea; and, as a corollary, lifted the prohibition on US travellers spending dollars in Cuba. On 5 April 1977 US Senators George McGovern and James Abourezk, both South Dakota Democrats, attended a basketball match in Havana between a Cuban team (which won) and a team representing the South Dakota universities (the first US sports team to compete in Cuba since 1960). Fidel Castro, now president, took the opportunity to urge the lifting of the trade embargo. But on this central issue nothing was accomplished. Various petty restrictions had been lifted by the Carter administration but it was clear that the squeeze on the Cuban economy would remain in place.

There were also other timely reminders that, despite US Democrat efforts to improve US–Cuban relations, Washington's fundamental hostility to the Castro regime remained intact. Thus a CBS television broadcast (10 June 1977), focusing on 'The CIA's Secret Army', acknowledged that CIA-orchestrated Cuban exile groups had maintained an unbroken series of terrorist attacks on Cuba for 18 years; Castro, interviewed for the programme, claimed that there had been at least 24 assassination plots against him and other Cuban leaders. Whatever the instincts of some elements in the Carter administration, efforts were still being made by powerful US factions to overthrow the Cuban regime by force. In this context it seemed unlikely that the trade embargo would be lifted.

On 16 June the Senate Foreign Relations Committee blocked moves to end the embargo. Carter himself opposed even a relaxation of the trade ban affecting foodstuffs and medical supplies, following State Department suggestions that this would weaken the US negotiating position. However the US government, under a Democrat presidency, had made a number of conciliatory moves. In September President Castro noted the 'lessening of tension' during the Carter administration, acknowledging such significant developments as the halting of surveillance flights (though spy satellites were now in use), US–Cuban agreement on fishing and maritime boundaries, the lifting of travel restrictions, and various diplomatic moves. Such developments, welcome as they were, failed to influence the shape of the trade ban. On 19 June 1979 Representative Ted Weiss, a New York Democrat, introduced legislation to end the economic embargo and to re-establish diplomatic relations with Cuba. But this initiative came to nought. Soon there would be a Republican in the White House: even the minor peripheral moves in the direction of a US–Cuban rapprochement would be abandoned.

In June 1984, following his trip to Cuba and Central America, the Reverend Jesse Jackson briefed members of Congress and announced that US–Cuban talks about migration would begin soon. President Ronald Reagan responded (in a 2 July recording for release on the Fourth of July) by questioning the legality of such missions to Cuba. The 'law of the land' (in fact the 185-year-old Logan Act), declared Reagan, prohibited diplomatic missions by private US citizens; though he failed to acknowledged that Jackson had conferred with the State Department, that the US authorities had agreed to process the visas of people that Jackson had brought out of Cuba, and that the State Department had allowed a Cuban plane to land on US territory. Moreover, the Reagan administration had already sent a communiqué to Cuba indicating that talks on migration would begin in July. A few days later Reagan admitted that he had gone 'astray' in doubting the legality of Jackson's visit to Cuba.

Now, under pressure from the American Right. the Reagan administration was moving to tighten the trade embargo. On 22 August 1986 the US Treasury Department introduced new measures, including 'crackdowns on trading with Cuban front companies located in Panama and elsewhere' and 'closer controls on organisations which organise or promote travel to Cuba'. At the same time fresh limits were imposed on the cash and gifts that Cuban Americans were allowed to send to their relatives in Cuba, while tighter regulations were imposed on companies shipping foodstuffs and care packages to Cuba. US politicians who visited Cuba and talked with Castro invariably moved in favour of looser restrictions on US–Cuban trade. Thus in January 1985 the Representatives Bill Alexander (Democrat), Mickey Leland (Democrat) and Jim Leach (Republican) talked for 37 hours with Castro in Havana; and on their return to Washington urged constructive negotiations with the Cuban regime. Even Representative Robert Torricelli, later of Cuban Democracy Act fame (see below), after he visited Havana in November 1988 with Representative Mel Levine, commented that in Cuba 'living standards are not high, but the homelessness, hunger and disease that is witnessed in much of Latin America does not appear evident'. Such testimony did nothing to deter a Republican administration intent on tightening the noose round the Castro regime.

In February 1990, at a time when the world was witnessing the progressive collapse of the Socialist bloc, the US State Department's Bureau of Public Affairs issued a document to reinforce the scope of the economic embargo on Cuba. It now declared that the embargo had been set in place because of the attachment without compensation of US property in Cuba; and confirmed that no Cuban products could enter the United States and that no US products could be exported to Cuba. On 28 February Senator Connie Mack, a Florida Republican, announced fresh moves to increase the pressure on the Castro regime. A principal aim would be to enlist the support of the new governments in Eastern Europe in tightening the anti-Castro economic embargo. In April Dante B. Fascell, Chairman of the House Committee on International Relations, following a similar Senate initiative by Mack and Robert Graham (a Florida Democrat), introduced a bill designed to increase the scope of the economic sanctions against Cuba. The Fascell bill included provisions for the prohibition of US companies allowing their foreign subsidiaries to trade with Cuba, and for the blocking of US aid to countries continuing to purchase Cuban sugar. In addition, US ports would be closed to all ships that had conveyed goods to Cuba in the previous six months. The Mack/Graham and Fascell initiatives represented further efforts to tighten the screws on the Castro regime, now in circumstances where Cuba could no longer rely on aid and favourable trade deals with a Socialist bloc of nations.

On 26 October 1990 the US Congress passed a trade bill that included the Mack Amendment (almost identical to the Fascell bill), designed to make it illegal for US companies abroad to trade with Cuba, even in goods of local origin. This was a highly significant development: at that time Cuba was trading with US companies in a dozen Latin American countries, a dozen European countries, Japan and Australia. Much of this trade, crucial to Cuba's social reforms, was in foodstuffs and medical supplies. Soon, however, it was clear that even under the reactionary administration of President George Bush the Mack Amendment would not have an easy ride. In the United States there was mounting domestic opposition to the strictures of an economic embargo that manifestly violated provisions of the US Constitution; and foreign governments were increasingly alarmed at fresh US efforts to interfere with their sovereign trading rights. On 5 June the American Civil Liberties Committee (ACLC) and several New York art bodies had lodged a suit against the government because the embargo included works of art, so violating not only the Constitutional right of freedom of expression but also a 1988 enactment exempting Cuban paintings, sculpture and drawings from the embargo. On 18 June a group of civic, political, religious and union organisations in Puerto Rico denounced Washington's mounting campaign of 'harassment and pressure' against the Cuban people. And there were growing uncertainties in the United States as to the practicalities of enforcing legislation such as the

Mack Amendment. Thus *The Miami Herald* (25 September 1990), despite its sensitivities to the local Cuban-exile community, noted the difficulties faced by the US Congress intent on enacting legislation that conflicted with laws in other nations.

The Canadian embassy in Washington confirmed the Mulroney administration's public expression of disagreement with the idea that US laws could be enacted to limit the trading practices of sovereign nations. Thus on 31 October, in response to the passing of the Mack Amendment in Congress, the Canadian Attorney-General Kim Campbell issued an order to block any US attempt to prevent US companies in Canada trading with Cuba. In the same spirit Joe Clark, Canada's Minister for External Affairs, denounced the provisions of the Mack Amendment as 'clearly unacceptable'; while the Canadian Foreign Ministry spokesman Denis Laliberte took pains to emphasise that the laws governing Canadian exports were a matter for Canada. In mid-November a report from Associated Press (AP) suggested that nominal friends of the United States (Britain, Canada and other countries) were complaining about US attempts to restrict the trade practices in their countries. Few nations were prepared to concede that Washington had the right to legislate in the attempt to control commercial activities outside its borders. In the event it proved useful to such objectors that the State Department had strong objections to other parts of the bill that contained the Mack Amendment. It now seemed increasingly likely that President Bush would move to veto the bill – for reasons that had nothing to do with US–Cuba trade. The deadline for presidential signing of the controversial bill passed, resulting in a *de facto* veto. The bill had fallen, but there remained powerful support for the Mack Amendment (for example, Senator Claiborne Pell, a Rhode Island Democrat, was now voicing his support for such a measure). Senator Mack himself declared that he would move to introduce the same text again in 1991. There was still a strong head of steam behind the Mack Amendment: legislation along these lines, sponsored by Mack or someone else, would not be long delayed.

The few constructive measures taken to improve US–Cuban relations under the Carter administration had now all been thrown into reverse. Carter had agreed fishing rights and other maritime accords, allowed US citizens to travel to Cuba, agreed the opening of Interests Sections in the two nations' capitals, and even contemplated an end to the embargo. Surveillance flights over Cuban territory were quietly brought to an end, and Pentagon war games at the Guantánamo base were cancelled. Just 22 days after Reagan assumed office, the new administration signalled the changed atmosphere by expelling a Cuban diplomat from Washington for allegedly encouraging US trade with Cuba. Throughout the Reagan years no constructive proposals were advanced to improve US–Cuban relations: with the collapse of the Socialist bloc it was inevitable that Republicans would move to intensify the anti-Cuban sanctions. The American triumphalism at the US victory in the Cold War added fresh fuel to the impulses behind the Mack Amendment. Now, reasoned many Washington strategists, it was time to settle the Cuba Question once and for all.

In September 1991 the Bush administration, having reacted with glee to the earlier Gorbachev promise that Soviet troops would be withdrawn from Cuba, now began to realise that the Castro regime was not about to collapse: the Cuban people were not about to fall like a ripe fruit into Washington's waiting hand. Hopefully, reasoned Defense Secretary Richard Cheney, the end was in sight: 'The Soviet withdrawal is an indication to Fidel Castro, who has kept himself in power all these years by brute force, that his own days are numbered.' But some observers of the changing scene were less patient. Said the Texas senator Phil Gramm: 'We cannot let this tide of freedom wash around the world and not drown Fidel Castro.'[4] Now there was little talk in the United States of a US-sponsored military invasion of Cuba, just the assumption that Castro would not be able to sustain the regime for long in the teeth of mounting economic deprivation.

Now the scene was set for enactment of the Mack Amendment or some equivalent legislation. The new torch-bearer was Robert Torricelli, a New Jersey Democrat, who in November 1988 had been impressed with the absence of destitution in Havana. On 5 February 1992, sharing a press conference with Bay of Pigs veteran Jorge Mas Canosa, now president of the anti-Castro Cuban-American National Foundation, Torricelli introduced the proposed 'Cuban Democracy Act of 1992' (Appendix 1). Part of the Torricelli strategy was to challenge President Bush to move to a strong anti-Castro position in election year; and it was useful also to attract contributions from the wealthy sectors of the Cuban-American community. An article in *Time* magazine (20 October 1992) revealed that the Foundation had spent more than a million dollars in recent years to buy influence in Congress: more than $26,000 had gone to Robert Torricelli himself, with some $57,000 being donated to the George Bush election campaign.

Features of the Torricelli bill, months in the drafting, include:

- the main idea of the Mack Amendment: an end to US corporate subsidiary trade with Cuba (70 per cent of which is in foodstuffs and medical supplies);
- a requirement that the president pressure Western allies to enforce the embargo;

- provision for sanctions on Latin American countries that trade with Cuba;
- preventing any ship that trades with Cuba from trading at a US port for the following six months;
- US government funds and supplies for anti-Castro groups both within and outside Cuba.

Once the bill had been introduced it was sent to six House of Representatives committees (Foreign Affairs, Energy and Commerce, Merchant Marine and Fisheries, Ways and Means, Post Office and Civil Service, and Banking, Finance and Urban Affairs). When it was found that lawmakers in Banking planned to block the bill, Torricelli deleted certain clauses to remove the bill from their jurisdiction. It has been reported that Torricelli's main financial backer is the 'Free Cuba' Political Action Committee, linked to the Cuban-American National Foundation.[5]

President Bush, sensitive to pressure from the Right, met with various interested politicians and the Cuban-American National Foundation, and then agreed to support the Cuban Democracy Act. Already Bush had signed an executive order banning foreign cruise and cargo ships from US ports if they also visited Cuba, in furtherance of his declared aim of bringing 'rapid, peaceful, democratic change' to the island. Now Torricelli felt sufficiently confident to remark that the US government 'has accepted the inevitability of the embargo being strengthened'. On 21 May the House Foreign Affairs Committee met to vote on the bill, but before the final verdict Representative Ted Weiss (a New York Democrat) proposed an amendment to exclude medicines and medical supplies. To Torricelli's horror, the amendment passed (11 to 10), whereupon he tagged on a mandate (clearly unacceptable to Cuba, as it would be to any country) that a US official must accompany any medicine sale to the island in order to oversee its distribution. Weiss then tried to exempt foodstuffs from the Act, but this further amendment failed. The Act was then passed in its entirety, embodying an effective ban on medicine and food exports from the United States and subsidiary companies to Cuba. Over the next few months the bill moved steadily through the various stages, until, to accelerate its progress, Senator Bob Graham managed to append the entire bill to the Defense Appropriations Act, which had already been approved by the House of Representatives.

Throughout this entire period the bill aroused substantial domestic and foreign opposition. Thus Victor Sidel, on behalf of the American Public Health Association (APHA), testified in committee that 'Cuba's accomplishments over the past 30 years are substantial in health, education and the eradication of extreme poverty.... Cuba has developed an exemplary national health system, which provides comprehensive, accessible health care to the entire population free of charge.' Such gains would be jeopardised by the bill: 'interference in the Cuban people's access to food and medicine is tantamount to the use of food and medicine as a weapon in the US arsenal against Cuba'. Surely, declared Sidel, the United States could devise a policy *that does not cause suffering among an entire population in order to accomplish our national political objectives'* (my italics).[6] A letter sent to House Speaker Tom Foley from his counterparts in Argentina (Juan Carlos Cafiero, Carlos Raimundi), Chile (Jaime Estévez), Bolivia (Hugo Carvajal) and Uruguay (Rafael Michelini) included the words: 'We believe that this new and total embargo will only bring new and bigger sufferings to the Cuban people. To introduce more conditions on the shipment of medicines would affect the right of life of those to whom it is purported to aid.' The pretensions underlying the new legislation violate 'the freedom of commerce' and affect 'the right to self-determination and of non-intervention in the internal affairs of third countries, universally recognised as basic principles of international law'. In the same spirit, Ricardo Valero, the head of the Foreign Relations Commission in the Mexican Chamber of Deputies, charged that the new measures *'confirm the United States as the leading violator of international law'* (my italics).[7]

Canadian parliamentarians continued to denounce the Torricelli bill ('unwarranted interference in other countries' commerce', 'the American government doesn't have any business telling a Canadian company or a French company or Spanish or Mexican companies or any other company... that they cannot do business with whomever they choose'). And even the normally supine United Kingdom found Torricelli too much to swallow: the then Trade Secretary Peter Lilley declared that it was 'for the British government, not the US Congress, to determine the UK's policy on trade with Cuba'. Said Lilley: 'We will not accept any attempt to superimpose US law on UK companies. I hope the Congress will think long and hard before seeking to interfere with legitimate civil trade between this country and Cuba.' Such comments did nothing to deter the Bush administration from pressing ahead with the Torricelli bill, or to discourage Bill Clinton (soon to be President-elect) from supporting this legislative development. Soon it would transpire that the new Democratic government intended to be as hawkish on Cuba as any of its Republican predecessors.

In May 1992 the Bush administration warned American fishermen planning to attend the annual Hemingway Marlin Fishing Tournament in Havana that they risked heavy fines and prison sentences if they violated the US embargo against Cuba. Richard Newcomb, head of the Office of Foreign Asset Control at the US Treasury, was duly despatched to Key West to inform about 60 fishermen that the United States 'will not betray 30 years of vigilance'. He informed the fishermen that, under the terms of the Trading with the Enemy Act: 'You will be subject to confiscation of vessels and criminal charges.' Said one charter-boat skipper: 'Hell, I fought for this country in Vietnam. I just want to go fishing, maybe have a few beers and come back' – an escapade that could attract a fine of $250,000 and a 10-year prison sentence (in 1990 a Texan, Don Snow, who had sold fishing trips to Cuba, was jailed for 90 days, made to perform 1000 hours' community service, made to pay $5,300 legal costs, and given five years' probation).[8]

On 4 June the US Senate Foreign Relations Committee approved the Torricelli bill, now widely seen as a mechanism to bankrupt the Cuban regime. Some observers were now suggesting that the new measures might provide a fresh refugee crisis (see 'The Exodus', below), and that this in turn would present Washington with new policy problems. The Reagan administration had suggested that normal relations would be restored with Cuba once Cuban–Soviet military links were ended, Cuban troops had been withdrawn from Africa, and Cuban support for 'terrorism' in Central America was ended. These conditions had now been fulfilled (though in circumstances that neither Reagan nor Castro had anticipated), but there was still no prospect of an end to US hostility. Now there was mounting evidence of growing international opposition to the terms of the Torricelli legislation. Thus even the British ambassador to Cuba, Leycester Coltman, was prepared to comment to the Cuban newspaper *Granma* that the Torricelli bill was an 'unjustifiable interference in international trade'.

As with the Carter administration, it was possible under the Clinton presidency to discern signs that suggested a hesitant step in the direction of rapprochement: in May 1993 Washington declared that it had no intention of invading Cuba; in June the US government announced a crackdown on the illegal activities of anti-Castro Cuban exiles; and Washington announced that funding for the anti-Castro TV Martí, the propaganda station beamed at Cuba, was to be ended. But in the context of the intensified economic embargo such moves were peripheral and inconsequential: all the efforts to force the Castro regime into bankruptcy and economic collapse remained in place. The Clinton administration continued to uphold legislative provisions that amounted to a *de facto* blockade of Cuba. It is useful to note the various themes in the Cuban Democracy Act and the associated legislation.

The US government was now committed to blocking imports of goods that contained even small amounts of Cuban input, even if thoroughly transformed in manufacture. Thus the French corporation Le Creusot Loire was informed that it would not be allowed to sell steel containing Cuban nickel in the US. This ban caused the company to cancel its contract with Cuba for the building of factories (for hardboard manufacture) in exchange for Cuban nickel. In the same vein, foreign confectionary companies using Cuban sugar are not allowed to export their chocolate bars to the United States.

If foreign companies produce goods that contain more than 20 per cent US input they are not allowed to export to Cuba, just as goods using US technological designs cannot be made available to Cuba. If a company's product contains between 10 and 20 per cent US input then export to Cuba is prohibited unless the company first obtains a licence from the US Treasury Department. This provision led to a block on the Swedish company Alfa-Laval exporting filtration equipment to Cuba, because a component filter membrane was a US product. In addition, foreign banks are prohibited from maintaining dollar-denominated accounts for Cuba and from conducting dollar-denominated commercial transactions that involve Cuba. US citizens who are directors of foreign companies are not allowed to deal with Cuba. And ships that stop at Cuban ports are not permitted to dock at US ports within six months of their infringement.[9]

The US government also uses threats and intimidation against other countries to discourage trade with Cuba. Washington may resort to legislation allowing sanctions against recalcitrant states; or direct communication (letters or phone calls) may be used to pressure particular trading companies into acquiescence. As one example, the Spanish conglomerate Tabacalera decided against planned investment in Cuban tourism after receiving notification that Washington would look unfavourably on any such commercial venture. In his address to the UN General Assembly in November 1991 (even before the enactment of the Cuban Democracy Act), Ricardo Alarcón, Cuba's UN ambassador, cited 27 cases of trade contracts sabotaged by US intimidation of foreign companies. In a televised interview in mid-1994 Fidel Castro himself admitted that the United States was succeeding in blocking 9 out of 10 of all trade deals negotiated between Cuba and foreign companies.

The specialist trade journal *Petroleum Economist* (September 1992) reported the common pattern of how the US State Department 'vigorously discouraged' such foreign companies as Royal Dutch Shell and Clyde Petroleum from investing in offshore oil exploration in Cuba. Such pressure is a typical US tactic. Thus Roberto Robaina González, the Cuban

Foreign Minister, gave details in a letter (25 June 1993) to UN Secretary-General Boutros-Ghali of how Washington was working to sabotage Cuba's trading efforts. Declared Robaina: 'The US government has been putting pressure on companies in third countries to cut off their economic ties with Cuba, invoking the restrictions imposed by the blockade and, more recently, by the Torricelli Act.'[10] Cited examples included:

- US pressure on the British sugar company Tate and Lyle to cut its economic ties with Cuba, after company representatives attended a meeting of sugar producers in Havana in May 1992;

- a US threat to the British Cable and Wireless company, working with a subsidiary on US territory, that any investment in Cuba would mean that a licence applied for (to operate in Europe and Asia using the US as an intermediate territory) would be rejected;

- a pressure from the US embassy in Mexico City on the Maria Isabel Sheraton Hotel to force the cancellation of a contract already signed with Cuba;

- pressure exerted by John D. Negroponte, US ambassador in Mexico, on the Monterrey Group to prevent the creation with Cuba of a joint venture in the textile industry;

- US pressure to prevent the sale to Cuba of respiratory valves, connections, pressure boxes, vaporisers, micro vaporiser flasks and so on – all of which are spare parts for the Bird respiratory machine, the most frequently used equipment of its kind in Cuba for intensive and intermediate care units, post-operative rooms, asthmatic units, and emergency rooms;

- US prohibitions (via the Cuban Democracy Act) on the Canadian medical company Eli Lilly Canada Inc. from selling its products to Cuba. The company, a subsidiary of the US corporation Eli Lilly & Co. (the world's main producer of insulin), is prevented from selling its medicines (used for vascular diseases, lung disorders and various cancers) in Cuba;

- US pressure on two major grain producers, Cargill SACI and the Continental SACINF Company, to stop exporting grain to Cuba. This meant an effective US block of $100 million-worth of sales of wheat, soya, beans and lentils alone. Company executives have stated that they were visited by US government officials making threats;

- US pressure resulting in a bill of lading for a ship carrying 25,000 tons of wheat to Cuba being withdrawn;

- US pressure to force a major Asian company shipping Cuban products to and from the Caribbean to cancel its contract, since the company's vessels could not avoid docking in US ports;

- pressure from US embassy officials in Mexico to prevent the transport of a ship full of oil to Cuba;

- US pressure to prevent Canadian travel agents reserving flights to and from Cuba, and between Cuba and third countries. A US company whose data bases were used by the Canadian reservation systems suddenly decided to cancel the service, so compelling Canadian firms to join the US blockade of Cuba, counter to their interests and intentions.

Foreign Minister Robaina, in presenting these and other examples of US activity, emphasised that the principal target of the Cuban Democracy Act was 'the supply of essential foodstuffs and medical products for the consumption of the Cuban people'; and that this could be verified in the information published in the US Treasury Department document, *Special Report: An Analysis of Licensed Trade with Cuba by Foreign Subsidiaries of US Companies*. Robaina concluded by expressing confidence that the United Nations would 'take an active role in ending an unjust and anachronistic situation' (see 'The Response – International', below).

The Clinton administration had made it plain that the economic blockade on Cuba would continue, despite the plight of a sovereign people 'trembling on the brink of famine and chaos';[11] and despite the damage being done to the trading activities of America's allies.[12] US efforts continued to be directed at intimidating foreign firms and countries that dared to trade with Cuba in exercise of their sovereign rights. Even the Clinton-sponsored bail-out package to relieve the Mexican financial crisis in early 1995 was linked to a number of significant political conditions, one of which was reportedly 'less support for Cuba'.[13] Despite such pressure the government of President Ernesto Zedillo, to its credit, continued to assert that it would accept no conditions which damaged Mexican sovereignty.

Nonetheless, a US draft of the proposed bill included strict conditions in terms of Mexico's foreign, economic and migratory policies.

The implementation of the Cuban Democracy Act and other pertinent legislation, the intimidation and blackmail of foreign companies, commercial pressure on allies, the abuse of aid and financial disbursements – even all this, designed to bring poverty and starvation to the Cuban people, proved insufficient to satisfy the vindictive appetites of the American Right. In early 1995, with the US Congress now securely in Republican hands, there were fresh moves to pull the noose yet tighter. In February the Senate Foreign Relations Committee chairman Jesse Helms and other influential lawmakers, convinced that the Castro regime was on the verge of collapse, introduced further legislation to strengthen the embargo. The proposed new bill would enable Americans whose property had been expropriated by Cuba to sue any foreign companies that now own it; officers and shareholders of those companies would be denied visas to enter the United States; and American banks would be prohibited from making loans to those companies. In addition, Cuban exiles would have to be compensated; and an amount (about $200 million) would be deducted from US aid to Russia to counter Russian payments to Cuba for the operation of the electronic listening post at Cienfuegos, essential for Russian monitoring of arms-control treaties. In short, the new bill would provide fresh legislative tools to pressure companies and the Russian Federation into political subservience to Washington's anti-Cuban policies. In this connection Senator Jesse Helms suggested on 15 February 1995 that it was time – via the mechanism of new punitive legislation – to tighten yet further the noose around Cuba. In April he was proposing a total naval blockade of the island as a way to depose Castro, 'an evil, cruel, murderous, barbarous thug' (*The Independent*, 19 April 1995). By now there was mounting international condemnation (including from the European Union) of the Helms Cuban Liberty and Democratic Solidarity (Libertad) Act of 1995 as a gross violation of international trade laws.

It was surmised that President Clinton would not oppose the new legislation. Keen to seek re-election in 1996, he had no wish to offend the powerful anti-Castro constituency in Florida. If anyone was looking for a signal on Clinton's intentions towards Cuba, they would have discerned one around the time when Helms was pontificating on further anti-Castro measures: the US State Department refused Cuba's UN ambassador permission to attend a 'national prayer breakfast' in Washington. With the Republicans tightening their grip on US foreign policy through 1995, there would clearly be no relaxation in US attempts to sabotage the Cuban economy. The campaign would intensify. It is useful, in this fraught political atmosphere, to note some of the main features of the revolutionary society that Helms, Fascell, Mack, Torricelli *et al.* are so keen to destroy.

THE TARGET SOCIETY

In February 1995 it was reported that the United Nations Children's Fund (UNICEF) had chosen to present Cuba as *a case of the positive achievements of a developing society* at the UN-sponsored Summit on Social Development, convened in Copenhagen in March 1995. This selection, seen as a great honour, served to signal the impressive social gains achieved by the Cuban Revolution. With an infant mortality rate of less than 10 per thousand live births, and life expectancy of 75 years, Cuba has won a prominent position among developing countries in general, and Latin American countries in particular. It is also the case that aspects of Cuban social achievement bear comparison with the situation in much of the developed world – a circumstances that, in the teeth of odious capitalist propaganda, advertises well the value of the progressive social philosophy underlying the Castro regime.

The social gains that followed the collapse of the Batista dictatorship are now beyond dispute. The revolutionary government inherited a depressed economy, high levels of unemployment and illiteracy (particularly in rural areas), widespread endemic diseases, and a crippling shortage of teachers, doctors and other professionals (many of whom preferred lucrative exile to service in the building of a new society). There then followed a period of reconstruction, investment in social services, the training of professionals – all with the aim of benefitting the Cuban people, too long accustomed to exploitation by (domestic and foreign) landowners, gangsters and capitalists. The subsequent social progress is universally recognised by aid agencies and UN bodies, and in academic analysis and journalistic commentary. Thus one observer notes that despite Cuba's growing problems (through the Socialist-bloc collapse and the US economic blockade), 'the health and education systems still represent an astonishing achievement in a Third World country, rivalling many developed countries in such key indicators' as adult literacy and infant mortality.[14] The bulk of the Cuban people are well aware that such gains 'would be forfeit under a wholesale conversion to a US-dominated market system'.[15]

The course of the Cuban Revolution, well documented in the literature, has been marked by experimentation, failures, retrenchments, advances, accommodations and successes. Early priorities were provisions for social welfare, the disbursement of national resources on an egalitarian basis, and measures to reduce the traditional urban–rural divide. By the early 1980s the peasant farmers working in the Agricultural Production Cooperatives (CPAs) became the beneficiaries of state social security provisions such as paid vacations, maternity benefits and pensions – the first time that peasant farmers had been granted government benefits to equal those afforded to state-salaried agricultural and industrial workers. The scale of this advance can only be appreciated by comparing the Cuban situation with that in most of Latin America, where peasant farmers typically subsist without social benefits on large private estates. Yet the very generosity of the Cuban scheme caused problems – a typical case of where experience led to policy revisions. By 1987, with some 35,000 CPA farmers having taken retirement, the pension scheme had incurred a substantial deficit; which in turn led to the National Association of Small Farmers (ANAP) endorsing government suggestions that farmers should delay retirement, in order to continue offering their expertise and to aid state finances. It is highly significant in this context that the welfare provisions were largely maintained in this difficult context, and that – with typical pragmatic adjustment to widely voiced criticisms – efforts were made to reshape the cooperative structure of agricultural production.[16]

By the late 1980s it was impossible even for opponents of the Cuban regime to deny the scale of the social gains, though it was argued that these were accomplished only at the expense of important human rights (see below), as if human rights did not include education and health provision. Thus a document issued by the Joint-Economic Committee of the US Congress, entitled 'Cuba Faces the Economic Realities of the 1980s', acknowledged the scale of the social achievements:

A highly egalitarian redistribution of income that has eliminated almost all malnutrition, particularly among children.

Establishment of a national health care program that is superior in the Third World and rivals that of numerous developed countries.

Near total elimination of illiteracy and a highly developed multilevel educational system.

Development of a relatively well-disciplined and motivated population with a strong sense of national identification.

The document suggested also that such social successes had 'themselves generated growing economic problems', not least the difficulty in providing jobs for the 'relatively well educated, rapidly growing labor force'.[17]

At the same time any unemployment is not allowed to affect the availability of welfare support: 'No person out of work, unable to work, or retired, is without means of livelihood. No sick person is without adequate medical care. No child, youth, or adult, is without means of schooling, higher education and self-development . . . social security in Cuba is an array of entitlements, financed and guaranteed by the government.'[18] Again it is useful to compare this situation with that obtaining not only in the rest of Latin America but in most developed countries (a bruised President Clinton, having failed in 1994/95 to bring 40 million excluded American citizens into US health care provision, might usefully reflect on the Cuban experience). The facts are plain enough. The Cuban Revolution has succeeded in creating a broadly egalitarian society, where disruptive social tensions arise through superpower sabotage of economic effort rather than through any particular features of social philosophy. Despite foreign subversion, the Castro regime managed to provide health care, education, jobs, and a rich cultural life for the Cuban people.

It is significant also that Cuba's social advances have been accomplished in the context of increased democratisation (see below), against US critics who suggest with manifest absurdity that only a polity resting on two plutocratic parties vying to protect the corporate interest can possibly be democratic. For example, through the 1970s the scale of worker participation in local enterprise and the national economy continued to develop in Cuba. Workers 'were increasingly consulted about national plans as well as their implementation at the enterprise level'.[19] It was reported that the number of workers involved in the discussion and amendment of economic proposals at the local level increased from 1.26 million in 1975 to 1.45 million in 1980. Workers in more than 90 per cent of all economic enterprises discussed the 1980 national plan, with consequent changes in 59 per cent of all enterprises.[20] In the same vein, a study produced by the Cuban International Economic Research Centre suggested even greater worker participation (24,000 proposals, with 17,000 approved) in the formulation of the 1984 economic plan. In this context the flexibility of the regime has been demonstrated by its sensitivity to worker proposals and complaints, and by such initiatives as the moves in 1975 to decentralise the state apparatus, periodic experiments with levels of private sector activity, and a flexible approach to debt servicing to avoid dislocations in overall economic activity.[21] The 'special period' of the 1990s is severely taxing the flexibility of the regime.

The social gains – health, social welfare, education, worker participation and the rest – have been achieved via the mechanism of an egalitarian socialist philosophy applied to realise well-defined national goals. For example, particular attention has been given to the elimination of the traditional disparity between the conditions of urban and rural life. A boarding school network of 'schools in the countryside' has been created as a means of integrating urban and rural education, with this policy of mingling children from disparate backgrounds helping to transform attitudes to rural life. In the same way particular emphasis has been given to the development of rural health programmes. One of the first initiatives taken by the regime in the 1960s was to develop a system of strategically sited cottage hospitals and rural clinics, with medical students required to work for at least two years in rural service after graduating.[22] This approach is one of various factors that has helped Cuba to avoid the drift to the cities, and the consequent urban blight, that is so common throughout the Third World. Today it is easy to identify the elements that contributed to such social progress: 'Socialist ideology has provided an impetus for broad-based economic development, where urban interests are not allowed to usurp rural needs. But it is political-economic control of state and society by the regime and international assistance which has made the ideal attainable.'[23] Today the missing element of 'international assistance' (that is, from the Socialist bloc) could be replaced by trade – which is why Washington is so keen to maintain the economic blockade.

A primary task was to develop a national education system. At the end of the 1950s only about half of all children aged 6 to 12 years attended school; but today, in contrast with much of Latin American, school attendance for this age group is universal and compulsory, with similar developments in place for the 13 to 16 age group. At the same time prodigious efforts were made to improve the *quality* of education, from that of the youngest children to that in the specialised institutes of higher learning and research. Thus Fernando García, Deputy Director in the Ministry of Education, commented in interview in 1983; 'To fully change a system requires more than a change in one of its elements; it requires a change in all of them.' In 1971 a national educational conference decided that a combination of study and work should guide *all* education, and that educational subsystems (beginning with daycare centres and pre-primary training) were essential to educational reform.

As an early step, following the suggestion of José Martí (see Chapter 4) that fortresses be turned into schools, the revolutionary government set about converting Batista's military garrisons and barracks into educational establishments. And as the gangsters and corrupt politicians fled the Castro regime their suburban mansions and palatial estates were quickly confiscated and turned into schools. Thus much of the plush Havana suburb of Miramar was converted into a 'school-city'; as was the notorious Moncada Fortress. For the first time free education was offered to everyone: whites, blacks and mulattos; girls and boys. The first childcare centre was opened in April 1961 in Ciudad Libertad, and soon the first literacy brigades were spreading out through the mountains and farmlands. Latin America had witnessed nothing like it before. The élitist factions throughout the continent had not welcomed such developments; and nor had Washington: the new childcare centres and schools were some of the targets bombed in the early 1960s by CIA-sponsored planes flying from US territory. But such responses did little to discourage the Cuban enthusiasm for radical social change. In the 1960s the national literacy campaigns transformed the country, enabling Cuba to achieve literacy rates superior to any in the rest of the Third World and equal to most in the developed countries. At the same time specialist institutes were established for the training of teachers (the first of these set high in the Sierra Maestra), doctors, engineers, scientists and other professionals.[24]

By 1995 Cuba had achieved a goal originally set for 1996: that of having 100 per cent of its 5-year-old children enrolled in kindergarten and more than 50 per cent of all its younger children (0 to 5) receiving some sort of pre-primary education. These achievements also meant that Cuba was three years ahead in meeting the goals specified in the National Plan of Action (PNA) based on resolutions passed at the UN-sponsored World Summit for Children. Luis Zuñiga Zárate, a UNICEF representative and director of resident programmes, commenting on these achievements, declared: 'Cuba has a very well-defined position and the political will when it comes to the development and well-being of its children. If one takes into consideration this country's educational trajectory, with a 30-year tradition in this field, there's no reason to be surprised at these achievements. . . . What is definitely unusual is that it is able to continue providing such extensive early education coverage within the framework of the enormous financial difficulties it has.'[25]

The importance of the Cuban achievements, in the context of characteristic Third World limitations, is that high-quality education is free to all children. Zuñiga: 'Here in Cuba education is the same for all children, and not just because it is free – in nearly all countries, public schools and private schools exist side by side. It is Cuba's intention to have its educational system equally accessible to all. UNICEF has great respect for the way the PNA was formulated here and for the way it is being implemented. It has one guiding principle: to be a genuine tool of social policy.' He emphasised also that every year the 'highest authorities in the country' review the programme, signalling the importance in which it is held.

At the same time few observers doubted that the US economic embargo was impacting on the situation of children in Cuba. Thus at a UNICEF-sponsored meeting on children and social policies, held in Bogotá (April 1994), the Cuban Minister of Education Luis Gómez Gutiérrez charged that the United States was violating the rights of children by denying them access to medicines and other essential goods. He pointed out that nonetheless Cuban advances in public health and education were recognised worldwide: Cuba had broken the measles transmission cycle in 1992, and had eliminated polio, diphtheria, tetanus neonatorum and tuberculous meningitis.

But it was inevitable that the economic embargo would affect the health of the Cuban people – as indeed Washington intended it to. When the US paediatrician Helen Rodríguez headed a delegation of the American Public Health Association (APHA) in a visit to Havana (April 1994) she declared that the measures taken against Cuba were an attack on the population's health. It is highly significant that Washington should want to undermine one of the most impressive achievements of the Cuban Revolution.

It is useful to contrast the US attitude to public health with the Cuban approach that has now persisted for 35 years. For example, at a time when Cuba was continuing to invest heavily in health the Reagan administration was introducing widespread cuts. The *New York Times* (17 January 1983) recorded this particular phase of cuts in the United States: 'In the last 18 months, every state has reduced health services for poor people, especially women and children. . . . Almost 700,000 children lost coverage under Medicaid . . . infant mortality rates are rising in Alabama, Maine, Michigan and Ohio . . . 47 states made cutbacks in maternal and child health programs . . . funds for health centers have been reduced by 13 per cent . . . 44 states reduced prenatal and delivery services to pregnant women or preventive health services for children . . .'. The contrast with Cuban medical practice could scarcely be more stark. Consider, for example, the trends in infant mortality in Cuba, set against 1995 figures for other Latin American countries, most of which are ideologically sympathetic to the United States (Table 1.1).

The 1994 figure of 9.9 infant deaths per 1000 live births again placed Cuba amongst the 25 countries with the lowest infant mortality figures in the world – a remarkable achievement for a Third World country during economic crisis. In the proud words of *Granma International* (18 January 1995): '*This achievement highlights the efforts of the health personnel working in mother–infant care, backed up by the unshakable political will of the revolutionary government to maintain the high levels of health care enjoyed by the nation, even in such difficult economic conditions.*'[26] Havana registered the lowest figure in its history, 'much lower, of course, than that recorded in the US capital . . .'. Another significant achievement during 1994 was the lowest infant mortality rate due to congenital malformation (2.3 per 1000 live births), achieved through the universalisation of prenatal diagnoses. The high incidence of breast feeding in Cuba is one of

TABLE 1.1   Infant mortality: Cuba and the rest of Latin America

---

Infant mortality in Cuba in the last 25 years* (per 1000)

1970	38.7
1971	36.1
1972	28.7
1973	29.6
1974	29.3
1975	27.5
1976	23.3
1977	24.9
1978	22.4
1979	19.4
1980	19.6
1981	18.5
1982	17.3
1983	16.8
1984	15.0
1985	16.5
1986	13.6
1987	13.3
1988	11.9
1989	11.1
1990	10.7
1991	10.7
1992	10.2
1993	9.4
1994	9.9

Infant mortality in Latin America† (per 1000)

Haiti	85
Bolivia	78
Guatemala	53
Brazil	52
Nicaragua	51
El Salvador	45
Ecuador	45
Peru	43
Honduras	43
Dominican Republic	40
Paraguay	28
Mexico	27
Argentina	24
Venezuela	20
Uruguay	19
Panama	18
Colombia	16
Chile	15
Costa Rica	14

SOURCES:
* National Statistics Department, Ministry of Public Health, Cuba
† *The State of the World's Children*, UNICEF, 1995.

the reasons why 40 of the 46 Cuban hospitals in which more than 1000 babies are born in a year have attained the international distinction of 'Baby Friendly Hospitals' (compared with, for example, Sweden's 41 out of 61 maternity hospitals achieving the same distinction).

The care of children in Cuba includes an extensive vaccination programme. Some 95 per cent of children continue to be immunised against a range of preventable diseases (tuberculosis, hepatitis B, poliomyelitis, diphtheria, tetanus, whooping cough, meningitis B and C, mumps, German measles, measles and typhus), despite all Washington's best efforts to prevent Cuba enjoying the benefits of sophisticated medical products. Cuba itself manufactures the meningitis B and C vaccine (the only country in the world to do so), and also the vaccines for hepatitis B, typhus and tetanus. Today the celebrated Finlay Institute, with other Cuban scientific institutions, is researching new vaccines; a leptospirosis vaccine is currently undergoing clinical tests. Again it is highly significant that the first certificate attesting to the eradication of polio in the Americas was bestowed on Cuba by an international evaluating committee. In the context of this evaluation the US scientist Dorothy M. Horstmann praised the technical work of Cuban specialists; and Dr Ciro de Quadros, coordinator of the Pan American Health Organisation (PAHO) immunisation programme and a special advisor to the World Health Organisation (WHO), declared that a principal factor in the historic eradication of polio in Cuba was the government's ongoing political will in that direction. Cuba's example provided the strategic basis for carrying out the polio-eradication campaign in the Americas (de Quadros: 'The lessons we learned from this country were essential political will and the participation of the people themselves in the campaign').

It was the same political will, mobilising Cuba's best scientific expertise, that brought the neuropathy epidemic under control in 1993. Then it was suggested, not least by US experts, that the economic blockade may have contributed to the incidence of the neural eye disease in 50,000 Cubans. Thus on 27 May 1993 Dr David Levinson, a San Francisco physician who had visited Cuba, stated that the US embargo was causing a severe shortage of medicines and 'effectively holding the health of the Cuban people hostage. . . . This is an inhumane, cruel policy which must be ended' (*The Guardian*, 28 May 1993). Even in the circumstances of a severe disease epidemic, Washington refused to relax the block on the export of medicines to Cuba: on 26 October 1993 Alexander Watson, US Assistant Under-Secretary of State for Inter-American Affairs, declared in a keynote speech that the blockade of Cuba would continue. By contrast, the World Health Organisation (WHO) and the Pan American Health

Organisation (PAHO) responded wholeheartedly to Cuba's request for assistance. With help from these bodies, and by dint of Cuba's political will and social commitment, the epidemic was quickly brought under control. Cuba has now produced extensive scientific documentation of the disease, with a book and other publications on epidemic neuropathy now made available to the international medical community.

Cuban specialists are now also researching minimum access surgery ('stereotaxis') for brain and other types of operations. Here, use is being made of computerised axial tomography (CAT) scanning and magnetic nuclear resonance techniques, in concert with computer programs developed by the International Neurological Restoration Centre (CIREN). This organisation is currently working in collaboration with the Hermanos Ameijeiras Hospital, the Scientific Research Centre (CENIC) and the Centre for Medical and Surgical Research (CIMEQ) to develop stereotaxic and other surgical techniques. Dr Luis Ochoa, CIREN's head of neurosurgery, claims that Cuban research has put the country 'hard on the heels' of Sweden, Germany, France, Japan, and the United States, the acknowledged world leaders in stereotaxic techniques.

Since 1982 Cuban biochemists have developed more than 100 monoclonal antibodies, one of these (ior-t3) now a registered drug used in the prevention and treatment of organ transplant rejection. In early 1995 tests were being carried out on monoclonal antibodies for the treatment of cancer of the lymphatic tissue (lymphoma) and cancers of the lung and brain. The establishment of the Molecular Immunology Centre (CIM) in 1994 represented a substantial contribution to this work. CIM director Dr Agustín Lage has emphasised that Cuba is no longer an underdeveloped country in the fields of education and health. Another Cuban organisation, the National Institute of Oncology and Radiobiology (INOR), is a world leader in the area of nuclear medicine. Here, for example, the researcher Dr Juan Perfecto Oliva González has developed the radioimmunolocalisation (or immunogammagraphy) technique that can use a monoclonal antibody against a tumor antigen 'pinpointed' with a radioisotope. In this context positive results have been obtained using a Cuban antibody (ior-cea-1) in the detection of colon and rectal tumours.

The Cuban approach to health care is impressive at all levels – from the scale of preventive medicine, through the treatment of disease by family doctor or hospital, to the highest reaches of fundamental research. One US observer draws attention to the Cuban health revolution that managed to achieve 'health indicators rivaling those of the developed countries. . . . By 1989 the country had 263 hospitals, 420 polyclinics, 229 rural and urban health posts, and two national research institutes . . . a health care standard unprecedented in Latin America, with modern tertiary health care facilities that included an extensive biotechnology industry, biomedical engineering institutes, genetic research programs, six cardiac centers, an ophthalmology hospital, and a network of immunoassay centers.'[27] Another American researcher, Milton I. Roemer, Professor Emeritus at the School of Public Health, University of California, compares primary health care and hospitalisation in California and Cuba, demonstrating Cuban superiority in important particulars: 'Admission to a hospital in both countries depends on the decision of a hospital doctor after a community doctor has made a referral. US hospital doctors would tend to discourage Medicaid admissions because reimbursements for Medicaid patients are very low; Cuban hospital doctors would have no reasons to discourage admissions.'[28] Again the stark contrast in US and Cuban political attitudes: in Cuba, unlike the United States, the immense advances in primary health care have been made possible 'because the government considered health a top priority'.[29]

In the contentious area of AIDS the Cuban approach has been typically thorough and multifaceted, marrying the need for individual health care with the necessity to protect the community. Here the policy of compulsory quarantine of HIV-positive individuals in state-run sanatoria has been widely criticised as an abuse of human rights.* The matter cannot be debated in detail here but it is useful to consider particular aspects. Sanatoria residents are allowed home at weekends, though chaperoned to prevent the spread of AIDS through sexual promiscuity. If after six months a resident is deemed trustworthy, unchaperoned home visits are allowed. Such conditions apply in the context of a massive HIV screening programme, the most comprehensive of any nation; and within the framework of specialist medical treatment – only if the individual is willing – using the most advanced drug therapies. Professor Nancy Scheper-Hughes, University of California, has observed that gays, women and children are 'especially protected by the Cuban AIDS programme. A strong and humane public health system has just as often protected the lives of socially vulnerable groups as it has violated their personal liberties.'[30] Today, after years of persecution of the homosexual community, official hostility to gays is much reduced. AIDS policy bears equally on heterosexuals and gays; and in 1992 the first open gay festival took place on the streets of Havana.

One important consequence of Cuba's emphasis on health care has been the export of doctors, drugs and other medical facilities – to Africa, Asia and the Americas. Cuban doctors accompanied the troops to Angola, and served also in Chile, Mexico, El Salvador, Nicaragua and many other countries. Interestingly enough, as a gesture of 'reverse internationalism' –

---

*The fact that tuberculosis sufferers in New York can be locked up is rarely cited as evidence of human rights abuses in the United States.

at a time when the Soviet Union was drastically cutting its aid to Cuba – some 3000 Soviet children, contaminated at Chernobyl, were being treated free-of-charge in Cuba. Said 10-year-old Axanna Kanuiyk from Kiev: 'I wish my mother and father and my friends could come here. Then I would not have to go home.'[31]

Advances in education, health, welfare, scientific research and other social sectors have been accompanied by progressive democratisation: not only in such areas as industrial decision making (where today there are levels of industrial democracy that are totally unknown in such capitalist countries as Britain and the United States), but also in the national political structures. By the mid-1980s the governmental structure comprised 169 Municipal Assemblies at the base, 14 Provincial Assemblies at a higher level, and the National Assembly at the peak. Representatives were elected to the Municipal Assemblies, which in turn elected the representatives at the higher levels. Large municipalities could elect more than one member to the National Assembly, in which case prominent sports figures or other celebrities could be chosen.

The entire political system embodies what the Cubans call 'Popular Power', a framework that encourages massive popular participation in the political process. At the same time public participation in Production Assemblies and enterprise Management Councils encourages the involvement of workers able to shape aspects of national planning policy. The Popular Power assemblies do not initiate plans, but consider and approve them, agreeing proposed amendments with enterprise directors, ministry officials, and representatives of JUCEPLAN, the national planning board.

The various elements of Popular Power (in both industrial planning and political elections) 'have the potential to permit significant levels of democracy'.[32] The level of public participation is generally seen as substantial, generating 'a visible degree of popular control over the development and administration of local plans (within the budgetary and resource limits set by the national plan)'.[33] At the same time there has been little opportunity for worker influence in setting the national planning goals. The need for improvement in this area and in the character of the Popular Power political system led to substantial constitutional changes in the early 1990s. The Cuban government had recognised the need to develop the degree of democratisation in the people's control of the highest organs of the state – and so encouraged the widest popular discussion. Between May and November 1990 3.5 million citizens took part in more than 800,000 assemblies, expressing their concern over national issues in general and Popular (or People's) Power in particular.

On 12 October 1991, after wide-ranging discussion at the Fourth Congress of the Communist Party of Cuba, approval was given to a resolution proposing various changes to the operation of the political structure. This in turn led to debate at the Eleventh ordinary session of the National Assembly (10–12 July 1992) on a new Constitutional Reform Law involving modifications to 76 Articles in the 141–Article constitution. One of the most important changes was the provision for the election, through direct and secret ballot, of the deputies to the National Assembly (where formerly the directly-elected municipal members had voted for National Assembly representatives).

The revised constitution allows a maximum of eight candidates to stand in a constituency, each individual being nominated and voted for in public meetings by a show of hands. Two observers, Trish Meehan and Dave Willets (from the Cuba Solidarity Campaign), have described the electoral procedure in the Cuban elections that took place in February 1993 according to the modified constitution: 'The commissions [for supervising the electoral procedure] consist of representatives of the various mass organisations such as the Federation of Cuban Women, the Cuban Workers' Congress, etc. . . . People then proposed candidates. One woman stood up and said she wanted to nominate the law teacher from the university. . . . The commissioners asked for a show of hands and so many were raised that the teacher was nominated. The existing delegate was renominated. . . . All Cubans over 16 living in the area had a vote.'[34]

The fact that about 80 per cent of candidates were members of the Communist party (with no other *political* group allowed to propose candidates) is evidence enough, in some perceptions, that the Cuban parliamentary system is inherently undemocratic; but particular considerations should be borne in mind. It is significant, for example, that there is today no *constitutional* block on non-Communists being nominated and elected – which means that a Cuban election could in theory yield a Communist *minority* in the National Assembly. In these circumstances a political system only permitting one organised party (with membership granted on the basis of civic responsibility and revolutionary commitment) is not necessarily undemocratic; particularly, as with the Cuban electoral system, when every successful candidate is required to win more than 50 per cent of the popular vote.*

Despite the manifest scale of democratisation in Cuba, in terms of both public participation in economic decision making and the evolving

---

*That the *two-party* political system in the United States is inherently undemocratic has been emphasised by many observers; drawing attention to the role of money in the electoral procedure. It might have been Fidel Castro himself who said that the US 'has one political party – the Money Party, with two wings, the Democratic and the Republican'. A variant on this theme suggests that the United States is a one-party state, but, being America, it has to have two of them.

character of the political system (especially in the context of recent constitutional changes), it is still deemed useful by hostile propagandists to depict Cuba as a 'totalitarian dictatorship' in violation of human rights. Washington has frequently tried to enlist international support for its charges against Cuba's human-rights record, though with little success. For example, on 11 March 1987, despite typical US diplomatic arm-twisting, the UN Human Rights Commission rejected (by 19 votes to 18, with 6 abstentions) a US resolution attacking Cuba on human rights. More credence should be given to Amnesty International reports criticising Cuba's treatment of political dissidents,[35] though here, Amnesty itself acknowledged that many of the cases involve 'an increase in delinquency and vandalism', widely perceived as one of the aims of the US economic blockade. Nor should it be forgotten that, by dint of the blockade and other tactics, the Cuban regime survives precariously in what is a *de facto* war situation. For example, the *Los Angeles Times* (16 November 1989) reported that the Bush Administration and Congressional oversight panels had agreed that the United States may participate in covert operations that might lead to the death of foreign leaders. Such assassinations, a well documented part of earlier US policy towards Cuba, would no longer be nominally illegal.

Attention should also be given to specific charges that the Cuban regime has targeted political activists, and to exposés of the appalling conditions in some Cuban jails.[36] But here too US outrage at advertised Cuban derelictions would carry more moral weight if the United States itself was not prepared to tolerate much worse human-rights abuses by its own allies (for example, torture of political dissidents in Turkey and Saudi Arabia, and in the Israeli-protected dungeons of Khiam in southern Lebanon) and if US police and penal institutions did not perpetrate their own gross abuses.*

Various Amnesty International reports have highlighted police torture in the United States, and the willingness of the US Supreme Court to allow the execution of juveniles and the mentally retarded.[37] Nor is

---

*One reported case concerns the treatment of a mentally-ill black inmate at the maximum security prison in Pelican Bay, California. When the prisoner smeared himself in faeces he was then handcuffed by warders and given a bath in scalding water. As his skin peeled off, one of the warders said: 'Looks like we're gonna have a white boy before this is through' (*The Observer*, London, 29 January 1995). This and many other flagrant abuses were exposed in a 345-page judicial ruling. There was 'little optimism that the prison will reform itself . . .'.

Washington's case against Cuba helped by the fact that the United States continues to abuse its own political prisoners.*

It is obvious that any US charges of Cuban human-rights derelictions should be considered in the context of America's pragmatic acceptance of gross abuses elsewhere, the appalling brutalities in US penal theory and practice,† and Washington's well-documented use of black propaganda (and other 'dirty tricks') against its political enemies. Nor has the US case been helped by a recent Central Intelligence (CIA) report suggesting that few of the Cubans seeking refugee status in the United States were doing so for political reasons: 'It is brazenly acknowledged by some of the reintegrated political prisoners that they apply for refugee status as a means to escape the deteriorating economic situation and not because of the current fear of persecution or harassment.'[38] It is the US economic blockade, a gross violation of UN resolutions (see 'The Response – International', below), that represents the most serious abuse of the rights of the Cuban people.

A PEOPLE UNDER SIEGE

The United States had resorted to terrorism, black propaganda, assassination attempts and military invasion (see Chapter 7) in its efforts to overthrow the revolutionary Cuban regime. All had failed, but the decades-long economic embargo, akin to a mediaeval siege would continue:

Assuming that initial storm had failed or was not feasible, the attackers were likely to settle for longer term success through a blockade. . . . No one wanted a siege to go on for months or years, so every avenue was explored. It was common to test the defenders as severely as possible in the early stages, battering them with men, engines and propaganda, but if all the various forms of pressure proved unavailing, then they might have to settle down to cutting off supplies and starving out the garrison.[39]

---

*One case concerns fifteen Puerto Rican independence fighters, including six women, regularly abused (their eyes, ears, mouths, rectums and penises or vaginas frequently searched – sometimes eight times a day – for 'security' reasons) and held in conditions of sensory deprivation and solitary confinement: one woman, Alejandrina Torres, was held in solitary confinement for two and a half years; a man, Oscar Lopez Rivera, for eleven years (*Granma International*, Havana, 8 February 1995).
† An important Amnesty International report (March 1995, AMR 51/25/95) focuses on torture and other abuses of human rights in US jails. Topics covered include: the execution of juveniles, deaths in police custody, beatings, sexual abuse, denial of medical care, prolonged shackling to beds, sensory deprivation, racism, political incarcerations, etc.

The progressive collapse of the Socialist bloc – that began in the late 1980s and ended with the demise of the Soviet Union in late December 1991 – provided Washington with the opportunity to tighten the economic block-ade of Cuba. The Cold War was over: now it seemed that only a few 'clean-up' operations would be necessary to make the world safe for global capitalism. Washington moved quickly to enlist the support of the former Socialist countries in its determination to crush the Cuban regime, at the same time working to tighten the relevant legislation. Now circumstances were conspiring against Cuba. Aid, already massively reduced by Gorbachev, continued to diminish; Washington was working to intensify Cuba's economic isolation; and the Republican victory in the mid-term US elections (November 1994) heralded an increasingly hostile US posture. It seemed that the defeat of Fidel Castro would not be long delayed.

Washington's hostility to the Castro regime had rendered Cuba increas-ingly dependent on the Socialist bloc; in particular, on the Soviet Union. This in turn had made Cuba highly vulnerable to Soviet political shifts. Castro himself had perceived that the Gorbachev reforms might bring immense difficulties to the Cuban economy, and this proved to be the case: aid and trade were cut back, and even agreed shipments, disrupted by *perestroika* ('restructuring'), arrived late or not at all. Shipments expected by January 1991 did not arrive until May; by September none of the expected rice, only 16 per cent of the normal quota of vegetable oil, and less than half the normal supply of butter had reached Cuba. At the same time expected shipments of raw materials, fertilisers for the sugar industry, wood, sheet metal, glass, paper, and spare parts for machinery and vehi-cles had been substantially reduced. Mineral rights were now being acquired by the former Soviet republics, further disrupting the supply of oil to Cuba. Castro himself said in a December 1991 interview that Cuba had received less than one third of the oil it had expected for the year.[40] The Cuban–Soviet 'special relationship' was at an end, and the effects were being felt in every area of Cuban life.

Washington seized on this chance to sabotage yet further the tottering Cuban economy. Throughout the world Washington was now intimidating companies into denying Cuba its legitimate trading opportunities. There are many examples of where US threats have forced companies around the globe to break their deals with the island:*

---

*See also the examples supplied by Cuban Foreign Minister Roberto Robaina to the UN Secretary-General (pp. 19–20).

- the US Treasury refused to license Medix (Argentina) to sell Cuba spare parts for medical equipment;

- Vickers (Brazil) has been prevented from quoting prices for hydraulic-pneumatic components;

- the US Treasury Department refused to allow Hoechst (Brazil) to sell plastic resins;

- the Ayerst Laboratories (Canada) has been blocked from supplying colyrum (for the treatment of gas and chemical damage to the eyes) to the Cuban health service;

- Federal Pacific Electric (Canada) has been prevented from supplying fuses;

- Pepsi Cola (Canada), though reprimanded by the Canadian Trade Ministry, has decided under US pressure not to make supplies available to Cuba;

- Square D (Canada) declared that it was no longer able to supply electrical switches to Cuba;

- CGR Thompson (France) has been denied a US licence to sell Cuba spare parts for X-ray equipment;

- Siemens (Germany) has been blocked from selling Gamma Cameras, an Ultra-sound system, and a Magnetic Nuclear Resonance system – all intended for use in the Cuban health service;

- Dow (Italy) has been refused permission to sell water-treatment resins;

- Toshiba (Japan) has been denied licences to sell medical equipment to Cuba;

- Crouse-Hinds Domex (Mexico) was pressured not to quote for iron components used in electrical installations;

- Piher Semiconductors (Spain), after selling Cuba US-made electrical equipment, was placed on a blacklist and then sued. After the settlement of $1 million, the company filed for bankruptcy a short time later;

- Alfa-Laval (Sweden) was blocked from supplying filtration cartridges to the Cuban health service.[41]

Such measures, and the many related US activities in the context of the Socialist-bloc collapse, had their inevitable consequences for Cuban society. Queues for even the most basic consumer goods – including foodstuffs – lengthened; while the list of rationed items continued to expand: since late 1990 eggs, fish, canned meat, biscuits, cream cheese, rum, undergarments and soap have all been added to the rationed list. Paper shortages have closed down newspapers and other publications; fuel shortages have resulted in frequent blackouts in Havana and other cities; bulls are being domesticated as beasts of burden to replace petrol-driven vehicles; and human power, via pushcart and bicycle (acquired from China), is increasingly used, as fuel and spare parts for cars, buses and trucks become increasingly unavailable. Social values are also being eroded: for example, the elimination of prostitution was once one of the proud boasts of the Revolution, but now it is clearly evident again in Havana and other cities. And there have also been growing signs of social dislocation: street protests, smashed windows in official buildings, a local party official reportedly killed.[42]

Today Cuba has only 14 per cent of the export levels it enjoyed in 1989, which means, since the country is denied even normal trade credit, that there has been a comparable cut in Cuban imports. Scheduled buses do not always arrive, power cuts – despite attempts to regulate their frequency – are unpredictable, and even rationed items (including food) are not always available in the shops. In general, 'shortages of food, transport, fuel, water, and electricity rule the day'.[43] All this has meant an inevitable decline in living standards and social cohesion, though many observers have remarked on how 'Cuba has managed to hang on to "normal" social life to a surprising degree'.[44] Few other societies would have survived such an economic onslaught.

The food situation in Cuba reached critical levels two or three years ago. One observer, Robert Lessman, noted that in the urban areas, 'one meal a day is the rule, and sometimes that consists of just boiled rice' (November 1993). Thus in 1992 calorie consumption *per capita* fell from 2848 to 2500, with the trend continuing downwards. By 1992 reporters were noting that 'Every day, Cuba dies a little',[45] with no end in sight. By now 'the cafes have nothing to sell',[46] and 'Cuba's terrible hunger' had 'reached a climax'.[47] Women were reported picking through rotting vegetables in the hope of finding palatable items, queuing two hours for bread (one bread roll), and then moving on wearily to queue elsewhere for tea. The average Cuban had lost between 15lb and 20lb in weight since the beginning of the crisis in 1990, the start of what Castro has called the 'Special Period', to mid-1993.[48] In May 1993 a journalist, living with her teenage daughter, was quoted: 'We live on rice and beans. And cabbage. We last had meat in this house in February. Everyone is hungry. It is all we think about'; and a clinic worker in Havana declared: 'When I see the tourists eating what they like, I don't hate them. But I want them to know we are hungry. I want foreigners to realise how the Cuban people live.'[49]

In mid-1995 the United States – by its unyielding campaign of forcing an international economic blockade – continued to use starvation as a political weapon against the Cuban people. The international protests at this inhumane and brutal policy were frequent (see 'The Response – International', below), but with the Republican domination of the US Congress there was even less hope than formerly of a relaxation in the food and medicine blockade. It is important in this context to remember Protocol I of the Geneva Convention:

Starvation of civilians as a method of warfare is prohibited.

Even legitimate attacks against the sustenance of enemy armed forces is only permitted in international law when such action cannot 'be expected to leave the civilian population with such inadequate food or water as to cause its starvation or force its movement'.[50] The US policy of economic siege – still maintained today after 35 years – works to do both.

THE RESPONSE – DOMESTIC

The first response of the Cuban government to the economic crisis was to admit the scale of the problems facing the country – an obvious requirement if realistic attempts were to be made to cope with the situation, but one that many other governments might have been tempted to disguise. In his letter (25 June 1993) to UN Secretary-General Boutros-Ghali, Cuba's Foreign Minister Roberto Robaina said that, 'according to conservative estimates made by experts', the economic blockade had cost Cuba more than $40 billion, about 20 times the country's 1992 account earnings. Said Robaina: 'The blockade effects have been felt in virtually all areas of the economy and have had a cumulative effect over more than 30 years, causing changes in the people's consumption habits, huge and otherwise unnecessary investments in industrial and transportation sectors, and creating obstacles to scientific and technological development, as well as great shortages in the number of products consumed by the population.'

One consequence is that foodstuffs, for example, have had to be acquired from wherever they were available – so adding to transportation costs. Thus it has typically cost an extra $23 for each ton of imported food. In late 1994 it was noted that over the past few years the cost of cereals, chicken and milk had increased from $500,000 to $41 million, that freight losses exceeded more than $85 million, and that fuel charges had increased by 43 per cent. Cuban telecommunications income had been frozen, causing losses of $102 million a year, with restrictions on Cuba's sugar sales resulting in losses of around $205 million. Because Cuba is prevented from pricing its sugar on the New York Commodities Exchange it has lost another $39 million. In the same way the need to obtain essential items from faraway places has resulted in between 30 and 40 per cent more being paid to middlemen, with a greater time lapse in obtaining essential products. As one typical example, medical products that could otherwise have been obtained from the US SIGMA company for $827 were eventually obtained elsewhere for $1938; another purchase of 24 medical products involved an additional expenditure of $986,386, without taking into account extra freight charges. One of the medicines (nifidipine, used to treat cardiovascular diseases) in this batch was listed in the Talgrex catalogue at $61.56 a kilogram, but the cost to Cuba was $111.67 a kilogram. And some products had become totally unavailable. The blockade had stopped the supply of many drugs, spare parts for medical equipment, and medical textbooks. Thus when Cuba's supplier of medical textbooks, the Spanish company Editorial Interamericana S.A., was taken over by the US company McGraw-Hill all transactions with Cuba were terminated.[51]

In the situation of mounting shortages the Cuban government progressively tightened the regime of rationing. (In June 1963 Che Guevara said: 'Normally, a shortage of commodities would have immediately produced an increase in market prices to bring supply and demand into equilibrium. Instead we instituted a strict price freeze and established a system of rationing.'[52]) Such measures averted the mass starvation that would have occurred in an unrestrained free-market economic system, but still the rigours of a rationing regime that was more severe than anything experienced by the British in the Second World War were increasingly difficult to bear (Table 1.2). The meagre allowances were inadequate in the early days of the rationing regime, but even these slender quantities have been progressively squeezed during the time of the Special Period. Moreover, even though an item is defined under the terms of the rationing regime it may not be available. People are required to queue to claim their entitlements; even then they may be disappointed. The increasingly desperate food situation became the most pressing concern of the Cuban government: if this problem could not be solved then nothing else would be possible.

By 1994 the list of rationed items had grown, with many products now available only on the black market. Clothes, like food, were rationed: one pair of shoes and one pair of trousers per person per year – though the waiting lists grew ever longer and many supplies were simply non-existent. In these circumstances the incidence of prostitution – formerly denounced as a decadent feature of the Batista regime – continued to rise, with girls as young as fourteen now resorting to *jinetear* ('looking for a tourist'), whereby sexual favours could be exchanged for a sandwich or a bar of chocolate.[53] And, in another development that suggested a return to the bad old days, the Cuban government entered into a joint venture with foreign capital to sanction the cruise ship *Santiago de Cuba,* equipped with the first casino in Cuba since 1959. Massimo Bessana, the director of

TABLE 1.2   Rationing in Cuba (1992)

Rice	5 lbs
Pulses	60 grammes
Cooking oil	$\frac{1}{2}$ lb
Lard	$\frac{1}{2}$ lb
Sugar	4 lbs
Soap (personal)	1 cake
Soap (washing)	1 cake
Coffee	4 ounces
Detergent	7 ounces
Eggs	4 per week
Bread	1 roll per day
Chicken or meat	1 lb per 9 days
Fish	1 lb per fortnight

Allowances per person per month
Milk available only to under-sevens and those on special diets

SOURCE: *The Guardian,* London, 15 July 1992

the Italian investors, Havana Cruises, said that it had been 'a struggle' to win Cuban approval for the floating casino; agreement was finally reached provided it remained closed while inside territorial waters.

It was now clear that the Castro regime would be forced to move to the right in order to survive. In 1991 there was growing speculation about what the Fourth Communist Party Congress would yield, with mounting expectation that increased private economic activity would be allowed, not least in the small service sector; and that, despite the unswerving revolutionary rhetoric, there would be renewed attempts to cajole foreign capitalist investors into joint venture projects. As one observer of the changing scene noted: 'The combined message reads: "Socialism or death – and how about building a hotel?"'[54] It was recognised that rationing and the redistribution of resources would not be sufficient to solve the economic problems. Efforts would have to be made to open up the country to foreign trade – the embargo permitting: joint-venture initiative would be intensified, the healthy tourist industry would be expanded to gain foreign exchange, and the thriving biotechnology sector would be encouraged to boost production. At the same time there was some tempering of the revolutionary rhetoric. On 8 November 1993 Castro declared, in contrast to the 'Socialism or death' slogans: 'The readiness to achieve success is more important than the readiness to die.'[55]

Some government reshuffling took place on 8 August 1993, with the possession of foreign exchange decriminalised a few days later; now Cubans, if they had the means, were allowed to buy goods in the foreign-exchange retailers previously restricted to the tourist trade. One aim was to deflate the growing black market, and thereby to swell the country's foreign exchange reserves. But the measure, however justifiable in economic terms, had disruptive social consequences: many Cubans, who had eschewed foreign exchange in the interest of the Revolution, now felt betrayed. There were growing signs that the new measures were eroding one of Cuba's most vital resources – the morale of the people.

On 8 September the Cuban government passed a law, 'Employment on Own Account', to allow 117 types of employment (extended to 135 on 22 October 1993) as a means of encouraging employment for the disguised number of unemployed. Still the prohibitions on private wage-related employment were retained: people were allowed only to sell those products they manufactured themselves, so that 'the emergence of intermediate dealers or parasites'[56] would be prevented. And the state retained the right to intervene to prevent 'excesses'. Any Cubans deciding to take advantage of the new law were required to pay a small monthly tax. In early 1994 some 140,000 Cubans were reputedly self-employed, many obtaining working materials on the black market and so scarcely operating on a legal basis. The Cuban press itself noted the uncertainty about 'what happens to persons who sell goods which were not manufactured from raw materials originating from the state' – a 'weak point of the law'.[57]

The government moved also (via a Politburo resolution on 10 September 1993) to convert most of the state farms (working 73 per cent of the land and accounting for 78 per cent of agricultural production) into cooperative enterprises. Here the aim was to preserve state ownership but to improve incentives by allowing the cooperatives a substantial element of autonomy in production and finance. At the same time plans were set in train to allow single persons (including pensioners) to own and farm previously unused areas up to half a hectare. Such developments, scarcely radical to most external observers, did in fact represent a significant departure from recent Cuban practice and philosophy. Castro had toyed with various free-market mechanisms in the past: now he was again supping with the Devil, albeit with a long spoon and from a small dish.

The new policies were achieving a measure of success in the strongest economic sectors. The numbers of tourists had increased from 336,000 in 1991 to 600,000 in 1993. Hotels were being built in Havana, Varadero and other tourist centres; and mounting numbers of foreign travellers (from Canada, Mexico, Europe and elsewhere – but rarely from the US because of the embargo) were bringing much needed foreign exchange. Cuba's substantial investment in education and biochemical research was now bringing further economic benefits, with such products as vaccines against meningitis and hepatitis and an anti-cholesterol drug (PPG) being successfully marketed in various countries, despite US hostility to such trade. One observer describes the work of the Imunoensayo firm, specialising in the use of computer-essaying of samples to allow diagnostic testing of entire populations; and now marketing the mail-in AIDS test-kit and other products in Latin America and Europe.[58] Sales from Imunoensayo and other high-technology enterprises earned more than $200 million in 1992.

The Cuban government had moved on several economic fronts. Joint ventures with capitalist investors were now being encouraged; the hard currency stores (the so-called *diplomercados*, for the diplomatic and tourist sectors) were now open to Cubans allowed to hold US dollars; the self-employment (*cuentapropista*) sector had been dramatically expanded (in such service areas as bicycle repair, TV repair, etc. and in arts and craft production); and some 1600 Basic Units of Cooperative Production (UBPCs) had replaced virtually all the state farms producing sugar cane. It is significant that all these reforms represented a movement in the direction of capitalist economic production. The joint ventures (see below), the expansion of private employment enterprise, the legalisation of US dollar holdings, the agricultural reforms – all represented a revolution in retreat. Today, for example, the UBPCs, unlike the traditional state farms, own their harvest and sell it to the state, albeit at government-fixed prices. Moreover, the cooperatives now own the agricultural machinery, bought from the former state farms using low-interest loans. Revenues are used to purchase seed, fuel, fertilisers and other supplies necessary for agricultural production. The land remains the property of the state: it cannot be sold, rented, inherited, mortgaged, or used as collateral for loans. Nonetheless, the reforms represent an unambiguous drift in the direction of privatisation, anathema to traditional supporters of the Cuban Revolution.

In February 1992 the government was forced to increase a range of prices, the first in three decades for some foods, in an attempt to reduce subsidies and to encourage local food production. At the same time Castro denounced the 'wave of savage neo-liberalism' sweeping the world, 'throwing people into hunger, into the street' – the consequence of free-market policies that were 'the most brutal violation of human rights'. By contrast, he claimed: 'We are dividing what we have among ourselves and each citizen feels secure. In spite of these catastrophic consequences, not a single child lacks school, the universities continue to be open, the hospitals continue to function, not a single patient lacks medical care.'

The 'decriminalisation' of dollar holdings in July 1993, seen as an inevitable reform to deflate the black market, brought its own problems. For example, there was an immediate upsurge in illegal dollar/peso exchanges, a growth in the illegal sale of goods (many stolen), and a rise in nominally illegal services (such as prostitution). The large number of pesos in the country, set against the shortage of peso goods, meant that most Cubans were virtually excluded from the dollar sector if they confined their 'illegal' activities merely to the conversion of their peso salaries into dollars.[59] Such circumstances inevitably encouraged the drift to crime.

In 1993 Cubans were reportedly moving to study various European languages (no longer Russian) as French oil companies began prospecting for oil offshore, Britain was investing in chemical plants, and a Spanish hotel overshadowing the old Riviera in Havana harbour was nearing completion.[60] Now there were some signs that progress was being made: a thriving tourist sector, increasing oil production (due to better recovery techniques), more nickel mines, foreign investment in hotel construction. Few doubted that the new developments were beginning to open Cuba up to market forces, but that the Castro regime still kept a firm grip on all the handles of power. In early 1994 it was possible to report that the dire economic situation – despite all Washington's best efforts – had improved. There was 'a visible lessening of economic pressure' in both Havana and the countryside; electricity blackouts had been reduced from 10 hours a day (in July 1993) to five hours every other day (in January 1994); and the streets of Havana, still replete with Chinese bicycles, were witnessing a slight increase in light petrol-driven traffic.[61] The aim, commented Raúl Taladrid, deputy minister for economic cooperation, was 'to preserve the basic achievements of the revolution, because if we lose that, we lose social stability'. There was 'a growing feeling that a new system is emerging'.

In March 1994 the Cuban government even went so far as to begin talks with the Cuban exile community. Now Castro was interested in encouraging the people he had always denounced as *gusanos* (worms) to invest in joint ventures to bring more of the coveted dollars to Cuban tourism and industry. At the same time there was increased pressure on the government to cut the country's vast money supply and so restore the buying power of the people. Castro declared that there would be no half-measures, but emphasised that the essence of socialism – free education and health care and egalitarian social policies – would be preserved. One consequence of the legalisation of dollar holdings was to dramatically devalue the peso. And again there was talk of raising the prices of heavily subsidised basic goods along with transport, telephone services and fuels. Now even the possibility of an income tax 'as soon as conditions permit' was being considered. In May Castro announced that the wealth of black marketeers would be confiscated and subsidies to loss-making industries would be cut as necessary moves to restore financial stability to the country.

Already there was talk of 'young capitalists' leading a new Cuban revolution: young upwardly mobile Marxists ('yummies') were reportedly acquiring control of crucial ministries and pushing through high-risk economic measures. For the first time there was serious talk of massive industrial lay-offs, an end to state subsidies, and capitalist-style taxes. Said one Cuban: 'All that will remain of the revolution soon could be the most advanced education and health care in the Third World.' Said Castro, reflecting the perplexities facing the revolutionary leadership: 'We are walking over broken glass and at times we don't know where to put our feet.'[62] The 'yummies', if such there were, continued to emphasise the need for further reforms. Observers keen to detect slippery slopes needed to look no further. Throughout 1994 the Cuban authorities redoubled their efforts to woo foreign investors. In June a business round-table in Havana,

organised by the *Economist* and called 'Cuba: Open for Business', was
widely regarded as a successful venture. Christine Stewart, Canada's
Secretary of State for Latin America, declared at the meeting: 'Canada's
aim is to promote peaceful and orderly change in the economic and political spheres in Cuba'; and Leycester Coltman, the British ambassador to
Cuba, expressed agreement with that policy. It is ironic that Canada and
Mexico (the Mexican firm Grupo Domos recently agreed a $1.5bn deal to
update Cuba's telephone system), both members of the US-dominated
North Atlantic Free Trade Organisation (NAFTA), are both prepared to
defy Washington on Cuba. A confidential British report (cited in *Time*,
20 February 1995) has commented that the Cuban reform process is now
'cohesive, systematic and unstoppable'. Canadian, Mexican and European
businessmen – increasingly impatient with the US blockade – were
showing themselves prepared to invest in Cuba's future. As one example,
at the end of 1994 the British Borneo Petrol Syndicate, an independent oil
and gas firm, signed a deal with the Cuban state oil company, Cupet, to
prospect 6000 sq km onshore near the Bay of Pigs for hydrocarbons.

Castro, according to one observer, had been forced to 'abandon fallen
gods'.[63] In return, against US pressure, the capitalists began to move in.
By 1995 Cuba had signed deals for 185 foreign joint ventures. Between
1991 and 1993, aided primarily by Spanish and German investment, the
Cuban tourist industry grew at a rate of 17 per cent a year; the Grupo
Domos deal meant that the foreign magnate Javier Garza-Calderón
would acquire a substantial interest in the Cuban telephone system; the
Dutch ING Bank, Cuba's first foreign financial company, has set up shop
in Havana; Unilever is now supplying toiletries and detergents to Cuba;
the Italian Benetton company now runs five retail stores on the island,
with more planned; Mitsubishi and Nissan today sell in Havana; and
Israel – still prepared to register its UN vote in favour of the American
blockade (see 'The Response – International', below) – has been
prepared to tolerate Israeli corporate investments in Cuban textile
manufacture.[64]

In mid-1995 it is too early to say whether the Cuban economic crisis –
occasioned by the linked problems of the Socialist-bloc collapse and the
US embargo – will finally be overcome; but there are many observers prepared to declare that the worst days are over. It also remains to be seen
whether economic survival will be purchased at too high a price. Even
Castro's detractors are forced to admit the durability of his regime and the
power of his message. Even when it is conceded that the cumulative mistakes of the regime have compounded Cuba's problems the achievements
of 35 years cannot be gainsaid: '. . . let us remember that it is precisely

because of the loftiness of its goals that the socialist ideal has been able to survive the wrath of its detractors, the blows and misfortunes of history, and the incompetence of its practitioners to remain a viable political alternative.'[65]

The privations suffered by the Cuban people continue today, artificially contrived by deliberate US policy. The economic embargo, directly affecting the Cuban civilian population, works to cause the two conditions – *starvation and forced movement* – specifically prohibited by the Geneva Convention (Pr. I, Art. 54). This circumstance should be remembered in any consideration of the plight of the Cuban boat people.

THE EXODUS

There have always been refugees from Cuba – from Spanish colonialism, from American invasion and occupation, from US-buttressed dictators, and from the ideology and privations of the Castro regime. The traffic has not always been one-way: with the victory of the rebel armies over General Batista in 1958/59 many people – torturers, profiteers, gangsters, corrupt officials – fled the island; and many former exiles returned to build a new society out of the chaos of social dislocation and neglect, and in the teeth of the abiding American hostility.

One of the largest waves of refugees began with the exodus of Cubans from Camarioca on 10 October 1965. Three weeks later (3 November), Cuba halted the boatlift, by which time perhaps 5000 Cubans had left the island for the United States. On 6 November Havana and Washington formally agreed to begin an airlift of Cubans who wanted to leave the island. The exodus continued over the coming years, substantially under the terms of Cuban–US agreement – until 1980, when events conspired to trigger a vast new wave of refugees from the island.

On 1 April 1980 a minibus carrying twelve Cubans seeking asylum crashed through the gates of the Peruvian embassy in Havana, causing the death of a Cuban guard and considerable embarrassment to the Cuban authorities. Three days later, Castro withdrew the Cuban guards from the embassy, whereupon the Peruvian chargé d'affaires declared that anyone wanting political asylum could enter the embassy. This led to some thousands of Cubans entering the precincts of the embassy and congregating outside. On 6 April the Peruvian authorities asked that further entry be blocked, and Cuba moved to close the surrounding streets – by which time there were tens of thousands of Cubans either inside the embassy grounds or outside wanting to enter.

A fortnight later (19 April), more than one million Cubans marched past the Peruvian embassy to demonstrate support for the Castro regime, while in New York anti-Castro demonstrators paraded to support the Cubans seeking asylum. By now the Cuban authorities had made it clear that there would be no block on Cubans leaving the island to go directly to Florida by boat. On 21 April small boats began arriving at Mariel, a small port 25 miles west of Havana, to pick up Cubans bound for the United States. At this time Washington did not term the fleeing Cubans (dubbed 'Marielitos') 'refugees' under the terms of the US Refugee Act of 1980; that is, they were not perceived as fleeing 'persecution . . . on account of race, religion, nationality, membership of a particular group or political opinion'. Instead it was decided that the Cubans should be classified as 'Entrants – Status Undetermined' and to intern them until such time as they were collected by relatives or sponsored by other interested parties. During this period it was reported that President Carter was planning massive military manoeuvres, 'Operation Solid Shield 80', involving the landing at Guantánamo of a further 1200 US troops as a deliberate provocation to the Cuban authorities. The planned manoeuvres were subsequently abandoned after mounting international pressure, including demonstrations in the United States. On 23 April the Carter administration announced that $1000 fines would be imposed on boat captains for every Cuban refugee brought to the United States without a valid visa. By mid-May some 40,000 Cubans (eventually to reach a total of around 125,000*) had arrived in Florida, while more than five million people, more than half the population of Cuba, were staging marches throughout the island in support of the Castro regime.

---

*In late 1994 a new film, *The Excludables* by the independent film-maker Estela Bravo, revealed how some of the Marielitos had been treated by the US authorities. The US Immigration and Naturalization Service (INS) had declared at least 5000 of the Marielitos 'excludable' from the policy of granting automatic asylum to Cuban immigrants. Some of the Marielitos were convicted of petty crimes in the United States and held for years until they were deported. One man was jailed for ten years after being sentenced to six months for a driving charge; another was imprisoned for 10 years for stealing $43. According to interviews conducted by Bravo many of the Marielitos were held at the Atlanta federal penitentiary, and were beaten and used in drug experiments. One Cuban was tied to a bed for 72 hours while drugs was administered; another was held in handcuffs for 18 days. The prison doctor, Bolivar Martineau, interviewed in the film, commented: 'The whole prison was a . . . social laboratory. It was just fabulous.' Today thousands of the Marielitos remain detained in 34 federal and state prisons throughout the United States (Rose Ana Berbeo, 'Film depicts plight of Cubans held in US jails', *Militant*, New York, 24 November 1994, p. 13).

In the early 1990s, stimulated by the US-induced privations in the islands, a fresh wave of Cuban refugees struggled to reach the United States. Between August and early September 1992 more than six hundred Cubans were picked up, often from makeshift rafts, in the Florida Straits. Said one spokesman for the US Immigration Service: 'Cubans are exceptional in our laws, above any nationality.' By 1993 more than 1000 refugees, many having made financial arrangements with intermediaries, had arrived in Florida: 'In contrast to the Mariel boatlift, the movement this year is a trickle and it appears to be organised more for profit than for humanitarian purposes.'[66] Throughout 1993, with mounting tensions between Washington and the Cuban government, the scale of the Cuban exodus continued to grow. Now few doubted that it was the United States that was causing the bulk of the problems: Cuba was not standing in the way of people wanting to leave the island but it was becoming increasingly difficult for Cubans to obtain visas from the US Interests Section in Havana. At this time the US was granting two types of visas: those giving regular immigration status (around 1800 granted in 1993), and those granting political refugee status. A Western diplomat was quoted: 'People considered to be persecuted here' will be granted political refugee status 'if they have Cuban exit visas. The Cubans give them exit permits with little problem. In fact they often force dissidents to leave, threatening them with jail.'[67] Through 1994 the exodus continued, with some Cubans even resorting to tactics that were reminiscent of the 1980 occupation of the Peruvian embassy: in early May more than 100 Cuban asylum seekers broke into the Belgian embassy in Havana, and on 13 June twenty-one Cubans smashed a truck through the gates of the German embassy. By the end of June there were still about 80 Cubans in the Belgian embassy, 21 in the German, and nine in the Chilean consulate. The official Cuban publication *Granma* suggested that US immigration policy had created a 'bottle-neck' for Cubans wanting to reach 'the promised land'.

In August 1994 Fidel Castro, angry at unprecedented riots in Havana, threatened to let the Cubans leave without restriction for the first time since the Mariel exodus. The disorder, according to Castro and many independent observers, had been caused by the US policy of limiting legal visas for Cubans while at the same time granting asylum to those prepared to flee. Washington expressed its deep concern at the threat: 'The US had stated repeatedly that we will not permit Fidel Castro to dictate our immigration policy or to create a replay of the Mariel boatlift. We urge the Cuban government to carefully consider all the implications.'

Now the situation was moving to a fresh climax. Foreign embassies had been occupied, the Cuban tugboat *13 de Marzo* had been hijacked on

13 July resulting in the drowning of 37 people, 700 Cubans had hijacked a Norwegian oil tanker (the *Jussara*) on 14 August, several hundred Cubans had attacked tourist hotels and looted shops on the Malecon seafront of Havana, and the wave of would-be immigrants to the United States was again escalating. All such events were exploited to fuel the inevitable anti-Castro propaganda in Miami and elsewhere. At the same time there was evidence of continued massive support for the Castro regime. Tens of thousands of Cuban workers spontaneously demonstrated against the Malecon riot of 5 August; on 7 August some 500,000 people demonstrated in Havana in support of Fidel Castro; around 30,000 people attended the ceremony (14 August) to honour the naval officer Roberto Aquilar who had been shot dead by boat hijackers; and on 7 September some 70,000 young people attended rallies to demonstrate their continued support for the Cuban government.

Throughout this period Washington was continuing to tighten the economic embargo, widely perceived as the principal reason for the new flood of would-be refugees. In September 1993 the US State Department had instructed all its embassies to pressure their host governments to prevent companies from trading with or investing in Cuba. The US intelligence services, desperate for new roles following the end of the Cold War, were given the job of tracking any possible negotiations between Cuba and potential capitalist investors. Businessmen in Britain and elsewhere have been approached by US embassy staff advising them to discontinue any plans to trade with Cuba; African countries have been told that trade with Cuba would mean a US veto of international aid for drought relief; and oil producers in Latin America and the Middle East have been warned that oil sales to Cuba would damage the prospect of financial credits being granted to them by the World Bank and the International Monetary Fund (IMF).[68] In these circumstances, at a time when Washington might have been expected to abandon its Cold War strategic postures, it was doing everything possible to cripple the Cuban economy. One inevitable consequence was the exacerbation of the Cuban refugee problem.

It was soon obvious that President Clinton intended to exploit the crisis to increase the pressure on the Castro regime. On 20 August he announced various measures to tighten the economic blockade yet further. These included:

- A ban on the Cuban-American community sending cash remittances to their relatives in Cuba (formerly this was a useful source of foreign exchange for the Cuban economy).

- Further restrictions on Cuban-Americans wanting to visit family members in Cuba (in 1993 some 50,000 people, mostly Cuban-Americans, had travelled to Cuba from the United States).

- Further restrictions on journalists and researchers wanting to visit Cuba.

- An increase in anti-Castro radio broadcasts, beamed into Cuba from US air force planes (total broadcasts then amounted to more than 1000 hours on 17 frequencies).

At the same time, while various US politicians were calling for a complete naval blockade of Cuba, right-wing Cuban-American groups were intensifying their preparations for further terrorist activities in Cuba (see Chapter 7). Washington was happy to feed the crisis by increasing the number of warships patrolling off Cuba and increasing the military presence at Guantánamo.

Yet again the United States had failed in its efforts to undermine the position of the Cuban government. On 5 August Fidel Castro, speaking on Cuban television, had made observations that no serious reader of the situation could have denied: 'Naturally they [the Americans] wanted bloodshed, gunfights and people killed – first of all as use for propaganda, secondly as an instrument of subversion, and thirdly as a means of intervention in our country. The US strategy is to create a situation, to promote as much discontent in our country as possible, to cause a conflict, a bloodbath. They dream about this, they long for it!' But there had been no bloody chaos, no brutal suppression, no ground for a propaganda-packaged US military intervention. The Cuban government, as ever working at a serious logistical disadvantage, had managed to contain the situation. The perennial American dream of a vast popular uprising in Cuba against the Castro regime had yet again been denied: the vast majority of Cubans had made plain their continued support for the government, and Clinton found that the United States was now burdened with 30,000 illegal immigrants with the prospect of more to come. In these circumstances, increasingly embarrassing to Washington, negotiations between US and Cuban officials yielded a new immigration agreement on 9 September 1994 (see Appendix 2).*

---

*In connection with the reference to 'Excludables' in the immigration agreement (Appendix 2), see the footnote on p. 48.

In 1984 the Cuban government had concluded an agreement with the Reagan administration to allow up to 20,000 Cubans to emigrate to the United States each year (in return Cuba had agreed to repatriate some of the Marielitos). In fact the US government repeatedly betrayed the terms of the 1984 agreement, allowing only 7 per cent of the specified number of visas (while Cuba granted visas to 99.9 per cent of all applicants). Now the new Clinton agreement reaffirmed the 1984 American pledge: 'The United States ensures that total legal immigration to the United States from Cuba will be a minimum of 20,000 Cubans each year, not including immediate relatives of United States citizens' (Appendix 2). The Cuban negotiators had secured an important diplomatic victory, but it remained to be seen whether Washington would honour the agreement in practice.

The United States now had to cope with the tens of thousands of Cubans that it had pressured to flee from the island. The immediate solution was to hold them at the Guantánamo base, suitably near to the problem and suitably distant from American shores. A nice irony: the Cuban refugees, denied access to the United States, were now being held in prison on Cuba by US troops. But would the Guantánamo camp be able to accommodate the growing number of refugees. Soon the Clinton administration was 'scrambling to find enough room' away from US shores to house the growing tide of Cubans.[69] Perhaps the US puppet regime in Panama might take a few. And what about the potentially useful camp on the British dependency of Turks and Caicos Islands? In the short term it was obviously necessary for the Americans to expand the Guantánamo facilities – to the point that a tented concentration camp ringed by razor wire was quickly provided for some 40,000 inmates. But still the American quest continued for other places to dump the hapless Cubans. US representations were made to Guyana, Surinam and Antigua. And perhaps Grenada and Dominica might take some. In early September 1994 the US began airlifting 10,000 Cubans to concentration camps in Panama. At least one US client state could be relied upon.

By now tensions were developing at the Guantánamo base. The imprisoned Cubans, sharing space with the Haitian refugees, were now denied the option of returning to their homes in Cuba: they had been incarcerated just as many of the 1980 Marielitos were still confined to the US state and federal penitentiaries. At Guantánamo minor uprisings took place and were quickly suppressed: on 6 September two US military personnel were injured in outbreaks of violence, and a fire was started, with at least one Haitian refugee seriously wounded. Now there were mounting protests in the US and elsewhere that the camp conditions – afflicting children and adults alike – were unacceptable. Perhaps, after all, the US would relent and accept some of the refugees as permanent immigrants. Then Cuban riots in the Panama concentration camps were reported, with US troops injuring some 28 people as they moved in to suppress the revolts and arrest the 'ringleaders'. Now more than 2000 US soldiers were patrolling the four camps, and 400 Cuban refugees were being interrogated by army personnel. Said General James Wilson, head of the refugee programme in Panama: 'This is a serious, serious situation.' Soon a policy reverse seemed the only option: at the end of January 1995 American troops armed with stun guns and pepper sprays began evacuating 7500 Cuban refugees from the Panama camps back to Guantánamo.

It was now being reported that the Cuban prisoners in the Panama and Guantánamo camps had organised hunger strikes, riots and mass escapes. In early November a group of 85 Cubans had broken out of the Guantánamo camp, with more than half arrested and put in detention. Some 39 reportedly jumped off a 40-ft cliff, swam a mile, managed to avoid mine-fields, and eventually reached Cuban territory.[70] About 1000 Cubans had asked to be allowed to return to Cuba, though most of the requests were blocked or delayed by court rulings. One of the refugees, Elsa Quintero, denouncing a blocking law suit introduced by a group of Miami-based Cuban-Americans, said: 'If they don't let us go, we are going to die in the sea. It is *our* decision to go back to Cuba.'[71] In January 1995 a resolution passed by the Panama Legislative Assembly demanded the 'cessation of unjustified confinement measures against detained rafters in the encampments', at the same time condemning the US troops for using excessive force. At the same time Panamanian parliamentary commissions were confirming the 'excessive' use of force to control the camps, and noting a 'patent and ostensible violation of human rights detrimental to Cuban citizens'. The former Panamanian presidential candidate, Eduardo Villarino (Christian Democratic Party) commented that the camps looked 'more like Nazi concentration camps' than places for refugees.[72] One of the refugees reported verbal and physical abuse by the US soldiers who, amongst other things, 'put their feet on [the rafters'] heads . . . made them kneel in the sweltering sun on a burning hot rock', and spat 'on the food'. The detained Cubans, reported the newspaper *El Panama America*, 'are being intentionally and spitefully bullied by the US armed forces'.[73]

By February 1995 conditions at the Guantánamo camp had deteriorated to the point that 41 refugees had either committed suicide or carried out 'suicide gestures' as a sign of their mounting desperation. These people had variously tried to hang themselves, set themselves on fire, cut their wrists, or swallowed bleach, shampoo, nails or razor wire. In the Panama

camps some 20 Cuban refugees had tried to commit suicide, with two
killed and 200 US troops reportedly injured when the rafters rioted in
December 1994.[74] Despite continuing US hostility and blocking law suits,
more than 400 Cubans had by now returned legally to Cuba. US officials,
embarrassed at the mounting disillusionment among the refugees, have
reportedly commented to the rafters: 'President Clinton made this policy,
not us.'[75]

THE RESPONSE – INTERNATIONAL

Throughout the last 35 years there has always been international opposition to the US economic embargo against Cuba. The Cuban Revolution
has always been able to attract a measure of support – fuelled by ideology
or idealism – from people around the world. Through the period of the
Cold War much of the support enjoyed by the Castro regime necessarily
derived from the Socialist bloc, a circumstance that had as much to do
with the strategic interests of powerful states as with the selfless desire to
support the building of a just society. At the same time private individuals
from around the world, albeit in relatively small and fluctuating numbers,
have been attracted to Cuba, keen to involve themselves in what they have
perceived as an idealistic and vitally important enterprise. As one
example, young US visitors, visiting Havana in 1969 to celebrate the 10th
year of the Revolution, discussed the idea of organising US citizens to
help with the Cuban harvest. Two months later Cuban officials approved
their proposal for a 'Venceremos Brigade' that would be drawn up from
American volunteers.

In December 1969 the first contingent of volunteers arrived in Cuba via
Mexico to work on the sugar harvest as an act of solidarity with the Cuban
people. Some 216 US citizens, defying the trade embargo and
Washington's efforts to discourage travel to Cuba, had set the pattern for
many volunteer initiatives in the years that followed. Volunteers were to
come from Latin America, Africa, Asia, Europe, Canada and the United
States. On one occasion ten Vietnamese fighters, straight from the war
against US forces in their own country, travelled to Cuba to help with the
sugar harvest (while Cubans journeyed to Vietnam to show solidarity with
the Vietnamese struggle against US agression). In 1970 a second
Venceremos Brigade, comprising 687 US citizens, reached Cuba, while
other volunteer brigades began arriving from many countries, including
Chile, Syria, Algeria, Egypt, the Soviet Union, East Germany, Bulgaria,

Romania, Guinea, Lebanon, North Korea and the People's Republic of the Congo. As soon as the second Venceremos Brigade returned to the United States it began organising a third. The pattern was set to continue. On 1 May 1989 more than 200 people, marking the 20th anniversary of the Venceremos initiative, participated in Havana's May Day celebrations. Today (mid-1995) volunteer workers are travelling to Cuba to show solidarity with the Revolution and with the struggle of the Cuban people.

With the ending of the Cold War, at a time when Washington saw an unprecedented opportunity to crush the Castro regime, it became easier for international opinion to condemn the US economic blockade. While the support from Eastern Europe had all but collapsed, massively affecting the Cuban economy, there began a significant growth in international opposition to US policy on Cuba. In November 1992, as one initiative among many, more than 100 US citizens, many of them from American churches, travelled to Cuba to meet a ship transporting 12 tons of food products, medicines, school supplies, bicycles and Bibles in defiance of the US embargo. The Cuban ship (the *Pinar del Río*), travelling from Tampico, Mexico, carried donations for Cuba collected in 90 US cities. The Reverend Lucius Walker, the head of the Pastors for Peace group responsible for the humanitarian effort, rejoiced at the breaking of what he considered to be an inhuman and unjust blockade: 'We won't back up until the devilish blockade ends.'

In July 1992 four celebrated British academics – Professors Patrick Collinson, Stephen Hawking, Joseph Needham and M. R. Pollock – issued a statement condemning the US blockade as '*a virtual state of siege for Cuba, resulting in shortages of every kind, from petrol to medicaments, machine parts to laboratory instruments*'. The statement included the following:

The Cubans are immensely and justifiably proud of their public health record and want to carry on the great advances made since 1959; they also want to trade freely, on an equal footing with every other nation. They view the US embargo as an act of war and cannot understand why it is tolerated by the international community.

We suggest that our own government should protest against the embargo to the American government, to the United Nations and to the European Community: Cuba is being treated most unfairly by having sanctions imposed – sanctions which deprive innocent people of the basic needs for a decent life, all in the name of freedom and democracy![76]

Academics elsewhere were also combining to denounce the terms and consequences of the US blockade. Thus in June 1993, a group of 120 French medical professors and doctors demanded at least a partial lifting of the embargo, declaring that shortages of milk and essential medicines were threatening the health of the Cuban people. In August a correspondent writing in the prestigious *British Medical Journal* applauded Cuba's achievements in health care, and then commented: 'The American blockade of Cuba gives rise to questions regarding the use for political purposes of measures that affect the health and wellbeing of a population. Medical societies around the world (as well as the World Health Organisation) should strongly condemn the sanctions, and demand the lifting of the embargo on medicines and food for Cuba.'[77]

In April 1993, in an effort to ease the growing shortages in Cuba, the first of a dozen boats sailed from Florida carrying eight tons of food, vitamins and hospital equipment. John Young, the leader of the *Basta* ('enough') group that organised the shipments, declared: 'They are our neighbours down there.' In July a group of 81 British Members of Parliament issued a statement drawing attention to the fact that 'the US trade embargo against the state of Cuba is in total disregard of international law'. Here it was pointed out that Thomas Richardson, the British ambassador, had recently informed the United Nations, on behalf of all the members of the European Community, that they considered the recently-passed Cuban Democracy Act 'to be a violation of a general principle of international law and the sovereignty of independent nations'. The MPs stated that it was 'the duty of our government (and the EC) . . . to urge the US President to modify his country's unfair policy towards Cuba'.[78] In October a group of 175 US citizens, risking fines and jail sentences by flying to Cuba, arrived in Havana carrying banners ('Freedom to Travel', in English and Spanish) in protest against US policy. In support of the chartered flight from Mexico, the African-American writer Alice Walker, Pulitzer Prize winner in 1983 for her novel *The Color Purple*, declared: 'I feel we should be able to visit Cuba because they are our neighbours. They are our sisters and brothers. I hope everyone who goes will have a real meeting with the people.' In December the American civil rights activist Jesse Jackson, citing the suffering of Cuban children, demanded an end to the US economic embargo.

In 1991 the Cuban Ecumenical Council adopted a resolution (dated 4 September 1991) condemning the American policy: 'We cannot be indifferent to the unjust economic embargo. . . . Because it disregards the supreme dignity of all people, because of its degrading implications for

health, the well-being and development, and because it violates the right
of every human being to life itself . . .'. On 14 August the Council of
Bishops of the Council of Methodist Churches in Latin America and the
Caribbean signed a declaration in Antigua, Guatemala, expressing solidarity with the Cuban people and urging:

1. An end to the unjust and prolonged blockade against Cuba, promoted by the United States of America, which is affecting the lives
   of our Cuban brothers.

2. The support of all the countries of the Americas and the Caribbean
   for the people of Cuba, so that they may freely and wisely determine their destiny, without pressure or threats of intervention.

A resolution issued by the General Assembly of the Latin American
Parliament, meeting in Cartegena, Columbia (31 July to 3 August), noted
the suffering of the Cuban people 'under a rigid economic and trade blockade, which even applies to food and medicine', highlighted US violation
of international law, and demanded an end to the blockade. In the same
spirit the Trade Union Federations of the Southern Cone (representing
Argentina, Brazil, Paraguay, Bolivia, Chile and Uruguay) issued a
statement on 12 March 1992 declaring 'the urgent necessity of ending the
economic blockade imposed on Cuba for more than 30 years'; on
29 September the Puerto Rican Teachers' Federation passed a resolution
repudiating 'the economic aggression against the Cuban people', demanding 'an end to US economic aggression', and demanding 'that the UN
General Assembly protect the rights of all people to self-determination,
independence and sovereignty and put an end to this unjust, illegal and
immoral situation which is an offense to all Latin Americans'.[79]
   In October 1992 the European Community condemned US policy on
Cuba as a violation of international law and of the sovereignty of other
countries. In response to the passing of the Cuban Democracy Act the
European Commission issued an unusually tough statement on behalf of
the member states: *'The extension of the US trade embargo against Cuba
has the potential to cause grave damage to the transatlantic relationship.
Although the EC is fully supportive of a peaceful transition to democracy
in Cuba, it cannot accept that the US unilaterally determines and restricts
commercial relations with any foreign nation [which has not been designated by the United Nations as a threat to peace or order].'* It was
reported that the Commission might file a complaint within the General

Agreement on Tariffs and Trade (GATT), and that individual member states might instruct companies based on their territory to ignore the US legislation.[80]

It has long been clear that international law protects the domestic affairs of states and their independence and sovereignty. Article 2(1) of the UN Charter affirms the 'sovereign equality' of all members of the United Nations; and subsequent UN Declarations confirm the spirit of this principle. Thus on 21 December 1965 the UN General Assembly adopted the 'Declaration on the Inadmissibility of Intervention in the Domestic Affairs of States and the Protection of their Independence and Sovereignty'. The principle was reiterated in the 1970 Declaration on Principles of International Law. In addition, on 9 December 1981 the General Assembly adopted by 120 votes to 22 (all Western states), with 6 abstentions, Resolution 36/103, the 'Declaration on the Inadmissibility of Intervention and Interference in the Internal Affairs of States'.

On 24 November 1992 the UN General Assembly passed Resolution 47/19 (Appendix 3) by 59 votes to 3 (United States, Israel and Romania), with many abstentions, calling for an end to the 'economic, commercial and financial embargo imposed by the USA against Cuba'. France, Canada and Mexico were among the supporters of Cuba; but Britain and most of the European Community countries abstained. On 16 September 1993 the European parliament passed a resolution urging the Commission to condemn the US policy on Cuba. It also called on Washington to repeal the Cuban Democracy Act, denouncing this legislation as an 'anachronism' and 'contrary to international law'.

The historic UN Resolution 47/19 was buttressed a year later when the General Assembly passed Resolution 48/16 (3 November 1993), condemning yet again the US economic blockade; and by the passing, a year after that, of Resolution 49/24 (26 October 1994), reaffirming the two earlier resolutions. What was particularly significant was the mounting support for Cuba. Resolution 47/19 was passed with a vote of 59 to 3; 48/16 with a vote of 88 to 4 (United States, Israel, Albania and Paraguay); and 49/24 with a vote of 101 to 2 (United States and Israel). It is important also that Resolution 49/24 (Appendix 3) draws attention to the Ibero-American Summits (July 1993 and June 1994) and to the Twentieth Council of the Latin American Economic System (June 1994), all of which condemned the US embargo against Cuba. Now, via GA 49/24, the vast majority of the UN General Assembly was combining to deplore the squalid and illegal policy of the United States.

In September 1994 the UN Secretary-General published a report following the request in Resolution 48/16(4) that he, 'in consultation with the appropriate organs and agencies of the United Nations system . . . prepare a report on the implementation of the present resolution in the light of the purposes and principles of the Charter and international law'. The report (published on 24 September)[81] includes a 12-page statement from Cuba, abundant support for the Cuban case from many other countries, and a comment from the United States that the US government policy in question 'is inappropriate to be the subject of multilateral consideration'. Of particular interest were statements provided by various UN organs and agencies:

> Indicators in the [Cuban] housing sector, as well as in the other social sectors, reveal a drastic worsening in the quality of life, impacting directly on the well-being of people, particularly the most vulnerable groups [as a result of the embargo] – *United Nations Centre for Human Settlements.*

> Among the negative effects on children . . . particular attention must be paid to the reduction in the availability of foodstuffs, the reduction in the availability of medical supplies, the reduction in the provision of public health services, the deterioration in nutritional levels . . . the lack of availability of school materials and the deterioration in the quality of drinking water. . . . UNICEF is particularly concerned over the scarcity of antibiotics and medicines related to childbirth . . . approximately 50 per cent of children between the ages of five months and five years now show signs of iron-deficiency anaemia – *United Nations Children's Fund.*

> The UNFPA local office has been reporting an increasing shortage of fuel, spare parts and other supplies that is affecting health-care service delivery and the implementation of a project aimed at improving the national capacity for oral-contraceptive production – *United Nations Population Fund.*

> The urban sector has been hardest hit by the current economic crisis and consequent food shortfalls – *World Food Programme.*

The position of the broadly-based UN community was plain: the votes in the General Assembly, the public speeches, the resolutions and declarations, the views of the various UN organs and bodies (UNCHS, UNICEF, UNPF, WFP, WHO and others) – all testify to Washington's growing international isolation on the Cuba issue. But in mid-1995 all the signs were that the US embargo, involving illegality and the gross abuse of human rights, was set to continue. The degree of UN impotence that this deplorable situation implied was one of many elements that invited criticism of the United Nations in its 50th anniversary year.

Even Washington's closest allies were now showing their unhappiness with the prevailing US policy on Cuba. Israeli companies were not averse to exploring the commercial possibilities in Havana; and on 7 September 1994 Ian Taylor, the British Trade and Technology Minister, left for Cuba. A British official declared that 'We are looking to do what we can to help the Cubans open up their markets'; while Taylor commented: 'There is a growing interest among British companies in the investment prospects now emerging in a country which could before too long become a significant market. The range of possibilities for taking a stake in Cuba's future has never been greater.'[82] At the same time the presidents of the leading Latin American countries, at the eighth summit of the Rio Group, were stressing the need 'for the lifting of the embargo' of Cuba. And an editorial in *The Guardian* (31 October 1994) commented: '*The virulence of the US vendetta against Cuba continues to embarrass its* [Washington's] *friends.*'

By 1995 there were growing signs that, despite all Washington's efforts, Cuba was becoming increasingly accepted within the international community. The island's relations with Latin America and the other Caribbean states had improved; there were signs of 'a revitalisation of relations with Russia'; China was continuing to provide support; and even many of the Cuban exile groups seemed to be changing their 'only-without Castro' stance.[83] Even a powerful thread of ideological support for Cuba in the international community could be discerned: as shown, for example, by the massive World Solidarity Conference held in Havana in November 1994. Here some 3072 delegates, representing 109 countries, were in attendance. 1995, it was resolved, would be the Year of José Martí and a time to coordinate activities worldwide against the US economic blockade.

Cuba's own internationalist credentials are well established. Many countries that have been served by Cuban teachers, doctors, engineers and other specialists have been grateful for Cuba's prodigious long-term investment in education, training and scientific research. The Cuban Revolution has always had an internationalist dimension, prepared always to consider the wider implications of radical reform in a small island. In July 1992 the Cuban government became the first in the world to incorporate the language of the Rio Earth Summit into its constitution. In 1977 Cuba set up its National Commission for the Environment and National Resources (COMARNA). Today Cuba is a member of the Convention on

International Trade in Endangered Species (CITES), and a fully participating member of various United Nations environmental commissions. The revised Cuban constitution charges the state with the responsibility to protect the environment for the 'safety and welfare of future generations'. It remains to be seen whether future Cuban generations will be permanently blighted by a malevolent and vindictive power committed to the use of starvation and disease to compel acceptance of social decay, economic exploitation, and needless human suffering.

Part II
The Long Subjugation

2 The Imperial Impact

But those mine enemies, which would not that I should reign over them, bring hither, and slay them before me!

Luke *19*, 27

Think not that I am come to send peace on earth: I came not to send peace but a sword

Matthew *10*, 34

When Columbus arrived here with his church – the Catholic Church – he came bearing the sword and the cross. With the sword, he sanctified the right to conquer; with the cross, he blessed that right

Fidel Castro[1]

The cumulative European invasion of the Americas in the fifteenth century and after was one of the key shaping factors of the modern world. But the early European explorers did not encounter a waste, an empty desolation: the lands in this part of the world already supported peoples, cultures and in some cases high civilisations. It was the misfortune of these peoples that they were destined to clash with foreign adventurers equipped with a superior military technology, an implacably racist ideology, and a merciless religious absolutism.

THE FIRST CUBANS

The original inhabitants of the Americas arrived some time before Christopher Columbus, during the last glacial period some 14–40,000 years ago. They journeyed from Asia, crossing in several phases from Siberia over the Bering Strait to settle first in North America, later (10,000 years ago) in Middle America (Mesoamerica), and later still in South America. It is historically and culturally significant that today the term *pre-Columbian* is used to denote the cultures of the first regions (the Caribbean area, Mexico and Peru) to be dominated by the European invaders.

Most of the pre-Columbian peoples lived in small nomadic bands subsisting as hunters and gatherers. Such primitive foragers used a simple technology, moved between dispersed settlements relying on the seasonal availability of food resources, and assumed the consensual leadership exercised by older (usually male) persons. The more advanced groups began the development of agriculture around 9000 years ago, which in turn led to the establishment of settled communities and the growth of relatively sophisticated tribal cultures. In a few regions of Mexico (the Aztecs), Central America (the Maya) and the Central Andes (the Inca), the agricultural techniques were sufficiently advanced to generate the surpluses that permitted the formation of towns and cities, key elements in complex states comprising hundreds of thousands (perhaps millions) of citizens. In contrast to the relatively peaceful nomadic peoples, the evolved states were preoccupied with predatory military expansion: the aggressive ambitions of the indigenous nations that were to be extirpated by the Europeans were limited only by the scope of their war-making technologies. But the Aztecs, the Maya and the Inca were not the only American peoples to be crushed by the power of European arms: even the most pacific indigenous communities were destined to suffer the ravages of Christian imperialism.

The early nomadic groups, many comprising only 30 or 40 people, gradually spread through North and Central America and thence the islands of the Caribbean. Cuba, the largest island of the Antilles, served as a geographical point of convergence for the wandering peoples of the region: it is likely that the aboriginal navigators, unlike Columbus, knew that Cuba was an island. The migrants sailed from Mexico in the west, from Florida in the north, and from the Antillean archipelago in the south. Many waves of aboriginal settlers came to populate Cuba, fleeing hostile neighbours or impelled by the economic necessities of the nomadic life. Anthropologists have long acknowledged that the geographical position of Cuba afforded the island importance for racial migration. Situated relatively close to both Florida and Yucatán (the Central American peninsula), and linked by a chain of islands (many within sight of each other), Cuba was also favoured by a good climate and teeming fauna.

Various groups of aboriginal settlers have been identified as the earliest inhabitants of Cuba. In pre-Columbian times much of the island was occupied by the Ciboney Indians,* a primitive people whose artefacts are

---

* Columbus, believing that he had reached the East Indies, lumped all the native peoples together as *Indians*. This conventional linguistic usage – signalling both the West Indies and all the disparate peoples in pre-Columbian America (and their descendants) – has long been unavoidable. Equally unfortunate was the decision of the Swedish taxonomist Carolus Linnaeus in 1735 to label the original inhabitants of the New World the 'American', or 'red', race.

today sometimes recognisable only by the skilled eye. The Ciboney arrived in Cuba in two separate migrations over the course of two millennia, and later disappeared leaving little trace. Their simple culture left few clues as to their origins. It is not known whether they sailed from Florida, from such Central American regions as Honduras and Nicaragua, or from South America, gradually progressing through the arc of the Lesser Antilles to the larger Caribbean islands.[2] The first Ciboney migration – that of the Ciboney-Guayabo Blanco, dated to around 1000 BC – focused on the central and western coastal regions of Las Villas, Matanzas, Havana, Pinar del Rio, and the Isle of Pines. Two thousand years later the Ciboney-Cayo Redondo settled on the south coast of Camagüey and around the estuarial regions of the Cauto River in Oriente.[3]

The Ciboneys – living, with other Indian groups, in what has been called a 'shell age' – preferred the coastal regions, mainly bays and estuaries, the offshore islets and keys. They fashioned the shells of large molluscs into various types of utensils and tools, such as jars, awls, knives and scrapers; moreover, the shells could serve as trumpets and horns, and as elements in mythology and religious practices. Some of the Ciboneys built small thatched dwellings, with others living in ravines or caves ('Ciboney' derives from the Arawak *siba*, cave, and *eyeri*, man). The dwellings helped to define temporary camps rather than permanent villages, though some permanent settlements were established in the later phases of the Ciboney period. Such people gathered wild fruits and nuts, caught animals in primitive traps, and lived off the sea, collecting molluscs and crustaceans, fishing, and hunting manatees and turtles. It is speculated that the Ciboney must have used simple boats, such as dugout canoes, but no remains have been found.

This was a simple culture, technologically primitive and ill-equipped to resist subsequent aboriginal migrations. Ciboney artefacts were no more sophisticated than the shell gouge and the stone mortar, fire was little used, and no traces have been found of basketry or pottery. Rough beads, simple artefacts of shell and stone, may have been used for personal adornment or in religious ritual; though nothing is known of Ciboney belief or superstition, and little of the language.

The Ciboneys were easily subjugated throughout much of Cuba by successive waves of Arawak Indians, themselves fleeing before the fierce Caribs, who have been historically associated with the practice of cannibalism. The Caribs nonetheless had certain inhibitions: they refrained from eating 'pigs lest their eyes should become small, nor turtles, to avoid becoming stupid'; instead they 'ate the bodies of their enemies', content to dry and smoke ('boucan') the 'more distinguished' ones so that they would be available 'to be gnawed at special festivals'. They reportedly ate the crew of a Spanish ship in 1564, and that of a French one in 1596 ('the French . . . made most delicate eating, while the Spaniards were the hardest to digest'). The Caribs emasculated captured Arawak boys and fattened them 'for eating'.[4] Thus Diego Alvarez Chanca, the physician to the second Columbus expedition, gave further details of Carib propensities: captive women of the islanders 'told us that the Carib men . . . eat the children which they bear them. . . . Such of their male enemies as they can take away alive they bring here to their homes to make a feast of them. . . . They declare that the flesh of man is so good to eat that nothing can compare with it in the world. . . . In one of the houses we found a man's neck cooking in a pot.'[5]

The Arawaks, having escaped the Caribs, set about enslaving the Ciboneys on Cuba or expelling them to the farthest reaches of the island. The first Arawak incursion, that of the Sub-Taíno, reached Cuba from Española (present-day Haiti) during the ninth century. Over the next hundred years the Sub-Taíno expanded westward into Camagüey, Las Villas and Matanzas, establishing settlements, driving away the Ciboney or reducing those who remained to serfs (*naborias*). Today around one hundred Sub-Taíno archeological sites are known in Cuba, mostly in Oriente province. The Sub-Taíno, like the Ciboney, erected thatched dwellings and relied upon shells and stones for the fashioning of artefacts. Each village was headed by a local chief (*cacique*), who lived in a palm-thatched hut (*bohios*) fronting a central open area surrounded by the loosely clustered dwellings. The Sub-Taíno rarely lived in caves but used them for religious rites, to conceal valuables, and as mortuary locations.

They also worked the land collectively, farming such diverse products as maize, potatoes, yucca, tomatoes, pineapples, and chilli and annatto (used both as condiments and as a source of dye). Tobacco was cultivated for smoking and religious ceremonies, and for its alleged medicinal properties. Wild animals were kept alive in captivity as a source of food, just as turtles were held in corrals in shallow waters and live mullet maintained in extensive pens.[6] Also the Sub-Taíno, with craft skills far beyond those of the Ciboney, produced ceramics, textiles, fishing lines and nets, ropes and cord, ornamental ear-plugs and pendants, and small figurine amulets. Cloth was woven from *ceiba* (silk-cotton) tree fibres, and there were many wood carvings and basketry and pottery artefacts. Canoes were made out of the boles of great trees and used for fishing.[7] In the villages the open area (*batey*) was used as a market place, for assemblies, and for festivities. Song and dance were employed to commemorate 'great happenings and . . . to transmit to the young people the traditions worthy to be preserved, the deeds of the ancestors, and the mystic vicissitudes of the race'.[8]

The *caciques* were aided by *behiques* who performed jointly the tasks of chiefs, priests, soothsayers and doctors. Women, despite polygamy, 'were anything but mere work horses'.[9] Some, familiar with the use of herbs and medicines, were doctors. The Sub-Taíno believed that natural medicaments could be effective remedies but there was belief also in magic and in the propitiation of supernatural beings. It is suggested, not least by Columbus, that the Cuban Indians were a peaceful people, despite their sufferings at the hands of the Caribs and (later) Christians and despite social hierarchy and the exploitation of subject tribes. But what has been perceived as a largely pacific Indian temperament was given little scope. The next Arawak migration into Cuba, that of the Taíno, began during the mid-fifteenth century, not long before the arrival of the Europeans. What the Arawak Indians may have made of Cuba in later centuries will never be known; all that can be known of the arrested Taíno development is revealed by the wealth of surviving artefacts and the interested testimony of contemporary Europeans.

In summary, archeologists in Cuba have collected artefacts and associated information on three basic cultural groups: the Ciboney (Guayabo Blanco and Cayo Redondo), the Arawak (Sub-Taíno) and the Mayarí, who settled in north-central Oriente province between the ninth and eleventh centuries. The Mayarí – with two sites (Arroyo del Palo and Mejia) excavated during the 1960s – are thought to have been supplanted by the Sub-Taíno migration. The Ciboney, dubbed *Guanahacabibes* by the Spanish, were the most primitive group that they encountered. Said the conquistador Diego Velázquez, conqueror of Cuba (see below): 'The life of these people is of the manner of savages, for they have neither houses nor village quarters, nor fields, nor do they eat anything else than the flesh they take in the mountains and turtles and fish.'

Some thirty Taíno sites have been identified, revealing a significant complexity in ceramic products, stone tools and shell artefacts. Such archeological sites have been investigated for well over a century. For example, one of the earliest researchers, the distinguished Spaniard D. Miguel Rodríguez-Ferrer, published his work on the *Natural History and Civilization of the Island of Cuba* in 1876, based on research conducted some thirty years earlier. Of this work it is worth mentioning his investigation in 1847 of what the people of Mayari called *piedras de rayo* (or 'lightning stones'), which they believed fell from heaven during thunderstorms. He concluded that these items were *hachuelas de piedra*, perfectly formed stone hatchets of diorite and serpentine, which he thought too advanced for the Indians found by Columbus. Later excavations revealed more such artefacts, products of the Taíno, in the same region.

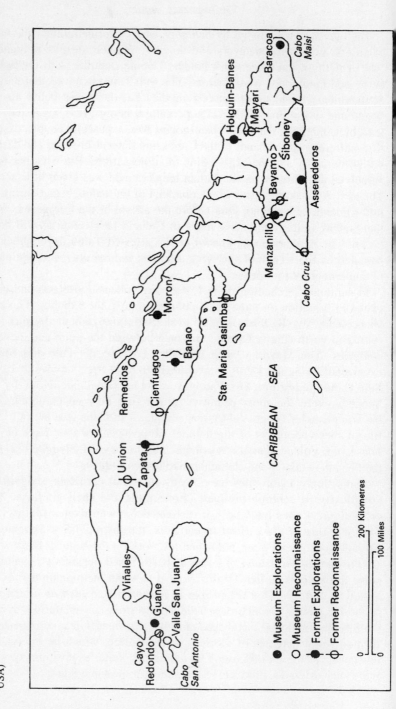

Figure 2.1 Archaeological exploration in Cuba, to July 1919

SOURCE: M. R. Hamilton, *Cuba Before Columbus*, New York, 1921 (courtesy of the National Museum of the American Indian, Smithsonion Institution, USA)

Rodríguez-Ferrer also describes two stone idols which he received as gifts: one a stooping humanoid figure weighing more than fifty pounds, and the other a ceremonial axe-head bearing what clearly purports to be a human visage. He suggests that this latter, with its almost identical sides, must have been 'made in a mould'; but he does not explain how this might have been accomplished. Another item described by Rodríguez-Ferrer is a clay figurine representing a night owl, held by the Indians in superstitious dread. In addition, he contributed to Cuban archeology by his careful explorations: of, for example, the small circular mounds ('caneyes'), found to contain many artefacts and other antiquities. He also found remains of Indians who had seemingly committed suicide by rope or poison to avoid the dreaded condition of slavery under the Spanish conquerors.[10]

Later archeologists have built on the vital work of the early researchers, exposing further Indian sites and enlarging our knowledge of the pre-Columbian cultures that developed on Cuba. The work has revealed settled communities featuring agriculture, a productive technology, a propensity for dance, mythology and religious ritual, a scheme for social order – many of the seeds that, left alone, can yield high civilisation. The American Indians who had made Cuba their home were not destined to be left alone. It is useful to glance at elements of the European culture that supplanted them.

IMPERIAL SPAIN

The Spain of the fifteenth century was anti-semitic, racially bigoted, religiously obsessed and ambitious for empire. This was the Spain that was to send a Genoese adventurer across the world in search of land, riches and possible allies in the interminable Christian jihad against the Muslim. The culture that Columbus was to introduce to the New World was not designed to benefit non-Christian communities with inferior war-making capacities.

The history of pre-Columbian Spain is largely the tale of conflict between the residual Christianity and the Moorish occupation. By 718 the Muslims, having defeated the Visigoths, controlled most of the Iberian peninsula. Many Christians prudently converted to Islam, and Arabs, Berbers and other Islamic groups moved to settle in Spain. The Umayyad caliphate ruled what the Muslims called al-Andalus, the rich lands of southern Spain, from 756 to 1031, though there was continual conflict between various Muslim factions and between the Muslims and small pockets of Christian resistance. Abd al-Rahman (891–961) reunited Moorish Spain and declared himself caliph of Cordoba. In the eleventh century the fragile unity again splintered, with al-Andalus later again reunited under the Almoravids (1086–1147) and the Almohads (1147–1212). Throughout this period the surviving Christian communities grew into powerful groups increasingly effective in challenging the Islamic occupation.

Charlemagne, Charles the Great (742–814), defeated the Saxons (772–804) and the Lombards (773–774), and fought the Muslims in Spain, here helping to establish the Spanish March that was destined to evolve into the future Catalonia. Aragon became an independent kingdom under Ramiro I (r. 1035–1063) and, in brief alliance with Navarre, expanded its territory at the expense of the Moors, with Catalonia subsumed by marriage under the Aragon crown. Castile, a principal force in the Christian reconquest, was united with the kingdom of Leon (in a subordinate relationship); and by the middle of the twelfth century about half of the peninsula had been reconquered from the Muslims. By 1188 King Alfonso VIII (r. 1158–1214) had expanded the Castilian frontier far to the south, and Europeans came to recognise the language of Castile as Spanish. Castile, supported by Aragon and Navarre, defeated the Muslim Almohads at Navas de Tolosa in 1212, and by 1248 only Granada remained in Muslim hands.

On 19 October 1469 the marriage took place between Ferdinand, King of Sicily and heir to the throne of Aragon, and Isabella, the heiress of Castile. Thus when Isabella I acceded to the Castilian throne in 1474 and Ferdinand II to that of Aragon in 1479, the two most powerful Spanish kingdoms were joined. An accident of dynasty fortune had yielded a strong Spanish unity. On 6 January 1492 the 'Catholic Kings', Ferdinand and Isabella, made their triumphal entry into the city of Granada, finally wrested from the Muslims after nearly eight centuries of struggle. The reconquest (*Reconquista*) was complete: at last the Moor was finally and conclusively defeated, and a long era was at an end. In that same epic year of 1492 all Jews were expelled from Spain, signalling the mounting racial bigotry and religious intolerance. At the same time the Catholic Kings launched the first phase of a historic overseas colonisation, the epoch-making intervention in the New World. A new era had begun.

THE CHRISTIAN DIMENSION – I

The centuries-long conflict between the Castile-led kingdoms and the Moors in Spain was in large part a religious struggle. At various times, not least in the early fifteenth century, the *Reconquista* faltered, rendering uncertain the eventual outcome. The fall of the Byzantine Constantinople to the Ottoman Turks in 1453 stimulated the crusading enthusiasm of Christendom; the Vatican made appeals to Christian leaders throughout Europe, whereupon Henry IV of Castile relaunched the *Reconquista* against the Spanish Moors in 1455. While the king exploited the papal calls as a pretext for raising revenue from his subjects, ordinary Castilians evinced a crusading zeal with passionate religious overtones. This Christian zealotry was exploited by the Catholic Kings, not only to consolidate their domestic power but also to fuel the overseas expansion.

Isabella used the church in an effort to centralise power in her hands. In 1480 the Spanish Inquisition began interrogating suspected heretics, converting Jews and other imagined subverters of the evolving Catholic orthodoxy. The original papal Inquisition had been formally created by Pope Gregory IX in 1231: convicted heretics were to be seized by the papally-authorised secular administration and burned. In Portugal and Spain the Inquisition underwent special development: in 1483 Pope Sixtus V sanctioned the creation of an independent Spanish Inquisition to be run by a high council and grand inquisitor with strong links to the Spanish state. The following year Pope Innocent VIII issued his notorious bull against witches, *Summis desiderantes affectibus* ('Desiring with the most profound anxiety').

The Spanish Inquisition, contrary to what Christian apologists may claim, was not an inexplicable historical aberration but a development that grew directly out of the mainstream Judeo-Christian tradition. By AD 430 the Christian civil code in the Roman Empire was ordering death for heresy, though the law was not always rigorously enforced; in 1144 Pope Lucius III instituted the first episcopal inquisition, with instructions to the bishops to make systematic enquiry (or *inquisitio*) into deviation from official church teaching. Half a century later, on 25 March 1199, Innocent III appointed *inquisitores* directly from the Vatican, with absolute power to override local administrators; and in the celebrated decree of 1215, *Excommunicamus* ('We excommunicate'), Innocent III further urged the secular authorities to pledge themselves to 'strive in good faith, to the utmost of their power, to exterminate from their lands subject to their obedience all heretics who have been marked by the Church'. In 1233 Pope Gregory IX proclaimed that the *inquisitores hereticae pravitatis* would henceforth be Dominicans, appointed by the pope and answerable to him alone.

We do not need to trace the appalling practices of the Inquisition.[11] It is enough here to note the systematic and prolonged use of torture,

sanctioned as a means to discover heresy by Pope Innocent IV in 1257 in
the bull *Ad extirpanda* and by later popes (the use of torture as an authorised inquisitorial tool was not abandoned until 1816). For our purposes it
is enough to note the prevailing religious climate, in which Christopher
Columbus was seeking the support of the Catholic Kings in his wish to
extend Spanish hegemony to the 'Indies'. To some extent the scene had
already been set. When the Portuguese Prince Henry the Navigator conquered the north-west coast of Africa in 1450, Pope Nicholas V supported
the new colonial acquisition: in his bull *Romanus Pontifex*, issued in 1454,
he declared that the subjugated territories belonged to Alphonsus of
Portugal and authorised the conquest and exploitation of other lands in
Africa and 'India' in the future. The pope was deemed to have authority
over the entire world, including the pagan world, and so he had the
assumed authority to dispose of all lands, those already conquered and
those waiting to be conquered. And in addition it was essential that all
the lands of the world be *Christianised*.

There was a minor complication when Columbus 'discovered' the
Americas in 1492 in the name of the Spanish rather than the Portuguese
crown. The pope responded a year later with the bull *Inter caeterae
divinae*, dividing the entire world between Spain and Portugal by drawing
a line on the map through the Atlantic from the North Pole to the South
Pole. Thus Pope Alexander VI, in a celebrated demarcation, assigned the
eastern half of the world to Portugal, the western to Spain. Ferdinand and
Isabella were granted full rights over the Americas and charged with the
task of evangelising the indigenous peoples. The tone of the times –
shaped as it was by the long Church struggle with Muslims and Jews, and
by the papal sanction for the torture and execution of heretics – is well
conveyed in the so-called 'proclamation of the conquistadores', read out to
the peoples of the Americas to induce them to surrender their lands,
possessions and freedom without a struggle:

God the Lord has delegated to Peter and his successors all power over
all people of the earth, so that all people must obey the successors of
Peter. Now one of these popes has made a gift of the newly discovered
islands and countries in America and everything that they contain to the
kings of Spain, so that, by virtue of this gift, their majesties are now
kings and lords of these islands and of the continent. You are therefore
required to recognise holy Church as mistress and ruler of the whole
world and to pay homage to the Spanish king as your new lord.
Otherwise, we shall, with God's help, proceed against you with violence and force you under the yoke of the Church and the king, treating

you as rebellious vassals deserve to be treated. We shall take your property away from you and make your women and children slaves. At the same time, we solemnly declare that only you will be to blame for the bloodshed and the disaster that will overtake you.[12]

The message, metaphysics apart, was simple: *We have come to steal everything from you. You will worship the God who makes this possible or you will suffer the consequences.*

COLUMBUS: CONQUISTADOR

National unity, signalled above all by the bonding of Castile and Aragon and the triumph of the *Reconquista*, now equipped Spain for a historic phase of overseas expansion. Portugal, unified before Spain, had already embarked upon the imperial enterprise of overseas exploration and conquest. The Canary Islands had been discovered in the fourteenth century, and Ceuta, on the north coast of Africa, was acquired by the Portuguese crown in 1415. Prince Henry the Navigator, obsessed with fabled kingdoms in Africa, despatched ships of exploration in 1419. New lands were discovered: the Azores (in 1431), Cape Bojador (1434) and the Cape Verde Islands (1445); by 1448 a Portuguese colony had been established at Agadir. In 1487 Bartolomeu Dias reached the Cape of Good Hope; and in 1497–99 Vasco da Gama established a trade route around Africa to India.

Where Portugal had looked to the Atlantic Ocean, Spain had initially expanded through the Mediterranean Sea. Catalan adventurers maintained the Duchy of Athens from 1326 to 1388; Pedro IV of Aragon acquired Majorca in 1349, and then Minorca. At the beginning of the fifteenth century Spain and Portugal contended for control of the Canary Islands; in 1480 Grand Canary Island was colonised by Ferdinand and Isabella – a prelude to a more ambitious phase of overseas exploration.

Now Christopher Columbus and his contemporaries appeared on the scene to participate in what has been called 'the Expansion of Europe', the historic period during which European adventurers would bring conquest and Christianity to the New World. The Genoese Columbus was born between 1446 and 1451, though some historians have disputed his place of origin. He himself, in the document defining his estate, urged his heirs 'to work always to enhance the reputation, welfare and growth of the city of Genoa', and to maintain a house there for a member of the Columbus family 'for I came from there and there I was born'. The Genoese city fathers, to counter competing claims, have sponsored the publication in photographic facsimile of fifteenth- and sixteenth-century material to confirm the Genoese origins of the Columbus family. In any event he did not remain long in Genoa.

There are suggestions that Columbus may have explored by land and sea before he arrived in Portugal around 1470, excited by the exploits of the Portuguese adventurers. In vain he sought support from the Portuguese king, and possibly also from England and France, for a westward exploration, and arrived in Spain in 1485. At first Ferdinand and Isabella, beset by financial and political problems, inclined to reject the proposals of the Genoese adventurer. In 1486, when Columbus first presented himself at court, the Crown was poor, heavily engaged in the last stage of the *Reconquista*. But Columbus had influential friends: not least, Ferdinand's secretary, Luis de Santángel, and a former confessor to the Queen, the Franciscan Juan Pérez. Moreover, as victory over Granada seemed increasingly likely Ferdinand and Isabella saw advantage in a westward exploration: such an adventure might help the Catholic Kings against Portugal and also replenish an empty treasury. And in particular Spain might gain fresh allies in the eternal confrontation with Islam. When Spanish noblemen pushed the Moors out of a region of Spain, they immediately established a military outpost, a *castellum*, and also a monastery. Similarly, any overseas hand-in-hand progress of the sword and the cross might be expected to deliver both secular riches and fresh forces to use against the heretic. The fall of Granada, celebrated throughout Christendom, gave fresh impetus to the enterprise proposed by Christopher Columbus.

On 17 April 1492 Columbus signed a contract with the Catholic Kings, which allowed him to launch his first westward exploration. He had said enough to convince the rulers of Spain that such a voyage would be worthwhile. Many of his theories were based on the *Book of Ser Marco Polo*, where the island of Cipangu (supposedly Japan) was judged to be 1500 nautical miles east of China; and he had calculated just how far he would have to sail to reach the East Indies. At the Portuguese court of John II, Columbus had argued with mathematicians who believed that Eastern Asia and Western Europe were separated by no less than 10,000 nautical miles. There were no skilled geographers in the Spanish court and there – to the advantage of Columbus – his ideas were subject to less scrutiny than in Portugal. Now he was granted the commission of Spain: 'It is our will and pleasure that you, the said Christobal Colón, after you have discovered and acquired the said islands and mainland . . . shall be our

Admiral and Viceroy and Governor therein and shall be empowered henceforward to call and entitle yourself Don Christobal Colón.'

Columbus set sail on 3 August 1492, in the hurricane season, with three ships – *Niña*, *Pinta* and *Santa María* (this latter his flag-ship) – and in command of a cosmopolitan crew of adventurers. On 8 September he left the Canary Islands, and, believing Cipangu to lie in the same latitude, held his course due west. Making good time with the easterlies, Columbus still lived in dread of the time when the crews of the three ships would fear to travel further in the uncharted waters. In early October the expected land was not sighted, and Columbus was forced to put down a mutiny on the *Santa María*. Then branches were spied floating in the sea, whereupon Columbus, desperate to reach land, allowed the ships to run before a gale. On 12 October, in the early morning, a sailor on *Pinta* saw white sand cliffs clearly discernible in the moonlight. The next day, the ships secure in safe harbour, Columbus held a service to thank God for their safe deliverance on the first island they had reached in the Americas. He named this island San Salvador (later known as Watling Island).

From 15 to 23 October Columbus encountered three more small islands. Having honoured God by naming his first discovery San Salvador, he now honoured the Virgin Mary, and the King and Queen of Spain by naming the newly-found islands, respectively, Santa María de la Concepción, Fernandina and Isabella. On these islands and others, Columbus noted various curiosities; for example, the *perros mudos* ('dumb dogs'), supposed canine creatures that did not bark ('Even when beaten or killed they did not know how to bark'). Perhaps, as some writers have suggested, the 'dogs' were really some form of rabbit or rodent. The Indians (the *Indios* of Columbus) ate such delicacies as fat spiders, succulent white worms bred in rotting wood, and raw fish; and were scantily clad, if at all (some women 'wear in front of their bodies a small piece of cotton which bearly covers their genitals'). Of particular interest were the frequent references made by the Indians to the largest land they knew, Cuba (or 'Colba'). Columbus, convinced that Cuba must be the famed Cipangu (Japan), set sail on 23 October in that direction. His journal entry (24 October) notes: 'At midnight last night I weighed anchor . . . and set sail for Cuba, which these people have told me is very large and busy, with gold and spices, and large ships and merchants. . . . I believe it to be the island of Cipangu, of which such wonders are told, and which lies in the region of the globes and the maps of the world which I have seen.' After encountering more small islands, Columbus reached Cuba on 28 October 1492 (Figure 2.2). His journal records some of his observations for that historic day:

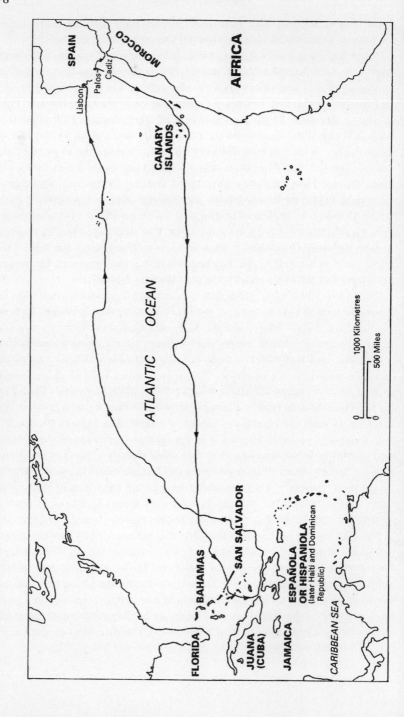

Figure 2.2   The first voyage of Columbus (Cuba reached on 28 October 1492)

I sailed SSW for the nearest point of the island of Cuba [present-day Gibara, in the province of Holguín], and into a fine river free from shallows and other perils. The sea along the whole coast along which I sailed is deep right up to the shore, with a clean bottom. . . . There are two beautiful high mountains, like the Peña de los Enamorados, near Granada, and one of them has another little hill on the top shaped like a handsome mosque . . .

I never saw a lovelier sight: trees everywhere, lining the river, green and beautiful. They are not like our own, and each has its own flowers and fruit. Numerous birds, large and small, singing away sweetly . . .

I jumped into the boat and went ashore, and found two houses which I think belonged to fishermen, who fled in fear. . . . In both houses I found nets of palm fibre, ropes, horn fish hooks, bone harpoons and other fishing equipment. I think many people must live together in each house. I gave orders for everything to be left alone, and nothing was touched. The grass is as long as in April and May in Andalusia, and I found quantities of purslane and spinach.

I returned to the ship and sailed a good way upriver. It is a joy to see all the woods and greenery, and it is difficult to give up watching all the birds and come away. It is the most beautiful island ever seen, full of fine harbours and deep rivers . . .

The Indians tell me that there are gold mines and pearls on this island, and I saw a likely spot for pearls. . . . I understand that large vessels belonging to the Great Khan come here, and that the passage to the mainland takes ten days. I have called this river and harbour San Salvador [yet again honouring God].[13]

Columbus soon began to doubt that he had reached Cipangu (Japan), but he then substituted an equally fanciful theory: perhaps Cuba was part of the mainland of Cathay (China) and the court of Marco Polo's Great Khan would be found in the interior. He even despatched a group, including a 'Chaldean-speaking' interpreter, to investigate, 'but, finding no signs of organised government, they decided to return'. Failing to locate the expected court of the Great Khan, Columbus began to focus on how Cuba and the other islands might be exploited and the indigenous peoples evangelised. He continued to savour the richness of the flora and fauna, and to contemplate the discovery of gold and other riches; but increasingly he turned to the vision of the Indians serving as the innocent raw material of a new Catholic community to be constructed in the Spanish dominions. The Spanish monarchs would 'leave their kingdoms in a very peaceful condition and free of heresy and malice, and shall be well received in the presence of the eternal Creator'. This vision served as a spur, were any needed, to the evangelising enthusiasms of the Europeans who would sail to the Americas in the following decades.

It was now clear that Columbus would not be able to deliver the letter from the Catholic Kings, written in Latin, to the Great Khan; nor would he be able to offer the personal gifts that had been carefully conveyed across the Atlantic, or strike up useful friendships at the court of Cathay. Despite his appreciation of birds and vegetation, Columbus had realised few of his ambitions in Cuba (which he had named Juana). The search for the court of the Great Khan had yielded nothing more than a village of fifty huts, and the 'inexhaustible' quantities of gold that Marco Polo had reported in Japan had not been uncovered. The Indians would be doubtful allies against the Muslim: Columbus was to comment that 'Ten Christians could put 10,000 of them to flight, so cowardly and timid are they.' Moreover, the Spanish crews, cheated of rich pickings, were growing increasingly restless: on 20 November Martín Alonso Pinzón, commanding *Pinta*, sailed off without leave in an act of what Columbus called 'treachery'. The reasons remain unclear: most commonly it is assumed that Pinzón, motivated by avarice, was off on a gold hunt. Now Columbus reasoned it was time to leave Cuba.

On 5 December Columbus reached Española (or Hispaniola, present-day Haiti). There he informed the first *cacique* (chief) that he encountered that he [Columbus] 'came from the monarchs of Castile, who were the greatest princes in the world'; and observed that 'the other would only believe that the Spaniards came from heaven and that the realms of Castile were in heaven'. To the Spanish monarchs Columbus reported: 'All the islands are so utterly at your Highnesses' command that it only remains to establish a Spanish presence and order them to perform your will. For I could traverse all these islands in arms without meeting opposition . . . so that they are yours to command and make them work, sow seed and do whatever else is necessary and build a town and teach them to wear clothes and adopt our customs.' Already the pattern was plain. The Indians, in part because they were not Christians, could be treated according to Spanish whim. Already Columbus had taken men, women and children and confined them in onboard servitude. On one occasion he took six young men from a canoe to add to the quota already captured; the next day, he collected seven women and three children, deciding that the men who were to be transported as slaves to Spain would do better with women of their own. Columbus had no doubt that the Christian church smiled on slavery (see Chapter 3).

He was still forced to admit that he had not found Cipangu: La Isla Española gave few signs of resembling the envisaged East Indies, though for once there was the compensation of gold. Columbus built a stockade at Puerto Navidad on the north coast of the island, and garrisoned it with thirty-nine Spaniards who were told to await the next expedition from Castile. On 24 December the *Santa María* ran aground and foundered off the present-day Cap Haitïen; on 6 January 1493 the *Pinta*, equipped with large quantities of gold supposedly obtained by trading, rejoined the *Niña* off Monte Cristi (in the present-day Dominican Republic). Now Columbus decided to return to Europe: in Española ('the best land in the world'), a land he thought larger than Spain, he claimed to have found an invaluable asset. On 16 January Columbus began the long journey home, without his flag-ship but bearing many items that would impress the Catholic monarchs of Spain: samples of gold, a few spices, tobacco ('highly esteemed among the Indians'), the hammock (from the Arawak *hamaca*), and an assortment of miserable slaves to display at court.

On 25 September, having accumulated privileges and titles, Columbus began his second voyage to the West Indies (Figure 2.3); this time he sailed with 17 ships from Cadiz. Now between 12,000 and 15,000 colonists, the largest such expedition ever to leave Europe, was heading west. The volunteers – soldiers, officials, priests, peasants, gentlemen and others – had far exceeded the capacity of the fleet. A principal aim was to explore Cuba to discover its precise nature (island or mainland), since 'the Sovereign sagely suspected, and the Admiral declared, that a mainland should contain greater good things, riches and more secrets than any one of the islands'. The monarchs and colonists alike remained hungry for gold.

When Columbus reached Española he found that the Navidad garrison had been massacred by the Indians, weary of the endless Spanish demands for food and gold. At the end of April 1494 he began his exploration of the southern coast of Cuba, by 18 July reaching the south-western extremity of the island (Cabo de Cruz). After some weeks of coastal exploration, Columbus decided to spend no more time investigating Cuba. He considered, wrongly, that he had explored some 370 leagues of coast, and that no island could possibly be so large. Thereupon he called on every man of the fleet to give their oath – to be recorded by the ship's scrivener – that Cuba was a mainland since no island of such size had ever been known. The men, faced with their master's evident frustration and fantasy, further swore that if they had persisted somewhat further they would have reached Cathay. Every man promised to abide by his oath on pain of a fine of

Figure 2.3 *The second voyage of Columbus (Cuba reached on 29 April 1494)*

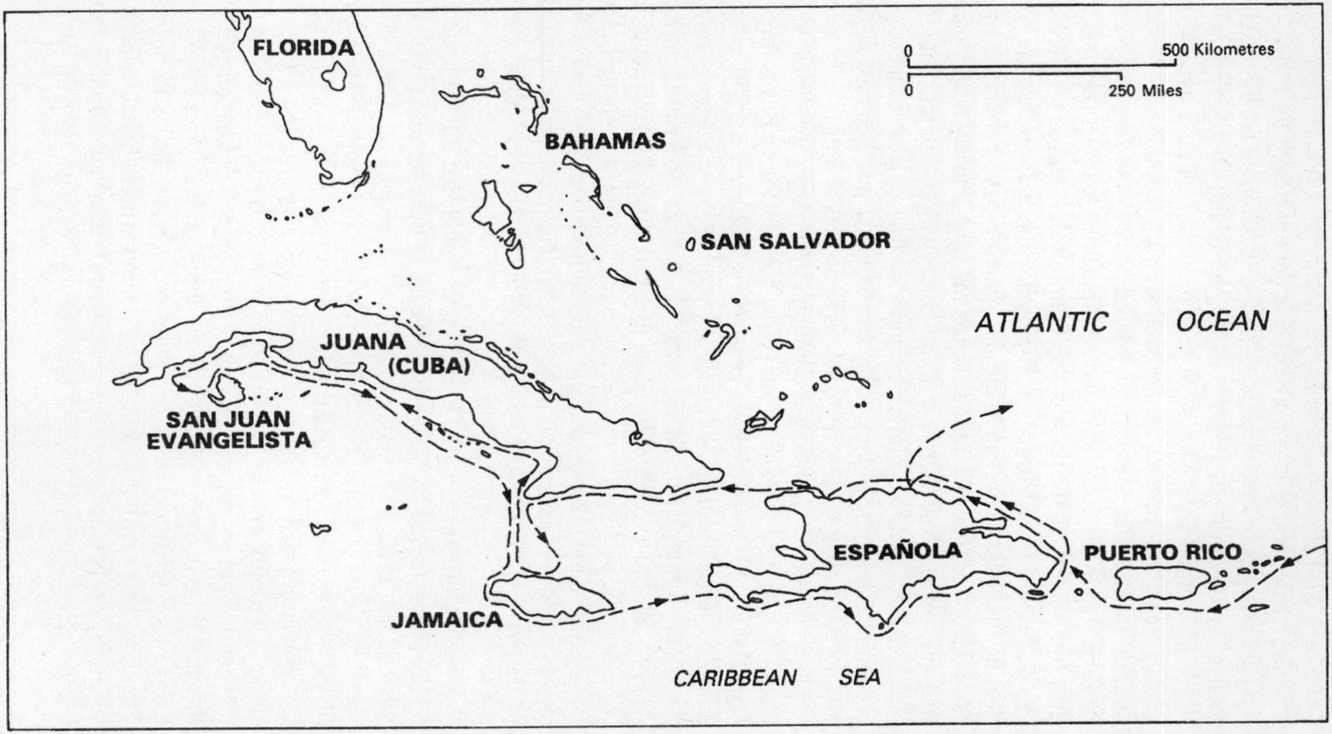

FLORIDA

BAHAMAS

○ SAN SALVADOR

JUANA
(CUBA)

SAN JUAN
EVANGELISTA

JAMAICA

ESPAÑOLA

PUERTO RICO

ATLANTIC   OCEAN

CARIBBEAN   SEA

500 Kilometres

250 Miles

10,000 maravedis and the excision of their tongues. Despite such wild measures, Columbus did not manage to sustain for long, in any mind but his own, the beguiling myth of a continental Cuba.

When Columbus returned to Española from Cuba in September, he found a situation of demoralisation and social decay: the settlers were roaming the land, attacking the Indians, stealing their possessions, and provoking resistance. Columbus himself felt compelled to organise military action against sections of the indigenous population: some five hundred Indians were captured and transported to Spain for sale as slaves. He then instructed the Indians to pay tribute to the Spanish authorities; they were required to pay either a hawk's bell full of gold dust or 25 lb of woven cotton every three months,[14] partly as a commercial tax and partly as a disciplinary pressure. Now the vassaldom of the Indians to the Catholic Church was to be made amply plain.

Columbus launched a series of campaigns against the Indians of Española, involving expeditions to every part of the island and justifying his later boast to have conquered the island: Columbus, despite the thrust of some biographers, was the first of the Spanish *conquistadores* in the New World. The interests of the Indians were ignored; the central aims were to appease the colonists and to bring booty to the Spanish crown. Forts were built, the Indians subjected to a harsh military regime, and despair and death visited on a hapless native population unused to either crippling taxation or forced labour. At one sham parley, the Indian chief Caonabó was reportedly persuaded to wear 'bracelets', which were really manacles. According to Las Casas, Columbus succeeded over a few brief years in exterminating two-thirds of the Indian population of Española.[15] The scene was set for the patterns of genocide and industrial slavery that would be visited on the American Indians – and on countless African men, women and children – by the Christian Europeans in the decades and centuries that followed.

On his third voyage (1498) and his fourth (1502) to the West Indies, Columbus gave little or no attention to Cuba. Instead he visited Jamaica, Central America, Trinidad and other regions, and continued his involvement with Española. In his later years he expressed a growing range of aberrant ideas, persisting in his firm belief that he had reached the East Indies; declaring, in addition, that he had been within a few days' journey of the River Ganges, that he had narrowly evaded bewitchment by sorcerers, that in Veragua he had discovered King Solomon's mines, and that he still harboured ambitions to convert the Chinese emperor to Christianity. He persisted in the belief that Cuba was part of China, and in the notion that he had been allowed by God to discover the earthly paradise. Throughout his life he remained a devout Christian, keen to demonstrate his piety by imposing harsh conditions on simple and uncomprehending peoples. His celebrated journal, preserved in large measure by Las Casas, begins with a Prologue bearing the heading *In Nomine Domine Nostri Jesu Christi* ('In the Name of Our Lord Jesus Christ') and addressing 'My Lord and Lady, most Christian . . .'. And the Prologue encapsulates the principal purpose behind the westward exploration sponsored by the Spanish monarchs: '. . . Your Majesties, being Catholic Christians and rulers devoted to the Holy Christian Faith and dedicated to its expansion and to combating the religion of Mahomet and all idolatries and heresies, decided to send me, Christopher Columbus, to those lands of India to meet their rulers . . . and to find out in what manner they might be converted to our Holy Faith. . .'. In a similar vein a letter (dated 14 March 1493) from Columbus to Lord Raphael Sánchez, after celebrating the discovery of the 'islands of India', concludes with the words: 'Therefore let the king and queen, our princes and their most happy kingdoms, and all the other provinces of Christendom, render thanks to our Lord and Saviour Jesus Christ, who has granted us so great a victory and such prosperity. Let processions be made, and sacred feasts be held, and the temples be adorned with festive boughs. Let Christ rejoice on earth, as he rejoices in heaven in the prospect of the salvation of the souls of so many nations hitherto lost. Let us also rejoice, as well as on account of the exaltation of our faith, as on account of the increase of our temporal prosperity, of which not only Spain, but Christendom will be partakers.'

In later life Columbus depicted his own Christian name in a four-line cypher:

.S.
S.A.S
X.M.Y
Xp̄o FERENS

There is uncertainty about the meaning of the first three lines,[16] but the meaning of the fourth seems clear. This shows a depiction of the Latin form of Christopher (Xp̄o a scribal abbreviation for *Cristo*), split to denote 'the bearer of Christ'. Thus Columbus used the myth of the saint who carried Jesus across the river to denote his own accomplishment in conveying the Christian faith across the seas. Murals in early colonial churches reflected this image of Columbus. We need to remember the human desolation that can be wrought by simple piety, by the purblind and arrogant bigotries of religious absolutism. Columbus was the first of the conquistadors, but soon the pious European adventurers were queuing to endure the westward voyage in search of land and riches, and as an expression of their Christian devotion.

VELÁZQUEZ: THE CONQUEST OF CUBA

For more than a decade after the first Spanish arrival in Cuba the island was left in relative peace. Columbus had disrupted Indian families, forced a few dozen people into slavery, and launched a few small-scale expeditions into the interior; but most of his extensive military campaigns had been confined to Española. Cuba, despite the Columbus rhetoric, did not at first seem an obviously exploitable asset. But there was still the lure of hidden riches. In 1510, following fresh reports that Cuba might be rich in gold, King Ferdinand ordered a new expedition to be sent to explore the island: 'Because we have some suspicion that in the island of Cuba there is gold, you should attempt to know it for certain.' In 1508 Sebastian Ocampo had circumnavigated the island, and so now the scale of the task was known. Columbus himself still maintained his *idée fixe* that Cuba was a mainland, the beginning of the East Indies, and the terminus for all those adventurers who wished to travel from Europe to the new regions of the world. Already Columbus was moving into history; it would be left to other Christian explorers to extend the imperial sway of the European.

Ferdinand instructed Diego, the son of Columbus and the governor-general of Española, to organise the conquest of Cuba. In 1511 Diego Columbus commissioned Diego Velázquez to undertake the task. Velázquez was well qualified: he had sailed with Christopher Columbus on the second voyage to Española in 1493, was already a wealthy landowner on the island, and had much experience in suppressing indigenous Indian populations. The conquest of Cuba was accomplished with ruthless efficiency. An initial wave of three hundred Spaniards under Velázquez sailed from Española to the region of Maisi at the eastern end of Cuba. Then Velázquez moved quickly to establish a secure settlement at Baracoa on the north coast. A second force under Pánfilo de Nárvaez sailed from Jamaica to the Gulf of Guacanayabo.

It may be surmised that the hapless Indians knew what to expect. Velázquez had commented to Captain Francisco de Morales, his second-in-command, that Columbus had found the Indians to be hospitable: 'I do not expect that they will receive us with hostility.' But Morales remembered how the Indians had been treated in Española. As José Martí, the nineteenth-century Cuban nationalist, was to write, of how the Spanish Christians had treated the Indians of Española: '. . . these cruel men hung them with chains; they took away their women and their sons; they put them in the depths of the mines to drag the weight of stone with their forehead, and divided them and marked them with a brand'.[17] Morales reasoned that if the Cuban Indians knew of such things, 'I do not believe that they will receive us with music and flowers.'[18] And so it proved.

The youthful Indian chieftain Hatuey had struggled to resist the Spanish incursions into Española, but when it became obvious that he could not fight effectively against a superior military technology he fled to the mountains. Even here it was obvious that Hatuey and the remnants of his people would not be able to survive long against the Spaniard; and so Hatuey, with a small band of miserable survivors, fled to Cuba to escape the conquistadores. Thus a small group of about 400 Guahaba Indians, with Hatuey in command, imagined that they would find sanctuary on an island not yet conquered by the Spanish. The historian Expósito described how the Indians – men, women and children – fled, 'full of terror, from their own soil, in order not to be victims of the atrocities of the Conquistadores'.[19]

Once in Cuba, Hatuey tried to organise resistance to what he now perceived would be the inevitable Spanish invasion. Bartolomé de las Casas recorded Hatuey's words to the assembled Indians: '. . . the Spaniards are ready to invade this island, and you are not ignorant now of the ill-usage our friends and countrymen have met with at their hands and the cruelties they have committed. . . . They are now coming hither with a design to inflict the same outrages and persecutions upon us . . . they are a very wicked and cruel people . . . these Europeans worship a very covetous sort of God, so that it is difficult to satisfy him; to perform the worship they render to this idol, they will exact immense treasures from us, and will . . . reduce us to a miserable state of slavery, or else put us to death.' Then, displaying a small basket of gold and jewels, Hatuey declared: 'This is their Lord. This is what they serve. This is what they are after.' It was essential to resist the Spaniards, even though 'they use the ray which wounds us from a point our arrows cannot reach. . . . But they are few and we are many. They are fighting in this foreign land, and we are on our own soil. They invoke a seditious God of blood and Gold, and we have, on our side, a just and wise God . . .'. But the Indian unity that Hatuey desperately tried to create was not forthcoming: the chiefs were suspicious of the non-Cuban interloper and could not believe the tales of atrocity that he told. When the Spaniards began their conquest of Cuba the Indians were ill-prepared.

Velázquez – accompanied by Morales and Hernán Cortés – arrived on what seemed to be a deserted beach; the Indians were waiting in the trees to attack the approaching Spaniards. The result was typical of all the bloody conflicts that were to follow: the Indians, valiant enough, could not contend with the firearms of the conquistadores. A few Spaniards were wounded but the Indians left many dead on the battlefield. The subsequent overland march from Carenas Bay, bringing death and destruction, ended with a massacre at Caonao in northern Camagüey. For a time, despite everything, the Indians continued to resist, using guerrilla tactics to delay the advance of the conquistadores. But the outcome was inevitable. When Hatuey, betrayed by an Indian who had once quarrelled with him, was captured by the Spaniards the Indian resistance was virtually at an end. Hatuey himself refused to capitulate. The circumstances of his death have echoed down the ages.

The fate of Hatuey was assured: as one who still refused to lead the Spaniards to hidden gold, and as one who had steadfastly resisted the imperial ambitions of the Catholic Church, he would be burnt at the stake. On a historic day, 15 February 1512, the stake and pyre were prepared. When Hatuey yet again refused to tell Velázquez where he would find the gold, he was tied to the post. A priest, Juan de Tesín, adjured Hatuey to die 'in the grace of God', and invited him to accept Christianity and be baptised before he died. Only in this way, declared the priest, would Hatuey be able to go to heaven. Hatuey responded with words which, in many versions and translations, reverberate to this day:

'And to heaven the Christians also go?'
'Yes, they go to heaven if they are good and die in the grace of God.'
'If the Christians go to heaven, I do not want to go to heaven. I do not wish ever again to meet such cruel and wicked people as Christians who kill and makes slaves of the Indians.'

Then Hatuey, having rejected all priestly appeals, was burnt to death on the pyre. His compatriot, Caguax, struggled to maintain Indian resistance, but his efforts were futile. The Indians were pursued wherever they sought refuge, killed or forced into slavery; the Cuban revolt, the first of many against foreign occupation, was at an end. King Ferdinand, true to the Christian spirit of the day, decreed that all the Indians who had supported the rebellion should be enslaved. They would be branded with hot irons on the forehead to show them and others the futility of resistance to the Catholic Church.[20]

After the creation of Baracoa in 1512 as the first permanent Spanish settlement in Cuba, six further settlements were established in this first phase of expansion through the island: Bayamo (1513), Trinidad (1514), Sancti Spiritus (1514), Havana (1514), Puerto Príncipe (1514), and Santiago de Cuba (1515). All, except Sancti Spiritus, were accessible by water. Santiago de Cuba, Bayamo, Trinidad and Havana (relocated on the north coast in 1519), facing the Caribbean, would play an important support role in later Spanish expansion into Central and South America. Trinidad and Puerto Príncipe (relocated to Camagüey in 1528) were sited, respectively, near supposed gold deposits and a large Indian population. The seven initial settlements were later followed by others.[21] The Spanish grip on Cuba, not to be broken for four centuries, was complete.

THE ROLE OF CORTÉS

Hernán (or Hernando) Cortés, resolved to seek his fortune in the West Indies, left Spain in 1504 to embark on the westward voyage. After a succession of heavy gales – filling 'all on board . . . with apprehensions and no little indignation against the author of their calamities'[22] – he eventually reached Española, and there travelled to the house of Nicolas Ovando, the governor of the island, whom he had known personally in Spain. Ovando was absent, and when an official assured Cortés that he would be given land he replied that he had come to get gold, 'not to till the soil, like a peasant'. However, he later accepted a grant of land with the usual *repartimiento* of Indian slaves, though keen to seek out adventure at every opportunity:'. . . the young adventurer first studied the wild tactics of Indian warfare: he became familiar with toil and danger, and with those deeds of cruelty which have too often, alas! stained the bright scutcheons of the Castilian chivalry in the New World'.[23] In 1511 Cortés took part in the Velázquez expedition to conquer Cuba, impressing the soldiers not only with his courage but also with his good humour and lively sallies of wit. When Velázquez, after the conquest, became governor of Cuba it was not long before Cortés was appointed as one of his secretaries. Soon Cortés was developing fresh ambitions.

In 1518 Velázquez decided to send a fresh fleet to Yucatán in the endless search for exploitable assets. His relation, Juan de Grijalva, was appointed Commander-in-Chief, and three other men – Alonso de Ávila, Francisco de Montejo, and Pedro de Alvarado – were each given command of a ship. After many adventures, including the inevitable battles with Indians (in which the Spanish suffered substantial casualties), the ships returned to Cuba bearing a moderate haul of gold and six hundred axes (thought to be gold but found to be copper).[24] Now Velázquez was considering sending another expedition under a new captain. Two favourites of Velázquez – his own secretary, Andrés de Duero, and Amador de Lares, Ferdinand's accountant – compacted with Cortés to share the spoil of gold if he be elected Captain-General of the fleet. With the aid of such influential friends, Cortés was duly appointed to head the new fleet, whereupon he began to collect not only the necessary munitions of war but also a compendium of religious regalia. Two standards and banners were made, worked in gold with the royal arms and a cross on each side and bearing the legend: 'Brothers and comrades, let us follow the sign of the Holy Cross in true faith, for under this sign we shall conquer.' The conquistador Cortés, like Columbus and Velázquez, resolved to slaughter the Indian in the name of the One True Faith.

Again it is useful to note the degree of religious absolutism that fuelled the endeavours of the Christian adventurers. One task was to gain knowledge about the unfortunate Christians who were being held in Yucatán. Another was 'to reclaim the natives from their gross idolatry and to substitute a purer form of worship. In accomplishing this he [Cortés] was prepared to use force, if milder measures should be ineffectual.' The Catholic monarchs wanted above all the evangelising of the Indian: 'There was nothing which the Spanish government had more earnestly at heart than the conversion of the Indian. . . . The sword was a good argument when the tongue failed . . . the spread of Mahometanism had shown that seeds sown by the hand of violence, far from perishing in the ground, would spring up and bear fruit to after-time. . . . The spanish cavalier felt he had a high mission to accomplish as a soldier of the Cross . . . to him it was a holy war.'[25] The Spaniards did not doubt, in such circumstances, that God and the saints would assist in battle – and so it proved. Thus St James and St Peter reportedly appeared on the battlefield, with Bernal Díaz forced to comment sadly that it was perhaps because he was an unworthy sinner that he was not able to see them.[26]

Cortés, despite his increasingly volatile relationship with Velázquez, had managed to use Cuba as a springboard for his conquest of the Aztec civilisation in Mexico. In Spanish perception, the power of God had ranged over the battlefields of the New World. In Española, Cuba, the myriad other islands and Mexico, the Christian sword had been granted a unique and terrible vitality. Throughout all the decades of carnage and destruction the conquistadores gave endless thanks to their god for bringing them bloody victories over seemingly impossible odds. For our purposes it is useful to remember that the Christian intervention in the

Americas, in the Caribbean and elsewhere, brought not only brutal suppression and endless misery but genocide. Our first detailed chronicles of life in Cuba tell of torture, desolation, plunder and death.

GENOCIDE

It is largely through the work of Fray Bartolomé de las Casas (1474–1566) that we know about how the Spaniards treated the Indians of Cuba and the other Caribbean islands. His father, as a common soldier, accompanied Columbus on his first voyage to the New World; and there acquired enough wealth to send his son to the University of Salamanca. There Las Casas was attended by an Indian whom his father had brought back from Española: the man who was to become a passionate advocate of freedom began his career as a slave-owner.

In 1498 Las Casas completed his studies in law and divinity, graduated in licentiate, and four years later sailed for the Americas. In 1510 he took priest's orders in Santo Domingo, and so became the first man to be consecrated in the Spanish colonies. Following the conquest of Cuba, Las Casas sailed to that island and became a curate in a small settlement. Soon he was striving to protect the subject Indians from vicious exploitation and dreadful torment. At that time the aboriginal population of the islands 'was rapidly melting away under a system of oppression which has been seldom paralleled in the annals of mankind'.[27] Las Casas, outraged by the privations and suffering of the Indians, returned to Spain to urge the government to take action. Ferdinand died soon after his arrival, but Cardinal Ximenes, sensitive to the efforts of Las Casas, created a commission of three Hieronymite friars with full powers to reform the colonial abuses. Las Casas was awarded the title of 'Protector General of the Indians'.

It was inevitable that the passionate Las Casas would soon grow impatient with the efforts of the pragmatic commissioners. He continued to rail against the manifest injustices meted out to the hapless Indians; but at the same time, in nice paradox, urged the importation of Castilian labourers and negro slaves to relieve the plight of the Caribbean aboriginals. Thus Las Casas, the uncompromising and fearless protector of the Indian, is associated with the development of the burgeoning Atlantic slave trade, a connection that he came to regret: in his celebrated *Historia de las Indias (History of the Indies)* he confesses with deep regret that his advice on this matter was erroneous, since 'the same law applies equally to the negro as to the Indian'. Las Casas had not been alone in advocating the importation of negro slaves as a means of ameliorating the conditions of the

Indians: there were plenty of contemporary advocates prepared to declare that 'the African was more fitted by his constitution to endure the climate and the severe toil imposed on the slave, than the feeble and effeminate islander'.[28]

Las Casas then proposed that he be allowed to establish a colony in Tierra Firme, where he would convert the natives to Christianity and administer a humanitarian regime. He suggested further that he be accompanied by fifty Dominicans, dressed in a characteristic way so that the Indians would not associate them with the cruel Spaniards. The debate was conducted in the presence of Charles V, Ferdinand's successor, with the traditional advocates declaring that, since the Indian was incapable of civilisation, the scheme was fantastic and unworkable. Las Casas, for his part, concluded: 'The Christian religion is equal in its operation, and is accommodated to every nation on the globe. It robs no one of his freedom, violates none of his inherent rights, on the ground that he is a slave by nature, as pretended; and it well becomes your majesty to banish so monstrous an oppression from your kingdoms in the beginning of your reign, that the Almighty may make it long and glorious.' Las Casas prevailed; in 1520, equipped with men and other resources, he again sailed for the Caribbean. In the event, after a period of uncontainable strife involving the continued Spanish oppression of the Indians, the scheme was abandoned. A disconsolate Las Casas took refuge in the Dominican monastery in Española; and there began, in 1527, the compilation of his celebrated *Historia*. It is essentially this work that immortalised the name of Las Casas, and preserved for all later generations a devastating chronicle of Christian perfidy.

Las Casas began collecting material for the *Historia* in 1502, concerned as he was with the oppression of the Indian and the questionable legitimacy of the Spanish presence in the New World. He relied to a large extent on the evidence recorded in Columbus's Journal, which the work of Las Casas helped to preserve for posterity. He worked on a copy of the journal, not the original, and Chapters 35 to 75 of the *Historia* draw heavily on material compiled by Columbus. It is the Las Casas summary of the journal, held in the National Library in Madrid, that is thought to be the best guide to the Columbus original.[29] For our purposes it is the information in the *Historia*, 'a work of extreme moral and political commitment',[30] that is of most interest.

The Indians, says Las Casas, were agile and could swim long distances, especially the women. There were no marriage laws: men and women came together and parted as they pleased, 'without offense, jealousy or anger'. If the women 'tire of their men, they give themselves abortions with herbs that force stillbirths, covering their shameful parts with leaves or cotton cloth; although on the whole, Indian men and women look upon total nakedness with as much casualness as we look upon a man's head or his hands'. Las Casas comments that the Indians were not completely peaceful: the tribes battled from time to time, but rather because of individual grievances than through the imperial ambitions of tribal rulers. They had no need for commerce, relying entirely on their environment for survival. At the same time the Indians were 'extremely generous with their possessions and by the same token covet the possessions of their friends and expect the same degree of liberality . . .'.

Las Casas notes the 'endless testimonies' that serve to prove 'the mild and pacific temperament of the natives'; yet the work of the Spaniards 'was to exasperate, ravage, kill, mangle and destroy . . .'. He records that Columbus 'was blind as those who came after him, and he was so anxious to please the King that he committed irreparable crimes against the Indians . . .'. The Spaniards 'grew more conceited every day', and after some time refused to walk any distance: Indians were commanded to carry them on their backs or, working in relays, to transport them in hammocks: 'In this case they also had Indians carry large leaves to shade them from the sun and others to fan them with goose wings'.

The cruelties committed by the Christians knew no limits. The Spaniards 'thought nothing of knifing Indians by tens and twenties and of cutting slices off them to test the sharpness of their blades'. On one occasion 'two of these so-called Christians met two Indian boys one day, each carrying a parrot; they took the parrots and for fun beheaded the boys'. When the Indians fled to the hills they were hunted down by dogs and killed or sent to the mines:

> they suffered and died in the mines and other labours in desperate silence, knowing not a soul in the world to whom they could turn for help . . . they dig, split rocks, move stones, and carry dirt on their backs to wash it in the rivers, while those who wash gold stay in the water all the time with their backs bent so constantly it breaks them; and when water invades the mines, the most arduous task of all is to dry the mines by scooping up pansful of water and throwing it up outside . . .

Las Casas records that after each six or eight months' stint in the mines, the time required to dig the required amount of gold, up to a third of the men had died; and while the men were confined to the mines the women were set as slaves on the land:

Thus husbands and wives were together only once every eight or ten months and when they met they were so exhausted and depressed on both sides . . . they ceased to procreate. As for the newly born, they died early because their mothers, overworked and famished, had no milk to nurse them, and for this reason, while I was in Cuba, 7000 children died in three months. Some mothers even drowned their babies from sheer desperation. . . . In this way, husbands died in the mines, wives died at work, and children died from lack of milk . . . and in a short time this land which was so great, so powerful and fertile . . . was depopulated. . . . My eyes have seen these acts so foreign to human nature, and now I tremble as I write . . .

'No tongue', wrote Las Casas, 'is capable of describing to the life all the horrid villainies perpetrated by these bloody-minded men.' He describes one incident where Spaniards on an expedition – having been given bread, fish and water by the Indians – finished their meal and then, turning on their benefactors, 'slashed, disembowelled and slaughtered the Indians until the blood ran like a river'. The head of the expedition, Captain Nárvaez, watched the massacre and then laughingly remarked to Las Casas, 'What does your reverence think of this that our Spaniards have done?' Replied Las Casas: 'You and them and all I offer to the devil.' When after a week the Spaniards departed from the area, there were few Indians left alive.

The Indians who heard of the massacre fled before the Spaniards; whereupon Las Casas, in a gross error of judgement, eventually urged them to trek homeward, 'men and women like sheep, each with his little bundle of poverty upon his back'. But then he was 'to see them whipped, tortured, castrated, murdered, the women raped, the villages burned, the children left to starve'. With the coming of the Christians, 'the land was expropriated, the native labour enslaved, the communal society extirpated, the population terrorised or liquidated . . .'.[31] The Spaniards, records Las Casas, set about 'with fiendish sport and mockery, hacking off their hands and feet, and mutilating their bodies in ways that will not bear description'; and feeding the Indians as meat to their bloodhounds: 'It was a fairly common sight to see armies accompanied by processions of slaves chained together to furnish food for the dogs. The more humane of the captains killed them first, but others turned the hungry dogs loose upon the terrified living naked victims.' The Spaniards, 'much given to the sport of hunting Indians', engaged also in contests of beheading Indians to test their blades and their own skills.[32]

In addition to the deliberate cruelties and exploitation, the Indians were driven to desperation and death in many other ways. They had lost control of their land and their economy. Where European farming did not replace the aboriginal agriculture, the Spanish released vast droves of livestock into a terrain with few predators and without the usual European diseases. Soon cattle, pigs, goats, horses, mules, donkeys, sheep and domestic fowl multiplied and spread on the grasslands and tended fields upon which the indigenous communities depended. The Indians, seeing their crops destroyed by this promiscuous animal onslaught, abandoned their cultivation in despair. The traditional communities collapsed, famine followed, and infanticide became widespread. Increasingly, individuals and entire families, plunged into ultimate despair, resorted to suicide – by eating soil, ingesting poison, or by hanging. One Spanish officer reported that there were days 'in which they were all found hanging, with their women and children, fifty households of the same village'.[33] And in these depressed conditions of malnutrition and misery, the Indians were inevitably susceptible to the European diseases carried by the Spaniards. There were frequent epidemics: smallpox, measles, typhoid and dysentery – in concert with the ravages of suicide and deliberate slaughter – all contributed to the extinction of the Caribbean Indian.

The Arawak Indians of Española, with only primitive weapons, had faced Spaniards equipped with armour, muskets, swords and horses. When the Spaniards took prisoners they hanged them, sliced them into pieces, or burned them to death. Hence the Arawaks, like other Indian groups in the Caribbean, resorted to mass suicide to escape the tortures inflicted by the Spaniards; infants were killed to save them from Christian cruelties. In a period of two years, the Indian population of 250,000 on Española had been reduced – through torture, murder and suicide – by a half; by 1515 there were around 50,000 Indians still alive; by 1550, a mere five hundred. A report issued in 1650 showed that there were no longer any Arawaks on Española.[34]

In Cuba an epidemic in 1519 reduced the population of some Indian communities by as much as two-thirds; in 1530 disease again ravaged the native population. On the eve of the conquest of Cuba the island supported around 112,000 Indians; as early as 1519 the indigenous population had shrunk to 19,000; and to 7000 by 1531. Twenty years later there were fewer than 3000 Indians on Cuba.[35]

The Spanish onslaught on the Indian communities of the Caribbean continued for some decades – until the extermination of virtually the entire Indian population of the islands stimulated the Spanish Christians to import slaves from Africa. The multifaceted European onslaught on the indigenous peoples had wrought nothing less than genocide. The Spanish monarchs continued to declare that the Spaniards were in the New World to promote the welfare of the original inhabitants, and that the colonisers should continue to persuade the Indians to adopt Christianity by humane and benevolent means. On 12 December 1512, King Ferdinand thanked Diego Velázquez for his conquest of Cuba, and for his 'humane treatment of the natives'.[36] Relatively little was known about pre-Columbian Cuba. Now the post-Columbian story of Cuba had begun.

3 The Slave Society

Everyone should remain in the state in which he was called.
Were you a slave when you were called? Never mind.

St Paul[1]

The first cause of slavery, then, is sin – that a man should be put in bonds
by another; and this happens only by the judgement of God, in whose eyes
it is no crime.

St Augustine[2]

If we take the modern history of Cuba as beginning at the start of the six-teenth century, then the island has had a well-defined political significance for almost five centuries. For nearly four hundred years of that period Cuba existed as a slave society. It is important to note the principal factors that encouraged and sustained this condition: not least, Christianity, free-enterprise business enterprise, and the rivalries of the European powers.

THE CHRISTIAN DIMENSION – II

For the vast bulk of its history, Christianity recognised slavery as an acceptable feature of the social order. At best, Christian moralists attempted to ameliorate the conditions under which slaves were forced to live; at worst, the Church ignored the brutalities perpetrated by the slave-owners, sanctifying their practices and in turn enjoying their support. In this attitude, sustained over many centuries, Christianity drew on its Jewish heritage. The ancient Hebrews sustained a slave class derived from various sources: captives taken in war, persons bought from other nations or from foreign residents in the land, the children of slaves, native Hebrews sold by their fathers, the native poor forced into slavery, and thieves unable to pay compensation.[3] St Paul followed in this tradition when he wrote: 'By one Spirit are we all baptised into one body, whether we be Jews or Gentiles, whether we be bond or free.'[4] And in the same vein St Peter urges servants to be subject to their masters 'with all fear' (I Peter 2, 18); St Timothy tells servants 'under the yoke to count their own masters worthy of all honour' (I Timothy 6, 1); and St Ignatius urges slaves not to desire 'to be set free at the public cost, that they be not slaves to their own lusts' (*Epistola ad Polycarpum*, 4).

A central feature of early Christian preaching was to stabilise the practice of slavery, an opportunistic posture that reflected the prevailing character of Roman society. Thus the feudal emperors, not fearing that Christianity would seek to overturn the hierarchical order of society, elevated the new religion to the level of a state orthodoxy: Constantine began the process in 313 and it was brought to completion in 380 by Gracian and Theodosius. Noblemen, newly sensitive to the demands of eternity, donated great estates to the Church; and in such a fashion the Christian bishops became the Empire's greatest land-owners with the greatest number of slaves. Some pagan moralists, reflecting a perennial theme in non-Christian philosophy, condemned slavery and demanded its abolition (see the *Orations* of Dio Chrysostom), but Christianity was deaf to such appeals. It was argued that the emancipation of the Church's slaves was impossible since it was not the clergy but God who was the owner – a principle that became law through the celebrated *Decretum Gratiani* (Gratian's Decree) in 1140, with reference to the slaves held by the monasteries. This enactment merely served to consolidate the patterns of slavery already established by the Church: the sixth-century pope, Gregory the Great, maintaining tens of thousands of slaves on his estates, had become the greatest slave-owner of the times. Throughout the Middle Ages the practice of slavery was defended by such leading Christian apologists as Thomas Aquinas, Duns Scotus and Albert the Great; with Thomas, for example, well prepared to applaud Aristotle's belief that the slave was an 'inspired tool of his master'.

Slaves who ran away from the Church estates were relentlessly pursued and brought back and then punished: as *fugitivi*, they were forced to wear around their necks an iron ring bearing Christian symbols. In Canon law, slaves were classified as Church property, and they were not allowed to assume the offices of the Church: the fifth-century pope, Leo the Great, ruled that no slave could become a cleric lest his 'vileness' should 'pollute' the sacred order. And it was also decided that slavery should be inflicted on people as a disciplinary measure. Thus in 1179, at the Third Lateran Council, all those who opposed the Church were threatened with slavery, even though it was often impractical to carry out such a gener-alised punishment: the popes imposed slavery on Venice in 1309, 1482 and 1506, on Florence in 1376, and on the whole of England in 1508.[5]

For our present purposes it is useful to note that the slave trade, already sustained in many manifestations by the pre-Columbian Church, was freshly invigorated at the end of the Middle Ages by the Spanish and Portuguese colonisations in the New World. In the bull *Romanus Pontifex* of 1454, Pope Nicholas V gave his blessing to the practice of enslaving conquered peoples; in 1487 Pope Innocent VIII accepted, as a gift from Queen Isabella, a large batch of slaves from Málaga; when, in 1493, Pope Alexander VI divided the world between Spain and Portugal he also sanctioned slavery; and in 1548 Pope Paul III granted to all men, including all members of the clergy, the right to keep slaves. The papal ships sailed out to hunt for people who could be enslaved, and thanksgiving prayers were offered throughout Christendom whenever a rich catch was made.[6] Papal philosophers, ever keen to debate important matters, seriously discussed the question of whether a pocket mirror was a just price for a negro. The Jesuits owned thousands of slaves on their plantations (a single Jesuit college in the Congo owned some 12,000 slaves in 1666); as late as 1864 the Benedictines in Brazil maintained slaves in the service of the Church.

The Church had never doubted the legitimacy of the slavery ethic. The Biblical sanction was unambiguous, brutally manifest in the Old Testament: a master shall bore a slave's ear through with an awl (Exodus *21*, 6), a man may sell his daughter into slavery (Exodus *21*, 7), slave-capturing expeditions are to be encouraged (Deuteronomy *20*, 10–15), female slaves may be violated and then discarded (Deuteronomy *21*, 10–14), and a slave may be beaten to death over several days, for the slave is only then man's 'money' (Exodus *21*, 20–21). A New Testament parable glorifies the master–slave relationship as a model of the relationship between God and man (Matthew *18*, 23–25); just as Paul, keen to uphold the institution of slavery, sent the runaway slave Onesimus back to his Christian master Philemon. The Europeans who sailed to conquer and colonise the New World were spiritually fortified not only by the excesses of the Christian inquisitors (see Chapter 2) but also by the long biblical and papal tradition applauding the exploitation of slaves in the service of God. To the religious sanction was added the full panoply of racist assumption, again fed by the long Christian confrontation with Moslem and Jew.

When the Spaniards encountered the Indians in the New World, they were quick to depict the indigenous peoples as children, beasts, savages and madmen; so making the torture, exploitation and murder of the native Americans a guiltless (even holy) matter. Learned Christian academics urged the European soldiers, torturers and executioners to persist in their humane efforts to bring Christian virtue to wretched pagans. European theologians and philosophers, keen to define the great hierarchy of beings created by God, were happy to place Indians, blacks and other non-whites somewhere near the most abject beasts and to place (male) whites somewhere near the angels. Aristotle, often helpful to the Church, had declared in the *Politics* that some people are 'natural slaves', a depiction that Christian thinkers had no cause to dispute.

An English observation from the 1630s suggests that the 'salvages' (sic) of America were 'a dangerous people, subtill, secreat and mischeivous'; the Pequot Indians slaughtered in 1637 received their just deserts, since they were 'barbarians, ever treacherous' and merited 'severe execution of just revenge'; and the Mohawks, in one description, were 'mad dogs'. The much-hyped American Declaration of Independence included the phrase 'merciless Indian Savages', just as George Washington characterised the native Americans as 'beasts of prey', similar to the wolf 'tho' they differ in shape'. Theodore Roosevelt, who was to become the twenty-sixth president of the United States, applauded the prospect of the extermination of the Indian: 'I don't go so far as to think that the only good Indians are dead Indians, but I believe nine out of ten are, and I shouldn't enquire too closely into the case of the tenth. The most vicious cowboy has more moral principle than the average Indian.'[7] In the same spirit an early debate in the Colorado legislature concerned the provision of bounties for 'the destruction of Indians and Skunks'. Governor Macduffie of South Carolina declared, without fear of contradiction, that no human institution is more clearly consistent with the will of God than slavery, and that every community should execute abolitionists as 'enemies of the human race'. Clerics would later be found among the abolitionists but in the mid-nineteenth century there were few religious bodies (notably the Quakers and the United Brethren) that were prepared to denounce slavery. One authority (Von Holst, cited by Westermarck[8]) noted that the American Churches, far from opposing black servitude, were 'the bulwarks of American slavery'.

Such was the character of the Christian ethic brought by the Europeans to the New World. This was the context – fundamentally shaped by racist assumption and religious absolutism – in which slavery was installed and developed in the Americas. It is useful to note this context in surveying the history of Cuba.

The Church saw its principal task in the New World as an evangelical one. In a classic clerical phrase the slaves were 'tools with souls': they would be required to serve their masters, clerical or secular, but at the same time they could be encouraged to save their (alleged) immortal souls. Here the Church was prepared to set the aboriginal Indians and the imported negro slaves on the same level; though because of the genocide of the aboriginal peoples the vast bulk of the evangelical effort was focused on the negro populations of the Caribbean islands. Since Cuba became the most heavily populated negro colony in Spanish America, it was Cuba that tended to set the pattern of church–slave relations in the region.[9] This pattern was of course itself substantially shaped by the prevailing character of Christianity in the Iberian peninsula.

The African negro imported into the Caribbean was necessarily regarded by the Church as a primitive or pre-religious person. Thus the *bozale* (the 'raw negro from Africa') was required to exist in a childlike condition, excluded from the priesthood but exempt (in law if not in practice) from the inquisitorial impulses of the Christian interlopers in the New World. A few clerics had disputed the legality of enslaving the Indians, so expressing doubts that did nothing to restrict the actual servitude of the native Americans; but the question of negro slavery was never in dispute. The enslavement of the negro was an established convention before the Spanish conquests in the Americas. Thus the Church, far from questioning a well-tried institution, developed its central role of securing souls for Christ. Hence at the start of the *Leyes de Indias*, a celebrated body of colonial legislation, the Church declares:

> We order and command to all those persons who have Slaves, Negroes and Mulattoes, that they send them to the Church or Monastery at the hour which the Prelate has designated, and there the Christian doctrine be taught to them; and the Archbishops and Bishops of our Indies have very particular care for their conversion and indoctrination, in order that they live Christianly, and they give to it the same order and care that is prepared and entrusted by the Laws of this Book for the Conversion and Indoctrination of the Indians; so that they be instructed in our Holy Roman Catholic Faith, living in the service of God our Master.[10]

The declaration was reinforced by colonial synods that worked to strengthen the close links that existed between civil and canonical law, and which in consequence generated an essential part of the legislation intended to regulate the working of the Cuban slave system. For example, a Dominican provincial synod convened in the early seventeenth century on Española, under the auspices of an Archbishopric that included all of the West Indies, Cuba, Florida and Venezuela.[11]

A main task of the synods was to frame the *sanctiones*, the laws and ordinances that emerged as the official civil code and canon law for a defined region. One of these *sanctiones* focused on the question of negro baptism. Had the negroes, as some claimed, been besprinkled with holy water by traders before arriving in the colonies? Or might they have to be baptised afresh? The negro slaves should be questioned on the matter. Had they received any knowledge of the sacrament? And had they 'willingly received' this holy water at the time it was offered to them? If any of the conditions were 'found to be lacking', it would be necessary to baptise the negroes anew. If, for any reason, a negro refused to be baptised, he would be given two or three months 'during which the fear of the doctrine must be found'. And as with baptism so with the other sacraments (confirmation, marriage, extreme unction, etc.): the use of indoctrination and any necessary pressure before they could be properly administered. The *Constitución IV*, published with others by a Cuban synod that convened in June 1680, ruled that all slaves be indoctrinated into the Faith and baptised within a year of arrival in the Indies.[12]

The Church had no objection to masters trading in slaves, provided that certain conditions were fulfilled: enslaved husbands and wives to be sold outside Havana had to be taken together, and masters were prohibited from selling slaves overseas or in remote parts to impede marital life. At the same time the clerical authorities gradually conceded that there was merit in the freeing of slaves (though the Church remained steadfast in upholding the slavery institution). Thus masters were encouraged to believe that the *manumission* (freeing) of their slaves would be pleasing to God on certain occasions: a slave might be freed as a tribute to God on a saint's day, when a master married, when his child was born, or when he recovered from a severe illness. On occasions the clergy would remonstrate with the masters for their bad treatment of the slaves, but were just as likely to criticise the negroes for their licentious and un-Christian behaviour. One Bishop Pedro Agustín Morel de Santa Cruz, working in Cuba in the mid-eighteenth century, denounced the negro clubs (*cabildos*) where men and women gathered to drink and to perform 'extremely torrid and provocative dances'. He visited each of the clubs to administer confirmations and to pray before an image of the Virgin Mary which he carried with him. Later he assigned members of the clergy to visit the clubs to indoctrinate the men and women with the Christian faith. In fact the *cabildos* often fulfilled a religious role, though not always one the Church approved: the *cabildos* participated in religious processions, akin to those of medieval Seville, but with the displayed figures and costumes tending to preserve elements of African mythology. One traveller describes 'free and enslaved negroes' assembling 'to do homage with a sort of grave merriment that one would doubt whether it is done in ridicule or memory of their former condition. . . . The only *civilised* part of the entertainment is – *drinking rum*' (original italics).[13]

The priests – interested above all in bringing slaves into the faith – served as the sole intermediary between the masters and the negroes. While the masters were concerned essentially with business and property, the Church was prepared to promote wider interests, providing these contributed unambiguously to the security of the Faith. To this partial extent the Church often succeeded in mitigating the miserable lot of the African slaves in Cuba and elsewhere in the Americas; but those wanting to achieve the total abolition of the wretched institution of slavery were forced to contemplate a total rupture with an important element in the centuries-long Christian tradition. And this was the dilemma that came to afflict many a would-be Christian reformer. In 1675 a companion of the parliamentarian George Fox criticised the Quakers for holding slaves in Maryland and Virginia (one slave ship was called *The Willing Quaker*), just as a number of the American Founding Fathers were slave-owners (inducing Samuel Johnson to ask: 'How is it that the loudest yelps for liberty come from the drivers of slaves?'). Thomas Jefferson might have denounced slavery but, in the words of the modern writer Peter Gay, he 'could still live with, and off it'. Similarly, the British abolitionist Charles Stuart complained in 1842 that America was making itself a spectacle in 'applauding liberty, yet keeping slaves!'.

Cuba, from the beginning of the European intervention, had been run as a slave society – a pattern that Europeans were keen to extend throughout the Americas. This is a crucial shaping factor of modern Cuban culture, one of the most important Christian contributions to the New World.

EARLY COLONISATION

Whereas the Spanish crown supported the Columbus expeditions to the New World, the subsequent conquests were largely a matter of private initiative. It was still necessary for the would-be entrepreneurs to have good court connections but in such circumstances the crown was prepared to agree a contract (*capitulación*), defining the adventurer's rights and obligations. He would be granted titles (typically that of *adelantado*, formerly a border lord in the time of the *Reconquista*), allowed to make money (from which the crown would take a cut), and entitled to give land and Indians to his followers. Some adventurers (for example, Cortés) ignored such preamble, made their conquests, and then sought royal assent on the promise of donating funds to the crown. The more successful conquistadores characteristically used earlier conquests to fuel later ones. Thus Velázquez used his pickings in Española to fund the conquest of

Cuba; he and Cortés used the wealth they had acquired in Cuba to facilitate the invasion of Mexico; and Hernando de Soto used the treasures of Peru to support his incursions into Florida. But the early successes of the conquistadores were reduced over time: the Spanish crown manoeuvred for legal advantage or bought out the adventurers. By the end of the sixteenth century, what had been the New World proprietary domains had been converted into royal provinces.

The colonists, in Cuba and elsewhere, were allowed a substantial measure of self-government, realised through the mechanism of the *municipality*. The Baracoa settlement, created by Velázquez in 1512 at the start of the Cuban conquest, quickly evolved into a well-defined municipality; as did the six other settlements established by 1515. The seven municipal governments, covering the whole of Cuba, were based on the *cabildo* (municipal council, not to be confused with the African *cabildos* mentioned earlier). Here the *cabildo* functioned as a court of law, a grantor of land titles, and a controller of prices, monopolies and import–export practices; as well as carrying out all the normal tasks of local government. Under Velázquez the settlers elected the first *cabildos*, out of which a representative assembly (along the lines of the Castilian parliament, the *Cortes*) emerged from the *procuradores*, the men elected to represent the municipalities before the Spanish crown. In the early days the Cuban assembly met once a year, usually at Santiago de Cuba (then the capital). The *procuradores* had an interest in extending Cuban autonomy, even in wresting the colony from Spanish control; the crown, keen to resist any threat to its authority, only granted limited concessions. For a variety of economic and other reasons the *procurador* assembly ran into decline; and by 1540 the *procuradores*, in their annual convention, represented only three of the seven municipalities. The crown, having tightened its grip on Cuba, encouraged the development of a powerful imperial bureaucracy.[14]

To this end the crown created *audiencias* (high courts), with powerful judicial–administrative roles; the first, established in Santo Domingo, Española, in 1511 soon developed jurisdiction over all of the West Indies and the north-eastern coastline of South America. Outside this region the administrative vice-royalties of New Spain (1535) and Peru (1544) were created. Such arrangements enabled the crown to revoke the early concessions made to Columbus. Cuba had fallen under the legal control of Diego Columbus, heir to his father's concessions and now the governor of Española; but the crown encouraged Velázquez to undermine Diego's control and so strengthen the hand of the monarchy. In due course the House of Columbus sold its rights to the crown for a pension. Throughout the islands the early *adelantados* had been replaced by royally appointed governors, with the Santo Domingo *audiencia* holding sway over much of the Caribbean region, including Cuba. The Cuban governor, a crown official, remained under close royal supervision: a career bureaucrat, his term of office was usually short. Furthermore, the colonials were almost totally excluded from the bureaucracy. Only fourteen *creoles* (native born) figured among the 602 captains-general, governors and presidents of *audiencias* during the colonial period; some 601 of the bishops and archbishops exercising power in the Americas during this time had come from Spain.[15] Thus the creoles, though enjoying local economic power, were almost completely excluded from political and social influence. The Castilian crown, aided by the Church against the Cuban white settlers, continued to consolidate its imperial control over the island.

Española remained important as the centre for administration of the Spanish Caribbean, with Cuba of special significance because of its position on the regular sea route to the Main. Havana, the chief Cuban port, commanded the Florida passage and so was crucial for defence. This port became a Spanish shipbuilding centre and a focus for the convoys sailing between Spain and the ports of the Empire. The Cuban colonists at first produced indigo and tobacco, later developing the vital sugar industry based on negro slavery. The *repartimiento* (later more often dubbed *encomienda*) system, whereby land and slaves (first Indian, then negro) were granted to settlers and their creole descendants, was developed in Cuba and elsewhere, and brought great profit to Spain.

In the early days there were enough Indians to satisfy the *encomienda* demand; but this phase did not last long. Following the efforts of Las Casas, steps were taken to deprive settlers of control of their *encomiendas* if they were found guilty of ill-treating their Indian slaves. At the same time efforts were made to mitigate the burden of tribute levied on the indigenous populations of the islands. But such reforms, limited and tardy, did little to address the rapid decline of the Indian population. The new laws, issued by Charles V on 20 November 1542, aroused such a storm of protest that they were quickly abandoned: the abused Indian population was soon reduced to a point at which the *encomienda* system faced serious labour problems. And the obvious shortfall could not be made up by immigrants from the Iberian peninsula.

The problems facing the Caribbean islands were particularly chronic, not least because new Spanish conquests were encouraging an unprecedented phase of white emigration: the catalogue of Spanish conquests and annexations included Panama (1519), Costa Rica (1519), Nicaragua (1522), Guatemala (1523), Honduras (1524), Ecuador (1525), Peru (1526), Venezuela (1527), Yucatán (1527), and Florida (1528). The white settlers were keen to follow the gold, or whatever other riches were advertised in the new lands of the Empire: in consequence, by 1574 only five hundred Castilian households remained in Española out of the original 14,000 settler inhabitants; by 1620 the total population of Cuba was estimated at less than seven thousand. Such circumstances gave an immense impetus to the negro slave trade, then seen as the only realistic means of populating the Caribbean islands to the advantage of Spain.

By the start of the sixteenth century the Spaniards were already experienced in purchasing negro slaves from the Portuguese, and now it was seen that the Portuguese monopoly of the Guinea trade was a serious limitation on Spanish imperial ambitions. At first the Spanish crown, keen to avoid the possibility of transporting heresy to the Americas, turned to the negro slaves already converted to Catholicism in Spain. On 3 September 1501 King Ferdinand, keen to supplement the diminishing Indian population in the Caribbean with negro slaves, wrote to the governor of Española: 'In view of our earnest desire for the conversion of the Indians to our Holy Catholic Faith, and seeing that, if persons suspect in the Faith went there, such conversion might be impeded, we cannot consent to the immigration of Moors, heretics, Jews, re-converts, or persons newly converted to our Holy Faith, unless they are Negro or other slaves who have been born in the power of Christians who are our subjects and nationals and carry our express permission.' Thus at the beginning of the Spanish slave trade, the traffic was only in Christian negroes – so that the New World would not be polluted by heresy or inadequate religious commitment. But this arrangement could not last: there were not enough suitably pious black slaves to meet the labour needs of the Americas.

One early problem was that the enslaved negroes died as rapidly as the Indians; in 1511 Ferdinand wrote to an official in Española that he could not understand 'how so many Negroes have died . . .'. The only solution was to increase the supply of slaves. In 1517 a contract (*asiento*) was agreed for the importation of 4000 negroes into the West Indies; in 1523 the Spanish crown ordered another 4000 to be sent to the Spanish colonies (of which 300 were destined for Cuba); and in 1528 Cuba demanded a further 700. At the same time European entrepreneurs were drawing up their own contracts for the supply of negro slaves to Cuba and the other Caribbean colonies; Las Casas suggests that by 1540 more than 100,000 slaves had been imported into the Caribbean colonies.

The early anxieties concerning the importation of heresy and the possibility of slave revolts (in 1506 the Spanish crown worried that the large numbers of slaves being imported into Cuba might stimulate rebellion) were rapidly submerged by the pressures of economic opportunism. There was now a substantial slave-based trade developing between Spain and its New World colonies. An annual fleet was sailing from Spain to Española, whence ships would sail to the other colonies. Later, after the conquest of Mexico and Peru, two regular fleets sailed together from Seville: one, the *flota*, stopped at Puerto Rico, Española and Cuba before reaching Vera Cruz in Mexico; the other, the *galleones*, headed for Cartagena on the mainland and Panama – after which the *flota* and *galleones* assembled at Havana for the return voyage to Seville. One estimate suggests that the combined size of the two fleets, dauntingly impressive for the day, amounted to around 10,000 tons.[16] In addition the islands were visited by supplementary ships that sailed each year in the main fleets: two to six vessels were assigned both to Española and to Havana, two to Puerto Rico, one to Jamaica and Santiago de Cuba combined, and one to Trinidad.[17] The commercial fleets dramatically shaped affairs in the Caribbean. As one consequence, Cuba became more important than Española, with Havana, 'the key to the Indies', increasingly perceived as a strategic port. The concentration of Caribbean production and population along the region of the trade routes led to the fading of the other Antilles, Jamaica and Puerto Rico, and to the relative neglect of the northern coast of Española and the southern coast of Cuba. But the strategic importance of Havana said nothing about the economic status of Cuba as a whole. The rise of Havana (made the Cuban capital in 1607) contributed to the decline of Santiago de Cuba and the eastern regions of the island.

The colonisation of Cuba had led to the extinction of the indigenous population, the importation of a large slave population, a strategic and economic focus on Havana to the detriment of distant communities on the island, and a focused economy based on only a few products. With official attention now directed at Havana rather than Santiago de Cuba, eastern Cuba was vulnerable to foreign ambitions: the French attacked Santiago and Bayamo in 1603, 1628 and 1633, occupying Baracoa and Remedios in 1652; the English sacked Santiago in 1662; the French sacked Sancti Spiritus in 1665; in 1668 Henry Morgan destroyed Puerto Príncipe; and in 1675 John Springer attacked the town of Trinidad.[18] Much of central Cuba remained sparsely populated and poorly governed, with little scope for commercial development that might have aided the national economy. The post-conquest economic depression had resulted in periodic subsidies (*situados*) being paid from Mexico to underwrite the Spanish military presence on the island (about 60 million pesos paid between 1766 and 1788). The economy gradually improved, though still rooted essentially in the export of tobacco and sugar.

The Spanish conquest also involved Cuba in the tensions between the European powers, and between them (especially Spain) and the United States. Furthermore, the dependence of Spanish Cuba on a large imported slave population (5000 negro slaves by 1650, 44,000 by 1774, 399, 800 by 1860) led to inevitable tensions, periodic rebellions, wars of liberation, and the eventual collapse of the Spanish occupation.

THE SLAVE ECONOMY

The first phase of economic exploitation of Cuba by the Spaniards was a relatively simple affair: the Indians were conquered and abused, and their possessions stolen, making the Spanish interlopers the effective 'hunters and gatherers' of Christian imperialism. Then, the early finds of gold quickly exhausted, the conquistadores put the Indians in the mines to maintain the flow of riches. In one account, about 62,000 pesos of gold were produced in the first four years, with some 100,000 pesos-worth being mined annually by 1517.[19] Efforts were also made to introduce the staple European crops and livestock, a process that further ravaged the indigenous communities. Then the further Spanish conquests drained Cuba of population and incentive, while at the same time the island's supply of gold began to give out.[20] The development of European-style agriculture had not managed to render the island self-sufficient; and that key product, sugar, destined to play such a central role in later Cuban commerce and politics, was at first slow to develop.

A principal reason for the importation of negro slaves to the Americas through the early decades of the Spanish occupation was that they were needed on the sugar plantations. In 1503 Pedro de Atienza and Miguel Ballester began producing sugar in Española; Atienza brought cane, and the two men constructed processing facilities for the production of molasses in Concepción de la Vega. Other colonists, soon seeing the economic possibilities, followed suit. In 1515 Gonzalo de Lellosa, a Spanish surgeon in control of some sixty-seven native labourers, imported technical experts to build a sugar mill. This machine (the *trapiche*) employed horses (or sometimes oxen or slaves) moving steadily in a circle to turn a main wheel to grind the cane. One early technological innovation was the use of water power as a substitute for human or animal power; the water-powered *ingenio*, cheaper to run than the *trapiche*, was obviously limited to particular geographical sites. The *trapiche* could handle 25–35 cartloads of cane every day to produce 840 pounds of sugar, while a hydraulic mill could cope with 40–50 cartloads and extract between 1120 and 1960 pounds of sugar during every 24-hour period.[21]

The burgeoning sugar industry in the Caribbean provided large profits to Spanish entrepreneurs; but then, as today, there were problems over capital investment. The Catholic Church, hostile to what it perceived as usury, maintained a ban on monetary interest, so restricting the availability of commercial capital. At the same time the wealth generated in the Caribbean often found its way into war expenditure and political corruption. The Spanish government, keen to exploit the expanding Empire, offered loans to entrepreneurs, agreed a moratorium on the debts of the sugar planters, cut the tithe due to the Church by a half, supplied sugar experts, exempted the machinery used in the sugar mills from import duties, and prohibited the attachment, seizure or sale of mills for debt.[22] The governor of Española, Rodrigo de Figueroa, was instructed by King Charles V to support the efforts of the sugar manufacturers in every way possible. Such support bore fruit: by 1520 six mills were operating, with another forty being built; and in 1522 Jean Florin made the first sugar export, a 25-ton load, to Spain. All the signs were that sugar production in the Caribbean would have a secure future. The tropical climate meant that there was no threat from freezing weather, and the abundant rainfall made irrigation unnecessary in many regions.

Sugar production, encouraged by government support, quickly spread from Española to the other islands of the Caribbean. Jamaica had sugar mills in operation by 1519; some thirty *ingenios* were working by 1523. Soon *ingenios* were being built in Puerto Rico, and cane was being taken to Cuba. Proposals were discussed for the production of sugar in Cuba but it was not until the 1570s that the first mills were built on the island, in Bahía Honda, near Havana. It was not until production spread to eastern Cuba, in the region of Santiago, that the Cuban sugar industry began to prosper towards the end of the sixteenth century.

Following the early exploitation of Cuba's natural riches, the island quickly ran into depression. The strategic position of the island continued to impress the Spanish crown, but there was less interest in the steady development of the Cuban economy. The tropical climate had not favoured the production of wheat, barley, grapes and olives, so the island was forced to continue importing not only manufactured items but also agricultural produce. The cattle and hogs brought by the first Spaniards thrived – to the point that cattle-product exports (hides, tallow, salted meat, and so on) became a principal trading commodity and the hunting of the herds emerged as an important settler pursuit. Large cattle ranches (*hatos* or *fincas*) developed throughout the island.

Other exports included woods from the island forests, and (later) tobacco. As with sugar production, the lack of investment capital restricted the development of the Cuban copper industry until well after the early colonial phase. The production of salted meats, vegetables and fresh fruit was important for the fleets calling at Havana prior to their long voyage across the Atlantic; and so the region saw the growth of shipyards, slaughter houses, taverns, lodges, eating houses and other facilities for the fleets. Such activities as gambling, prostitution and smoking were stimulated by the crews visiting Havana (with smoking, spreading to Europe and the colonies, eventually creating the massive demand for Cuban tobacco). In 1581 Gabriel de Luján reported to the Spanish crown: '. . . this place [Havana] is the most expensive in all the Indies; this is because of the great number of ships that pass through here, and the people traveling on them who cannot refrain from spending even if they wanted to'.[23] Such developments offered Cuba clear economic benefits and helped to compensate for the exhaustion of the gold resource.

The slave population on the island helped to underpin these activities, just as it was essential for the working of the plantations. Some negroes accompanied the Spaniards on their fresh conquests, so swelling the Cuban exodus, but the importation of slaves continued to increase. In 1532 there were around 500 African slaves on the island, by 1535 about 1000, and by 1606 some 20,000. Thus in 1542 the Cuban *procuradores* were able to declare: 'Here the principal property are the Negroes.' It had taken the negro slave a mere three decades to become a major factor in the economic life of Cuba. In contrast, there was limited white migration to the island in the first two centuries of Spanish colonisation, not least because of the crown's exclusion of many 'new Christians' and non-Castilians. Moreover, there was no Spanish equivalent to the English indenture system which encouraged the migration of thousands of labourers.

The white settlers in Cuba also had a significant interest in escaping from manual work, so sacrificing their skills, in preference to living off land worked by slaves. Hence, because of what was known as the *hidalguismo* ideal, white craftsmen were prepared to teach their skills to black slaves, if this meant that the whites could accumulate capital and 'retire'. Thus the negroes were able to acquire important skills and to practise these, first as slaves and later as freedmen. This meant that later waves of white immigrants in the nineteenth century were at a disadvantage when forced to compete with the skilled black workers in the Cuban economy. The negroes had been forced into the mines, following the demise of the Indian population, but later they began to acquire the skills associated with such work: by 1546 a German expert was offering the slaves apprenticeships in copper mining and smelting. The negro continued to live a life of penury, with few rights and little political influence, but gradually the black population was acquiring the skills and confidence that would lead to eventual emancipation.

In the seventeenth century tobacco emerged as the first modern commercial crop, a product of the small tobacco farm (*vega*) on which poor white farmers commonly worked alongside their slaves in the field. Many of the workers were poor whites and free blacks, with some slaves even managing to rent *vegas* for a fixed sum payable to their masters. In 1717 the Spanish crown created a monopoly for tobacco production and introduced fiscal policies that discouraged the large-scale importation of slaves. One consequence was that the 8 million pounds of Cuban tobacco produced in 1717 was scarcely exceeded by the 9 million pounds produced in 1788. Nonetheless the tobacco industry has remained a crucial part of the Cuban economy up to the present day.

By 1763 some 60,000 negro slaves had been transported to Cuba, with the rate set to increase over the next three decades. In a single year in the 1770s some 17,000 slaves were imported into the island; between 1763 and 1790, around 41,000 slaves were brought to Cuba, with no less than 320,000 brought to Havana alone between 1791 and 1825. Many of the slaves transported to the other islands were then conveyed to Cuba. Thus in an attempt to capture the slave trade with foreign islands British entrepreneurs first brought slaves to a British territory and then transported them to Cuba, Puerto Rico, or elsewhere. While the number of slaves brought into Cuba from the British islands is not known for certain, 'it is quite clear that this was Cuba's most important source of slaves'.[24] Of some 90,000 slaves imported into the British West Indies between 1784 and 1787, about 20,000 were re-exported. The Cuban slaves found themselves occupied in every sector of the island economy, from the many urban enterprises to the small farms and vast plantations.

At the end of the eighteenth century the erosion of industrial activity in Española boosted commercial activity in Cuba. The coffee industry, significant at the beginning of the century, saw rapid expansion; unlike tobacco it was soon being produced on large plantations, a pattern of crop production that demanded substantial investment. In 1790 production was around 7000 *arrobas* (a 25-lb measure), but in 1815 some 28,000 slaves produced a crop of 900,000 *arrobas*. After the middle of the nineteenth century the Cuban coffee industry, in the face of growing foreign competition, went into steady decline.[25] The world price of coffee had doubled between 1792 and 1796, and newly arrived French coffee planters settling around Santiago and Guantánamo had succeeded in transforming the island into a major world producer of coffee. By 1833, before the subsequent decline in the industry, coffee exports had reached around 2.6 million *arrobas*. But it was in sugar production that the most spectacular advances were to be achieved. Estimates for 1825, when sugar production was beginning to overtake coffee as the dominant Cuban crop suggest that with 140,000 slaves employed in staple crop production some 66,000 were engaged in the sugar industry (another 73,000, 28 per cent of the total, were employed in urban work). Even then, the sugar industry, despite massive expansion never involved a majority of the rural slave population (Table 3.1).

The sugar producers were keen to respond to the sudden explosion of world prices: the zones of cultivation in Cuba expanded, as they did elsewhere; and between 1792 and 1806 the number of sugar mills in the region of Havana soared from 237 to 416, planters favouring regions where they could use water transport to convey their products to the capital. The disappearance of entire forests signalled that sugar had become 'king' in Cuba: for the planting of cane and the building of mills, an estimated 1700 acres a year were being cleared in the late eighteenth century, expanding to an annual 3500 acres being cleared over the next two decades and some 13,000 acres a year being cleared by the 1840s.[26] And deforestation was only one of the impacts of the burgeoning sugar industry. The roads and tracks, without adequate infrastructure investment, ran into disrepair and decay. One observer (Humboldt), writing of the sugar zones around Havana, commented that in 'no part of the world do the roads become more impassable during the rainy season, than in that part of the island, where the soil is a decomposing limestone ill adapted to the making of wheel-roads'.[27] Eventually the demands of the sugar industry led to the improvement of roads and the building of the first railways (the first line, 51 miles long and built to link Havana with Guines, was working in 1838); by the early 1860s 400 miles of railway had been built to connect the

TABLE 3.1   Rural slave population in Cuba (1830)

Type of agriculture	Number of slaves	Value of slaves
Sugar plantations	50,000	$15,000,000
Coffee plantations	50,000	15,000,000
Small farms and cattle ranches	31,065	9,319,500
Tobacco farms	7,927	2,378,100
	138,992	$41,697,600

SOURCE: Herber S. Klein, *Slavery in the Americas: A Comparative Study of Cuba and Virginia* (London: Oxford University Press, 1967) p. 152

sugar producers with the provincial ports. Such developments led in turn to a widening of the export market, a decrease in transport costs, and a transfer of various tasks from slaves to rail. In 1817 steam power was first introduced into Cuban sugar mills; between 1846 and 1860 steam-powered mills, having increased in number by 20 per cent, comprised nearly three-quarters of the total. Other technological developments included the replacement of wooden rollers by iron ones, the introduction of vacuum boilers during the 1830s and 1840s, and the introduction of the centrifuge to aid sugar purification.

Over the period from the 1760s to the 1830s, Cuba had evolved from an underpopulated island of small towns, cattle ranges, and small tobacco farms to a thriving land of large sugar and coffee plantations based on the exploited labour of African slaves. Many factors contributed to this radical evolution; not least the shifts in world market demand, the English occupation of Havana in 1763–64, the reforms introduced by Charles III (1759–88), the collapse of the French colony of St Domingue, and the prodigious efforts of the Cuban independence agitators. And with the historic agricultural development came other changes: new ways of organising slave labour, new attitudes to international market possibilities, and a growing impatience with the restrictions imposed by the Spanish crown. The English occupation of Havana helped to convince Charles III that the colonial administration was ripe for reform (see 'From Reform to Abolition', below), and to set in train the vortex of social and economic forces that would eventually lead to Cuban emancipation.

A central economic problem facing the Spanish government was that there was now a vast and widening gap between the Cuban demand for slaves and the available supply. The property owners had traditionally bought their slaves from the English, the French, the Dutch and the Portuguese; *asientos* (contracts) for the supply of slaves were awarded to individuals or countries, and later to the joint-stock companies and the French, the Portuguese and (after 1713) the British.[28] In addition to the *asiento* system, a parallel inter-island slave trade thrived throughout the Caribbean: privateers ran their own trade, and the Cuban owners were able also to purchase slaves in such places as Jamaica and Dominica. The Spanish authorities, outflanked by such enterprise, were resentful; and so moved to create their own chartered companies to improve matters. Thus the Real Compañía Mercantil de La Habana was created in 1740 to transport African slaves to Cuba for sale (cash, credit or pledged crop volumes). Over a 26-year period the company transported and sold 9943 African slaves in Cuba. Other chartered companies (for example, the Caracas Company operating along the Venezuelan coast) were active in various parts of Spanish America. But the Real Compañía and its counterparts failed to solve the slave-supply problem.

The Spanish crown responded by granting permission for an unrestricted number of slaves to be brought to the island. In particular, a royal *cedula* of 28 February 1789 allowed Spaniards and foreigners to market as many slaves as they could in a specified number of free ports, including Havana. Taxes were suspended for a period of three years, and merchants were encouraged to respond to local market circumstances. These developments, together constituting a nice example of free-trade licence, delighted the planters and encouraged them to press for further reforms. In 1792 the Spanish authorities extended the free-trade provisions for a further six years, and between 1789 and 1798 a total of eleven royal pronouncements worked to expand the transportation of African slaves to the Spanish Indies. This gave an enormous boost to the development of plantation society in the Caribbean and elsewhere.

The sugar and coffee plantations in Cuba quickly expanded to erode the tobacco and cattle holdings; tobacco remained the main crop in a region to the west of Havana, with sugar now dominating the central plains and the area around Santiago and coffee retreating to the eastern mountainous region. Such trends increased the pressures for reform of the landholding system. The early conquests had consigned the bulk of Cuban land to the Castilian monarchs, who then distributed it to deserving settlers. At the same time the crown struggled to retain control over the situation, deriving income from its dispensations and maintaining regulations over land use. The tensions built up: as the rate of white immigration increased and the Spanish treasury ran into its own financial problems the Cuban landholders pressed for clarification of the rules governing land ownership and exploitation. In 1791 the Havana Economic Society, created by twenty-seven Creole landholders, received its royal sanction and worked to expand landholder rights. The Society was most successful during the terms of office of Luis de Las Casas y Arragori (1790–96) and Alejandro Ramírez (1816–19), Cuban landholders able to exert political influence in Madrid.

A royal *cedula* of 1800 dismantled the hereditary pattern of the *señorios* (large estates), and allowed land previously held in *usufruct* to be directly owned – so stimulating for the first time a real-estate market in royal land. Subsequent royal decrees (for example, in 1815 and 1816) further liberalised the land position, allowing landholders to use and trade their land without legal constraint and to clear the hardwood forests in the interest of plantation expansion. This led to real-estate speculation, the growth of the plantation economy, and the creation of new towns (Guira,

Alquizar, Nueva Paz, Palos, Guines, and others) settled largely by immigrants. At first the forests enjoyed a measure of protection as a husbanded source of fuel and building materials, but later industrialisation accelerated the deforestation process: the cane growers found it profitable to clear the forests and plant cane, and thereafter to import lumber, firewood and coal. By the middle of the nineteenth century much of the central region of Cuba had been deforested.

Sugar production increased dramatically through the nineteenth century (Table 3.2). New strains of sugar cane were introduced, and new techniques of production were developed. Mills increased their output dramatically: from an average of 72 tons per mill in 1830 to 120 tons in 1841, and reaching an average of 316 tons by 1860; from around one thousand sugar mills in 1827 the number had doubled by 1868. Cattle ranchers and coffee producers were hard hit, with the coffee growers affected also by a series of devastating hurricanes between 1844 and 1846 and by the tide of international competition, mainly from Brazil. Now the coffee producers were finding it increasingly difficult to buy slaves. Coffee production fell from around $80 million in 1829 to $40 million in 1849; from 1680 *fincas* (coffee farms) in 1846, the number fell to 782 in 1861; and exports fell from 2.5 million *arrobas* in 1833 to 154,208 in 1867.[29]

Now Cuba was developing an economy dependent upon a single crop export: in 1840 sugar accounted for 60 per cent of total export earnings, in 1860 as much as 74 per cent. The United States was increasingly influencing the shape of Cuban production strategies; North American entrepreneurs were supplying slaves and manufactured goods, and accept-

TABLE 3.2 Growth in Cuban sugar production
(1790–1868)

Year	Tons
1790	15,423
1800	28,761
1805	35,238
1815	45,396
1829	84,187
1840	161,248
1850	294,952
1860	428,769
1868	720,250

SOURCE: Manuel Moreno Fraginals, *El ingenio: complejo económico social cubano del azúcar* (3 volumes, Havana, 1978, vol. III, pp. 43–4)

ing payment in sugar and molasses. The number of North American ships trading with Cuba gradually increased (150 in 1796, 1886 in 1852), and the Spanish commercial monopoly was broken. American ships arriving at Cuban ports brought such products as staves, caskets, barrels, nails, tar, textiles, salt, fish, flour and rice; and took in turn coffee, tobacco, molasses and sugar. By the middle of the nineteenth century England, Spain and the United States accounted for almost 80 per cent of Cuba's foreign trade, with Cuban–US trade representing 39 per cent of the total (England 34 per cent, Spain 27 per cent); by 1860 the US share had grown to 48 per cent, with Cuba soon exporting 65 per cent of its sugar to the United States and a mere 3 per cent to Spain. By 1877 more than 80 per cent of Cuba's total exports were going to the United States.[30]

It was conventional for the traders, entrepreneurs and interested politicians to consider such economic trends with scant regard for the welfare of the vast Cuban slave population upon which all the commercial enterprises depended. It was normal for the owners to discuss the merits of looking after slaves (and so deriving most benefit from their toil), as against working them to an early death (and then going to market for fresh labour); such debates were a purely economic affair. One observer notes that the rural field slaves were 'allowed but five hours of sleep';[31] another, Richard R. Madden, comments that the amount of sleep the slaves were allowed 'was about four hours. . . . Those who worked at night in the boiling-house worked also next day in the field. . . . The treatment of the slaves was inhuman, the sole object of the *administrador* being to get the utmost amount of labour in a given time out of the greatest number of slaves that could be worked day and night, without reference to their health or strength, age or sex'; and another observer, a coffee grower cited by Madden, suggested that slaves 'required . . . three or four hours sleep, not more; and if they had more time they would not employ it in sleep, they would go out wandering or stealing'.[32]

To such oppression were added the wretched living conditions and the remorseless floggings and beatings designed to intimidate through terror; and such factors as malnutrition and preventable disease also contributed to the high levels of mortality. On many of the Cuban plantations of the nineteenth century the slaves were not expected to live for more than seven years from the time of arrival; annual death rates were often as high as 10 to 12 per cent, emphasising the need for a constant supply of new labour. The essential priority for the traders and planters was to maintain the productivity of their business enterprise; politicians prepared to support unrestricted free trade in slaves were important allies in this cause, as were all the lawyers, law-enforcement officers, local officials, clerics and others prepared to sustain the bondage of the African slave.

On 26 August 1833, pressured by English abolitionists and perceived empire interests, the British parliament passed the Emancipation Act abolishing slavery in the British colonial territories. Some £20 million was offered as compensation to British planters in the West Indies; slaves were nominally converted into apprentices (a 6-year apprenticeship for field hands, a 4-year apprenticeship for others). This meant that, despite technological advances, the West Indian planters faced increased production costs while the Cuban producers could still rely on a relatively cheap labour force. Some purchasers of sugar transferred their business from Jamaica to Cuba, a development that encouraged the British to work for total abolition of the slavery system. Thus a British Commission in the 1840s reported that the ruin of the British West Indies 'would be complete and immediate' if the Cuban slave traffic was allowed to continue. Now Britain was opposing the international slave trade because it saw itself at a commercial disadvantage. But agreements with foreign governments, even if acting in good faith, were often insufficient; for example, the United States, via the instrument of the 1842 Webster–Ashburton Treaty, agreed to ban the use of the American flag in the slave traffic, but American ships continued in the lucrative trade of bringing slaves to Cuba. In fact the prosperity of Cuban slave society had been aided by both Haitian independence (1804) and the nominal British abolition of a large part of the slave traffic. Spain itself, despite treaties with Britain, continued to connive in the importation of slaves to Cuba. The Queen Mother in Madrid had a financial stake in a slave-smuggling company; and the Spanish Captains-General in Cuba and their officials continued to receive a financial 'cut' for every African slave they brought into the island.

By 1827 slaves constituted more than 40 per cent of the Cuban population, a proportion that had declined to 36 per cent in 1846 and 28 per cent in 1862, partly because of laws that allowed slaves to buy their freedom. Significantly the *working* population of Cuba was largely constituted by slaves for most of the nineteenth century prior to abolition in Cuba. This is shown for 1846, where the total Cuban population of 896,294 included a working population of 431,258 (Table 3.3). This meant that long after the Haitians had achieved their independence and abolished slavery, and in the teeth of the European abolitionist agitation, Cuba continued to depend upon a large slave population. This in turn depressed white attitudes to work; if poor whites were unable to find employment in the professions (law, the Church, medicine), cattle-raising or the army, they preferred to be idle – which in turn led to vagrancy problems. Thus Juan J. Reyes, in an 1851 study of vagrancy, commented that unemployed whites would continue stealing and living off the land as long as they looked 'not only with repugnance, but also with horror, on that kind of labour which habit

TABLE 3.3   Composition of Cuban working population (1846)

	Urban	Rural	Total
White	58,806	54,504	113,310
Free Negro	47,162	18,252	65,414
Slave	44,951	207,583	252,534
TOTAL	150,919	280,339	431,258

SOURCE: Charles Albert Page, 'The Development of Organised Labour in Cuba', unpublished Ph.D thesis, University of California, Latin American Studies, June 1952, p. 4 (cited by Philip S. Foner, *A History of Cuba and its Relations with the United States,* vol. I: *1492–1845* (New York: International Publishers, 1962) p. 187)

commonly associates with slaves'.[33] Hence the miserable lives of slaves had consequences far beyond those forced into servitude: the entire social order, solidified in hierarchical oppression, represented a distorted and baleful structure, even for those not nominally constrained by its demands.

The slaves on the plantations remained at the foot of the social hierarchy. Though important to the business economy, they remained miserably treated, often denied the necessities of life and routinely abused by vindictive overseers. Travellers remarked not only on the wretched lives of the field slaves but on such phenomena as the frequency of suicide among them: the negroes, like the Indians before them, often used their own hand to escape the dismal cruelties of their existence. It was reported that hanging, strangling, and even swallowing the tongue were common means of suicide: all methods that the owners tried to prevent by subjecting the slaves to further intimidations, shackles and constant surveillance. The travellers also noted the circumstances that led the slaves to despair: the miserable food and housing, the punishments for minor insubordinations, the beatings and floggings, the hideous use of chains, pronged collars and tin masks. Much of the history of Cuba is the tale of slavery and the social, religious and economic crimes committed in its name.

FROM REFORM TO ABOLITION

The dismal chronicle of slavery in Spanish America included periodic attempts – on behalf of the crown and other authorities – at humanitarian reform: the Spanish monarchs, impelled by elements of Christian conscience and secular agitation, made desultory efforts to mitigate the harsh consequences of free trade in human lives. Such efforts were largely inconsequential. It was one thing to issue an ordinance; quite another to guarantee its observance. With the Spanish crown wedded to the business interest, any reforms – even then enacted in the teeth of bitter commercial opposition – were necessarily tardy and piecemeal. The Church continued its pretence of viewing black souls as equal to white, and there were various means whereby the slaves, particularly in the towns, could enjoy a relatively liberal regime, or even win their freedom; but it was obvious that the injustices and brutalities of the slave system would not be comprehensively swept away without abolition. In the event the collapse of slavery came relatively late in Cuba; and even now, at the end of the twentieth century, its baleful legacy has not been wholly extirpated from the Cuban consciousness.

Many of the ordinances and enactments issuing from the Spanish crown served to consolidate, rather than mitigate, the condition of African servitude. Thus an order issued by the viceroy of New Spain in 1535 outlawed the possession of a weapon by any negro, free or slave; a 1552 statute specified that 'at the sound of a trumpet' (that is, at sundown), all slaves had to be off the streets; and other statutes banned slaves from riding horses or from travelling from one place to another without their master's permission.[34] In supposed protection of slave rights, decrees issued in 1544 and 1648 declared that slaves must not be worked on Sundays and holidays, but the masters were not punished if they failed to comply. Similarly a 1545 decree urging that slaves be well treated included no steps to be taken against derelict slave holders. Later *cedulas* instructed slave-owners to provide religious instruction, to sell slaves who had suffered mistreatment, and to accept constraints on their power over their charges; colonial officials were encouraged to punish brutal and sadistic owners. It has been suggested that such instructions did nothing to ameliorate the conditions of the slaves. Madrid was far away, and local officials were powerless against the business interest.[35]

In 1785 the Santo Domingo *audiencia* promulgated the *Código negro carolino* (the 'Black Code of Charles [III]'), enacted as a general law four years later. This *código*, enacted specifically for Española, had ripple effects in much of Spanish America. Its stipulations on the rights of slaves gave incidental clues as to how they were being treated in the colonies:

- the owners were to provide religious instruction for their slaves;
- slaves were to be given proper food and clothing;
- slaves were to be given a *conuco* (garden plot) as their private property;
- slaves were not to be interrogated under torture, and the mutilation of their physical features was prohibited;
- slave-owners failing to fulfil such obligations were to be punished.

At the same time the *código* made it plain that nothing must be done to erode the basic institution of slavery: slave mothers would not be allowed to keep their children; all negroes, both slave and free, '*will be humble and respectful to each white person as if each was his master or lord*'; and the establishment of '*the most comprehensive subordination*' on the part of the slave '*toward the white population*' was '*necessary*', for this was to be '*the fundamental basis of the internal policy of the colony*'. In such a context it is easy to conclude that stipulations protecting the rights of slaves were largely specious.

On 31 May 1789 Charles IV issued the *Código negro español*, incorporating elements from both the 1785 statute and the French *Code Noir* of 1685, and intended to define the master–slave regimen for all the Spanish-American colonies. The new *código* included the following provisions:

1. Slaves must be given education in religious matters; the master must provide for this.
2. Slaves must have 'Christian and decent clothing'.
3. Mutilations of the slaves' bodies are prohibited.
4. Slaves must receive adequate housing.
5. Whippings must henceforth be limited to twenty-five lashes for each penalty.
6. Owners must report the death or escape of the slaves within seventy-two hours after the event occurred.
7. Masters and overseers violating these stipulations could be fined up to 200 pesos for each offence.
8. The office of protector of slaves (*procurador síndico*) was to be created in each urban centre to investigate violations and argue the case for the slave in civil court. If a master mistreated a slave, the *procurador síndico* could demand that the slave be sold or, if permanently injured, supported for life by the master.

9. Officials of the *audiencias* and the Church were to conduct inspect-
    ions two or three times a year to hear slave complaints and see that
    the code was enforced.[36]

The 1789 *código* still allowed the splitting up of slave families, said
nothing about how slaves might win their freedom, and rested on the basic
assumption that the slave system would be protected. Slaves would still be
transported and sold, though, enforcement problems apart, the excesses of
their mistreatment would be prevented. But even such a *código*, one that
essentially reaffirmed the legitimacy of the slave system, could not be tolerated by officials and slave holders deriving benefits from African servitude. A torrent of protest swept across the Atlantic, urging Charles IV to
abandon the *código* or at least to make crucial amendments. The result
was that the 1789 provisions were only partially implemented, if at all. In
various colonies, including Cuba, the code was never issued in its entirety;
and even where particular provisions were issued it seems they had little
effect. The historian Jaime Jaramillo Uribe, declaring that the new legislation 'did not modify in any significant manner' the life of the negro
slave, examined a number of legal suits charging slave holders with mis-
treating their slaves. Typical is the case of Casimero Cortés, charged in
1796 with torturing his slaves and forcing them to kill their own children.
The Bogotá *audiencia* recommended legal action, but no steps were ever
taken to punish Cortés. The *código* was powerless to mitigate the abuses
inherent in the entrenched slave system protected by the business interest.

At the same time it was becoming increasingly clear that Spain would
not be able to resist international pressures for ever. In the eighteenth
century 'enlightened' European opinion had swung heavily against the
slave trade, and even Pope Benedict XIV felt obliged, in 1741, to follow
his predecessors (Pius II in 1462, Paul III in 1537, and Urban VIII in
1639) and make a routine but inconsequential condemnation of the evil.
The famed Catalan missionary St Peter Claver, who spent a large part of
his life ministering to slaves at Cartagena, was a typical representative of
the priesthood: at bèst the lot of the slaves should be ameliorated, while
nothing should be done to abolish the system in which they were
imprisoned. For the most part the pressure for abolition came from secular
agitators and pious individuals outside mainstream Christianity. Such
pressure mounted at the end of the eighteenth century, following the legal
ruling of Lord Mansfield in 1772, prohibiting slavery in the British Isles.
Events in the Caribbean were also helping to undermine the slave system.

After the French established the colony of Saint Domingue on the
western end of Española in 1697 there was a rapid increase in the slave

population. By the 1780s some half a million African slaves were working the sugar and coffee plantations in this French 'pearl of the Antilles'. The provisions of Louis XIV's *Code Noir* were largely ignored; and in August 1791 the oppressed slaves, forced to work in appalling conditions (and now out-numbering the white population by ten to one), rose up against their masters. Inspired by the example of the French Revolution, the negro Toussaint L'Ouverture succeeded in gaining control of the colony. In January 1794 the French National Convention decreed the abolition of slavery, but eight years later Napoleon I despatched an army under General Charles Leclerc to subdue the rebellious negroes. Toussaint was captured but the negro forces under Jean-Jacques Dessaline and Henri Christophe defeated the French. On 1 January 1804 the colony, renamed Haiti, was declared independent. In 1844 the Spanish-speaking group in the eastern part of the all-island Haiti broke away and established the Dominican Republic. The Haitian negroes had, by their own efforts, struck a great blow against the international slave system, and again the ripples ran out through the Caribbean and beyond.

On 1 May 1807 the British government finally abolished the trading in slaves throughout its dominions (though the practice of slavery in the British Empire was not abolished until 1833). Britain then moved to pressure the other European powers to follow suit, not least because some British commercial sectors now felt at a trading disadvantage. In 1815 Portugal agreed to prohibit the slave trade north of the equator; and Spain signed two treaties (1817 and 1835) with Britain to refrain from trading in slaves, but the treaties were widely ignored. Now many of the Spanish-American colonies were finding their way to independence, and so to a fresh sympathy with the anti-slavery movement. Slavery was abolished in Venezuela (1821), in Chile (1823), in Mexico (1854), in Peru (first in 1821 and finally, having been reinstated by General Gamarra, in 1854), and in Puerto Rico (1873). Slavery survived in Cuba until 1880, at which time around 150,000 slaves were working in the island.

The Portuguese and Spanish agreements with the British were important milestones, though widely flouted. The 1835 treaty, building on earlier enforcement provisions, stipulated the search and seizure of suspected slave ships, the punishment of guilty shipowners and crews, and the confiscation and disposition of captured vessels; further measures were introduced in Spain's 'Law of Abolition and Repression of the Slave Trade' (1845). Such measures failed to stop the flow of slaves into Cuba, but dramatically increased the prices that could be charged; illicit trade supplanted the open market, and in the circumstances of greater risk the costs rapidly inflated. From the early 1800s to the 1860s the price of a male slave rose from 300 (to 600) pesos to as much as 1500 pesos.[37] There was now an increased incentive for planters to look after the health of slaves already in their possession.

The Cuban planters were now becoming concerned that Spain was moving towards the abolition of the slave system. The continued acquisition of contraband slaves would itself be undermined if the very use of slaves was to be prohibited; indeed, with the slave trade banned in law, it followed that an increasing proportion of working slaves must have been illegally obtained and so were entitled to their freedom. Thus legislation not specifically framed to achieve the abolition of slavery was in fact contributing to that end. By the middle of the nineteenth century a majority of Cuban slaves had arrived after May 1820, the date after which slave acquisitions were defined as illegal under the terms of the 1817 agreement between Britain and Spain. In such dire circumstances the Cuban planters contemplated a radical move: annexation with the United States, where the institution of slavery seemed secure (it was not until the ratification of the Thirteenth Amendment to the Constitution on 18 December 1865, after the Civil War, that slavery was abolished in the United States). Such an option gained encouragement from the fact that a substantial body of American opinion, peaking in the 1840s, was focused on the desirability of a US acquisition of Cuba (see Chapter 5).

However, despite such planter anxieties and political calculations, the flow of slaves into Cuba continued unabated. Spain was showing a new resolve in ignoring British anti-slavery pressure, and with the slave trade ban only loosely enforced the planters continued to see profit in their traditional practices. By the middle of the century, with the United States itself increasingly involved in its own slavery debate, the annexationist movement had passed its peak, forcing the Cuban planters to acknowledge that a salvation from across the seas was an unlikely prospect. In fact, between 1856 and 1860 an estimated 90,000 contraband slaves were brought to Cuba, one of the greatest volumes for any 5-year period in the history of the island. But the political dilemmas remained. The planter class seemed trapped in an increasingly impossible position. The impulse towards independence from Spain seemed incompatible with the preservation of the slave system: the Spanish authorities had threatened that a decree of emancipation would follow any challenge to Spanish rule. Thus the crown was promising social and economic turmoil in Cuba unless the planters and the class they represented continued to acquiesce in their colonial status. In the event the turmoil was not avoided, the institution of slavery collapsed, and Cuba won its independence from Spain – only to fall under the more direct sway of the United States.

During the early part of the nineteenth century there was a growing recognition in Cuba that the institution of slavery would have to come to an end, but it still seemed unclear how such a seismic change to the Cuban social order could be accomplished. The Cuban dilemma had been thrown into focus by the treaties of 1817 and 1835; and by the efforts of such abolitionists as David Turnbull who, in a crucially important work, described the status of the Cuban slave as 'desperately wretched' and that of the *emancipados* ('freed' slaves) as 'worse than ordinary slavery'. It was Turnbull who, on 3 November 1840, arrived in Havana as British Consul and Superintendent of Liberated Africans (*Negros libertos*); this latter post went unrecognised by Spain but was deemed necessary by Turnbull to provide 'present comfort and future freedom of the Negroes captured by our cruisers, and brought with the slaver to Havana, preparatory to her condemnation'.[38]

Turnbull had brought with him Francis Ross, another British abolitionist, as Vice-Consul; and it was inevitable that the pair would be greeted with much hostility by the slave-owners in Cuba and their class. Thus the powerful Royal Board of Promotion of Agriculture and Commerce protested to the Captain General that Turnbull's ideas would only create distress in a country where the salves in the towns participated 'in the domestic comforts' and where there was a 'relaxed discipline among those destined to cultivate the land'. Moreover, any spreading of the insidious doctrine of freedom would 'create irretrievable evils, as was the case of the bloody Negro insurrection in nearby Santo Domingo'.[39] Turnbull, insisted the businessmen, must be expelled from the island. In the event Captain-General Tacón did not agree this; but, concerned about his own pickings from the slave trade, he decided not to recognise Turnbull as Consul. We may assume that this did not surprise Turnbull, and it certainly did not deter him. He moved at once to insist that the Cuban authorities enforce the 1817 and 1835 treaties, and to compile a census of the slaves brought to Cuba after 1820: such information would expose the numbers of slaves transported illegally, and the Cuban slave system would be struck a mortal blow.

The Spanish government, alarmed at the drift of events, resolved to block Turnbull's demands. The Council of State asserted that the relevant treaties were being enforced, and that the Cuban slave population was maintained not by traffic but by breeding. Moreover, if the slaves brought to Cuba after 1820 were to be released then the island would be overrun by ignorance, idleness and debauchery, as had happened in Haiti and Jamaica; and this would clearly 'ruin the production of sugar'. The Spanish Council of State expressed sadness that an 'old ally and friend' could suggest any such course. In the same spirit the Board of Promotion in Cuba warned that Turnbull's proposals would leave 'the territory abandoned to the disaster of general misery and the commotions of the Negro against the white'; and the *Ayuntamiento* (Municipal Council) in Havana declared that free negroes, left to themselves 'in the ignorance and stupidity in which we maintain them for our convenience, would retrograde naturally to a savage state . . .'. The whites would not allow the sacrifice of '400,000 whites for a measure that would make even unhappier 500,000 coloured people'.[40] But the Cuban whites were now on the defensive: in 1841 Tacon was replaced by Gerónimo Valdés, supposedly the only Captain-General of the time who failed to derive an income from the slave trade. Valdés, to the outrage of the slave holders, agreed to recognise Turnbull officially as the British Consul.

Soon there were fresh moves for Turnbull's dismissal. Valdés, though sharing the opinion that Turnbull had encouraged slave uprisings, resisted such pressure; and in London Palmerston supported Turnbull's efforts, declaring that the British government had 'the right to request from Spain the dismissal of all the employees in Cuba, starting from the governor himself, because they all protect notoriously and openly all the slave merchants in violation of the obligations of the treaty of the Spanish Crown'. Two further ships were despatched to reinforce the British Antilles squadron in support of Turnbull's efforts to secure the slave census; but on 12 February 1842 Lord Aberdeen, Palmerston's successor, assured Madrid that the British government would not press for a census and at the same time ordered Turnbull not to pursue the matter. Turnbull, incensed by this turn, now began to agitate for Cuban independence as the only realistic route to the emancipation of the slaves. The Spanish government, predictably outraged by such endeavours, demanded that Turnbull be removed from his post: Aberdeen bent before the Spanish pressure, and on 8 June 1842 Turnbull left the island, commenting in his letter of farewell to Captain-General Valdés that though his [Turnbull's] 'zeal for the cause of liberty' may sometimes have provoked resistance, he had 'not mistaken the path that inevitably must be followed in the not too distant future'. Valdés, in a suitable reposte, suggested that what Turnbull had called 'the spirit of the century' might 'carry its beneficial influx to change the situation of the unfortunate people of Ireland and those in the colony of India . . .'.[41] On 16 October 1842 Turnbull returned to Cuba in a ship manned by negroes, and was arrested when he arrived at Cardenas; his negro associates were shot down, and after a short period in prison Turnbull was put on board a British steamer and told that he was never again to visit Cuba 'under any pretext whatever'. Then the British government abolished Turnbull's cherished position of 'Superintendent of Liberated Africans'. The Cuban slave holders had achieved a victory of sorts, but it was short lived. The island could not escape Turnbull's 'spirit of the century', slave uprisings continued to shake the social fabric, and it would not be long before emancipation had been finally accomplished.

The question of emancipation had become inextricably linked to the issue of continued Spanish control of Cuba. Britain had indicated that it was prepared to support Spanish sovereignty, even against the wishes of the United States, but only if Spain agreed to suppress the slave traffic. Thus on 23 September 1853, under this pressure and fearing American intervention, the Spanish government charged the new Captain-General of Cuba, the Marqués Juan de la Pezuela, with the task of suppressing the slave trade. As governor of Puerto Rico (1849–1851), Pezuela had condemned the slave trade and supported the slaves in many ways. He arrived in Cuba on 3 December and three weeks later issued the first of several decrees to improve the lot of the negroes: anyone caught importing slaves would be fined and banished from Cuba for two years; and provincial governors prepared to tolerate clandestine landings would be removed from office (under this ruling various governors, including those of Trinidad and Sancti Spiritus, were subsequently removed). Pezuela faced predictable opposition from the slave-owning class, and there were practical difficulties: for example, Madrid was forced to issue new directives authorising Pezuela to search the formerly inviolable plantations in search of contraband slaves. Now he was able to issue a decree (3 May 1854) authorising his officials to enter the plantations, creating a slave register, stipulating penalties for failure to notify slave landings, and subjecting slave smugglers to a two-year exile. Pezuela denounced 'the impunity of a few capitalists' and the 'avaracious interests that place private gain above the national interest'.[42]

The slave owners responded by denouncing Pezuela and all his works. The 'barbarous' negroes would, in due course, submerge the white population; morality would collapse, and Christian civilisation would perish in the island; and such a 'diabolical' *Africanisation* would reduce Cuba to a 'howling wilderness'. Again the slave-owners urged an American annexation of Cuba as the only means of preserving the slave system. So in March 1854 the US Secretary of State William L. Marcy sent a secret agent, Charles W. Davis, to ascertain whether the dreaded Africanisation of Cuba was likely, whether the British were involved in the 'conspiracy', and what action should be taken by the United States. Marcy's worst fears were realised: there was evidence of such a conspiracy, and this could only bring bloody racial conflict and commercial loss to the Union. The

Cuban whites increasingly favoured the annexation option, while US racists demanded American military intervention to protect Christian values (that is, slavery and oppression) in the island. But in the event the Pierce administration, preferring the option of an American purchase of Cuba from Spain, discouraged initiatives that might antagonise the Spanish authorities. A countervailing expedition organised by General John A. Quitman, Governor of Mississippi, came to nothing: he lost his chance of dovetailing an invasion with an insurrection in Cuba, and Pierce and Marcy took steps to prevent any freelance annexationist initiative.

The mood in Cuba began to focus on the prospect of eventual emancipation. In 1865 the Reformist Party, created by some of the planters who had formerly advocated annexation, petitioned the Spanish parliament on four basic demands: reform of the tariff system, Cuban representation in the Spanish parliament, judicial equality with the *peninsulares* (to end discrimination against the creoles), and suppression of the slave trade. At that time, Leopoldo O'Donnell, a former Captain-General of Cuba (1843–48), ruled Spain, and was well disposed to Cuban demands: elections were authorised and the Junta de Información de Ultramar was established as a reform commission to propose changes to the colonial regime. At the polls the Reformist Party secured twelve of the sixteen seats on the commission, a result that represented a significant victory for the Cuban creoles.

Now the labour system was undergoing radical change as a prelude to emancipation. Over the two decades leading to the early 1870s some 125,000 Chinese had been imported to work under indenture in Cuba; while during the same period there was a growing influx of white immigrants. A growing division between field and factory enabled the various sectors to focus their efforts and improve productivity; white workers gradually extended their control of urban work at the expense of the free blacks; and new social classes began to emerge (including, for example, those labour groups with an interest in the creation of mutual aid societies organised along national and racial lines). Labour militancy began to grow.

The Junta de Información, despite the high Creole hopes that it carried, made little headway; the party newspaper *El Siglo* suspended publication, and the party itself was dissolved soon after. A wave of reaction resulted in increased military powers, higher taxes, and protectionist measures imposed from Madrid that did nothing to mitigate a plunging recession, in 1866 reaching its lowest point in fifteen years, while sugar production dropped from 620,000 tons in 1865 to 597,000 tons two years later. These and other economic developments combined to create a general air of political instability. Abolitionist pressure on the slave trade was mounting, though not all the reformers were in favour of negro emancipation. Francisco Montaos, the editor of *La Prensa*, urged the gradual freeing of the slaves, with scales of compensation to be paid to the slave holders; but some reformers opposed the scheme on the ground that it would antagonise such conservative bodies as the powerful *Partido Incondicional Español*. But slavery in Cuba did not have long to run. the last authenticated slave voyage to the island – the last recorded slaveship journey to the New World – took place in 1865. Thereafter the price of slaves rose to prohibitive levels: in 1872 a correspondent on the London *Times* reported slaves being sold at £400 ($1700) a head. Slaves still worked in the Cuban towns and on the land, but it was no longer possible to maintain their number through breeding or trade. On 7 October 1886, with only 26,000 slaves remaining in Cuba, the Spanish government abolished slavery on the island.

The struggle for emancipation had been long and bloody, with countless unknown victims lost to history on the painful road. The enslaved Africans, the first-generation slaves and their descendants, had staged protests, strikes, uprisings – laying the basis for two Wars of Independence in which the vital issue of negro emancipation was inextricably linked with the question of national sovereignty. We need to acknowledge that the centuries of violent struggle in Cuba, as elsewhere, are too rarely advertised in the West; that England's efforts to suppress the Spanish slave trade were as much a commercial as a humanitarian priority; and that it was the Cuban people themselves that were at the heart of the freedom struggle. The struggle continues: at the end of the twentieth century it is not yet over.

4 The Violent Struggle

The centuries-long struggle for emancipation and independence in Cuba was part of a much wider historical process: the ebbing and flowing war of national peoples throughout the world against imperial oppression. In particular, the Cuban struggle was a crucial element in regional resistance to European ambition. The early uprisings were against slavery, the most manifest symbol of imperial exploitation; later, the struggle matured to demand national independence, the essential condition for any people's dignity and freedom.

It is a remarkable fact that in each generation men and women are prepared, whatever their sacrifice, to challenge the arrogance of power. The long Cuban struggle, despite all the reforms ceded by pragmatic imperialism, has inevitably been one of blood and violence: history has shown that oppressors are signally deaf to other appeals.

THE SPECTRUM OF RESISTANCE

The slave-owners in the Caribbean and elsewhere ruled through terror. Any perceived offence – even an insolent look or word might qualify – could bring whipping, chaining, denial of food, mutilation, and other abuses. Nominal protections for the slaves, according to this or that code or decree, were empty gestures that perhaps served to ease consciences but which had no practical effect; for example, restricting whippings to a mere thirty-nine heavy lashes brought scant benefit if the punishment could be repeated a short time later. In some colonies the murderer of a slave might be fined (about £57 in the early eighteenth century), but many slaves died under brutal treatment and the masters typically faced no punishment. An extract from a law passed by the Assembly of Antigua in 1723 conveys the climate of the time:

> Several cruel persons, to gratify their own humours, against the laws of God and humanity, frequently kill, destroy or dismember their own and other persons' slaves, and have hitherto gone unpunished, because it is inconsistent with the constitution and government of this island, and would be too great a countenance and encouragement to slaves to resist white persons, to set slaves so far upon an equality with the free

inhabitants, as to try those that kill them for their lives; nor is it known or practised in any of the Caribbee islands, that any free person killing a slave is triable for his life.[1]

Here the law stipulated that in any event a man should never be fined more than £300 for the killing of a slave, and never more than £100 for a dismemberment. Minimum penalties (£100 and £20 respectively) were stipulated also, but convictions were rare. The slaves, forced to live in conditions of extreme privation, faced the daily prospect of unremitting toil, beatings, mutilations and early death – a dismal plight that provoked various responses.

Many of the negroes, like the enslaved Indians before them, sought escape through suicide. Since the slaves were economic properties, essential to the commercial system, suicide was a powerful means of striking at the heart of the imperial fabric. Thus the Royal African Company, sensitive to economic priority, issued instructions in 1725 to ensure that negroes remained fettered on the slave ships to prevent them jumping overboard. It is not hard to imagine why, political gesture apart, the hapless negroes would want to bring an end to their misery. In transit many of the slaves were sick; all were hungry and terrified. Dysentery, 'the bloody flux', was rife on the slave ships; and with the captives forced to defecate where they lay chained to each other for weeks or months on end the grim reality of such an existence can be imagined. One Olaudah Equiano, looking back thirty years, remembers: 'I was soon put down under the decks, and there I received such a salutation in my nostrils as I had never experienced in my life: so that with the loathsomeness of the stench and crying together, I became so sick and low that I was not able to eat . . .'[2] Such circumstances, added to the strictures of discipline and inadequate food, produced many fatalities during transportation; the option of suicide was removed from many.

Many negroes, having survived the dreadful sea passage, took their own lives on the plantations; or they sought relief in flight. In 1717 the Barbados authorities ruled that any slave who had been in the island for a year and then absented himself for thirty days or more should have one of his feet cut off; in 1776 the French West Indies ruled that slaves sheltering runaways should themselves be given thirty lashes and eight days in gaol; and for this offence St Vincent prescribed fifty lashes for the first violation, one hundred for the second, and one hundred and fifty for the third. Sometimes a colonial authority was willing to shelter runaway slaves from a foreign territory as a welcome injection of labour. Thus in 1768 the

Governor of Cuba refused to surrender slaves who had escaped from Jamaica. Similarly, in 1773 the Spanish authorities ruled that slaves who had escaped from British Tobago to Spanish Trinidad were to be kept for work in public enterprises.[3]

The slaves also had the option of revolt, an offence that invited the severest penalties. One estimate suggests that revolts occurred on as many as one in fifteen slave ships sailing from Nantes. In 1775 the ship *Diane* was captured by the 224 negroes on board; on the *Concorde* the slaves killed all but three of the white crew. On land, where the slaves could not be kept chained for ever, uprisings were common. In 1639 some sixty negroes fled in the French part of St Kitts, and built a mountain fort; only to be eventually overwhelmed by French troops, many of the rebels then being burned alive and their severed limbs displayed in various parts of the region. In 1649 eighteen slaves were executed in Barbados when one of their number revealed a planned uprising; and six years later a revolt led by two slaves from Angola occurred at Capesterre in Guadeloupe. This latter plot failed when slaves from another part of West Africa refused to support the insurrection; the two Angolan leaders were captured and quartered, their supporters variously flogged, hanged and torn to pieces alive. In 1679, as a violent prelude to the later emancipation, an uprising took place in Saint Domingue, only to be suppressed with the aid of mercenary buccaneers; and in 1690 three hundred slaves at Clarendon in Jamaica seized arms and provisions, killed an overseer, and fought against the local militia. More than one hundred of the Jamaican slaves were killed in the fighting, and when the rest were finally subdued a number of them were executed.

In 1729 an uprising took place in Cuba, followed by a revolt in 1731 when negro slaves in the Santiago copper mines combined to take up arms and proclaim their freedom. Here the negroes declared that the Cuban authorities were suppressing a royal decree that gave them their freedom. The Dean of the Cathedral of Santiago tried to convince the slaves of their error: 'Although I explained the facts to them several times, I could not make them see their error, for, in addition to their deficient intelligence, they were very anxious for their freedom, and thus they laughed at everything which was opposed to it.' At the same time the Dean was aware that it was the brutal treatment of the slaves that had occasioned the revolt. The uprising was suppressed, but the negro agitations and revolts showed no sign of abating. Slave revolts in the eighteenth century included ones in Jamaica (1733, 1746, 1760, 1765, 1769, 1776), St John (1733), Antigua (1736), Guadeloupe (1737), Martinique (1752), Nevis (1761), Surinam (1763, 1772) and Montserrat (1776).[4]

The widespread uprisings were stimulated not only by the inevitable brutalities and exploitation of the slave system but also by the sheer excesses of cruelty perpetrated by sadistic masters. The abuses in Saint Domingue, where slaves were first to taste a triumphant emancipation, had repercussions throughout the region, not least in Cuba. The French slave masters in Saint Domingue perpetrated some of the worst excesses. It was here that punishment by torture was a common daily practice: '. . . few slaves escaped floggings with all manner of whips, including nail-studded wooden paddles and brine-soaked bull's penises. They were also burned with boiling cane, chained, branded with hot irons, buried alive, manacled and smeared with molasses so ants would devour them, mutilated and crippled by amputation of arms, legs, and buttocks, raped, starved, and humiliated.'[5] Forced to toil naked in the sun, given tiny amounts of miserable food, the wretched slaves were granted no respite. In Haiti alone the French Christians killed one million Africans; thousands committed suicide to free their spirits for a joyous return to their distant African homes.

The 1791 insurrection in French Saint Domingue traumatised the slave-owning classes in the Caribbean and beyond. Here, it seemed, was the shape of the future: abused and tortured peoples combining in revolt to throw off the shackles of European imperialism. A decade of bloody turmoil followed the 1791 rebellion. In June 1793 the French fleet evacuated the entire French population, whereupon troops from the Spanish sector and from British Jamaica, fearing the consequences of an unprecedented negro rule in the Caribbean, occupied the island. The negro general Toussaint drove out the Spanish in 1794, and a few years later the British were forced to withdraw. On 29 November 1803 the negro former slaves forced the surrender of the eight thousand survivors of the 43,000 men sent by Napoleon to restore slavery under clear French domination. In 1805 the victorious negroes proclaimed their Republic of Haiti, the first of its kind in the world. Such events had a profound effect upon the people of Cuba.

One of the first consequences of the Haitian insurrection was a boost for the Cuban economy. Prior to 1791 Saint Domingue had been a leading supplier of coffee, cotton, tobacco, indigo, and sugar; by the second half of the eighteenth century the French colony was rapidly becoming the world's leading producer of sugar. The rebellion destroyed the major sugar and coffee plantations, leaving the field open for a massive expansion of the Cuban sugar industry – from 14,000 tons in 1790 to around 34,000 tons in 1805.[6] In the same way a massive boost was given to the Cuban coffee industry. From 1795 to 1805 Haitian planters and their slaves, amounting to an influx of around 30,000, flooded into Cuba to escape the insurrection in their own country. In the eastern end of the island they developed coffee production to the point that it became a vital element of the Cuban economy. At the same time the fleeing Haitian whites regaled the slave-owning Cubans with fearsome tales of what had transpired in Saint Domingue. Could the same happen in Cuba?

Slave revolts had already broken out in 1792 and 1793 on sugar plantations around Havana, Puerto Príncipe and Trinidad; and in 1795 the free negro Nicolas Morales began an insurrection that quickly spread through eastern Cuba. This uprising, surprisingly supported by both negroes and whites, was suppressed by Spanish army contingents led by Captain-General Las Casas. In 1796 an uprising on the Boca Niguia plantation was crushed, the leaders were executed, and the Spanish king was told: 'The punishment imposed on these uprising negroes and the warning examples of these evil-doers will assure repose and tranquillity to the public.' The Cuban slave holders were not convinced: there had been revolts before and they were not yet at an end. The repression intensified, and as the rate of slave mortality increased in the worsening conditions the planters relied on the profits from a booming economy to buy replacement negroes.

The crushing of the Cuban insurrections following the collapse of slavery in Saint Domingue was a temporary expedient. Slavery in the Caribbean and elsewhere was a doomed institution, but the protracted Cuban struggle would have to run on for some decades. Despite the shaking of the slave system occasioned by the Saint Domingue rebellion, the Cuban slave holders managed to preserve the island in a condition of relative isolation from dramatic events in Mexico, Central America, South America, and elsewhere in the Caribbean. Even after the establishment of the negro Republic of Haiti, Cuba remained seemingly secure as Spain's chief base in the region. A powerful military garrison facilitated military expeditions to the mainland, and guaranteed that any Cuban revolts would be quickly suppressed. Moreover, the wealthy creoles, benefiting from the growth of the sugar industry, were fearful that agitation to overthrow the *peninsular* Spaniards might hasten a negro insurrection: for the influential creole class, Cuba was better a secure Spanish colony than an unstable black republic. But such a posture could not be long preserved. The nineteenth century was to see repeated revolts, mounting instability, and nationwide wars of independence.

THE CUBAN UPRISINGS

From the beginning of negro slavery in Cuba in the early sixteenth century there were frequent uprisings, all suppressed with merciless brutality. The first revolt known to chroniclers, in 1533 at the Jacabo mines, involved only four slaves. The Governor-General, determined that the rebels be given exemplary treatment, sent a large military contingent from Bayamo to restore order. The four negroes refused to surrender, but the outcome was inevitable: they fought to the death, whereupon their severed heads were conveyed back to Bayamo to hearten the anxious colonisers. But the revolt had alarmed the whites. If the privations, chainings and whippings had failed to intimidate a handful of blacks then perhaps there would be further uprisings in the future. The slave-owners quickly urged the Spanish crown to prevent negroes carrying knives longer than 'a palm's length' or moving in parties from one place to another.[7]

In 1538, while Havana was being attacked by French pirates, groups of negro slaves rose up and destroyed much of the city. Again the Spanish authorities quickly put down the uprising, killing many blacks and forcing others to flee. Sporadic acts of defiance continued in the hills; not least, acts of group suicide to deprive the slave masters of an economic resource and in the traditional belief that the blacks would find themselves resurrected in their African villages. To discourage this latter practice the slave masters dismembered and decapitated the corpses to convince the living that the dead Africans would be resurrected in a mutilated state.

A black revolt occurred in 1727 at the Quiebra-Hacha sugar mill to the west of Havana. Here large troop contingents were despatched to suppress some three hundred rebels. Four years later there was a black uprising at the copper mines of Santiago del Prado. Again the Spanish authorities responded with overwhelming military force, the predictable response that did little to discourage further revolts. In due course the Spanish crown decided that some amelioration of the slaves' miserable lot might stabilise the situation. Thus a new slave code, decreed by Charles III on 31 May 1789, stipulated improved conditions for the enslaved blacks and required the masters to provide their captives with religious instruction. The code was submitted to but not complied with (*se obedece pero no se cumple*); the rules bearing on the slaves were rigidly enforced whereas the obligations imposed on the masters were ignored. Bribes were sufficient to induce officials to ignore the relevance of the code to the slaves' condition. In some estimates the plight of the blacks worsened; with more revolts and more escapes to the hills, the masters responded by housing the slaves in virtual prisons. On some plantations there were block houses and watchtowers, with hired troops on constant alert: a regime of containment and repression that must have resembled the concentration camps of the twentieth century. Despite all such measures, the revolts continued.

Many slaves, determined to maintain their religious commitment to sorcery, sought vengeance on their masters through the use of charms, spells and other magical means.[8] One runaway slave described a sacred pot containing earth that, while contained in the vessel, was supposed to keep a master ill.[9] Yet more resorted to flight or violent rebellion. By the end of the eighteenth century there were vast numbers of black slaves in Cuba, a repressed and bitter population, 'intractable, undisciplined, resentful, and with a memory of their lost freedom'.[10] Some 385,000 slaves arrived between 1790 and 1820; 272,000 between 1820 and 1853; and another 175,000 between 1853 and 1864. Most of the imported slaves were males; and many were from the same cultural groups, the African Carabalis and Lucumies (Yorubans), with strong military traditions.[11] The scene was set for frequent attempts at insurrection.

The very size of the slave population in Cuba was now increasing the scale of the slave conspiracies and rebellions. Spontaneous disturbances could involve one or more sugar plantations; and in addition there were many planned insurrections. Often free negroes conspired with captive slaves to organise large-scale uprisings: between 1795 and 1843 there were nine major revolts at the provincial level, as well as many smaller incidents.[12] A rebellion in Camagüey in 1805 was crushed with severe repression, as were the further revolts on the sugar plantations in Puerto Príncipe, Holguín, Bayamo and Trinidad in 1812. These events followed a large uprising organised the year before by José Antonio Aponte, a free black carpenter, in Havana, and involving whites, free negroes and slaves in Oriente and Puerto Príncipe. Again the rebellion was crushed, but only after overseers, whites and slaves had been killed and sugar mills and coffee estates destroyed.

An 1825 revolt in Matanzas Province was crushed, but fifteen whites and forty-three blacks were killed; this insurrection resulted in the destruction of some twenty-four plantations. In 1843 Matanzas saw more uprisings, suppressed with much loss of life and destruction of property. One of these revolts involved three hundred slaves from more than fifteen sugar plantations; here the local squadron of Spanish lancers was used to defeat and disperse the insurgents. Yet another rebellion in the same year began with two hundred slaves on the *Triunvirato* plantation in Matanzas and quickly spread to neighbouring estates. Hundreds of slaves were killed during these insurrections, with the survivors severely punished and fugitives hunted down by trained bloodhounds. The Spanish authorities concluded that the *Triunvirato* was a widespread conspiracy involving thousands of whites, free blacks and slaves; and set about making more than four thousand arrests of suspected plotters.

There followed a period of severe repression: whippings, beatings, mutilations, and executions. Some estimates suggest that as many as a thousand slaves and free negroes were garroted, or hung, drawn and quartered – often after prolonged torture and whippings. Dr J. G. F. Wurdemann, in Cuba during that period, wrote that 'slaughter-houses' were established in Matanzas and Cardenas, 'where the accused were subjected to the lash to extort confessions. . . . A thousand lashes were in many cases inflicted on a single negro; a great number died under this continued torture, and still more from spasms, and gangrene of the wounds.'[13] The conspiracy became known as '*La Escalera*', after the ladders to which the prisoners were tied for flogging.

The agitations and attempts at insurrection continued through the nineteenth century, though not always with the aim of abolishing slavery. Thus in 1809 an independence conspiracy headed by Ramón de la Luz, a wealthy Mason in Havana, and Joaquín Infante, a Bayamo lawyer, tried to gain creole support by assuring the planters that the institution of slavery would be protected. An independent Republic of Cuba would be run by the landowner class: the suffrage would be limited to property holders, Roman Catholicism would be the official state religion, and all army officers would be *personas pudientes* (wealthy people). Despite its declared support for slavery, the conspiracy gained the support of some slaves and free negroes, who saw the movement as contributing to their own struggle against the Spanish authorities. The Aponte rebellion, already mentioned, was an entirely different affair. Here too there was pressure for independence, though an ending of slavery was the principal objective.

José Antonio Aponte, a religious man, saw himself as a Cuban Moses destined to lead his people out of bondage. He followed the *Cortes* debates on the slave trade, and also established contact with Jean François, a negro general in Haiti. Aponte now believed that the time was ripe for a successful rebellion: Spanish forces had been transferred to the mainland to suppress revolts in various regions, and he reasoned that with Haitian help he would be able to stage a successful insurrection and then repel any returning Spanish contingents. In 1811 Aponte established the Central Revolutionary Junta in Havana, with subordinate juntas set up in other towns and cities. But before any insurrection could be launched, Captain-General Someruelos overheard two negroes in Havana discussing the forthcoming rebellion. The negroes were imprisoned and then tortured by means of the *cepo*, a machine that tightens around the neck and limbs, whereupon they named Aponte as the head of the planned revolt. In February 1812 Aponte and eight of his companions, three slaves and five free negroes, were seized and later sentenced to execution by hanging. The Someruelos proclamation (7 April) of sentence includes the words: '. . . the heads of Aponte, Lisundia, Chacón, and Barbrado will be hung in the most public and convenient places as a warning to those of their kind. With this is avenged, for now, the offended public and scandal which these culprits have brought to this tranquil people.' The sentence was duly carried out on 9 April 1812, and the heads of the victims were displayed in the specified manner: Aponte's head was locked in an iron cage in front of his home on the San Luis Gonzaga highway, while one of his hands was nailed on another street. Many other South American heroes met the same fate at the hands of the Spanish Christians, their bodies dismembered and displayed to advertise the folly of opposition to the Catholic crown.

One of the most celebrated revolutionary organisations was *Los Soles y Rayos de Bolivar* (the Suns and Rays of Bolivar), established in 1821. The founders included José Fernández Madrid, a Columbian agitator, Sévère Courtois, a Haitian revolutionary, and José Francisco Lemus, a native of Havana who headed the group. Lemus had risen to the rank of Colonel in the Columbian army, but returned to Cuba in 1820 to work for its independence. By October 1822 a nationwide network of cells, some involving leading members of the community, had been established throughout Cuba. Lemus arranged for selected members of the group to infiltrate the Spanish-led militia, thereby to acquire weapons, with the aim of joining the rebellion at the right moment; and he prepared three proclamations, for release one after the other once the uprising had begun, to explain the reasons for the insurrection.

The first proclamation, a significant document declaring the creation of the Republic of Cubanacan, is addressed to 'Peoples of the World'. It includes the words:

> As the fortunate sons of the new Republics of Paraguay, Chile, Lima, Buenos Aires, Columbia and Mexico, full of honour, valour and justice, have shaken off the ancient and heavy yoke of servile dependence, so the valiant islanders of fertile Cubanacan, for the same causes, and to end the same scandalous abuse and suffering under Spanish rule will make our country take the position that it merits among the nations of the world, augmenting the number of American Republics.[14]

At last the ranks and hierarchies 'that foster arrogance and ignorance and are opposite to the virtuous character of free men' would be abolished, and the slave system would be brought to an end: 'Let us treat gently those unfortunate slaves, alleviating their horrifying destiny while the representatives of our country propose the means of happy redemption, without prejudice against individual interest. They are the children of our own God.' In this fine endeavour the Minister of the Altar merited 'the highest consideration', but should not forget 'that the law of the good Jesus is purely Republican'. Thus in contrast to many of the other independence programmes, the Lemus plan involved the abolition of slavery: the enslaved blacks were not 'ignorant and debased', as the slave-owners maintained, but would be invited to join in the struggle for independence and liberty.

In the second and third proclamations, Lemus addressed the report that England had purchased Cuba from Spain; advised the Spanish monarch that no attempt to crush the Cuban independence movement would succeed ('*We are ready to live free and independent of all nations and neither the absolute Government nor the Constitutional Government of Spain, can ever hope again to make us the sad objects of their negotiations*'); and defined the aims of the new Republic. Addressing his fellow Cubanacanos, Lemus declared that the whole world knew that the political transformation of the island was now inevitable, and that such a transformation 'is the only means of re-establishing among its sons moral customs, of bettering the public administration, by appointing men of capacity and virtue, and of guaranteeing a good income, well distributed, without the burdens which tyrannically oppress the day labourer, the farm hand and the seaman. . . . Neither the army which follows me, nor I, have been impelled by any kind of selfish ambition, nor any interest other than our common salvation and happiness.'

Now, while Lemus contemplated an idealistic future and prepared the insurrection, the Spanish authorities moved to crush the conspiracy. Already, spies of Captain-General Vives had penetrated the secret revolutionary organisation, and he was able to report to Madrid that agents from abroad 'have been able to seduce with all their arts and mysteries, only many youths, men of the field, and a few Negroes on whom they count to raise the cry of independence (*el grito de independencia*)'. The important planters, reported Vives, had remained loyal, steadfastly unaffected by 'the fallacious doctrines and democratic principles unveiled in the discussions of the different Republics which are constituted on the Continent' and which had 'hallucinated many heedless men and stimulated the ambitions of young Cubans'.[15]

Soon Captain-General Vives was in a position to strike. Lemus and two dozen other leaders of the organisation were seized, while many of the other conspirators fled the country. Some slaves attempted uprisings in sugar mills in various provinces, but such desultory revolts were soon crushed. Now most of the leaders of *Soles y Rayos* were captured or in exile, and the conspiracy collapsed. Yet again an attempt to generate a nationwide rebellion against slavery and for national independence had been suppressed. Vives, fearful of fresh revolts, tightened his grip on the island: the press came under the total control of the Spanish authorities, any literature deemed subversive was forbidden, and hundreds of Cubans fled abroad. One such, José María Heredia, through his revolutionary poems, remained a potent symbol of the struggle for Cuban independence; another, Father Felix Varela, was condemned to death by Spain but sought refuge in the United States, where in 1824 he began publishing the newspaper *El Habanero* favouring the independence cause and brought to Cuba for secret distribution throughout the island.

The Spanish repression did not prevent all further attempts at insurrection, though it would still be decades before a measure of Cuban independence would be won. In 1824 a conspiracy led by Ensign Casper A. Rodríguez was put down; and Vives was encouraged to demand extra powers. In 1825, with the courts superseded by the Permanent Executive Military Commission, his demands were met. Now the military was authorised to survey and control every aspect of Cuban life: commerce, travel, law and order, social affairs, and even many personal activities. The press was censored, public meetings banned, mention of *independence* ('the inciting word') prohibited, and any discussion of slavery or political reform banned. On 8 April 1826 a special decree outlawed the importation of 'all books which oppose the Catholic religion, the royalty, rights and prerogatives of the sovereign, or which, in any other manner, defend the rebellion of vassals or nations'. In such a fashion the traditional union between Catholic authority and the institution of slavery was unambiguously reaffirmed.

Varela, fearing that his efforts might intensify the repression, stopped publishing *El Habanero* in 1826; now also Lemus and most of the other revolutionary leaders were out of the picture. Some 40,000 Spanish troops were now roaming the island, terrorising the local population and punishing anyone suspected of dissidence. But even now it proved impossible to extirpate all impulses to rebellion. Even the Masonic lodges, prohibited by royal decree in 1824, continued to agitate for independence; and there could always be found recalcitrant nonconformists, keen to struggle for national liberation. In April 1826 two young men were condemned to death and hung at Puerto Príncipe for (according to the *Niles' Weekly Register*, 29 April) 'attempting to revolutionise the country'. The two men, Manuel Andrés Sanchez and Francisco de Aguero y Velazco, had planned to organise a revolt in Cuba which would be supported by an invasion from Columbia. Again Spanish spies run by Vives uncovered the plot and led to further executions. Aguero and Sánchez were executed on 16 March 1826; and so in some judgements became the first martyrs, one white and the other black, of Cuban independence.

In 1827 the *Gran Legión del Águila Negra* (the Grand Legion of the Black Eagle), formed by Cuban exiles in Mexico and Columbia, began plotting the independence of Cuba. The secret society established branches throughout the island, but in 1830 the movement was uncovered and crushed. Suspected conspirators were seized and, unusually, sentenced to long prison terms rather than execution. But again the impulse to insurrection was not wholly suppressed. On 5 November 1843 a female black slave, Carlota, led a black rebellion in which she died (on 5 November 1975 Cuba named its campaign in Angola 'Operation Carlota' in honour of this woman).

Now the persistent agitations, conspiracies and revolts were inexorably shifting the Cuban political climate. Each new suppression organised by the Spanish authorities brought more people into the movements for emancipation and independence. The horrors of *La Escalera* had delayed further attempts at widespread insurrection, but stimulated debate on the slavery issue. Thus Ramón de la Sagra, a representative of the peninsular Cubans, noted in 1845 a new responsiveness to his agitation against the slave trade. At the same time the slave holders desperately urged annexationism with the United States (see Chapter 5) as the strategy most likely to preserve the Cuban slave system. Then the American Civil War (1861–65), fought in part over the slavery issue, undermined all such ambitions. The outcome of the war profoundly affected Cuba; the scene was set for a further eruption of violence and political turmoil.

THE TEN YEARS' WAR

On 12 February 1867 the Spanish government imposed new taxation on Cuba, a 6 per cent levy on net property incomes, with the colonial government authorised to raise such taxes to 12 per cent to cover administrative costs – and this at a time of severe economic depression in the island. Some taxes were abolished but not the burdensome customs duties. The agitations of the reformers were suppressed, and it became obvious that no ameliorative measures would be taken by the Spanish crown; Lemus, Pastor and other reformers, then in Madrid, tried to influence the government, but to no avail. Protest grew throughout Cuba, with many of the Creoles now preparing for armed rebellion. In Oriente Province the wealthy Creoles established conspiratorial centres via the Masonic lodges of Bayamo, Manzanillo, Holguín, Las Tunas, and Santiago de Cuba; while the lodges of Havana and Camagüey offered support to the growing movement for national independence. The outbreak of the Ten Years' War, Cuba's first War of Independence, was imminent. Various groups were now organising to stage an armed revolt. To channel these activities, Francisco Vicente Aguilera arranged a meeting on 4 August 1868 at a farm in the district of Las Tunas. Carlos Manuel de Céspedes, the oldest delegate (born on 18 April 1819 at Bayamo), presided over the gathering. Educated at the University of Barcelona, he had become involved in revolutionary activity in Madrid, after which he was banished to France; on his return to Spain he was imprisoned. Then Céspedes sailed to Cuba where, with Aguilera, Pedro (*Perucho*) Figueredo and others, he began working in Oriente for independence. At the gathering organised by Aguilera, Céspedes declared: 'Gentlemen, the hour is solemn and decisive. The power of Spain is decrepit and worm-eaten; if it still appears great and strong to us, it is because for more than three centuries we have contemplated it from our knees.'[16] The delegates remained undecided: over various matters, but not least on the question of slavery. They all acknowledged that the negroes would demand emancipation but not all the delegates were prepared for such a decisive step. A new meeting was scheduled, at which it was hoped all outstanding matters would be resolved.

Events in Spain were now moving to create political instability and to encourage the agitators for reform. On 18 September 1868 *La Revolución Gloriosa* (the 'Glorious Revolution'), led by liberals and various military factions, forced the collapse of the Spanish monarchy. The Queen fled to France, whereupon the Provisional Government announced various reforms and a promise that the Revolution was not carried out only for 'the inhabitants of the Peninsula, but also for our loyal brothers overseas'. While many Cuban reformers hoped that the new political climate would reduce the pressure for independence, the revolutionaries saw their new opportunity. On 10 October 1868 Céspedes, accompanied by thirty-seven Oriente planters, proclaimed, via the historic *Grito de Yara*, the independence of Cuba. At the same time he freed the thirty slaves on his plantation (*La Demajagua*) and enrolled them in his small army, now totally all of 147 men. Then he issued a proclamation that included the words: 'We only want to be free and equal, as the Creator intended all mankind to be . . . we believe that all men were created equal.' But slavery was not to be abolished at a stroke: his support for 'the gradual, indemnified emancipation of slaves' was enough to rally men to his cause. By the end of October Céspedes, now commanding an army of 12,000 men, had captured Bayamo and Holguín, and was sweeping through Oriente. Now Figueredo proclaimed a martial song, the 'Freedom Anthem', that was later to become the National Hymn of the Republic of Cuba:

Al combate corred bayameses!
Que la patria os contempla orgullosa!
No temais una muerte gloriosa
Que morir por la patria es vivir!

To the battle, Bayameses!
Let the fatherland proudly observe you!
Do not fear a glorious death,
To die for the fatherland is to live!

The ragged patriot army grew by leaps and bounds as men, white and negro (free and slave) rushed to join Céspedes. The cattle farmer Ignacio Agramonte, aided by a Cuban veteran of the US–Mexican war, General Manuel de Quesada, joined the rebellion in Puerto Príncipe. Dominican exiles, including Máximo Gómez, Luis Marcano and Modesto Díaz, provided instruction to the rebel army in military tactics and strategy. On 9 February 1869 General Féderico Cavada, a Colonel in the US Volunteer Service in the Civil War, led a revolt in the Las Villas district. And with every fresh victory, more and more men expressed their allegiance to the Céspedes banner.

Now the Reformers were rallying to the cause: a fruit of Céspedes' cautious approach to slavery. A key element in the war was the conflict between the *creoles* and the *peninsulares*, with negro emancipation not always a primary concern. On 24 October 1868 some forty leading businessmen of west Cuba called upon Captain-General Francisco Lersundi to urge him to meet with the rebels. He refused and the meeting broke up in disarray, whereupon a number of the Reformers – José Manuel Mestre, Morales Lemus, Miguel Aldama, and others – joined the rebellion (some went to New York to raise money and support). Lersundi, at that stage ill-equipped to launch effective military action against the insurgents, was beginning to alarm Madrid. Perhaps, reasoned the Spanish authorities, a more conciliatory approach to the Reformers might have defused the crisis. The successive Madrid governments of Generals Serrano and Prim were struggling to achieve political stability in Spain: the mounting turmoil in Cuba was not their first priority.

It soon became clear that Spain was facing a grave threat to its colonial authority, whereupon Lersundi moved to crush the growing insurrection.

He launched a military force under the Count of Valmaseda to attack the self-proclaimed independence government in Bayamo; and at the same time he activated the *Voluntarios* (the Volunteer Corps) and declared a state of martial law. All rebels would be brought before Military Commissions and regarded as traitors. The Volunteers, composed mainly of adventurers who had left Spain to find their fortune, soon embarked upon a campaign of repression and mass murder. In this fashion, from 40,000 to 73,000 Volunteers, drafted to supplement the 7000 regular troops on the island, managed to contain the rebellion until reinforcements arrived. The Volunteers, with Lersundi as their hero, continued a policy of extermination until their excesses began to alarm the Madrid authorities. Far from crushing the insurrection, Lersundi's extremist tactics were fomenting rebellion throughout the island. Finally Lersundi was removed, and a liberal governor, General Don Domingo Dulce, sent to Cuba to treat with the rebels.

On 4 January 1869 Dulce arrived in Cuba, authorised 'to modify taxation and to govern by liberal standards'; and bearing with him a moderate reform programme for freedom of the press, freedom of assembly, and representation for Cuba in the Spanish *Cortes*. He also proposed an amnesty for all rebels who surrendered within forty days, and despatched peace envoys to meet Céspedes. But Dulce had reckoned without the intensity of feeling among the *peninsulares*. These groups, now led by Julián de Zulueta, wanted no dealings with insurrectionists: Céspedes, who had even freed his own slaves, was not to be trusted. Moreover, the reactionary groups were heartened by the outcome of the battle of Bayamo, the first major battle of the war and one in which a force of 4000 rebels under Donato Marmol had been comprehensively defeated. Generals Valmaseda and Weyler had inflicted 2000 casualties on the rebel force, and the rest had fled, allowing the Spanish troops to re-enter Bayamo. It now seemed likely that the rebels could be crushed, and that placatory talks would be unnecessary.

The Volunteers were becoming increasingly influential in Spanish colonial policy; by the beginning of January 1869 they numbered more than 20,000 infantry and 13,000 cavalry, and by sheer weight of numbers forced Dulce to accede to their wishes. On occasions they denounced Dulce for his supposed sympathy with the rebel cause, and in general pursued their own inclinations irrespective of the wishes of Madrid. They sacked Miguel Aldama's mansion, fired into a theatre to disperse rebels, and blocked the gates of Havana to block the movement of rebel sympathisers. Within a month Dulce himself, intimidated by the Volunteers' show of strength, suspended the political guarantees offered to the

Reformers and acquiesced in a new phase of repression. Suspects were seized, imprisoned and beaten; the press was again censured; and the Volunteers were allowed to behave at whim. After the massacre of men, women and children in the theatre, the Volunteers roamed the streets throughout the night, attacking the homes of suspected rebel sympathisers. The pro-Spanish press applauded such activities, blaming the carnage and destruction on the rebel factions. The Volunteer publication *La Voz de Cuba* continued to denounce Dulce as betraying the Spanish cause.

Dulce, now with little option, issued a proclamation urging the rebels to surrender their arms by 20 February 1869; and at the same time began the wholesale deportation of suspected persons. A youth of eighteen, rash enough to shout '*Viva Cuba libre!*' to a crown of departing exiles, was sentenced before a military tribunal and shot. Dulce also endorsed a proclamation (4 April) issued by Valmaseda decreeing that all males over fifteen caught absent from their plantations in rebel areas would be shot, that houses in such areas not occupied by Spanish forces or displaying a white flag would be burned, and that all women and children not already living in approved accommodation would be consigned to special fortified camps. The Volunteers were still not satisfied with Dulce's performance. They continued to agitate for his resignation, finally breaking into his palace to demand his departure; on 5 June 1869 General Dulce left the island.

General Caballero de Rodas was soon named as the new Captain-General to replace Dulce, but several weeks elapsed before he arrived: in the interval the Volunteers moved to consolidate their position still further, founding the *Casino Español* (the Spanish Club) as a centre where the Volunteer leaders could meet with the rich sugar planters to determine colonial policy. The new Captain-General, when he arrived on the island, quickly showed his sympathies with the Volunteer forces, headed by two rich sugar planters, Manuel Calvo and Julián de Zulueta. Caballero had already crushed rebellion in southern Spain, on the principle of 'if we don't devour them, they will devour us'; and there was little doubt that soon he would be prepared to move against the Cuban insurgents. Any tentative steps towards political reform were now abandoned; the policy of the blood-stained Volunteers was now the policy of Madrid. It was deemed essential to keep the Castilian flag flying over Cuba, the 'Pearl of the Antilles'. No Madrid government would be prepared to oppose the Spanish Party in Cuba and their Volunteer allies: the way was open for a war of extermination.

By late 1869 the Spanish forces on the island numbered about 40,000 trained soldiers, augmented by substantial Volunteer contingents and mercenary *guerrilleros* in the rural areas. Spain despatched her best generals and officers to command these forces, sending men and supplies on fourteen warships, and supplying the Spanish army with Krupp artillery of the latest design. Already a fleet of fifty vessels with 400 guns was based on Cuba, an effective means of minimising the supply of arms and men reaching the Cuban rebels from abroad.

The insurgents, forced into retreat, adopted the only strategy open to native bands facing a powerful conventional army: guerrilla warfare. The new circumstances threw up fresh leaders to supplement the command of such men as Céspedes and Agramonte; for example, the ex-slave Guillermon (described by the Irish writer J. J. O'Kelly[17]), a gigantic guerrilla leader with a harem in the Sierra Maestra; and the Dominican Máximo Gómez, with his 'character of iron' and his mastery of guerrilla war. Now only a quarter of the rebels had rifles; the rest relied upon machetes, metal daggers, or wooden (indigo) blades sometimes dipped in poison. In many parts of the island the rebel Cubans were faced with a substantial Spanish military build-up, and the plight of the insurgents became increasingly desperate. A Volunteer leader, Ramón de la Tottiente, commented: 'Lately we are receiving plenty of troops from home; all of us expect for an early end of the robbers who are all badly tiring us further than men's patience can endure.' The rebels were forced to abandon various centres of insurrection, the civilian populations – in such areas as Santiago, Manzanillo, Bayamo and Puerto Príncipe – then condemned to exist in virtual concentration camps. The Spanish troops and the Volunteer factions often executed prisoners taken in battle, and there were many reprisals against civilians and fugitives deemed to have helped the guerrillas. Torture and executions of suspects were common, with women and children still prepared to act as spies and to aid the independence struggle in other ways. Even in these conditions, sugar production continued to expand; and, according to the British Consul, the price of slaves – at £500 to £650 – 'kept up wonderfully'.[18]

There were many instances of Spanish brutality and harsh punishment. One case was that of the schoolboy José Martí, sentenced to six months' hard labour for writing a letter accusing a fellow student of treachery for marching in a Spanish parade. Martí spent the full sentence stone-cutting in the government quarries, an ordeal that left him physically disabled, half blind and suffering a hernia caused by a blow from a chain. In 1871 the Spanish authorities expelled the teenager Martí from Cuba to prevent his further participation in revolutionary activity. The measure did not succeed.

It now seemed clear that the Spanish troops and their Volunteer allies, despite vastly superior military resources, were unable to defeat the guerrillas – and so they resorted to the types of behaviour that history has shown are typical of conventional armies in these circumstances. Harsh reprisals were taken against civilian populations: helpless men, women and children – many hungry, exhausted and traumatised – were forced into prison camps; many areas, thought to harbour rebels, were put to the torch; in some villages, all the male inhabitants were executed; arrests mounted throughout the island; in the region of Santiago peaceful civilians were slaughtered so that their houses and crops could be plundered by the military; and rebel prisoners, shown no mercy, were given 'the usual four shots in the back'.[19]

The Madrid government continued to assert that the Cuban 'problem' would be solved, and there was much talk of famous military victories. At the same time there were hints that the war might drag on for years, that the Spanish soldiers were reluctant to confront the guerrilla tactics, that there was gross inefficiency in the military high command, and that, according to some Madrid newspapers, Spain might even be losing the war in Cuba. In January 1870, A. E. Phillips, the American Consul in Santiago, wrote 'that it is impossible to suppress the insurrection, and the only inducement for continuing the war is that the commanding officers are filling their pockets'.[20] On 24 March 1870 an editorial in the Madrid newspaper *La Discusión* spoke of the 'very difficult and bloody struggle in Cuba', noted the $40 million spent, and asked 'who can conquer a people fighting for liberty?'. It was certain, despite the reported Spanish victories, 'that the contest will be ceaselessly renewed'.[21] And so it proved.

The Madrid administration under General Juan Prim now began to realise that concessions would be necessary if the Cuban war was ever to be brought to an end. In May 1870 his Minister of the Colonies, Segismundo Moret, wrote to Captain-General Caballero to point out that France and Britain would not help Spain 'while we are slave-holders, and this one word [slavery] gives North America the right to hold a suspended threat above our heads'; and introduced a new law whereby slavery could be abolished under certain conditions. The decree stipulated that all the children of slave mothers would henceforth be free, with baby slaves born in the previous eighteen months to be bought by the state for $125; the slaves in these categories would be fed, brought up, and trained in a craft skill, until they reached eighteen, by their old masters now required to operate a patronage (*patronato*) system. One consequence of this arrangement was that the slave masters still had the right to exploit the labour of their young charges; up to eighteen, no wages would be paid, and after that the negroes were only entitled to 'half the wages of a free man'. The Moret law also freed slaves over sixty – which meant that, as old freedmen (*libertos*) they would be turned adrift unless they desired to remain with their masters, in which case they were required to labour in the house or on the plantation. The new law, while it did not itself alter the character of the slavery institution, acted to undermine further the traditional climate in which black servitude was the normal condition.

General Prim made further efforts to negotiate a Cuban peace, but then all his efforts were abruptly terminated: on 27 December 1870 he was mortally wounded by an assassin in Madrid, to die three days later. On the very day of Prim's death, Valmaseda had Zenea, Prim's poet envoy in Cuba, seized and thrown into gaol; several months later, with Zenea's safe conduct violated in the field, he was shot. The Volunteers rejoiced, and with King Don Amadeo now seated uncertainly on the Spanish throne the Captain-General of Havana was left with a *de facto* autonomy in the island. Now the brutal Caballero de Rodas had been succeeded by the equally harsh General Valmaseda, whose deputy, General Crespo, had executed eight students accused of desecrating the cemetery of Gonzalo Castañón, the founder of the Volunteers' newspaper, *La Voz de Cuba*. An English merchant commented that maintaining order in such a fashion was 'a capital job'. The rebels were in no doubt that an end to the brutal regime would be brought only by independence.

After the execution of the students (one of whom had been in a different town at the time of the desecration), and the sentencing of thirty others to chain gangs for up to six years, there were widespread protests throughout Cuba. The military repression had rendered the insurgents incapable of useful initiatives through much of 1871; but on the first anniversary of the executions printed posters throughout Madrid advertised the 'terrible day on which eight sons were stolen from the earth and a people wept at the grave of eight martyrs'. The statement, *El 27 de Noviembre de 1871*, was written by José Martí; he emphasised also that there was 'a limit to weeping over the graves'. Nothing would suffice but the resolute struggle for Cuban independence.

The rebels were on the defensive. Ignacio Agramonte continued to maintain a guerrilla presence in Puerto Príncipe, but other areas were abandoned under the mounting pressure from the Spanish forces. Máximo Gómez and Féderico Cavada urged Céspedes to take a military initiative to advance the rebel cause, but he declined and Gómez withdrew unhappily to the Guantánamo region. There were some rebel victories in Oriente but morale among the guerrillas remained low. Some 1500 to 2000 rebels had fled to Jamaica, and the total guerrilla numbers stood at only 10,000 to 12,000 at most.[22] Antonio Maceo, one of the most successful guerrilla leaders, continued to win praise from Gómez for his 'valour, skill and activity'; but nothing more than a military stalemate seemed possible. When General Martinez Campos, with 1000 men, failed to defeat Maceo the Spaniard declared that it was 'impossible to end the war by means of arms'. Céspedes, for his part, acknowledged Maceo's successes in paralysing the Spanish operations around Guantánamo, and paid tribute to 'the sort of glory that is justly associated with your name and which is confessed and recognised by all'. But any successes of Maceo and other rebel commanders were limited to specific regional initiatives: there was little prospect of a nationwide victory.

Céspedes was now being blamed for rebel failures, despite the tactical successes in Oriente and elsewhere. His gradual movement towards total black emancipation was angering his more cautious supporters, while the radicals were demanding more positive initiatives. Now Céspedes, 'nearly blind, ill-dressed and ill-fed, attempting to sustain a ghostly government through arrogance and pride alone', was demanding fresh powers. On 27 October 1873 a rump meeting of the tottering rebel 'House of Representatives' resolved to remove Céspedes from control of the movement. Military commanders from Guantánamo, Santiago, Holguín, Jiguani, Bayamo and Las Tunas, accompanied by more than 2000 soldiers, attended the gathering. Céspedes was removed from power *in absentia*, and was later killed in an ambush at San Lorenzo in March 1874. The mantle of the instigator of the first Cuban War of Independence was now assumed by others.

The new head of the rebel 'government', Salvador Cisneros Betancourt, was a cattle farmer from Camagüey; when he named his 'cabinet' it was clear that the planter class was now in control of the movement. Gómez again urged an invasion of the west, with the aim of carrying the revolution to Havana; but the new leadership rejected his demands on the grounds that the situation in Oriente was too unstable to allow the despatch of rebel forces in a western adventure. Nor, in the aftermath to the Don Carlos insurrection of 14 April 1872 in Spain itself, did the well-entrenched Spanish forces in western Cuba seem inclined towards vigorous military initiatives.

In 1873 the new Republican government in Madrid, preoccupied with the Carlist war in the north and rural insurrection in the south, had little interest in addressing the Cuba problem. Cándido Pieltaín, the new Captain-General in Havana, began with a fresh military campaign, which led to the death of Ignacio Agramonte in Puerto Príncipe on 11 May 1873. But this victory, without real commitment from Madrid, did nothing to convince Pieltaín that the war against the rebels could be won; he soon asked to be relieved, and was followed by General Joaquín Jovellar, previously the Spanish Minister of War, as the new Captain-General. The war dragged on, with some territorial shifts, mounting casualties, and various dramatic incidents (not least the capture by the Spanish of the rebel supply ship *Virginius* sailing under the US flag), but with no final outcome in sight. On 10 February 1874 some 500 rebel soldiers under Gómez defeated 2000 veteran Spanish troops led by General Manuel Portillo and equipped with artillery. A week later, at the battle of Las Guasimas, the rebels launched 200 cavalry and 50 infantry against an artillery-equipped Spanish column of 2000 men. The Spaniards, despite reinforcements that swelled their force to some 6000 soldiers, were made to retreat. The Spanish suffered more than a thousand casualties; the total of 174 rebel casualties included Maceo, wounded during the victorious battle. The engagement had lasted five days, and what had seemed a remarkable rebel triumph had in fact severely depleted the rebel resources: the unusual departure from guerrilla tactics had proved a costly enterprise.

The rebel movement also faced other debilitating problems. As Gómez and Maceo at last began to march their small army to the west, the conservatives again started to express concern at the prospect of black liberation. If Maceo, the hero of the negro population, were to liberate the slaves as he moved through Cuba, would he not emerge as the leading figure in the island? Fuelled by this anxiety, the conservatives launched a propaganda onslaught on Maceo, accusing him of wanting to establish a black republic. One consequence was that rebel troops in Las Villas refused to accept Maceo as their commander, so forcing Gómez to recall him to Oriente. This meant that the western invasion plan, long opposed by the conservatives, was abandoned: typically, Morales Lemus, a spokesman for the wealthy planters, commented that a march to the west would be 'the policy of the incendiary torch', and would jeopardise any chance of gaining American support for the rebel cause. Morales pointed out that the Spaniards were spreading propaganda in the United States that a successful rebel movement to western Cuba would result in black domination of the island.[23] The Morales strategy was a failure: there was no likelihood of US support for the insurgents, and the conservative reluctance to move west meant that the revolution was confined to the least important economic region of the island.

On 6 January 1875, in a dramatic attempt to break the military and political stalemate, Gómez belatedly crossed the *trocha*, the long fortified line erected by the Spaniards to prevent access to the west. Then, to 'snatch the slave from the domination of his master', Gómez (*el hombre de la tea*, the man of the torch) set about burning the plantations and mills that sustained the enemy. In six weeks he burned eighty-three plantations in the Sancti Spiritus area, freeing the slaves, and leaving much of Oriente and Camagüey in rebel hands. But despite such substantial gains, the rebel leadership was again plagued by factional division. A new campaign of slander was launched by the conservatives against Maceo, and a large number of men was detached from his army. In late 1876 General Carlos Roloff informed Gómez that since he was a Dominican the officers in Las Villas would no longer accept him as their commander. Gómez responded by turning over to him the command of the force with which he had expected 'to fight the last battle against the Spanish Army'.[24] He then retired to the plantation, *La Reforma*, his heart 'broken by so many deceptions'.[25] Now, with the rebel leadership split and with the Spanish monarchy firmly re-established, the Spaniards in Cuba resolved to go on the offensive. At last there was the will to bring to an end the inconclusive years of conflict on the island.

At the end of 1876 General Arsenio Martínez Campos had arrived in Cuba with some 25,000 troop reinforcements; now he headed 70,000 men distributed between eight main Spanish commands. In March 1877 Martínez Campos launched a vigorous offensive, driving the rebels back beyond the *trocha*; while at the same time he worked to exploit the political divisions in the rebel camp. In the new circumstances there was low morale among the rebels, now exhausted by years of fighting. Some officers had already deserted the rebel groups, and their numbers swelled when Martínez Campos offered an amnesty to all except the leaders who surrendered before the end of the war. In addition he offered land to all 'ex-soldiers, volunteers . . . needy residents who had remained faithful', and to rebel soldiers who were prepared to surrender.

By now the rebel forces were desperately battling for survival. In September the Spaniards almost captured Maceo; and Eduardo Machado, the head of the rebel 'legislative chamber', was killed. In October Estrada Palma, the rebel 'President', was captured, whereupon his place was taken by Vicente García. Soon García was indicating that he was prepared to discuss terms with the Spanish authorities; and now even Gómez was beginning to admit that the rebel forces could not endure for much longer. On 5 February 1878 the rebel leaders met with the Spanish generals to discuss how the war might be brought to an end. Immediately after this inconclusive meeting, García and the 'House of Representatives' resigned, and a *Comité del Centro* (Committee of the Central Department) was formed to conclude the talks. On 9 February Martínez Campos proposed a package of terms for the ending of hostilities: a general pardon for the rebels, Cuba to be given political equality with Puerto Rico, the liberation of the rebel negroes and Asians, and liberty for all the rebel leaders prepared to leave Cuba. The rebels proposed that a 'general amnesty' would avoid the element of guilt implied by a 'general pardon', and demanded that Cuba be given the same 'status' as the provinces of Spain. Eventually the phrase 'forgetting the past' was substituted for 'general amnesty' and, once Martínez Campos had pointed out that Puerto Rico and the provinces of Spain enjoyed 'substantially the same status', agreement was reached.

On 11 February 1878 the rebel leaders met with Martínez Campos at Zanjón, a village in Camagüey, and both sides accepted the terms and conditions specified in the *Pacto del Zanjón*. The agreement included eight articles: Cuba to have the same status as Puerto Rico; no action to be taken against anyone for political offences committed from 1868 (and freedom for those under indictment or gaoled, and for Spanish deserters); freedom for insurgent slaves and Asians; no-one who submitted to Spanish authority to be forced into military service before the establishment of peace over the whole island; freedom for anyone to leave Cuba; each force to capitulate in uninhabited spots; insurgents from other departments to be offered free transportation within the Central Department; and the pact with the Comité to be judged to have been made with all the departments of the island.[26] In February 1878 Maceo and a few rebels stated that the Zanjón terms were unacceptable since they did not abolish slavery or establish Cuban independence. A subsequent meeting (16 March) between Maceo and Martínez Campos was inconclusive. The demands made by Maceo at this 'Protest of Baragua' (near Santiago) were rejected in their entirety by Martínez Campos, who then asked whether hostilities would be renewed. Maceo responded by declaring that the war could restart immediately. Finally, an eight-day truce was agreed (Maceo: 'On the 23rd, hostilities break out').

Maceo had dramatically rejected the Pact of Zanjón, and with this act he had breathed new life into the struggle for Cuban emancipation and independence. The Spanish saw the act as indefensible arrogance, but Maceo had now won international acclaim. In New York *La Verdad* (6 April 1878) commented: 'The hero of the day is Maceo, and it appears it is up to him to raise Cuba again to the pinnacle of its glory.' A month later the same newspaper published a message to Maceo from S. R. Scottron, the black Secretary of the American and Foreign Anti-Slavery Society and Chairman of the Cuban Anti-Slavery Committee. It included the words: 'Few men in the history of the world have had the good fortune of finding themselves in such an honourable position as that which you now occupy. And none have occupied one more noble.' At the same time the Anti-Slavery Society of London, citing the protest of Baragua, urged the British government to intensify the pressure on Spain for the emancipation of the Cuban slaves.

The Spanish authorities put further pressure on Maceo to accept the Pact of Zanjón, even offering bribes for him to lay down his arms and leave the island – all to no avail. With exhausted and heavily depleted forces, Maceo again began a series of military initiatives against the Spanish. At first Martínez Campos, urging an optimistic campaign of passive resistance, instructed his soldiers not to fight and to respond to all attacks with shouts of: *'Viva Cuba! Viva la Paz! No hagais fuego, pues somos hermanos'* (Long live Cuba! Long live peace! Don't shoot, we are brothers). But the peace strategy could not be long sustained: soon Maceo and his small forces faced the full onslaught of the reinforced Spanish army. In May 1878 Maceo was forced to capitulate, but with the intention of renewing the struggle however he could. On 10 May a Spanish ship with Maceo on board left Santiago de Cuba for Jamaica. Maceo had thanked Martínez Campos for his considerations, but continued to emphasise that he (Maceo) was not compromised: 'I will do what I can to come back and then undertake my work anew.' From Jamaica, Maceo sailed to New York, where he worked to raise money for the Cuban rebels. When it was clear that the 'government' he represented no longer existed he abandoned his efforts and returned to Jamaica.

The first Cuban War of Independence was over – at a cost to the Cubans of about 50,000 dead, and to the Spanish 208,000. Countless more Cubans had been killed by Spanish atrocities; and tens of thousands were left wounded, mutilated, exhausted and traumatised. The Ten Years' War had cost $300 million, a sum that the Spanish authorities added to the Cuban debt.[27] The Cuban revolutionaries had been forced to accept the Pact of Zanjón. Slavery had not yet been abolished in Cuba, despite its demise elsewhere in the Americas; and Cuba still lay under the Spanish crown. But it was soon to emerge that the Zanjón agreement was no more than a truce: the war, despite all the reverses for the rebel cause, had imbued the struggle for emancipation and independence with an irresistible momentum. It would not be long before slavery was abolished in Cuba, and the Spaniards evicted from the island. Even then it would emerge that the long struggle for freedom and dignity was far from over.

THE ROLE OF JOSÉ MARTÍ

José Martí (1853–95) is one of the few leading figures in the pantheon of heroes who fought in history for Cuban freedom and independence. Today

Martí – the 'most brilliant of Cubans',[28] the '"Apostle" and father of Cuban independence'[29] – ranks with Ernesto 'Che' Guevara de la Serna and Fidel Castro Ruz in Cuban hagiography: with photographs and busts adorning homes and public places, Martí continues to occupy a sacramental place in Cuban consciousness.

Both Martí's parents were Spaniards. His father, from Valencia, was a sergeant in the artillery who later became a minor city official and then a policeman in Havana; his mother was a Canary islander from Tenerife. José had six sisters and no brothers. During his formative years he was influenced more by the schoolmaster Rafael María Mendive, a romantic poet and supporter of Cuban independence, than by his parents; José Martí himself became a poet and journalist, even writing a novel and publishing a magazine for children, as well as becoming a leading political philosopher and activist.

At the start of the Ten Years' War in 1868, Martí was a schoolchild and already politically active. Aged sixteen, Martí founded the newspaper *La Patria Libre* in January 1869, for which he wrote romantic and political pieces; one significant contribution was *Abdala*, a long poem 'expressly written for the fatherland' and in which 'Nubia' (Cuba) was fighting for its freedom. Then Mendive was accused of agitating against the Spanish authorities, and was exiled to Spain; during his time in a Cuban goal, Mendive was visited by Martí – providing yet more information, if more were needed, of the youngster's subversive inclinations. Following the courtmartial of Martí and Fermín Valdés Domínguez for writing a letter denouncing a fellow student for 'apostasy' in supporting Spain, Martí was sentenced to six years' hard labour and Fermín given six months' imprisonment. On 5 April 1870 Martí began his sentence in the stone quarry of St Lazaro in Havana, but after six months was sent to the Isle of Pines to recover and was then exiled to Spain.

Martí never fully recovered from his time in the quarry: forced to wear a chain from waist to ankle and to cart heavy blocks of stone, he suffered a permanent groin lesion. He was appalled also by the sadism of the guards and by the constant physical and mental abuse heaped upon the prisoners. In a vivid political tract, *Political Imprisonment in Cuba*, written when Martí was eighteen, he denounced the Spanish government's brutalities in Cuba and graphically depicted the plight of particular prisoners he had known: how beatings had turned the back of a seventy-six-year-old man into a suppurating wound; a boy of twelve with smallpox serving ten years' hard labour; a Chinese who died of cholera; a negro driven insane; others forced in desperation to attempt suicide.

The young Martí was now active in Madrid's revolutionary politics. At the Central University of Madrid, like many revolutionaries, he studied law, and then moved to the University of Saragossa where he graduated in 1874. On 11 February 1873 the *Cortes* had proclaimed the First Spanish Republic, and, soon after, one of the Spanish deputies reaffirmed the status of Cuba as a Spanish colony. Five days later, Martí sent his tract *The Spanish Republic and the Cuban Revolution* to Prime Minister Figueras, in which he argued that a republic could not countenance colonialism. Cuba, declared Martí, could not be part of the Spanish fatherland:

'Fatherland is something more than oppression. . . . Fatherland means a community of interests, unity of tradition, unity of goals, the sweetest and most consoling fusion of loves and hopes. . . . Cubans do not live as Spaniards live. . . . They are nourished by a different system of trade, have links with different countries, and express their happiness through quite contrary customs. There are no common aspirations or identical goals linking the two peoples, or beloved memories to unite them . . .'[30]

The Spanish premier expressed vague approval of the principles expressed by Martí, but then the matter was shelved. A short time later the fragile First Spanish Republic was swept away by a military coup.

In early 1875 Martí travelled via Paris to Mexico, where his parents were then living and where he stayed until his return to Cuba in January 1877. In Havana, at a time when the war was continuing with great ferocity, bringing massive casualties to both sides, it was clear that the conflict could not be long sustained. After a stay of less than two months, Martí then went to Guatemala, where he tutored in languages and philosophy, and unromantically abjured his love for a daughter of an ex-president in favour of the more suitable Carmen Zayas Bazán, the daughter of a rich Cuban sugar planter, whom he later married in Mexico. Now the revolutionary Martí was linked by marriage to the Cuban oligarchy that would soon be swept away. In 1878, then aged twenty-five, he returned to Cuba but seemingly did not much like Havana. To a friend he commented in 1879: 'If Cuba were not so unfortunate, I would love Mexico more than Cuba.'

A peace, of sorts, had been established throughout the island. The disputed Pact of Zanjón (19 February 1878) had been concluded, Céspedes and Agramonte were dead, and Maceo and Gómez were in exile. Martí and his fellow revolutionaries continued to agitate for independence (Martí: rights are 'to be taken, not requested; seized, not begged for'), while at the same time the Spanish authorities spread the usual propaganda in an attempt to undermine the independence movement. Spies infiltrated the revolutionary groups, the rebels were often forced into premature initiatives to avoid exposure, and the Spanish authorities worked to arouse fears that the negroes in Cuba and elsewhere were plotting a race war for the extermination of the white population. The propaganda campaign was aided by those Cubans still deriving profits from slavery, and by the various new Cuban parties committed as 'moderates' to the suppression of revolutionary groups. Now the non-revolutionary reformers were spreading the charge that a new insurrection was being planned 'by 4000 Negroes who proclaim not only the flag of separation but also a war of the races'.

On 26 August 1879 a fresh revolt, *La Guerra Chiquita* (The Little War), erupted throughout Cuba. It started in Santiago, and was quickly followed by further actions in the rest of Oriente and elsewhere across the island; the rebel forces, negro and white, were quickly supplemented by large numbers of runaway slaves. The exiled Calixto García and Antonio Maceo, preparing to land in Cuba, urged all Cubans to fight for freedom, and all negro slaves to join the struggle:

. . . your comrades who fought in the last war achieved their liberty because they embraced the Cuban flag which belongs to all Cubans alike. Get together again under the same flag, and you shall obtain freedom and your civil rights, and after that, you shall be able to make a common cause with those that today want to redeem you from the degraded situation in which you find yourselves now.[31]

In Havana a Central Committee was established, with Martí as president, to support the revolutionary struggle: steps were taken to channel resources to the rebels in Las Villas and Oriente, and to prepare a similar revolt in the province of Havana.

There were now growing signs that the Spanish authorities feared that they would not be able to protect the slave system. Thus the US Consul in Havana, Henry C. Hall reported Spanish anxieties that unless the insurrection was quickly suppressed it might be 'seconded by the slave population who, it is said, are becoming, day by day, less reconciled to their condition'. In these circumstances the Spanish government reacted in the usual way. Any Negroes suspected of having any sympathy with the new rebellion were arrested: some 350 blacks were arrested in Santiago alone, taken to Havana, and thrown into the Morro Castle dungeons prior to overseas penitentiaries.

On 25 September Martí was again arrested and deported, 'under surveillance', to Spain. He did not remain there long: again, via Paris, he travelled back to the New World, where he arrived in New York to become president of the Cuban Revolutionary Committee. On 24 January 1880, before a Cuban audience assembled in Steck Hall, Martí made his first public speech in the United States. He applauded the Negro contribution to the Cuban revolutionary struggle, denouncing as propaganda the Spanish claims that the blacks intended to launch a race war. Martí, as much as anyone, had seen the suffering of the Negroes in Cuba. He had written: 'What man who has seen a Negro whipped does not ever after consider himself his debtor? I saw it, I saw it when I was a child, and my cheeks still burn with shame.' Above all, Martí called for the unity of all Cuban patriots, regardless of race or colour. Later that year the Spanish government, now acknowledging that the slave system could not be indefinitely prolonged, moved to regulate its gradual abolition under the controversial *patronato* scheme. When slavery in Cuba at last came to an end in 1886, Brazil was the only remaining slave state in the Americas.

It soon became clear that *La Guerra Chiquita* would not be another ten years' war: the rebels were poorly resourced and there were divisions among their ranks. In October 1880 Martí was acknowledging the lack of agreement among the military leaders, and writing to Emilio Núñez, the last of the active leaders in the field, to lay down his arms. The war was unwinnable and now the struggle would have to be continued by other means. Martí continued to write copiously, not least for a wide range of South American newspapers, and to travel, making speeches and building his revolutionary contacts. On 20 July 1882 he wrote to Gómez and Maceo, neither of whom had ever abandoned their commitment to militant struggle, and outlined an ideological strategy for the winning of freedom in Cuba. Now he was 29, prepared for patient years of preparation and acknowledging that *the possibility of a Cuban annexation to the United States represented the greatest threat to the island's independence*: 'In Cuba there has always been an important group of cautious men, proud enough to abominate Spanish domination yet timid enough not to put their personal well-being in danger by fighting against it. These kinds of men . . . are vehemently in favour of the annexation of Cuba to the United States. All the timid people, all the ones lacking in decisiveness, all the superficial observers, all those attached to wealth, have marked inclinations to support this solution, which they believe to be cheap and easy . . .'.

With his travels and writings, Martí had now won an international reputation: in 1884, in part to acknowledge his growing fame, Uruguay made him their Vice-Consul in New York, a nominal post that at least offered a regular income. Martí was writing on every great event: political, economic, cultural (his novel *Amistad funesta*, written in seven days, has been judged as purely autobiographical: it did not do well). Morale remained low among the revolutionaries after *La Guerra Chiquita*, and it was not long before Martí himself was in dispute with the other leaders of the movement. Gómez and Maceo had arrived in the United States from Honduras, where they intended to organise a fresh force for an invasion of Cuba. Martí had agreed to the creation of a governing junta, despite his doubts about the authoritarian character of such a group; but when Gómez, discussing a projected trip to Mexico to drum up support, curtly declared that Maceo would be in charge and that Martí should confine himself to obeying orders, he [Martí] countered with a strong personal attack: 'A people is not founded, General, in the same way one commands a military camp. . . . The man that uses a great idea to serve his personal aspirations to glory or power, although he may be putting his life at risk for them, is to be abominated. To sacrifice one's life is only a right when it is sacrificed disinterestedly.' The rift was never healed. It has been suggested that Martí's death – caused when he rode recklessly towards Spanish troops against Gómez's orders – came as a consequence of earlier insinuations that Martí was a mere intellectual who could not be compared with the military heroes of the past.

The revolutionary leadership continued to be racked by internal divisions. Maceo and Gómez fell into dispute: over money, tactics and other matters – with Maceo eventually disputing Gómez's fitness as a commanding officer (Gómez then broke off the friendship: 'There remains only one thing in common between us, a sacred thing which I have made mine – the cause of our country'). Martí, in an attempt to heal the festering wounds in the revolutionary movement, combined with other activists in New York to issue a five-point programme: democratic procedures were essential; military organisation outside Cuba must be co-ordinated with organisation within the country; the émigré centres must be democratically united; no one group, class or race should be allowed to twist and enslave the revolutionary sympathies in Cuba; and annexationist propaganda should not be allowed to weaken the revolutionary struggle. Maceo and other revolutionary leaders quickly expressed their broad agreement with the circular publicising the programme.

Now Martí was recognising the growing threat posed by the United States. Some Americans wanted to buy Cuba, others wanted to go to war over it. Perhaps, commented Martí, Cuba would be left to bleed until such time as the United States could grab it with its 'selfish and disrespectful hands'. Already Martí was envisaging the catalogue of US interventions that would take place in the years ahead. Increasingly he came to recognise the impossibility of reconciling the interests of the two halves of the American continent. In a famous letter (18 May 1895) Martí wrote on the eve of his death to Manuel Mercado he declared that *his one aim in life had been to free Cuba and so to stop the United States from falling on the nations of Latin America.*[32] Increasingly he saw the United States as the 'colossus of the north', as a 'monster'.

In January 1890 Martí founded *La Liga de Instrucción*, a kind of training school for revolutionaries, in New York; Martí himself lectured at the school, declaring that the next Cuban revolution would not be one for the planters but one for the people. Maceo again visited Cuba, nominally to inspect property but with the task of contacting potential revolutionaries. Now Martí, his fame spreading, was offered the consulships of Argentina and Paraguay; and in 1891 represented Uruguay in the first inter-American money conference, held in Washington; here Martí opposed US plans and so 'thwarted the design of the Department of State'. The United States developed a growing interest in José Martí. On 25 November 1891 he arrived in Tampa, Florida, and gave revolutionary speeches to expatriate Cuban tobacco workers; in December he travelled to Key West to deliver the same revolutionary message. It was in Key West that the Tampa resolutions were amplified into a set of basic principles for the creation of the Cuban Revolutionary Party (CRP).

The Cuban Revolutionary Party (*El Partido Revolucionario Cubano*) was formally approved by local Cuban revolutionaries on 5 January 1892, after two full years of detailed preparation. *La Liga* had served as an important stepping-stone, a means of bringing the Cuban Negroes into the active struggle and of laying the basis for racial harmony in the Cuban Republic. The Tampa resolutions, drafted by Martí, were intended to contribute to 'the foundation of a just Republic open to all, one in territory, in law, in work and in cordiality, established with the collaboration of all for the good of all'. Then a Tampa *Liga de Instrucción*, modelled on the New York *Liga*, was formed to allow Negro exiles to gain an education and to prepare themselves for the revolutionary struggle. After the founding of the Revolutionary Party, José Martí, with the agreement of the CRP leadership, drafted the *Bases* of the new organisation – to define the reasons, justifications and political ideals of the movement. The aim was 'a generous and brief war, undertaken to ensure the peace and labour of the inhabitants of the island'; this would be 'a war of republican spirit and method', designed to establish 'a nation capable of assuring the lasting good fortune of her children and of fulfilling in the historical life of the Continent the difficult duties which her geographical situation assigns her'. Democratic processes would be established; and Cuba would, as far as possible, be freed from dependence on the outside world.

The 'secret Statutes' of the Party, also drafted by Martí, specified the internal workings of the organisation. Individuals and associations, provided they accepted the Party programme and agreed to pay the assessed dues, could join the Party. Elected councils would be set up in each locality, to carry out specific tasks and to serve as intermediaries between Party members and the national headquarters. A principal duty was to be the collection of funds for the revolutionary war and the payment of regular contributions into the action fund. Elected delegates were expected to fulfil defined duties, including working assiduously for the cause in Cuba itself and submitting to elected treasurers all transfers from the action fund. These requirements and the other associated principles and conventions were intended to combine grass-roots democracy with efficient executive action: an example of 'democratic centralism', akin to the organisation of the modern Cuban Communist Party.[33]

Martí had now succeeded in uniting many of the disparate elements in the revolutionary movement. Even Gómez, often inclined to dispute Martí's efforts, wrote in his *Diary* that the triumph of the Cuban revolution 'is a matter of concord and unification, and, in my opinion, the work that Martí has done up to now is quite consistent, for he is gradually obtaining the unification of the discordant elements'; Martí, perceived Gómez, was 'an intelligent and persevering man . . . a real defender of the liberty of his country'. Now Martí was moving to tie the military wing of the movement to the democratic statutes that he had framed. In April 1892, once elected a delegate, Martí ordered elections to be held amongst the military veterans in order to select the head of the armed forces. When Gómez, predictably enough, was elected, Martí wrote to invite him to take up the post: now, at least in theory, the army had been subsumed by the Party. In June 1893 Martí visited Maceo in Costa Rica and succeeded in recruiting him to join the army leadership. Soon Gómez and Serafín Sánchez, along with other veterans from 1868, were also on board. It would soon be time to launch yet another struggle for Cuban independence.

In the autumn of 1893 the Cuban employers in the Florida tobacco factories tried to cut the workers' wages, whereupon strikes were called. Then the Spanish authorities in Cuba agreed to help the Florida planters by providing Cuban labour. The Florida workers appealed to Martí, who, with Horatio Rubens a young New York lawyer, succeeded in showing that the importation of labour was against the US Contract Labour Act of 1885. The workers thus won a total victory, an outcome that encouraged yet more workers in Cuba and elsewhere to flock to the Martí banner.

With growing popular support, Martí had intended to name February 1894 as the next (and hopefully final) Cuban uprising against colonial Spain; but here he was forced to delay because sympathetic planters wanted first to complete the harvest. On 30 September 1894, after yet more delays, Gómez wrote to Maceo (then recovering from a wound inflicted by Spanish assailants) that there must be immediate action after 15 November. Martí was impoverished and ill, possibly suffering from tuberculosis, and yet he 'laboured as one inspired. . . . The organisation of the conspiracy in Cuba was crystallising. . . . Cigar workers responded nobly. . . . At the end of October Martí let it be known he would have $5000 more.'[34] Still the revolutionaries moved with care: no rebellion would be attempted until at least four of the six provinces were ready. In Florida, revolutionary expeditions preparing to sail to Cuba were caught by the US authorities on 14 January 1895, a blow that nonetheless indicated the scale of Martí's organisation: Martí was not just a poet and a philosopher but a highly competent activist.

On 29 January Martí signed the order for the start of the new insurrection, and two days later he left New York to join Gómez in Santo Domingo. On 24 March Martí and Gómez issued a joint manifesto in which they promised a 'civilised war': private rural property would be respected; non-combatant Spaniards would not be attacked; negroes would be welcome to join the rebellion; and Cuba would emerge as a republic 'different from the feudal and theoretical ones of Hispano-America' since Cuba was 'different from the peoples previously liberated'. Such differences derived from the 'civic responsibility of its warriors; the culture and magnanimity of its artisans; the appropriate and most up-to-date use of a vast number of skills and riches; the strange moderation of the peasant, seasoned by both exile and war'. The new economic system would give work to all in a free nation; no longer would Cuba be a humiliated country subject to tyranny and exploitation. The manifesto concluded with the words *La Victoria o el Sepulcro* (Victory or the Tomb), a descendant of Garibaldi's cry of *Roma o Morte* and an ancestor of Fidel Castro's *Patria o Muerte* and (later) *Socialismo o Muerte*.[35]

The new document, the *Montecristi Manifesto*, had defined the aims of the revolution; but it was one thing to spin words, quite another to achieve military victory. The revolutionaries encountered difficulties from the beginning – of logistics, morale and leadership. Martí relates some of the problems in his *Campaign Diary*; as when a guerrilla was courtmartialled and executed for robbery and rape, and when an acrimonious meeting took place to consider the shape of the future Cuban government (even now the rebel leaders in the bush were jostling among themselves for political advantage). What exactly would be the shape and powers of the future political

Assembly? What role would the army have? Who would be president? For Martí it transpired that such questions were no more than academic.

At the beginning of May 1895, Martí discussed with Gómez and Maceo the critical question of civilian or military control of the revolution. Maceo, against Martí, wanted a military junta to have full powers until victory. Martí, now demoralised by the persistent splits in the leadership, gave a final interview to a journalist from the *New York Herald* and then rode off with Gómez. On 19 May a Spanish Colonel, Ximénez de Sandoval, acting under the newly returned Martínez Campos, surprised Gómez in a skirmish. Martí, against Gómez's orders, rode towards the Spaniards and was shot down and killed by three bullets.[36] The man who almost certainly would have been the first president of a free Cuba did not live to see the independence of his country. Nor, in one sense, did any of his contemporaries. It would not be long before the Spanish were finally evicted from Cuba; and then the Cuban people would soon learn that there were other forms of colonialism.

TOWARDS INDEPENDENCE

Martí was dead, but now the new revolution, the War of 1895, was gaining momentum. The rebels liked to think that this time it would be different; they had learned from the Ten Years' War and *La Guerra Chiquita*. The Ten Years' War, declared Máximo Gómez, had originated from 'the top down, that is why it failed'; the new war 'surges from the bottom up, that is why it will triumph'. In the Ten Years' War the rebel leaders had been largely men of patrician origins; in 1895, by contrast, many of the separatist leaders came from the ranks of the disgruntled creole petit bourgeoisie, from the liberal professions, including engineers, teachers, physicians and lawyers. The army officers originated from the working class, from the burgher ranks (shopkeepers and merchants), and from the ranks of the impoverished gentry. And for the first time there was substantial Negro representation in the higher echelons of the revolutionary forces: blacks amounted to around 40 per cent of the senior ranks of the new Liberation Army.[37] A nation was on the move.

The disparity between the contending forces seemed to give the Spaniards a clear advantage. It is estimated that in June 1895 the revolutionary forces numbered between 6000 and 8000; where the Spaniards had 52,000 troops supported by nineteen warships, six of which weighed more than 1000 tons.[38] But the figures tell only part of the story: the Spaniards were confronting a mass eruption, a genuine revolution, rather than a conventional war. The rebels, supported by the local population, operated freely in the rural areas, recruiting 'revolutionary bandits' and judging when it was useful to harass the enemy forces. The Spanish, without heavy reinforcements, travelled only on the roads and kept to the towns, so rendering themselves vulnerable to ambush and encirclement. Now tens of thousands of non-combatant civilians (*pacíficos*) were supporting the liberation struggle.

Gradually the war began to expand from the remote eastern districts to the key western zones. In 1896 and after, the Liberation Army was confronting the entire colonial system – attacking Spanish troops, disrupting communications, and striking at the heart of the colonial economy. In July 1895 Gómez had announced a moratorium on all economic enterprise: all commercial activities – trading, manufacture, agriculture, ranching, sugar production, and the rest – would be stopped, either voluntarily or under the compulsion of the rebel forces. The Gómez decree warned of the consequences of ignoring the proclamation: 'All sugar plantations will be destroyed, the standing cane set fire and the factory buildings and railroads destroyed. Any worker assisting the operation of the sugar factories will be considered an enemy of his country . . . and will be executed.' Thus *la tea* (the torch) became the favoured revolutionary weapon. Said Gómez: 'It is necessary to burn the hive in order to disperse the swarm.'[39] There was some resistance to the decree, and plantations and factories were burned. One producer, noting the shift of fortunes towards the rebels, wrote in early 1896: 'If anyone had told us four months ago that [Gómez] would be able to stop the crushing of cane in the province of Havana, or even in Matanzas, we would have laughed in his face. Today not a planter disobeys his orders.'[40]

In these circumstances Martínez Campos, the veteran Captain-General, decided that the only effective strategy was one of complete ruthlessness; though now he had serious misgivings: 'Even if we win in the field and suppress the rebels . . . before twelve years we shall have another war.' And he was forced to acknowledge that the new insurrection was 'more serious and more powerful than early in 1876. The leaders know more and their manner of waging war is different from what it was then.' In July 1895 Martínez Campos had confronted Maceo in Oriente, almost intercepting him between Bayamo and Manzanillo, but the Spanish initiative ended in failure: a Spanish general, Santocildes, was killed, and Martínez Campos himself was almost captured at Peralejo. In August a fifth of the new Spanish troops sent to Cuba were ill with yellow fever.

Spain responded by increasing its Cuban army to 200,000 officers and men; and by appointing General Valeriano Weyler to crush the insurgency

(Weyler: 'I believe that war should be answered with war'). He arrived with 50,000 fresh troops, and at once introduced a reign of terror. The rural population was forced to evacuate the countryside and relocate in fortified sites akin to concentration camps; while at the same time subsistence agriculture was banned and livestock owners were made to bring their herds into the cities. Spanish soldiers roamed over the countryside, destroying crops and entire villages, burning food reserves, razing homes, and slaughtering what livestock could not be driven to secure Spanish zones. The aim was to depopulate the rural areas, to remove any sign of human habitation: vast regions became empty wastelands. One traveller to Cuba wrote:

> I travelled by rail from Havana to Matanzas. The country outside the military posts was practically depopulated. Every house had been burned, banana trees cut down, cane fields swept with fire, and everything in the shape of food destroyed. . . . I did not see a house, man, woman or child, a horse, mule, or cow, nor even a dog. I did not see a sign of life, except an occasional vulture or buzzard sailing through the air. The country was wrapped in the stillness of death and the silence of desolation.[41]

Hundreds of thousands of Cubans, driven from their homes, crowded the towns in desperate confusion. Some 300,000 Cubans (*reconcentrados*), denied adequate food and shelter, were crammed into abysmal resettlement camps. The inevitable consequence, deliberately contrived or not, was mass deaths. The Spanish government, denying all responsibility, contemplated the situation in which Cubans died by the tens of thousands – from disease, hunger and abuse. Even now, Weyler had failed to crush the Cuban spirit. Thus the rebel General José María Rodríguez wrote in March 1896 that the sending to Cuba of the 'ferocious Weyler' had been counterproductive for Spain since formerly pacific Cubans 'are found today swelling our ranks'; and Maceo commented that the Revolution had no better ally 'than Weyler himself'.

Much of Cuba had been turned into desolation. The sugar estates were idle, the rural areas depopulated, and the Spanish colonial forces increasingly demoralised. The bulk of the male population had taken up arms, whether for or against the Revolution, as an alternative to starvation. Hundreds of thousands of destitute families, often denuded of the menfolk, struggled to subsist in the filthy camps. On 11 July 1896 a certain Captain Beal, the *colón* of Cienfuegos, wrote to Edwin F. Atkins:

No sanitary measures have been adopted. Smallpox extends to all parts of the city. . . . The rags used for the sick are thrown into the streets, where they are carried up and down by the wind and curs. . . . Smallpox and pernicious fevers are very fatal, particularly to children . . . a large trench has been dug in the cemetery, where the dead are thrown in during the night and covered with quick lime. . . . The death rate from this disease [smallpox] is now on the wane, I suppose from lack of victims. Yellow fever is very epidemic and of an alarming type . . .[42]

In the midst of this chaos and despair the Spanish army plundered and abused the Cuban population, seeking to make money at every turn. Commanders demanded money from plantation owners for protection; a Spanish judge in Manzanillo arrested a number of citizens, and demanded money before he would release them; once they had paid, he arranged for them to be rearrested and again imprisoned. Similar practices were reported for various parts of the country.

The depopulation of the rural areas had done nothing to help the pro-Spanish planters, newly deprived of their labour force. Under attack from both insurgents and rebel troops, the national economy approached collapse. Unemployment had rocketed, taxes had soared, and the massive increase in inflation had affected the entire population. When the Spanish government printed money with abandon, the merchants refused to accept the depreciated currency; whereupon the army responded by confiscating goods under military decree. By 1897 it seemed that the Spanish colonial regime was running into terminal collapse: Martínez Campos had been unable to confine the rebellion to the eastern regions of the island; and Weyler, despite policies that had produced virtual genocide, had been unable to totally crush the insurgents in the west.[43]

At the start of 1898 all the signs were that the Cuban Revolution would triumph.

5 The US Involvement

the Island of Cuba . . . would be an easy conquest

Thomas Jefferson[1]

the faith is true and adorable which leads a soldier to throw away his life in obedience to a blindly accepted duty, in a cause which he little understands . . . under tactics of which he does not see the use

Oliver Wendell Holmes[2]

The United States, through most of its history, has looked at Cuba with covetous eyes. There were times – pre-eminently the period of the Civil War (1861–65) – when politicians and profiteers had other matters on their mind. But the natural resources of Cuba, the bountiful produce of the island's slave plantations, the post-slavery commercial potential, the real estate, the strategic siting of the 'Pearl of the Antilles' – all have tempted the northern colossus. Even the long Spanish occupation could not block the growing US commercial interest in Cuba; while talk of adding Cuba – by purchase or by conquest – to the expanding American empire continued unabated for more than a century.

Much of the growth of the United States was at the expense of Spain; and the increasingly precarious position of Spanish colonialism in Cuba at the end of the nineteenth century gave America a fresh opportunity. Spain had repeatedly refused to sell Cuba to the United States. Now, with Cuba on the brink of independence, a new military conquest was the obvious answer.

THE MOUNTING INTEREST

On 13 August 1762 the British captured and occupied Havana – one of the consequences of the Seven Years' War.* The city was given back to Spain the following year in exchange for Florida but the brief British occupation had lasting effects. The British had opened Havana to free trade, selling merchandise and slaves at reduced prices, and facilitating the arrival of freemasonry, which was to stimulate the revolutionary impulse in the fol-

---

*War (1756–63) fought in Europe and in the colonial domains. It initially pitted Britain, Prussia and Hanover against Austria and France; and later involved Sweden, Russia, Saxony and Spain.

lowing decades. Traders and consumers had tasted the benefits of liberal trade, and now the Spanish government found it impossible to reimpose the former constraints of Bourbon rule.

The lessons of the British occupation of Havana were not lost on the Spanish king, Charles III (r. 1759–88), the successor to Ferdinand VI and wisely perceived as an 'enlightened despot'. It now seemed that the Spanish government was prepared to accept administrative reform and commercial change; and that such developments would bring benefits to the Cuban economy. Thus a commercial decree of August 1764 expanded Cuba's trading rights, and the following year Havana was authorised to trade not only with Seville and Cadiz but also with seven other Spanish cities (Barcelona, Alicante, Cartagena, Málaga, Coruña, Gijón and Santander). A monthly mail-packet service had begun between Havana and Coruña in Spain, and the Cubans were now permitted to search for new markets using their own ships. In these changing circumstances Cuba was well prepared to respond to the opportunities provided by the American rebellion (1776–83) against British colonialism. In 1778, as a further blow to Havana's commercial dominance, three further ports (Santiago, Trinidad and Batabanó) were permitted to trade directly with Spain and with the other Spanish colonies.[3]

During the rebellion against Britain, American privateers sailed into Caribbean waters in search of friendly ports. Spain, welcoming any attacks on England and Portugal, encouraged their presence; and, through a royal decree issued on 5 November 1776, opened Cuban ports to direct trade with North America. Now the rebel vessels could trade with Cuba under their own flag, able to obtain much needed supplies in exchange for cash, bills of exchange, or negro slaves. This was important trade for the American rebels since they were now denied access to the commerce of the British Caribbean colonies; Cuba in turn – now a vital source of sugar, molasses, coffee and tobacco – thrived on these economic developments. In 1779 the official entrance of Spain into the struggle against Britain gave a further boost to trade between Cuba and America. Soon afterwards the first official US agent in Latin America, Robert Smith of Baltimore, was despatched to Havana to assist American traders (Smith and his successor, Oliver Pollock, were refused official recognition by the Spanish authorities). But already there were signs that Spain's encouragement of Cuban–American trade would not last. Even during the reign of the liberal Charles III, the wealthy Spanish merchants continued to press for a restoration of Spain's commercial monopolies.

In January 1784 the Spanish government, now highly sensitive to commercial pressures, issued a spate of decrees prohibiting trade between

Cuba and all countries except Spain. Oliver Pollock, instructed by the US Congress to intercede where possible with the Spanish authorities, was expelled from Havana, along with other foreigners keen to expand trade links. An American appeal that the new republic be allowed to trade with Cuba on the basis of reciprocity was rejected. In Madrid Don Francisco Rendón, the Spanish agent at Philadelphia, argued that Spanish commerce would be at a disadvantage with American; if concessions were granted to US traders, the Cuban economy would soon be dominated by the United States – and Spain was determined to resist any such development.[4] Some clandestine Cuban–US trade continued, but the flourishing commerce rapidly declined. For a decade the situation remained unchanged – until events in Europe again impacted on the colonial economies.

The various conflicts precipitated by the French Revolution (1789–99) had wide-ranging consequences for the European colonial powers. In 1793, fearing domestic upheaval in the event of a French republican victory, Spain joined the royalist allies against the French revolutionaries. French privateers immediately responded by attacking Spanish merchant ships, so effectively disrupting commerce between Spain and her colonial territories. Cuba, with Spain no longer able to meet the island's trading needs, again turned to the United States; Spain's monopoly policies were changed without reference to Madrid. On 23 February 1793 Captain-General Las Casas decreed that American trade would be permitted in clothing; in June the Madrid government acquiesced and even authorised concessions for trade in foodstuffs. But the limited commercial freedoms forced on a reluctant Spain by war were quickly rescinded at its end. On 22 July 1795 the Spanish government signed the Treaty of Basel with the French Republic; and then moved quickly to restore the Spanish monopoly over Cuban trade. On 12 June 1796 a proclamation was issued to prohibit commerce between Cuba and the United States – and then yet again a European war disrupted Spain's colonial trading policies.

In August 1796, through diplomacy following the Treaty of Basel, Spain became an ally of France – a move which on 6 October involved a Spanish declaration of war on Britain. This led the British navy to attack Spanish shipping, just as the French privateers had done earlier in the decade. Again Spain's commercial links with its colonies were interdicted, forcing the government to modify its monopolistic trading policies. A royal decree of 18 November 1797 opened the Cuban (and other Spanish colonial) ports to neutral trade on a temporary basis: the Cuban economy was given access to foodstuffs, lumber, naval supplies, manufactured goods and slaves in exchange for sugar, coffee, tobacco and other products.[5] The United States was again a principal beneficiary of the new economic policies.

Cuba was now obtaining a wide range of products from the United States (such as flour, wine, lumber, iron, clothes and furniture) in exchange for the typical Cuban products. American ships were also carrying Cuban exports to Europe, and then returning with cargoes destined for Cuba and elsewhere. Spain resented such burgeoning commerce but had no option beyond heavy taxation. This did little to discourage the flourishing trade; by 1798 the volume of American trade with Cuba surpassed the amount of Cuban–Spanish commerce. Then, the European war at an end, the *peninsular* merchants close to Madrid exerted pressure for an ending of the new commercial arrangements. On 18 April 1799 a fresh royal decree revoked the 1797 ruling, a move designed to curtail US commercial access to the ports of Spanish America. This further policy shift impacted on Cuban–US trade but not decisively: the Captain-General, facing local anger at the revocation decree, continued to allow US ships into Cuban ports – until the coming of the European peace in 1801 encouraged the Spanish government to insist on a total prohibition of American ships in Cuban ports. Captains who ignored the ban were jailed. Such harsh measures had the desired result: over a two-year period the volume of Cuban–US trade plunged (between 1801 and 1803 the number of ships arriving in Philadelphia from Cuba dropped from 98 to 20), and Spain began to reassert its commercial dominance over the island. And yet again a European war – renewed between Britain and France in 1803, with Spain later joining France – interrupted the fresh phase of commercial development.

This was the pattern of affairs. The *peninsular* merchants, often close to the Madrid government, saw the obvious virtues of a Spanish trading monopoly; whereas the Cuban creole planters and entrepreneurs perceived the advantage of free trade without imposed restrictions from Madrid. The tensions between the two camps, much influenced by the tempestuous oscillations of European politics, helped to fuel the Cuban independence movement; and encouraged at the same time the covetous opportunism of American entrepreneurs. There was moreover the growing US sensitivity to the strategic importance of Cuba, a consideration that was itself highly relevant to secure commerce. The US acquisition of Louisiana (1803) and Florida (1819) served to emphasise the strategic value of the Caribbean shipping lanes – a clear perception that served to intensify American interest in establishing some sort of permanent control over Cuba.

THE ANNEXATIONIST OPTION

The most obvious way to control a territory is to occupy it: to absorb it into a larger political entity or to run it as a colony, dominion or protectorate. With some such options the (military) occupation need not be permanent: for example, a protectorate may function as a supine proxy in the absence of foreign troops on its soil, though there is the assumption that external military pressure is available to guarantee obedience. There is a long history of American debate about how Cuba can be best subdued, controlled and exploited in the virtuous interests of the United States. John Adams, the second US president, was one of the first American leaders to express what would prove to be a long-running strategic policy: Cuba should remain a Spanish colony until such time as it could be grabbed by the United States. On 23 June 1783 Adams commented in a letter to Robert R. Livingston that Cuba was a natural extension of the American continent, and that therefore an American annexation of Cuba was indispensable for the continuation of the United States. In the same vein John Quincy Adams (1767–1848), not to be confused with the earlier John Adams (1735–1826), contemplated the Cuba Question when he was Secretary of State in the James Monroe (1758–1831) administration and when he succeeded him in 1825 to become the sixth US president. John Quincy Adams perceived that it was a virtual law of nature that Cuba was destined to fall one day into the warm embrace of the United States: '. . . if an apple, severed by the tempest from its native tree, cannot but fall to the ground, Cuba, forcibly disjoined from its unnatural connection with Spain and incapable of self-support, can gravitate only to the North American Union, which, by the same law of nature, cannot cast her off from its bosom'. And even if propitious laws of nature could not always be relied upon, there was always the divinely-contrived *Manifest Destiny* whereby the unique American link to an imagined deity would always guarantee the virtue of any American imperialism.

Thomas Jefferson (1743–1826), the slave-holding third US president, had firm views on the status of Cuba: he was, observed one authority, 'a constant spokesman for incorporation of Cuba into the Union'.[6] In November 1805 he declared that the prospect of war with Spain would not be allowed to deter the United States from seizing Florida: 'East and West Florida and successively the Island of Cuba . . . would be an easy conquest.' In 1808 General James Wilkinson was despatched to Cuba to hint to Captain-General Someruelos that his interests would be best served by allowing the United States to acquire Cuba. The Spanish authorities summarily rejected the proposal but this was far from the end of the matter. Jefferson never relinquished the idea of a US acquisition of the island, and repeatedly counselled his successor, President James Madison (1751–1836), as to how Cuba might be acquired. Madison, however, saw problems; not least that a conquest of Cuba might be difficult to sustain in the light of English ambitions. At the same time he was clearly prepared to countenance a future annexation: the US consul in Havana, William Shaler, was instructed to discover how the Cubans themselves would regard annexation. In fact the wealthy planters, reported Shaler, saw a close connection with the United States 'as necessary for their happiness and prosperity' (that is, they saw annexation as a means of preserving slavery).

The movement in Cuba for annexation (*anexionismo*) began around 1810 when spokesmen for the planters began talks with the US consul. At that time the United States was reluctant to give guarantees that British and Spanish interventions would be resisted. A revival of the *anexionismo* cause in 1821 again came to nothing. There would come a time, judged the United States, when the Cuban apple would land in the American lap; until then the main priority was to keep Cuba out of the hands of the Cubans. The annexationists received a boost in 1837 with the publication of a powerful essay* by the exile José Antonio Saco, criticising the Spanish administration of the island and declaring that if Cuba was forced 'to throw herself into foreign arms' she could not 'fall with more honour or glory than in those of the great North American Confederation', where she would find 'peace and consolation, strength and protection, justice and liberty'.[7] The early 1840s saw a rapidly developing annexationist movement: slave uprisings in Cuba had frightened the planters at a time when American agitation for incorporating the island into the Union was growing.

In Cuba the annexationist cause was promoted by the *Club de la Habana* (the Havana Club), a group that included writers, intellectuals and other professionals but which comprised largely the slave-holding planters; and by groups in Puerto Príncipe, Matanzas and Las Villas. Many of the rich Cuban families were now sending their sons for education in the United States, where they were impressed with the mercenary attitudes of American politicians and entrepreneurs. The Cubans would then return home to press for annexation – a development that led the Spanish authorities in 1849 to ban the education of Cuba's wealthy sons in the United States. At the same time there were mounting commercial pressures for annexation as American entrepreneurs penetrated the Cuban market. The Cuban planters raised loans in the United States, while much of the new machinery now being used on the plantations was supplied by

---

Paralelo entre la isla de Cuba y algunas colonias inglesas (Parallel between the Island of Cuba and some English colonies).

American factories; and already many of the plantations were American-owned. In 1844 gas lighting was installed in Havana by a New Orleans company; five years later the telegraph concessions were obtained by Americans; and now the first Cuban railroad, built by an American engineer using English funds, was encouraging economic development.[8] It was inevitable that such economic penetration should encourage the activists – in both Cuba and the United States – in the annexationist movement.

On the US side, President James Knox Polk (1795–1849) offered to buy Cuba from Spain for $100 million in 1848, but the offer was rejected. Six years later, President Franklin Pierce (1804–1869) raised the offer to $130 million, again without success. In the same year, meeting in Ostend, Belgium, the US ministers to France, Britain and Spain (respectively, John Y. Mason, J. Buchanan and P. Soulé) urged the US government to press its offer to Spain. This 'Ostend Manifesto', later disavowed by Secretary of State W. Marcy, warned that if Spain declined to sell, 'then, by every law, human and divine, we shall be justified in wresting it [Cuba] from Spain if we possess the power'. Again the Spanish government, keen to retain what was left of its American empire, refused to trade. But now the pattern was plain. The United States would buy Cuba if it could; if not, the option of military conquest would be given serious consideration. In the event, later US presidents – James Buchanan (administration 1857–1861), Ulysses S. Grant (1869–1877), and William McKinley (1897–1901) – tried to buy Cuba, but to no avail. McKinley made the final offer just prior to the first American invasion of the island (see below). At last the Cuba Question was addressed in military terms.

Spain's early rejections of America's purchase offers did little to erode the enthusiasm of the annexationists; on the contrary, buoyed by the sentiments of *Manifest Destiny*, they redoubled their efforts to achieve annexation in any way possible. Such efforts inevitably generated a countervailing reaction; according to the *New York Times* (22 October 1852), the Cuba Question had become 'the leading one of the time'. Judge J. C. Larue of Louisiana had no doubt that Providence 'had carved out a destiny' for the United States; and that this meant that 'Cuba, by Providence's decree, belongs to the United States and must be Americanised.' It was all part of the inexorable process whereby, according to the New Orleans *Creole*, the 'Hispano-Morescan race will quail and disappear before our victorious march. The inferior must yield to the superior . . .'; and whereby, according to the New Orleans *Delta,* the absorption of the Cuban people would be 'all due to the inevitable dominance of the American mind over an inferior race'.[9] At this time the American annexationists hoped to strengthen the slave system in both Cuba and the United States, and to bolster the South's political weight in the Union. Any foreign efforts (for example, by Britain) to force Spain into abolishing slavery in Cuba could be represented as a direct attack on the 'peculiar institutions' of the South; but slavery should be preserved under American, rather than Spanish, administration. In one (American) account the Spanish rule over Cuba was 'one of the veriest despotisms Christendom ever knew'. How much better for virtuous Americans to be in a position to run the Cuban slave economy.

The annexationist issue, an involved controversy in Cuba and the US, thrust many partisan advocates to the fore, not least the controversial Spaniard General Narciso López, who was variously dubbed a fighter for Cuban independence and, by others, a promoter of annexation.[10] In September 1851 a new conspiracy against Spain, the 'Order of the Lone Star', was organised by several former associates of López, including Francisco de Frías, López's brother-in-law. The conspiracy boasted a 'supreme council', and 'chapters' in many North American states; in mid-1852 a branch of the Order was uncovered in Cuba. The conspirators were now pushing for annexation by any means possible – which in turn led to an inevitable Spanish reaction. The Spanish authorities announced that the North American mail steamer, the *Crescent City*, would not be allowed to berth in Cuba because the ship's purser, William Smith, was one of the members of the Order. George Law, the president of the US Mail Steamship Company, was himself an annexationist and 'perhaps hoped that war between the US and Spain would swiftly follow', with the subsequent peace giving him a chance 'to extend passenger traffic to the island'.[11] Spain relented; the *Crescent City* and its purser were allowed to dock in Havana. Now it seemed that a war between Spain and the United States was a real possibility. At one indignant meeting in New Orleans, 'War! War! Give us War!' was the mob cry; while Senator Judah P. Benjamin declared, to tumultuous applause, that if Spain did not comply, then the United States had the right 'to appeal to the God of battle and annex Cuba'. There was talk of a 'crusade' that would be led by Law to expel Spain from Cuba; and in October 1852 the Order of the Lone Star announced that a brigade was being raised for war, and that the 'grand password' – 'Action! Action!! Action!!!' – had been declared.[12]

President Millard Phillmore then ordered the mails to be withheld from the *Crescent City* when the ship sailed for Havana with Smith on board; whereupon Law responded by sending the newer ship *Cherokee* to Havana with Smith on board but no mail. Phillmore protested that Law had no right to 'threaten war on his own account', and announced that he would not be protected if he persisted. Purser Smith then declared his innocence of writing any pro-annexationist literature and disseminating it in Cuba. Captain-General Valentín Canedo diplomatically accepted Smith's affidavit to this effect, and the crisis was defused: Law had not managed to provoke a Spanish–American war. Now the annexationists were obliged to try another tack. With the great Democratic Victory of 1852, Franklin Pierce, by no means unsympathetic to annexation, was president-elect: banners celebrating his victory proclaimed the need for the 'Acquisition of Cuba', urging that 'the Queen of the Antilles Be Added to Our Glorious Confederacy'. General John A. Quitman was selected by the annexationists to replace the 'martyred Lopez'.

On 18 August 1853 General Quitman, the governor of Mississippi, accepted an invitation from the *Junta Cubana* (the New York group of Cuban exiles) to head a new invasion of Cuba; he was promised $1 million, if successful. The aim was for Cuba, like Texas, to first proclaim itself independent and then to accept annexation to the United States. Slavery, one of Cuba's 'domestic institutions', would be preserved. Such plans were boosted when the Spanish government, in a remarkable departure from precedent, appointed the anti-slaver Marqués de la Pezuela as Captain-General. One of his first initiatives, after his arrival in Havana in December 1853, was to encourage a series of articles in the *Diario de la Marina* encouraging the observance of the treaties outlawing the slave trade. An important decree (23 December), shattering to the slave holders, stipulated that the *emancipados* should be freed, that slave traders would be fined and exiled, that black–white intermarriage should be encouraged, and that governors and lieutenant-governors aiding the slavers would be dismissed. Under the spur of this decree the wealthy Cuban planters rushed to support Quitman, then in New Orleans planning to invade Cuba in February 1854.

Again the US administration, now led by President Franklin Pierce, was prepared to discourage freelance attempts to annex Cuba – but only because the administration had schemes of its own. Thus Pierre Soulé, the US minister to Spain, conveyed in Madrid the sentiment of Secretary of State William L. Marcy that the US government expected that Cuba 'in one way or another' would 'release itself or be released from its present colonial subjection, whereupon the island would 'fall, necessarily, into the American continental system . . .'. One of Soulé's initiatives, in addition to fighting a duel with the French ambassador, was an attempt to convince the queen mother María Cristina that her Cuban interests – extending to 8700 acres over four plantations – would be best served if Cuba were sold to the United States. There is some evidence that she agreed the sale,[13] but the Spanish government was less accommodating. Soulé was making no progress with Spain; Quitman, his original plans delayed, was still scheming in March 1854; and the Pierce administration, noting the seizure of the US steamer *Black Warrior* and its cargo in Havana Bay, used the incident to foment war (said Pierce on 15 March to the House of Representatives: 'I shall not hesitate . . . to insure the observance of our just rights to obtain redress for injuries received and to vindicate the honour of our fiat' – soon afterwards *Black Warrior* was returned to its owners).

On 3 April Soulé received fresh instructions from Secretary of State Marcy: now he was to offer Spain $130 million for Cuba, though there was ambiguity as to what American policy would be adopted in the event of a Spanish refusal. If Spain declined the offer then Soulé was expected to seek 'the next most desirable object, which is to detach that island from Spanish domination and from all dependence on any European power' – an opaque formula that fell short of threatening war but at the same time failed to disavow the military option. By now, Quitman and his 50,000 supporters, still scheming in June, were bound over for $3000 not to violate the Neutrality Act. On 13 November, following the Democrats' loss of control of the US Congress, Marcy informed Soulé that if Spain were obdurate then talks should end, in which event the United States would not invade the island. Soulé, dismayed and also impatient with what he dubbed his 'languid impotence', resigned. The pressure for a solution to the Cuba Question had abated for a time. Even the fervent annexationist Lewis Cass, sensing the shifting mood, declared: 'We cannot get Cuba honestly at present. We have nothing now to do but to sit still.' The matter was on hold. The instructions to August Caesar Dodge, Soulé's successor, included the observation that the US president regarded 'the incorporation of Cuba into the American Union, essential to the welfare both of the United States and Cuba, as one of those inevitable events the occurrence of which is merely a question of time'. The Pierce administration had tried purchase offers and various forms of provocation: all had come to nought.

Similarly the procrastinatory Quitman enterprise had foundered, despite the urging by Senator Alexander Stephens, the future vice-president of the Confederacy, that Quitman act 'while England and France have their hands full in the East' (the Crimea); eventually a group led by Domingo Goicuría and José Elias Hernández broke with Quitman and launched a futile invasion of Cuba. By now the enlightened Captain-General Pezuela had been replaced by General Gutiérrez de la Concha. The annexationist tide had ebbed and the institution of Cuban slavery had a new lease of life.

In December 1857 President James Buchanan, a co-author of the controversial Ostend Manifesto, began the third presidential attempt to buy Cuba from Spain. He had proposed in his inauguration speech that Cuba be added to the Union; and now the Philadelphia banker Christopher Falcon was suggesting that he might use his connections with European bankers – Rothschilds, Barings of London, and Leon Roth of Paris (all of whom held Spanish bonds) to press for annexation. It was argued that a sale of Cuba would enable Spain to pay its interest and to reduce its principal. Falcon, authorised to proceed, found the bankers helpful but the Spanish politicians reticent. Buchanan agreed that the Spaniards should be bribed into acquiescence. William Preston, an ex-congressman for Kentucky, was despatched to Madrid; and duly reported back that the sale of Cuba could be arranged by means of $30 million-worth of bribes. In the event nothing came of this plan: the Republicans were sceptical, and soon the United States was sliding into the Civil War. The South had hoped that annexation would preserve slavery, but the historic domestic conflagration removed that option once and for all.

The dream of *anexionismo*, long favoured by the motley assortment of imperialists and slave holders, had seemingly collapsed for good, but it was destined for resurrection: Cuba was too close to the United States, too tempting, and already too enmeshed in American economic enterprise to be ignored. The northern colossus observed the Cuban Ten Years' War and the ensuing rebellious chronology with keen interest. Already the Cuban turmoil was threatening the security of US investments in the island. Spain had long resisted American efforts to buy Cuba: speeches in the *Cortes* that any such sale would be an insult to Spanish honour had been greeted with thunderous applause. But the Cubans were set to accomplish what successive US governments and assorted American brigands had failed to do: to break the hold of Spanish colonialism over the island. Then, at long last, the imperial United States would have its chance.

Many Cuban patriots, not least José Martí, were well aware of what the US wanted to accomplish. In his letter (19 February 1888) to Manuel Mercado, Martí deplored the general 'onslaught' being waged by public and private interests in the United States on the nations of Latin America. Here he notes the declaration, 'already almost official', that yet again the US 'is attempting to propose to Spain the purchase of Cuba'. Of this prospect, Martí commented in despair: 'I do not know if that were to happen, how I should stay alive.' A year later, in a letter (15 February 1889) to his Uruguayan friend Enrique Estrazulas, Martí declared: 'I am beside myself, because what I have been fearing for years and announcing is bearing down, and that is the United States' policy of conquest . . .'. Martí's fears were well founded.

American opinion was mixed. For example, the Philadelphia *Manufacturer* (16 March 1889) considered the arguments for annexation, and then rejected them. Yes, Cuba was strategically placed, and had great commercial potential; but the island's population was lazy and barbaric, 'immoral pigmies', and so Cuba was not fit to become an equal state of the Union. The New York *Evening Post* (21 March) similarly decided that the conversion of a million Cuban blacks into US citizens would compound the negro problem in the United States. Annexation would do more harm than good, though the island might be converted into an associate territory or dependency (as was to happen with Puerto Rico after the US intervention in 1898).[14] But such reservations carried little weight with successive US administrations. As the Cuban War of Liberation escalated towards the end of the nineteenth century, the government of President William McKinley was yet again considering the acquisition of Cuba. The US minister in Madrid again discussed the possibility of a sale; and on 17 March 1898, just prior to the first US invasion of Cuba, wrote to the Secretary of State that 'if we have war we must finally occupy and ultimately own the island'. A purchase would be the preferred option: 'If today we could purchase at reasonable price we should avoid the horrors and expense of war.'[15] In subsequent debates in Congress it was pointed out that *'for three-quarters of a century this Government has persistently asserted its right to control the ultimate destiny of Cuba'* (my italics).[16]

The situation had moved to some sort of climax. At last the Cuban patriots had broken the power of Spanish colonialism in the island; at last the centuries-long struggle for *Cuba Libre* seemed near to victory. But the northern monster, in whose entrails José Martí had developed his bitter wisdom, was not prepared to tolerate an independent Cuba. The United States had on occasions helped Spain to maintain its hegemony over the island. The collapse of the Spanish presence was imminent. After all the proposed purchases, the attempts at bribery, the provocations and talk of war – spread over more than a century – it was now necessary for the United States to invade Cuba. The reason, at root, was a simple one: capitalism, ever intent on sweeping all peoples into its insatiable maw, had its own imperative.

THE CAPITALIST IMPERATIVE

American capitalism, notoriously indifferent to any ethical pressures, has always been prepared to prosecute any effective means for the maximisation of profits. It is not surprising to find that the earliest American trade with Cuba was via the congenial mechanism of piracy, a practice which was to sire many of today's wealthy American families. Thus the privateer George Cabot of Boston subsequently became a wealthy US senator; the privateer Israel Thorndike, in 1832 at the age of 75, left a fortune 'the greatest that has ever been left in New England' (the legacies to the members of his family amounted to some $1,800,000); the privateer Joseph Peabody came to own eighty-three ships that traded around the world; and Asa Clapp, who at his death in 1848 aged 85 was the richest man in Maine, began his entrepreneurial career as a privateer and later commanded a shipping business and various banking interests.[17] Such individuals (the list could easily be extended) were well prepared to attack merchant vessels, to plunder and kill, in the furtherance of mercenary interest. They were also prepared to smuggle – foodstuffs, raw materials, weapons, slaves – in defiance of prevailing law. Any relaxations in trading law were quickly exploited, such that – in the case of US trade with Cuba – the American merchants had a growing interest in Spain's periodic inability to police its trading routes to the American empire. The activities of the American pirates and smugglers first saw a rapid expansion between 1778 and 1783 when Spain had an interest in supporting the American war for independence.[18] In the 1890s decrees were enacted to open Cuban ports to neutral ships carrying various goods, leading to a further expansion in trade. At this time a growing number of Americans began to settle in Cuba: the laws against foreigners meant that the presence of such settlers could not be officially acknowledged, with the welcome consequence that they avoided taxation.[19] By whatever mechanisms, the American commercial involvement with Cuba developed progressively from the mid-1700s to the middle of the twentieth century.

It was Americans – project organisers, share jobbers, engineers and overseers – who built the Havana-to-Guines railway, the first in Cuba, in 1837 using an English loan. American planters introduced much of the steam-engine machinery in such regions as Matanzas and Cardenas. The growing American commerce in the island was sufficiently alarming to the Spanish authorities to provoke a Spanish decree (1834) imposing duties against American flour; but despite this and other discriminatory enactments few observers doubted the gradual Americanisation of the burgeoning Cuban economy.[20] By the middle of the nineteenth century the United States accounted for about a third of the island's trade, a proportion that exceeded Cuban commerce with Spain: the US was exporting around $8 million-worth of goods to the island each year, and receiving in return some $12 million-worth. By now, more than half the merchant ships entering Cuban ports carried the American flag. At a time when sugar products represented more than three-quarters of Cuba's total exports, the American consumption of sugar increased fourfold. Annexationists were happy to contemplate some future time when – with Cuba joining sugar-producing Louisiana in the expanding American empire – the United States would control the world's supply of sugar. By the 1880s six regular shipping lines (the Ward, Munson and Plant lines the best known) were providing merchant and passenger links between Cuba and the United States.[21] Sugar was at the heart of this rapidly expanding trade.

At the same time the American traders were keen, for obvious commercial reasons, to maintain their access to non-Cuban sources of sugar products. European beets were available, and in 1876 duty-free sugar from Hawaii entered the American market. American producers, under prodding from the Department of Agriculture, began experimenting with domestic sugar production – leading President Rutherford Birchard Hayes (1822–1893) to predict, wrongly, that the United States would no longer need to import foreign sugar. Fortunately for Cuba, home-grown US sorghum failed to affect sugar imports to the United States. American investors continued to pump money into sugar refining processes, most of them relying on Cuban sugar exports. In 1888 nineteen US refineries were combined under the leadership of Henry O. Havemeyer to become the mighty American Sugar Refining Company (the so-called 'Sugar Trust'). This company, supplying from 70 to 90 per cent of the refined sugar sold in the United States, represented the vast bulk of the American market for Cuban sugar.

Under pressure from mounting demand, and at a time when the collapse of the slave system and oppressive fiscal policies had dramatically increased labour costs and tax burdens, the Cuba sugar industry experienced an industrial revolution. Newly-available technologies (for example, hydraulic presses from the Scottish manufacturers Stewart and Macdonald) were introduced, while sugar production evolved under the parallel '*central*' (large grinding centre) and '*colono*' (decentralisation of management) systems.[22] The *colono* system, devised in part as a response to the emancipation of the slaves, involved contracting the *colono* to plant cane and to deliver the product to the mill-owner (*hacendado*). The *central* mills, supplied by the *colono* producers, dealt with *colonos* forced to sell quickly to satisfy creditors and labourers. Such developments served to secure the Cuban sugar industry, but inevitably had a negative social impact: the population depended increasingly on the fortunes of the sugar industry, the Cuban market was 'locked in' to the demands of the US Sugar Trust, and American capital came to dominate sugar production.

American merchants, bankers, industrialists and shipowners now dominated key sectors of the Cuban economy. Spanish and other foreign companies continued useful levels of trade with the island, but by now Cuba had been drawn inexorably into the dominant orbit of American commerce. The problems experienced by the Spanish in maintaining slavery and, after its abolition, in resourcing the moribund colonial system often served American interests. After the Ten Years' War (1868–1878) the dislocated economy presented American entrepreneurs with fresh opportunities: merchants homed in on the sugar plantations, often acquiring dominant control; and other properties and real estate were offered to Americans at knock-down prices. Vultures from the northern colossus hovered over a desperate people struggling for independence.

A typical case was that of the Sarria family, unable as a Cuban sugar producer to repay debts to American investors at the end of the Ten Years' War. The consequence was that the Soledad estate was taken over by E. Atkins and Company of Boston who, through the Torriente Brothers firm in Cienfuegos, invested in Cuban planters. By 1893 the expanded Soledad plantation comprised 12,000 acres (5000 planted with cane) with 23 miles of private railway track.[23] Another substantial venture was launched by Hugh Kelly, a West Indian trader, and Franklin Farrell, an iron industrialist from Connecticut; they began the Santa Teresa *central* facility near Manzanillo, prior to the establishment of other American *centrales* after 1891 when a treaty with Spain allowed Cuban sugar free entry into the United States. Similarly an organisation of New York sugar traders, principally the Rionda family, established the Tuinucua Cane Sugar Company in 1893 for processing cane near Sancti Spiritus. The various enterprises often consolidated links between each other where mutual interests could be served. The Atkins refinery, for example, was one of the operations amalgamated into the Sugar Trust.[24]

American and other foreign groups invested also in non-sugar sectors of the Cuban economy. Thus for much of the nineteenth century the *El Cobre* copper mine near Santiago was owned by an English company. In 1883 the Juragua Iron Company, controlled by the Pennsylvania Steel Company of Steelton and the Bethlehem Iron Works of Bethlehem, Pennsylvania, opened mines of chrome iron ore in the same region; just as in 1889 a manganese and nickel iron ore mine near Daiquiri was purchased by American interests (one authority notes the irony that this mine supplied the material for the armour plate used by the US forces that later landed at Daiquiri).[25] Another Pennsylvania firm, the Ponupo Manganese Company, was operating near Santiago. This meant that Cuba was being used to source the armour used by the American armed forces in their subsequent invasions of Cuba and other states in the region.

The US Secretary of State Richard Olney estimated in his annual report (7 December 1896) that American investments in Cuba totalled around $45 million ($12 million in Cienfuegos, $9 million in Matanzas, $9,229,000 in Sagua, and $15 million in the Santiago mines). There were in addition various tobacco and other interests worth around $5 million. Other foreign states continued to maintain substantial Cuban holdings: the British had invested heavily in Cuban railways; and the Spanish, despite the weakening colonial grip, still ran many other commercial operations. Tensions between Spain and the United States affected tariff policies, which in turn impacted on the level of trade.

The Foster–Canovas trade agreement (1891), for which the creole producers had long worked, stipulated that Cuban products would receive customs benefits in exchange for Spanish tariff concessions for American exports. This agreement now stimulated a rapid expansion in sugar production and beyond. From 1890 to 1893 Cuban exports to the United States increased from $54 million to $79 million, with exports to the US twelve times larger than exports to Spain; and by 1894 the US was taking almost 90 per cent of all Cuba's exports.[26] Cuba's mounting economic dependence on American capital and markets was transparent – which meant that any shift in US trade policy could have dire consequences for Cuban producers. Thus in 1894 the United States rescinded its tariff policy on Cuban exports, so abandoning the reciprocal US–Spain agreement. Spain responded by denying duty concessions to American imports, whereupon in mid-1894 the island was surrounded by a firm protectionist wall. Cuba's expanding trade with the United States was thrown into reverse: in particular, sugar exports plummeted – from $64 million (1893) to $13 million (1896). The Cuban producers decided to blame Spanish tariff policy. In November 1894 the influential Círculo de Hacendados y Agricultores convened to petition the Ministry of Colonies to rescind the anti-American duties, and then the planter élite took to the streets for a peaceful protest. The economic crisis in Cuba, affecting all social strata, fuelled civil unrest and encouraged the activists preparing for what many observers thought would be the final war of independence. Throughout the period foreign entrepreneurs, as always, watched for the main chance.

In 1896 President Stephen Grover Cleveland (1837–1908) summarised the scale of the US economic interest in Cuba: 'It is reasonably estimated that at least from $30,000,000 to $50,000,000 of American capital are invested in the plantations and in railroad, mining, and other business enterprises. . . . The volume of trade between the United States and Cuba, which in 1889 amounted to about $64,000,000, rose in 1893 to about $103,000,000.' The scale of the American interest meant that any threat, such as that posed by the Cuban rebels, was a grave matter – not least because, as the American and European racists feared, a successful insurrection might lead to the establishment of another black republic such as Haiti. Thus in 1896 the imperialist Winston Churchill wrote in *The Saturday Review* that it would be better for Spain to keep control of Cuba, even though such an outcome went against the wish of the Cuban people: 'A grave danger presents itself. Two-fifths of the insurgents in the field are negroes. These men . . . would, in the event of success, demand a predominant share in the government of the country . . . the result being, after years of fighting, another black republic.' What, to the racist mind, could be worse? Particularly if there were also a threat to capital!

It now seemed increasingly likely, in 1898, that the United States would go to war to protect the American commercial interest (see below). In New York the *Commercial Advertiser* (10 March), in the spirit of the mounting fervour, urged the United States to invade Cuba for 'humanity and love of freedom' but *'above all'* (my italics) so that 'the commerce and industry of every part of the world shall have full freedom of development . . .' . In the same vein, the *Journal of Commerce* commented that the Teller amendment, the congressional pledge that the United States would not invade Cuba, 'must be interpreted in a sense somewhat different from that which its author intended it to bear'; in short, it was time to contemplate invasion. The Chamber of Commerce in Pittsburgh urged war, and the *Chattanooga Tradesman* reported happily that the possibility of an invasion of Cuba had 'decidedly stimulated the iron trade'; moreover, 'actual war would very decidedly enlarge the business of transportation'. Reports from Washington noted that a 'belligerent spirit' was evident in the Navy Department, stimulatd 'by the contractors for projectiles, ordnance, ammunition and other supplies, who have thronged the department since the destruction of the Maine'[27] (see below). The banker Russell Sage remarked that if war were to come, 'there is no question as to where the rich men stand'. The rich men, it may be judged, were interested above all in becoming richer: a survey revealed that John Jacob Astor, William Rockefeller, and Thomas Fortune Ryan were 'feeling militant' (though presumably not sufficiently militant to hump their personal army packs through the disease-ridden Cuban tropics). The banker John Pierpont Morgan, with investment in military manufacture, was reliably reported as believing that further talk with Spain would be a waste of time. On 21 March 1898 Henry Cabot Lodge wrote to President William McKinley, saying that 'bankers, businessmen, editors, clergymen and others' wanted the Cuban question solved; in the same spirit, an advisor to McKinley noted by telegram (25 March) that the 'big corporations' would all 'welcome' war 'as relief to suspense'.[28]

In the event the American invasion of Cuba in 1898 'gave the American capitalists what they wanted'.[29] The newly 'independent' Cuba, despite its effective victory over Spain, was denied a seat at the US–Spain peace talks in Paris; special tariff reductions were imposed on Cuba to aid American business; Cuba became in essence a US protectorate, with American forces granted the 'right' to invade again when they chose; and the United States achieved a permanent 'legal' naval base (Guantánamo) on the island. The scene was set for further military tyrannies in Cuba, but now charged with the task of protecting American capital. It was no accident that the bloody dictator General Gerardo Machado Morales, who terrorised Cuba from 1925 to 1933, was a local executive of the John Pierpont Morgan financial empire. In the early part of the twentieth century, American capital flowed into Cuba: the process well under way during the last decades of Spanish colonialism now accelerated apace. By 1905 American citizens owned a quarter of all Cuban land; by 1922 American mills were processing half of all Cuban sugar; and by 1926 a half of all Cuban sugar was actually owned by seven US companies. Now the great American capitalist families and their proxies had come to own much of Cuba (for example, the Rockefellers had substantial holdings in the Cuba Company and the Cuban-Dominican Sugar Corporation). What José Martí had dreaded had come to pass. It is useful to profile the prelude to war, and the ensuing events, that shaped this historical period.

THE PRELUDE TO WAR

The decades-long prelude to a US war in Cuba must be regarded in the context of mounting American arrogance in the region. It was easy (and still is) to see the Caribbean as the 'American Mediterranean',[30] a geographical circumstance that has long afflicted (and continues to afflict) the smaller states in that part of the world. Pressure for an imperial attack on Cuba was well evident in the early 1800s, and it grew through the century. Successive US administrations gradually assumed 'rights' and 'entitlements' in the region that only naked military power could sanctify. This was the time of the *Monroe Doctrine* and *Manifest Destiny*, those symbiotic constructs designed to license American dominance and imperial virtue.

On 2 December 1823 President James Monroe (1758–1831), in his annual address to Congress, outlined the three central points that would come to shape American foreign policy for the rest of the nineteenth century and after:

> the American continents, by the free and independent condition which they have assumed and maintain, are henceforth not to be considered as subjects for future colonisation by any European powers;

> we should consider any attempt [by the nations of Europe] to extend their system to any portion of this hemisphere as dangerous to our peace and safety;

> in the wars of the European powers in matters relating to themselves we have never taken part, nor does it comport with our policy to do so.

The principles, not called the *Monroe Doctrine* until 1853, were not officially invoked until 1895 (in connection with the Venezuela Boundary Dispute); but they had already helped to shape the climate of the times. Put succinctly, the Monroe principles suggested that if there were to be imperialism in the region it would not be European. That it would be American was implied by the notion of *Manifest Destiny*, already encountered in the present book. Americans began using the concept of Manifest Destiny in the 1840s as a cloak for US imperial expansion. The Americans – they were not the first – found it congenial to wrap their aggressions in celestial garb: who would dare to gainsay the wishes of the Almighty? This was the role of *Manifest Destiny*, conceived in part to grant divine permission for imperial expansion.

It was in 1845 that the New York editor John L. O'Sullivan wrote that it was 'the fulfillment of our manifest destiny to overspread the continent allotted by Providence for the free development of our yearly expanding millions'. At that time it was primarily Texas that was in O'Sullivan's mind, but Americans were happy to extend the notion to wider domains: it came to be used as a general justification for US imperial expansion, and more specifically in connection with the Mexican War (1846–48) and the Alaska Purchase (1867). In particular, for our purposes, the doctrine of *Manifest Destiny* served as one of several apologist justifications for the US invasion of Cuba in 1898. It is useful also to note that this was the period of the great capitalist 'robber barons', that hallowed free-enterprise epoch when American entrepreneurs relied upon crime and corruption in the amassing of fortunes to be left to their posterity,[31] an important shaping factor on the modern world. In short, much of nineteenth-century American culture was imperialistically inclined and commercially rapacious. In such a climate the frequent calls for a military solution to the Cuba Question would not be ignored for ever.

For some decades after Monroe's famous 1823 declaration the Americans were preoccupied with expanding their empire to the west coast and absorbing millions of European immigrants. In the 1860s the turmoil of the Civil War temporarily diverted American attention from the option of imperial expansion overseas; with the expansion of the Union, at the expense of the Confederacy, it again became practical to consider adventures in foreign lands. In particular, Cuba was in turmoil, an intractable problem for the Spanish authorities: it seemed clear that before long an American 'solution' would be found. By the 1890s, with a new Cuban rebellion imminent, American nationalism was swollen with self-righteous arrogance. The Europeans were complaining about aggressive American commercial enterprise, while the United States celebrated its growing economic strength. The 1890s saw the creation in the US of countless patriotic societies (such as the Sons of the American Revolution and the Daughters of the American Revolution), mounting racism (as evidenced by the 'Whitecap' movement and the swelling Ku-Klux Klan), and the newly-sired cult of the national flag. Speakers at public functions competed to laud the power and virtue of the United States. Thus said one speaker at a veterans' convention in 1896: 'The place of this nation is at the head of the column of civilisation. . . . Our idea has always been and is now to point to other nations the way to come up higher.' In the same spirit, Admiral Alfred T. Mahan, author of the seminal work *The Influence of Sea Power Upon History* (1890), urged that America acquire the navies, colonies and markets that would enable it to compete with the other imperialist powers of the time. In 1893 Mahan declared: 'Whether they will or no, Americans must now begin to look outward' – a view shared by such political figures as Theodore Roosevelt and Senator Henry Cabot Lodge and such influential editors as Walter Hines Page and Albert Shaw.[32]

The mounting expansionist interest in America was already spreading alarm – not only among fighters for independence in small states (such as Cuba), but also among the other imperial powers. Spain had long resented American imperial ambitions in the Caribbean and elsewhere; and in 1872 Benjamin Disraeli, British Prime Minister (1868, 1874–1880), chose to observe that the New World was 'throwing lengthening shades over the Atlantic' and creating 'vast and novel elements in the distribution of power'. It had been noticed that by the end of the Reconstruction period America had begun to evince a marked interest in the Pacific islands and, 'even before the Civil War, her interest in such Caribbean territories as Cuba had been intense'.[33] While Britain 'dreaded the rise of a great

American maritime empire based on the Caribbean',[34] the United States itself was concerned that Britain might want to grab territory in the Spanish Americas – a further spur to American expansion. But, by the time of the fresh Cuban rebellion of 1895, the British attitude – perhaps in recognition of *realpolitik* inevitabilities – had mellowed. In October 1897 Lord Robert Salisbury, then British Prime Minister and keen to prosecute his own imperialist agenda (not least the 1899–1902 Boer War in South Africa), informed US Secretary of State John Hay that British interests in Cuba were purely commercial; and that moreover Britain would welcome any policy which might restore peace in the island. On 9 February the Cuban insurrectionists published an indiscreet private letter written by de Lôme, the Spanish Minister in Washington, asserting that Britain was encouraging a Spanish–American war in order to block US economic expansion. Perhaps surprisingly, this exposé helped to cement Anglo-American relations; the New York *Tribune* commenting that 'English comments on the Spanish Minister's breach of international etiquette have been inspired by a sense of justice and a spirit of good-will toward the United States.' And then, when an American invasion of Cuba seemed unavoidable, and despite an appeal from the Spanish Queen-Regent to Queen Victoria, Lord Salisbury made it plain that the British government would not intervene in the cause of peace.[35] Subsequently Britain declared its satisfaction with the post-war Spanish–American peace treaty (signed on 10 December 1898). The concerns of the Cuban patriots, excluded from the peace negotiations, were not mentioned.

José Martí had anticipated the course of events. In the United States he had become increasingly horrified by the features of the developing capitalist culture. Via the 'cult of wealth', big business had succeeded in corrupting 'the courts, the legislatures, the church and the press' to create 'the most shameful of oligarchies'. In a letter to the New York *Evening Post* (25 March 1889), Martí deplored 'the evil conditions that, like worms in the heart, have begun in this mighty republic their work of destruction'; and he denounced the 'excessive individualism' and the 'reverence for wealth' which could not be expected to create a 'nation of liberty, where no opinion is to be based on greed, and no triumph or acquisition reached against charity and justice'. Above all, from Martí's perspective, the United States was about to launch an imperialist offensive to absorb Latin America; and this campaign would begin by engulfing Cuba.

The United States had remained broadly neutral during the Ten Years' War; but with the fresh outbreak of Cuban revolt in 1895 the fragile state of neutrality would soon be at an end. The Cleveland administration had been prepared to recognise the condition of Cuban insurgency, but had not recognised the Cuban rebels as *de jure* belligerents; but in 1896 (by a vote of 64 to 6 in the Senate; 246 to 27 in the House of Representatives) the Congress acknowledged that Cuba was in a state of war and offered mediation. Cleveland ignored the vote, and in 1897 McKinley inherited the problem. It was soon made clear that he was well prepared to build on Cleveland's view, as revealed in his last annual message to Congress, to the effect that if Spanish colonialism had collapsed in Cuba then 'a situation will be presented in which our obligations to the sovereignty of Spain will be superseded by higher obligations which we can hardly hesitate to recognise and discharge'.[36] In short, the time would soon be ripe for an American conquest.

On 24 December 1897 the US Under-Secretary of War, J. C. Breckenridge, sent written instructions to Lieutenant-General Nelson A. Miles, the Commander of the US Army, regarding government policy towards the Hawaiian islands, Puerto Rico and Cuba. In this document there is reference to 'the upcoming campaign in the Antilles with certain observations on the political mission that will fall to you as general in charge of our troops'. After discussion of what were obviously projected annexations, Breckenridge declared, of Cuba:

> The island of Cuba, a larger territory, has a greater population density than Puerto Rico, although it is unevenly distributed. . . . The inhabitants are generally indolent and apathetic. As for their learning, they range from the most refined to the most vulgar and abject. Its people are indifferent to religion, and the majority are therefore immoral. . . . Since they only possess a vague notion of what is right and wrong, the people tend to seek pleasure not through work, but through violence. As a logical consequence of this lack of morality, there is a great disregard for life.

It would of course be 'sheer madness' to annex such a dissolute and depraved people into the virtuous United States – until appropriate steps had been taken: 'we must clean up the country, even if this means using the methods Divine Providence used on the cities of Sodom and Gomorrah. We must destroy everything within our cannon's range of fire. We must impose a harsh blockade so that hunger and its constant companion, disease, undermine the peaceful population and decimate the Cuban army.' Then Breckenridge commented on matters of military strategy, before noting that 'there will be a phase of indeterminate duration, of partial pacification in which we will continue to occupy the country militarily, using our bayonets to assist the independent government . . .'. But such 'assistance' was conceived as simply a means to the objective of annexation:

> To sum up, our policy must always be to support the weaker against the stronger, until we have obtained the extermination of them both, in order to annex the Pearl of the Antilles.

Breckenridge anticipated that the campaign would begin in October 1898. At last Cuba would feel the benefits of what Cleveland had depicted as America's 'higher obligations', the Christian offspring of *Manifest Destiny*.

There is a sense, albeit the trivial one often voiced with regard to military conflicts, in which the American invasion of Cuba could have been avoided. Even after the sinking of the *Maine* (see below), the US Secretary of the Navy could state in the *Boston Journal* (15 April 1898) that President McKinley had 'succeeded in obtaining from Spain a concession upon every ground which he has asked'.[37] Every American prisoner had been released; 'Butcher' Weyler and de Lôme had been recalled; an armistice ordered; and new policies introduced. Only the question of independence for Cuba remained unaddressed – and that of course was the most vital matter of all. By now the McKinley administration was intent on supplanting Spanish control over the island: Cuban 'independence' was no more, in contemporary American thinking, than a fig-leaf for an expanded US hegemony.

In the United States the war propaganda mounted, though the American press was mixed in its attitude to what seemed to be the imminent US invasion of the island. The press baron William Randolph Hearst talked about 'furnishing the war', providing his cartoonist, Frederic Remington, supplied the pictures; Hearst later admitted that he backed the war because it would improve his papers' circulation.[38] Then, in the great spirit of American black propaganda, the Hearst *Journal* (12 February 1897), under a vast headline *Does Our Flag Protect Women?*, carried a story of how three Cuban women had been strip-searched by Spanish policemen on the US ship *Olivette*; Remington provided a picture of a demure and naked girl surrounded by men. The picture provoked congressional resolutions in both houses, and the war-mongers were much encouraged; the girls later denied in Joseph Pulitzer's *World* that they had been searched by men. The propaganda had served its purpose and the war fever mounted. When Hearst ran another story that a US citizen might have been beaten to death in a Havana gaol, McKinley's new Secretary of State, the ageing Senator John Sherman, was quoted as saying (though he later denied it): 'If the facts are true ; . . and American citizens are being murdered in Cuba in cold blood, the only way to put an end to the atrocities is to declare war on Spain.' The accompanying *Journal* editorial (22 February 1897) opined that war 'is a dreadful thing but there are things more dreadful even than war and one of them is dishonour'. Hearst went so far as to fund yachts loaded with cargoes of medicine, ammunition and reporters, waiting for a chance to run to Cuba.[39]

In 1897 the pro-war newspapers (primarily those of Hearst and Pulitzer) had a circulation of around 1,600,000; whereas the anti-war papers (*Herald, Tribune, Post* and *Times*) reached around 225,000. The Cuban Junta had friends in Washington and the press, but by now the national mood was much in favour of a US war of intervention. McKinley himself increasingly favoured the war option, partly to free America from 'European domination' but also because of *'the benefit done to our people by giving them something to think of which isn't material gain and especially the benefit done our military forces by trying both the army and the navy in actual practice'.*[40] And Theodore Roosevelt, then McKinley's Secretary of the Navy, was prepared to urge war with an enthusiasm that one authority considered to reveal a state of mind 'bordering on the pathological'.[41] Thus on 2 June 1897 he gave a speech at the opening of the Naval War College, Newport, Rhode Island. Here he remarked that a 'really great people . . . would face all the disasters of war rather than purchase that base prosperity which is bought at the price of national honour'; 'Cowardice in a race' was 'the unpardonable sin', with 'tame submission to foreign aggression of any kind . . . a mean and unworthy thing'. Roosevelt had no doubt where America stood: 'We feel that no national life is worth having if the nation is not willing . . . to stake everything on the supreme arbitrament of war, and to pour out its blood, its treasure and tears like water rather than submit to the loss of honour and renown.'[42] Many prominent Americans shared such sentiments. Thus Senator Thurston of Nebraska was pleased to declare where he stood:

War with Spain would increase the business and the earnings of every American railroad, it would increase the output of every American factory, it would stimulate every branch of industry and domestic commerce, it would greatly increase the demand for American labour, and in the end every certificate that represented a share in an American business enterprise would be worth more money than it is today.

And there was more to war than mere commercial advantage. Senator Money of Mississippi reckoned that 'after one generation of the profoundest peace' it was time for a war to improve the condition of America: 'War brings out . . . all the best traits of character . . . devotion, self-abnegation, courage.' Congressman Peters of Kansas agreed that 'a war would be a blessing to the world'; while Senator Harris of Kansas applauded the just war that 'promotes and preserves all that is highest and best in national life'.[43]

At the same time there was much business opinion opposed to war. The *Commercial and Financial Chronicle* (2 April 1898) represented much Wall Street opinion when it declared that the proposition for war was 'a stain on our country's good name'; just as many of the businessmen with interests in Cuba showed little enthusiasm for military involvement: the powerful Sugar Trust, for example, was happy to treat with any stable Cuban regime. But public opinion, well in accord with various powerful business sectors, had become sufficiently agitated – not least by the fulminations of the pro-war press – to make war inevitable. One of the main events that served to shape American public opinion was the sinking of the *Maine*, a dramatic event of great use to the pro-war advocates.

REMEMBER THE *MAINE*!

In December 1897 various rumours began to emerge from Havana: for example, that Spanish Army officers were attacking anti-Spanish newspapers, and that 'an extensive and dangerous' anti-American conspiracy was being hatched. In consequence General Fitzhugh Lee, the US Consul in Havana, suggested that a strong American naval force be concentrated off Florida Keys ready to sail to Cuba 'at short notice'. His earlier suggestion to this effect had been rejected, but now the American government was increasingly sensitive to the developing course of events. The *Cincinnati* and a number of other South Atlantic cruisers were ordered into equatorial waters, while a small force was stationed at Lisbon to monitor Spanish naval activity. At the same time the North Atlantic Squadron joined the *Maine* at Key West and proceeded to take on coal. Reports of riots in Havana – despite Lee's claims that all was quiet – encouraged McKinley in the view that action should be taken to protect American lives and property.

The *Journal* (13 January 1898), under the headline 'NEXT DOOR TO WAR WITH SPAIN', reported US citizens taking refuge with the Consul; the *World* shrieked that 'THE RIOTS IN HAVANA MEAN REVOLUTION'; and the *Sun* stoked the fire by reporting continuing riots in the Cuban capital. All the reports were untrue.[44] But now, with mounting war fever at home, McKinley decided that some action had to be taken. On 24 January Judge Day of the State Department asked the Spanish minister, Enrique Depuy de Lôme, whether the *Maine* could be sent to Havana 'purely as a mark of friendship'. The minister, sensitive to the demands of diplomatic etiquette, quickly agreed to the request. McKinley, deciding to despatch the *Maine* on its questionable 'friendly visit', was responding to public opinion, impressed with the idea of sending a US battleship to Havana. Not all American observers thought this a prudent policy: the Democrat Senator Mark Hanna commented that sending the *Maine* to Havana 'is like waving a match in an oil well for fun'. Fitzhugh Lee himself, well aware of how passions had been inflamed by a mendacious press, urged delay. Too late; the *Maine* had sailed.

On 25 January 1898 the *Maine* arrived in Havana harbour. Spanish officials received the vessel with polite but chilly courtesy; Captain Charles D. Sigsbee, wanting to encourage accord, denied his crew shore leave; and Lee was pleased to cable the message, 'Peace and quiet reign'. Then an event occurred that was well designed to shatter the fragile peace. Some weeks earlier, Minister de Lôme had commented in an (undelivered) letter to a Spanish friend that McKinley was 'weak and a bidder for the admiration of the crowd, besides being a would-be politician [*politicastro*] who tries to leave the door open behind himself while keeping on good terms with the jingoes of his party'. The New York press knew how to react to this new Spanish slur on American dignity. The *Journal* (9 February), under the headline 'WORST INSULT TO THE UNITED STATES IN ITS HISTORY', published de Lôme's letter; and demanded 'action immediate and decisive'. Madrid hurriedly recalled de Lôme, and it seemed that the new crisis had passed. However, there was worse to come.

The *Maine*, still on its supposed 'peace mission', continued to ride at anchor in Havana harbour. Many observers had expressed doubts about the wisdom of the visit; Mrs Richard Wainwright, the wife of the cruiser's executive officer, had agreed with Senator Hanna in declaring that 'You might as well send a lighted candle on a visit to an open cask of gunpowder.' But with the *Maine* still in Havana, and seemingly untroubled, the anxieties had abated. Then, on 15 February 1898, the ship exploded in harbour – so fulfilling the mysterious prediction of Henry Cabot Lodge only a fortnight before: '*There may be an explosion any day in Cuba which would settle many things.*'[45] Captain Sigsbee immediately sent a telegram to Secretary of State Long in Washington: 'MAINE BLOWN UP IN HAVANA HARBOR AT NINE-FORTY TONIGHT AND DESTROYED . . . MANY WOUNDED . . . DOUBTLESS MORE KILLED OR DROWNED . . . NO ONE HAS

CLOTHING OTHER THAN THAT UPON HIM . . . PUBLIC OPINION SHOULD BE
SUSPENDED UNTIL FURTHER REPORT.' Some 254 men had been killed
instantly, with eight more so badly burned and injured that they later died
in hospitals ashore, bringing the death toll to 262. Most of the Maine had
disappeared; only a few blackened vestiges of the superstructure could be
seen above water.

At that time there was uncertainty about the reason for the explosion,
though the war-mongers predictably had no doubts. The next day
(16 February) Theodore Roosevelt, then Assistant Secretary of the Navy,
wrote privately: 'The *Maine* was sunk by an act of dirty treachery' – a
view that the press advocates of war were happy to endorse. But Secretary
Long, not prepared to assume Spanish culpability, wrote in his diary of the
'intense difference of opinion as to the cause. . . . In this, as in everything
else, the opinion of the individual is determined by his original bias.' The
US Navy immediately set up a Court of Enquiry, and American and
Spanish officials seemed content to wait upon its findings. It was reported
that the Governor-General, Ramón Blanco y Erenas, had wept openly in
his palace at the tragedy, while the bishop of Havana took pains to conduct
and expensive and dignified ceremony for the dead.

The (first) US enquiry concluded that the *Maine* had been destroyed 'by
the explosion of a submarine mine which caused the partial explosion of
two or more of the forward magazines'; so, it was said, deliberate action
had been taken to sink the ship, though the court was 'unable to obtain
evidence fixing the responsibility . . . upon any person or persons'. Lee
assumed that 'unknown conspirators' had been responsible, a view that
McKinley, Long and Day regarded as 'probable'. The Spanish enquiry,
hampered by lack of cooperation by the US authorities, concluded that the
explosion had an internal rather than an external cause. A second US
investigation, after the *Maine* was raised in 1911, confirmed the earlier
American report in concluding that an explosive device 'exterior to
the ship' had been detonated; though the new report fixed the site of the
explosion in a different place to that suggested by the 1898 report. The
Maine was then towed out to sea and ceremoniously sunk. The Spanish
had disclaimed all responsibility; the Americans concluded that either the
Spanish had deliberately placed the mine or, by their negligence, had
allowed someone else to sabotage the ship.

In fact the likely cause of the explosion derived from the design of the
Maine, a conclusion that accords with the early Spanish verdict.[46] A report
to Secretary Long noted: 'There are some bunkers in which a fire would
involve great danger; namely, those adjacent to magazines.' Two ships
with a similar internal design had suffered fires that had charred the wood-

work of the magazine; had the fires 'not, fortunately, been discovered in time, there might have been in each case a terrible disaster'.[47] A further enquiry, carried out in 1976 under Rear Admiral Hyman G. Rickover, found 'no technical evidence in the records examined that an external explosion initiated the destruction of the *Maine*'. Here it was concluded that the evidence was consistent 'with an internal explosion alone'; and that the most likely cause was 'heat from a fire in the coal bunker adjacent to the 6-inch reserve magazine'.[48] The Rickover enquiry confirmed 'what other nations had believed for three-quarters of a century'.[49] It seems that one of the crucial incidents that helped to propel the United States into a war in Cuba was – far from being what the Hearst press blazoned as clear evidence of *Spanish Treachery* – a simple but catastrophic accident. Bad ship design had helped to cause the 1898 war.

The pro-war press was not interested in evidence or enquiry: its mind was made up. The *Journal* (17 February 1898) carried a dramatic headline 'THE WARSHIP MAINE WAS SPLIT IN TWO BY AN ENEMY'S SECRET INFERNAL MACHINE'; and a short time later the first US investigation seemed to support the *Journal* line. This was the verdict that the American people – and much of the press and business – wanted. But McKinley had doubts, just as Queen María Cristina of Spain expressed her anxieties: 'The Americans intend to provoke us and bring about a war, and this I would avoid at all costs. But there are limits to everything, and I cannot let my country be humbled by America.' Now the American public, despite the expressed reservations of Long and McKinley, were determined to believe the worst of Spain; and in this they were encouraged by the sensational press.

The *Journal* despatched yachts (*Buccaneer* and *Anita*) and the tug *Echo* to Havana, along with a team of special correspondents. In addition it promised a reward of $50,000 'for the conviction of the criminals who sent 258 American sailors to their death'; and inaugurated a fund for the building of a memorial to the *Maine* victims. The *World*, not to be left out, chartered its own tug and hired divers to investigate the wreck, but was denied permission to do so. The *Journal* publicised what it deemed 'Strong evidence of crime', and in the same issue (17 February) declared that there were many 'Spanish officers and privates who hate Americans to the point of frenzy'. Moreover, once the Spanish guilt had been established, 'the brutal nature of the Spaniards will be shown in that they waited to spring the mine until after all men had retired for the night'. The next day a leading Journal heading read 'THE WHOLE COUNTRY THRILLS WITH WAR FEVER'; an accompanying report stated that the governors of many states were signalling the eagerness of the militia for service; and a picture carried the caption, 'Divers searching for the dead and the evidence that they were murdered under the murky waters of Havana Bay'. A few days later the *Journal* (20 February) headlined 'proof of a submarine mine', but no evidence was offered in the accompanying text. The *World* adopted the same approach. The explosion was, it declared (17 February) 'caused by a bomb'; and there was 'suspicion of a torpedo'. Three days later, the *World* claimed that its discoveries had proved 'the mine theory'; and the next issue (21 February) boasted that the US government had accepted the 'mine theory of *World*'.[50]

The American press was far from unanimously pro-war. Even the *World*'s first editorial (17 February) on the issue of the *Maine* was quite pacific, recalling that there had been former accidents to iron-clad ships. The *Sun* demanded 'no lynch law for Spain' and denounced the 'purely professional shriekers of sensations'; the general Cuban question, the Sun urged (26 February, 2 March), should be considered separately. The *Times* (19 February) was prepared to accept the accident theory, having already (17 February) commented that Spain should not be held morally accountable 'for the crime of an irresponsible wretch'. The *Times* and other New York newspapers (*Evening Post, Tribune, Mail and Express, Journal of Commerce* and others) hoped that war might yet be averted.

Things had gone too far. The incident of the *Maine* represented a dramatic contribution to the mounting agitation; but it was only one element in a complex scene that had been shaped over decades. On 11 April 1898, in the circumstances of a mounting clamour for war, President McKinley, ignoring a joint note from the European Powers urging that he negotiate with Spain, delivered his war message to Congress (extract given in Appendix 4). This included a request that Congress 'authorise and empower' him 'to take measures to secure a full and final termination of hostilities' between the Spanish government and the Cuban people, '*and to secure in the island the establishment of a stable government, capable of maintaining order and observing its international obligations, insuring peace and tranquillity and the security of its citizens as well as our own, and to use the military and naval forces of the United States as may be necessary for these purposes*'.

On 19 April the Congress, responding to McKinley's request, passed a joint resolution (42 to 35 in the Senate; 311 to 6 in the House of Representatives):

First. That the people of the Island of Cuba are, and of right ought to be, free and independent.

Second. That it is the duty of the United States to demand, and the Government of the United States does hereby demand, that the Government of Spain at once relinquish its authority and government in the Island of Cuba and withdraw its land and naval forces from Cuba and Cuban waters.

Third. That the President of the United States be, and he hereby is, directed and empowered to use the entire land and naval forces in the United States, and to call into the actual service of the United States the militia of the several states, to such extent as may be necessary to carry these resolutions into effect.

Fourth. That the United States hereby disclaims any disposition or intention to exercise sovereignty, jurisdiction or control over said Island except for the pacification thereof, and asserts its determination, when that is accomplished, to leave the government and control of the Island to its people.

The Spanish government interpreted this joint resolution as a declaration of war: on 21 April 1898 Spain severed diplomatic relations with the United States, and followed this on 24 April with a formal declaration of war. The next day the United States declared war on Spain.

THE FIRST US INVASION

The United States had been forced to confront the intolerable – the prospect of genuine Cuban independence. American presidents since the time of Thomas Jefferson had opposed any transfer of Cuban sovereignty to another power; how much more unwelcome was the prospect of a transfer of Cuban sovereignty to Cubans! McKinley's war message to Congress had made no reference to the rights of the Cubans. Here there was no support for *Cuba Libre*. All that interested McKinley at this juncture was that he be given the powers to launch a 'forcible intervention'. And Congress was happy to oblige. The Cuban war of liberation was converted into 'a US war of conquest'.[51] The pundits and politicians (and most later historians) knew how to describe this war: since it had nothing to do with Cubans it was no more than an element in the Spanish–American War (Figure 5.1). The Cubans would be denied the fruits of their struggle: soon the long centuries of Spanish colonialism would be supplanted by a new form of subjugation.

15 February	**The sinking of the *Maine*. The first US enquiry concludes that external device was the cause.**
11 April	**McKinley delivers war message to Congress.**
19 April	**Congress resolution gives McKinley full powers.**
22 April	**Admiral Sampson imposes blockade of Havana.**
24 April	**Spain, interpreting Congress resolution as war declaration, declares war on United States.**
25 April	**United States declares war on Spain.**
27 April	US Asiatic Squadron, under Commodore George Dewey, sails for Philippines.
29 April	**Admiral Pascual Cervera, with 4 modern cruisers and 3 destroyers, sails for Cuba.**
30 April	Dewey steams into Manila Bay at night.
1 May	Dewey attacks Spanish squadron under Admiral Montojo anchored off Cavite; captures Cavite and blockades Manila, awaiting troops.
May to July	**Sampson imposes blockade of Santiago de Cuba.**
14 June	**US V Corps (17,000 strong) under General Shafter leaves Tampa, Florida, for Cuba under escort.**
22 to 25 June	**US troops land at Daiquiri and attack Santiago.**
30 June	General Merritt and 10,000 troops reach Manila.
1 July	**Battle of San Juan and El Caney. The charge of Roosevelt's 'Rough Riders' becomes war legend.**
3 July	**Cervera overwhelmed by US ships in Santiago Bay.**
17 July	**General Toral surrenders Santiago to US forces.**
25 July	Troops under General Miles land in Puerto Rico.
13 August	Manila capitulates to General Merritt.
10 December	**Treaty of Paris. Spain agrees to end sovereignty over Cuba,** to cede Puerto Rico and Guam to the US, and to sell the Philippines to the US for $20 million.

Figure 5.1   Main events in Spanish–American War (1898)

(events relating to Cuba shown in bold)

On 22 April 1898 Acting Rear Admiral William T. Sampson, heading the US Navy's North Atlantic Squadron (2 battleships, an armoured cruiser, 3 further cruisers, 5 gunboats, 7 torpedo boats, and 3 monitors), began hostilities by imposing a blockade on Havana. The Governor-General Ramón Blanco suggested that his people were not unduly perturbed by this move; but nonetheless he cabled Madrid to say that if people 'should become convinced' that the squadron of Admiral Pascual Cervera was not on its way, 'disappointment will be great'. In fact Cervera had been ordered to sail west, bringing panic all along the East Coast of the United States. The American ships had sailed off to police the Havana blockade, and the US ports and harbours felt defenceless. Now the US Navy was required to protect the East Coast, to maintain the blockade, and to locate Cervera when he arrived in the Caribbean. A 'Flying Squadron' (2 battleships, an armoured cruiser, and one other cruiser) under Commodore Whinfield, based at Hampton Roads, was created as a rapid-response force. Lighter vessels were ordered to maintain the Havana blockade, while Sampson took ten ships and went looking for Cervera.[52] At Puerto Rico, seen as a likely first stop for Cervera, Sampson found nothing, but registered his presence by bombarding the port of San Juan (May 12) for several hours. Then he returned to Key West while the elusive Cervera was heading for Santiago de Cuba.

It was towards the end of May that Sampson learned of Cervera's location; on the morning of 3 June Sampson arrived at Santiago – and decided that it might be possible to block the harbour entrance. Volunteers were ordered to sail a 333-ft, 7000-ton collier into the winding approach to Santiago and, using underwater charges, to sink the vessel in the narrow channel. The plan, reasonable in theory, failed in practice: as the vessel approached, its steering gear was shot away, most of the charges failed to explode, and when the vessel sank it offered no obstruction. A month would pass before the decisive battle between the Spanish and American naval forces.

On 24 April, four days after signing the Cuba resolution, President McKinley issued a call for 125,000 volunteers to supplement the 28,000-man US Army. In particular, he proposed three regiments 'to be composed exclusively of frontiersmen possessing special qualifications as horsemen and marksmen'. The command was offered to Theodore Roosevelt, already active in the War Department and a man who in 1886 had relished the thought of leading 'harum-scarum roughriders' into battle; but Roosevelt declined the command, preferring what he saw as the more active post of lieutenant-colonel. On 15 May Roosevelt reached Camp Wood in San Antonio, a sign at the railway station already signalling, 'This Way to Camp of Roosevelt's Rough Riders'. By the end of May the Rough Riders had been trained to constitute an effective cavalry regiment: able, according to Roosevelt, to 'whip Caesar's Tenth Legion'. On 29 May the Rough Riders struck camp, following a telegram from Washington, and proceeded to Tampa, Florida, en route to Cuba.

The progress of the troops was far from trouble-free. The difficulty of loading some 1200 horses and mules onto several trains had brought delays; and on 2 June recalcitrant railway employees refused, six miles from Tampa, to take the Rough Riders any farther. They completed their journey on horseback, dragging their equipment behind them, and eventually reached the Fifth Corps campground in the dead of night. When, some days later, more than 16,000 troops embarked, a telegram arrived from Washington: 'WAIT UNTIL YOU GET FURTHER ORDERS BEFORE YOU SAIL. ANSWER QUICK. R. A. ALGER, SECRETARY OF WAR'. It seems that warships had been detected at sea, waiting for the American invasion fleet. General William Rufus Shafter ordered the American ships back to quayside – and 'for the next six days sixteen thousand men baked like sardines in their steel ovens'.[53] On 14 June the largest armed force ever to sail from America set course for Cuba.

The American strategy called for troop landings at Daiquiri, as a prelude to the capture of Siboney, seven miles to the west, and a march to Santiago. General Shafter had decided that there was no room on the transport ships for horses, except for those of senior officers: if Roosevelt's Rough Riders were going to seek glory they would have to do it on foot! By sunset of 22 June around 6000 US troops were on Cuban soil, and not a single shot had been fired to oppose the landings. On 24 June Spanish fire brought the American forces to a halt outside Siboney, and the first US fatality of the war was recorded: Hamilton Fish, the grandson of Secretary of State (Hamilton) Fish. Roosevelt noted in his diary: 'we struck the Spaniards and had a brisk fight for two and a half hours . . . we lost a dozen men killed or mortally wounded and sixty severely or slightly wounded . . . the fire was heavy at one or two points where the men around me went down like nine-pins. . . . The Spaniards shot well but they did not stand when we rushed. It was a good fight.'

On 1 July (Roosevelt: 'the great day of my life') the only major land battle of the war took place. Generals Kent and Wheeler were ordered to attack Spanish positions on the hill known as San Juan, whereupon Kent's infantry (3000-strong) moved forward to confront the Spanish forces (numbering about 250 men). Now General Sumner headed the cavalry, including the Rough Riders led by Roosevelt, with an ill General Shafter struggling to command the developing battle from his bed. At the same time a US division under General Lawton was facing 600 Spaniards with two cannons. As the fire became heavier, Roosevelt was wounded in the wrist by a shrapnel burst, while around him four Rough Riders were wounded, and the leg blown off a Regular. More shells wounded and killed 'a good many', whereupon Roosevelt ordered his men into jungle cover.

Bloody exchanges lasted for several hours: until Gatling guns and cavalry charges at last subdued the Spanish forces. Two regular cavalry units (one negro), to be followed by Roosevelt and his Rough Riders (most on foot), charged the enemy position. Roosevelt himself described his charge up the hill, an event that was to become part of military legend. Said he: 'All men who feel any power of joy in battle know what it is like when the wolf rises in the heart.' He heard the sound of shouting and cheering, and the sound of bullets 'like the ripping of a silk dress'. Now with only one man, his orderly Bardshar, beside him, he drove to attain the height. Using a revolver salvaged from the *Maine*, he shot a Spaniard who fell 'neatly as a jackrabbit'. In such a fashion Roosevelt reached the pinnacle of Kettle Hill, which afforded a view of the final US assault on San Juan. Soon, impatient with being a mere observer, he started down the hill to approach the other heights. Having ascended yet another peak Roosevelt found himself overlooking Santiago.

On 3 July, two days after the main land battle, the US naval fleet under Admiral Sampson engaged Admiral Cervera's ships at Santiago. Slowly and deliberately, Cervera's few remaining ships, 'dressed as for a regal parade or a festal day', emerged from their anchorage: four cruisers and two destroyers, in the gallant expectation of unavoidable defeat, prepared to engage the superior American forces. From the US battleship *Iowa* Robley ('Fighting Bob') Evans observed Cervera's flagship, *Infanta María Teresa*, with 'her magnificent battleflag'. The American sailors were even constrained to cheer the Spanish display, until 'they came at us like mad bulls'.[54] In four hours more than 300 men were dead, six ships had been overwhelmed, and the battle was over. Cervera later commented: 'There was no doubt in my mind as to the outcome, although I did not think that our destruction would be so sudden.'[55] As soon as the battle was concluded, Commodore Schley sent the exuberant signals, 'glorious victory' and 'great day for our country'. The Cuban part of the Spanish–American war was almost over.

Immediately after the victories at San Juan the siege of Santiago began; the Spanish fleet seemed impotent and faced imminent destruction. Santiago waited. But the final triumph was not easily achieved. The city was heavily fortified, and manned by some 5000 Spanish troops with abundant stocks of ammunition. Moreover the American soldiers were now considerable weakened as wounds, dysentery and malaria took their grim toll. Roosevelt commented, in a letter to Henry Cabot Lodge: 'Tell the President for Heaven's sake to send us every regiment and above all every battery possible. We are within measurable distance of a terrible military disaster.' At the same time, Shafter, trying a desperate ploy, sent a message to General José Toral, the commander of the Santiago garrison: 'I shall be obliged unless you surrender, to shell Santiago de Cuba. Please inform the citizens of foreign countries, and all women and children, that they should leave the city before 10 o'clock tomorrow evening.'

Then Toral heard that Cervera's fleet had been destroyed; the capitulation of Santiago seemed unavoidable, despite the influx of 3600 more Spanish troops and the city's abundant stocks of ammunition. Toral, not perceiving the weakness of the US forces, continued to negotiate. Reinforcements brought in to Santiago, without extra food and munitions, had merely exacerbated Toral's problems, and now he seemed to be searching for a way out; on 11 July General Shafter stated that if the Spanish army surrendered unconditionally they would be returned to Spain at American expense. The next day Captain-General Blanco urged Toral to attack the US lines, but the time for any such military initiative was over: on 17 July the final terms of surrender were agreed. Santiago de Cuba would be handed over to 'the authority of the United States' (Blanco later denied that he had authorised the surrender). For the most part, the war in Cuba was over.

The US Secretary of State John Hay described the Cuban conflict in words that conveyed the prevailing American attitude:

> It has been a splendid little war; begun with the highest motives, carried on with magnificent intelligence and spirit favoured by that fortune which loves the brave. It is now to be concluded, I hope, with that . . . good nature which is . . . the distinguishing trait of the American character.

The 'splendid little war' had produced some tens of thousands of fatalities, but only a minority from direct enemy action (Table 5.1). The American people, cajoled by a largely war-sympathetic press, were happy to accept the war in a spirit of light-hearted patriotism. Bands played Sousa's new piece, *The Stars and Stripe Forever*, and every pianist strummed the ragtime march, *There'll Be a Hot Time in the Old Town Tonight*. A new national fervour helped to erode some of the traditional tensions between North and South, while there was widespread rejoicing at news of each fresh victory.

TABLE 5.1   US and Spanish casualties in Cuba conflict (1898)

US casualties

	Officers			Men		
	Killed in action	*died of wounds*	*Died of disease*	*Killed in action*	*died of wounds*	*Died of disease*
Regular army	24	7	51	270	114	1,524
Volunteers	17	3	114	188	78	3,820
	38*	10	165	458	192	5,344

* 3 officers of regular army also held commissions in volunteer regiments and are deducted from the total.

Spanish casualties

	Killed in battle with the enemy	*Died of wounds*	*Died of yellow fever*	*Died of other diseases*
Casualties	1 general			
	81 *oficiales*	463	313	127
	704 soldiers	8,164	13,000	40,000

SOURCE: Hugh Thomas, *Cuba or The Pursuit of Freedom* (London: Eyre and Spottiswoode, 1971) pp. 405, 414)

Some observers noted that the American triumph was won against a weary and demoralised foe. The Spanish authorities had mustered 200,000 troops in Cuba, but they were badly led and had little stomach for yet more conflict after the long decades of Cuban insurrection. Nor, to shrewd observers, did the reputation of the United States emerge unscathed from the Cuban conflict. The US War Department was badly mismanaged, to the point that its head was later sacked; and the high number of deaths due to disease reflected badly on the army medical branch in particular, and on US health services in general. Despite the victory over Admiral Cervera, it was acknowledged that US naval gunnery was inadequate (after the war it was taken in hand). The background to the American victory in Cuba was 'a record of bureaucratic corruption, inefficiency, and bungling which seemed to reflective citizens highly discreditable'.[56] Even the patriot Theodore Roosevelt dubbed the conflict the 'War of America the Unready'.[57] The shortcomings of the American military administration were graphically exposed in connection with the disease question, what one authority has called 'one of the worst disasters in the annals of American military medicine'.[58]

No serious estimate had been made of the extent to which Cuba's diseases would impact on the American soldiers. Roosevelt informed General Shafter that in his (Roosevelt's) group alone there were fifteen hundred cases of malaria. When he learned that the War Department had decided to leave troops on the island as an army of occupation Roosevelt wrote in horror that the policy 'will simply involve the destruction of thousands'. In the letter to Shafter, also sent to the Associated Press, Roosevelt commented: 'The whole command is so weakened and shattered as to be ripe for dying like rotten sheep when a real yellow fever epidemic . . . strikes us and it is bound to if we stay here.' The War Department responded by moving some men from Cuba, but the politicians still wanted to play down the mounting crisis. Their pliant tool, Surgeon-General George Miller Sternberg, the acclaimed author of a textbook on bacteriology, emphasised for political reasons that the fevers were of a 'mild' type that would soon clear up. When the troop ships began reaching the United States it was obvious that the truth was rather different.

When the *Concho* reached Hampton Roads, Virginia, the ship was found to be rife with typhoid, malaria, dysentery and yellow fever; 157 passengers, out of the 190 on board, were sick. Soldiers had already died – from 'haemorrhages', from over-eating after not having eaten, from blood poisoning after army vaccination, and from various unnamed causes at sea. Dr A. Monae Lesser, working for the Red Cross, complained that the food given to sick men 'would have sickened well men'. Captain Samuel Risk, the *Concho*'s captain, had wanted to visit Jamaica to take on provisions before sailing north. Shafter denied the request, and once in Hampton Roads there was further delay in official directives: more soldiers died, until *Concho* was ordered to sea to bury its dead. Then the ship was instructed to sail to New York. By now the vessel was filled with the stench of rotting flesh; filthy, sick men lay on the deck, often in their own excrement. When the *Concho* eventually reached New York, Dr Alvah H. Doty, the port's health officer, declared that it was no responsibility of his to determine the nature of the men's illnesses. In the same spirit Surgeon-General Sternberg stated that it was no business of his. On 3 August the army authorities reported that some 4104 soldiers were ill, with 3212 of them suffering from fever.

Eventually the government began to show some interest in the dreadful state of affairs. McKinley himself wanted information, while Secretary of War Russell A. Alger decided that it was all probably the fault of the victims: 'At the time they left Santiago, the general desire of the convalescents to come home doubtless overcrowded the ships'; and it had to be remembered that 'a large number of civilians rushed aboard to get away and they occupied many staterooms that should have been given over to the soldiers'. The 'civilians' were in fact Red Cross personnel. The War Department, well prepared to echo the *Sentinel* (from Boise, Idaho) in its editorialising ('Men who go to war . . . do not expect feather beds'), spread the word that the complaints about the *Concho* were a fuss about nothing. But the *Concho* was not the only disgrace to the American administration. Other ships arrived full of sick men, often with little food and no medical facilities. Anyway, stated Adjutant-General Corbin, perhaps the men dying in droves did not really have actual diseases but were suffering from 'homesickness' and 'nostalgia'. He assured concerned citizens that once the convalescent soldiers had been sequestered on Long Island (at the Wikoff camp, Montauk Point), all would be well. It was certainly the case that nostalgia was not at all contagious.[59]

The conditions at Montauk Point were appalling: disease spread through the camp, and the men were reduced to pitiful beggars. A woman named Chadwick wrote in protest to the *Star*: 'These starving men whom we are feeding, who are so reduced that they come to me and beg . . . who are they? Paupers reduced to want through their own fault? No! but the members of one of the finest armies the world ever saw . . . the victors of Santiago, come home to die for want of food.' By 22 August there were thousands of sick camped at Wikoff, with typhoid spread through the camp. The sick, lacking shelter or adequate food, died in the rain and mud. When Secretary of State Alger visited the camp in late August he remarked to reporters how 'agreeably surprised' he was at the conditions he found there: 'The sick seem to be quite cheerful. When asked if he could find substance in the complaints that had emanated from Wikoff, he replied, 'None!'

McKinley himself visited the camp, and was somewhat noncommittal about his findings; but not long afterwards he appointed General Grenville M. Dodge to investigate the War Department. Wikoff was eventually dismantled; the dead, often naked, crammed into small coffins. Secretary Alger summed up the tragedy: 'The whole trouble has been in the volunteer troops not knowing how to care for themselves and carelessness in warding off disease.' The Dodge Commission duly deliberated and finally blamed bad beef for all the problems. Alger, it concluded, should be applauded for his performance.

The 'splendid little war' was over. The ordinary troops and some officers, American and Spanish, had suffered severe privation, disease, mutilation and death. Their desperate adventures had been conducted not in defence of their respective homelands but to establish or protect an imposed sovereignty over a foreign nation. No heed was paid to the wishes of the inhabitants of the island. The Cubans were ignored, nonpeople in the midst of the frantic imperialist struggle over their territory. Spanish colonialism in Cuba was now at an end. The Cuban people would be forced to confront yet another foreign attempt at subjugation.

THE US OCCUPATION

The American war in Cuba had been represented by the US government as a selfless campaign designed to end Spanish atrocities in the island and to secure genuine Cuban independence. The joint resolution passed by Congress had given President McKinley full war powers; but had also incorporated the so-called 'Teller Amendment' (see Part Four of the resolution, p. 193), asserting that the United States had no intention of establishing sovereignty over the island. It was not long before the hollowness of this assertion emerged, one of the first of what would be many exemplifications of US moral hypocrisy in international relations.

The US government had refused to recognise the political status of the insurgent movement that had all but defeated Spanish colonialism in Cuba: a clear sign, if any were needed, that the United States had no intention of allowing the establishment of a truly independent Cuba so close to American shores. At the same time the American military commanders were well prepared to exploit insurgent resources in their attack on the island. At first this seemed to be a mutually beneficial arrangement. The rebel Council of Government, perhaps unduly neglectful of Martí's earlier warnings, had instructed Máximo Gómez and his subordinate General Calixto García to place themselves under the orders of American commanders wherever this was practical.[60] The American forces landed at sites recommended by the insurgents, and enjoyed their protection: some fifteen hundred Cuban troops covered the landing beaches, while other insurgent units continued to confront the Spanish forces elsewhere in the island.

García already had his doubts about the policy of cooperation urged by the revolutionary Council of Government. McKinley had invaded Cuba without recognising the Council: so what would be its status after the inevitable US military victory? At least García might hope that if the Cuban forces 'fight at the side of the Americans in the first line' then 'before the campaign ends, all the people of the United States will be convinced that we do not lack the conditions to govern ourselves'. The dream was soon shattered. From the start it was obvious that the Americans were not prepared to grant the Cuban insurgents any meaningful military or political significance. García soon learned that the Cubans were expected to work as 'pack-mules' for the US forces, carrying supplies and digging trenches; while Shafter, complaining that 'the Cuban forces are not to be depended upon for severe fighting', was soon virtually ignoring the insurgent deployments. Then, with the surrender of Santiago, the US political posture became plain: no Cuban was allowed to take part in the conference leading to the city's surrender, and all armed Cubans were forbidden from entering Santiago. Said Shafter, following a meeting with the outraged García: 'I explained to him fully that we were at war with Spain, and that the question of Cuban independence could not be considered by me.'[61] Already, only four months after the passing of the joint resolution in Congress, the pledge on the freedom and independence of the Cuban people (Part One of the resolution, p. 192) had been abandoned.

When the hostilities ended in August 1898, both Shafter and General Lawton, the newly appointed military commander of Santiago Province, made it clear that they regarded the Cuban forces as a threat to American interests (Shafter: 'A dual government cannot exist here; we have got to have full sway of the Cubans . . . war is no longer possible to them except with ourselves'). A letter from President McKinley, via the Adjutant-General, to Lawton (16 August) emphasised that the Cubans must recognise the military authority of the United States: 'Interference from any quarter will not be permitted.' When García demanded food and rations for his men, General Leonard Wood (Lawton's successor) said: 'I told him they could have neither, while they remained under arms.'

The Cuban forces had made a substantial contribution to the American military victory. While US propaganda had represented the war as focused mainly on San Juan, the Cubans had fought over many years throughout the island; and continued to do so after the American landings. Throughout the brief campaign some 8000 Spanish soldiers at Holguín were contained by Cuban rebel forces; and a further thousand Cubans had helped the US troops to contain 6000 Spanish soldiers based at Guantánamo. Now the Americans, already deeply mired in post-slavery racism, dismissed the impoverished and ragged Cuban fighters, many of whom were negroes, as 'dagoes'.[62] Moreover, wrote a *Manchester Guardian* correspondent, the Americans used the Cubans 'as scapegoats for the errors and ills of the campaign'.[63]

The American public was now encouraged to believe that the Cuban people were no more than an anarchic rabble unfit for freedom. Shafter had commented that the Cubans were 'no more fit for self-government than gun-powder is for hell'; and the *New York Tribune* conveyed the prevailing mood when it roundly announced that any assumption that the Cubans were equipped for self-government was 'false and unsubstantial'.[64] The *Detroit Tribune* recognised the need for 'the military subjugation' of the Cuban people; the *Hartford Post*, published by John Addison Porter, McKinley's private secretary, spoke of 'these good-for-nothing allies of ours'; while the Cleveland *Leader*, relieved that the Cubans had 'displayed their worthlessness thus early in the struggle', judged that 'it may be absolutely necessary for us to keep Cuba and make it a part of the United States'.[65] Carl Schurz, the celebrated professional liberal, represented the public mood when, in a speech in New York to a National Conference on Foreign Policy, he noted the 'multitudes of Americans who say now that if they had known what a sorry lot the Cubans are, we would never have gone to war on their behalf'. In such an atmosphere any thought of genuine Cuban independence was an unrealistic dream. The Teller Amendment, in helping to sanctify the US invasion of the island, had played its part: there would be little reference by American policy makers to any such idea in the years to come.

The war in Cuba officially ended on 12 August 1898 when representatives of the United States and Spain signed a preliminary protocol: Spain agreed to relinquish sovereignty over Cuba and to evacuate the island. The US government still refused to allow the Cuban leadership any political status, though it was clear that some accommodation would have to be made once the Spanish forces had departed. On 1 October the peace conference opened in Paris, intended to confirm the *de facto* aspects of the Cuban peace, to address the other elements of the Spanish–American War (Figure 5.1), and to settle particular matters (for example, the so-called Cuban debt) that had formerly received little attention. Spain suggested that the United States might assume sovereignty over Cuba, so allowing Spain to unload the Cuban debt (nominally around $400 million). The United States, unsurprisingly, balked at any such proposal – which meant that a direct annexation of the island, which might involve unwelcome financial liabilities, would not be favoured. The United States was determined to work out its own relationship with Cuba, one that would maximise the opportunities for commercial exploitation and strategic control but which at the same time would minimise the attendant costs.

It was now clear that the US government intended to institute a military administration in Cuba. This further exacerbated tensions between Cubans and Americans, and between Cubans and residual Spaniards, in the island. On 11 December riots broke out in Havana and lasted for several days, resulting in many casualties. In these circumstances General John

R. Brooke, appointed the first US military governor of Cuba, decided that the Cubans should not be allowed to stage their planned victory parade in Havana on 1 January 1899. Senator Henry M. Teller (of Teller Amendment fame) protested that to deny the Cubans their celebration would 'create a false idea of what our course is to be dealing with them, and our difficulties are quite great enough now without any additions'. In fact Brooke's policy was quite consistent with the strategy of the US government: the Cubans would recognise their place in the new military regime, or face the consequences. Some Cuban commanders were allowed to attend the transfer-of-government ceremony on 1 January, but Máximo Gómez and his army were absent: the Cubans were allowed no great victory parade in Havana.

General Brooke, one of the three most senior US officers before the war and now governor of Cuba, received the keys of Havana from Jiménez Castellanos, the last Spanish Captain-General in four centuries of colonial rule. Brooke then issued a proclamation addressed 'To the People of Cuba', stating the purposes of the American occupation: 'The object of the present Government is to give protection to the people, security to person and property, to restore confidence, to encourage the people to resume the pursuits of peace, to build up waste plantations, to resume commercial traffic, and to afford full protection in the exercise of all civil and religious rights.' It was emphasised that the civil and criminal codes formerly administered by the Spanish authorities would remain in force, except for such changes as might be required. The Cuban people should cooperate with the new government and show 'moderation, conciliation and good will' towards one another. The situation was plain. The United States had authority in Cuba through 'the law of belligerent right over conquered territory' (McKinley), and Cubans would question this authority at their peril.

By one reckoning Brooke's military administration was 'benevolent, without being assertive'.[66] He had encountered, on his arrival, 'a state of desolation, starvation, and anarchy' prevailing 'almost everywhere',[67] but with six and a half million rations distributed over an eight-month period the food situation was reportedly much improved. The military administrators had been confronted with an appalling situation, in Havana and throughout the country: the war had crippled the economy and reduced thousands of people to destitution. In Havana the municipal services had collapsed, and the city stank. Sick and starving people roamed the city or lay in the gutters; streets were littered with the corpses of horses, dogs and human beings. General Ludlow reported that even the most imperative requirements of a city government – 'to clean the streets, rescue the dying, even to bury the dead' – had been abandoned. The destruction of the interior estates in Santiago Province and elsewhere had left a wilderness. Throughout the island people confronting the aftermath of war struggled for survival.

One of the most controversial (and paradoxical) measures of the first few months of the US occupation was Senator J. B. Foraker's amendment to the Army Bill designed to limit the commercial concessions granted by the American military regime. The amendment, passed by the Senate (47 votes to 11) in March 1899, was intended by Foraker to facilitate an early US withdrawal from the island. The extent to which the amendment was successful can be judged by the build-up of American commercial interests in Cuba (see below). Efforts were made also to diminish the role of the Catholic Church in the island: divorce matters were henceforth to be judged in the civil courts; and all marriages, even if ecclesiastical, had to be civil also; and religious parades were banned, though funerals (with no women present, as in the past) continued to be held. Some reforms – for example, Brooke's decision to have postal revenues remitted to Havana (so impacting on General Wood's cash flow) – served to generate tensions within the US military administration. Wood even went so far as to protest to Theodore Roosevelt: 'I am kept extremely busy doing all I can to preserve order and harmony. . . . The new order of things is not conducive to such conditions here.' On 1 March 1899 Roosevelt, then governor of New York State, replied that he and John Cabot Lodge had been to see the president 'and told him that we thought you ought to be in command of the whole island'.

A key point at issue was the question of Cuba's future. Wood seemingly believed in the notion of 'annexation by acclamation': that is, after a period of notional independence the Cubans would ask to be joined to the Union. Thus Roosevelt commented in a letter to Lodge (21 July): 'Wood believes that we should not promise or give the Cubans independence: that we should govern them justly and equitably, giving them all possible opportunity for civil and military advancement and that in two or three years time they will insist on being part of us.' By contrast, General James Wilson, then governor of Matanzas and Santa Clara, argued that the United States should leave the island, setting up a Republican-style government, and keeping coaling facilities. The various views can be debated,[68] but the principal consideration, common to virtually all the main commentators, was that the concept of *Cuba Libre* could not be countenanced. American hegemony over the region was a necessary condition: the only realistic debate was the precise nature of the Cuban subservience.

The tensions between the Cuban leaders and the US military government continued to grow. The funeral of General García on 11 February

1899, at which an American cavalry unit had mistakenly occupied a place intended for the Cuban army and the Cuban Assembly, had not helped matters. Failing to gain satisfaction, all the Cubans had withdrawn from the ceremony: again it had seemed that the Americans were intent on humiliating the Cuban people and monopolising public events, even the funerals of Cuban heroes. When, on 24 February, Cuban troops were at last allowed to parade, talks between Brooke and Gómez took place with unaccustomed cordiality. It did not last long. The Cuban Assembly was soon charging that Gómez was not acting with its authority: it then stripped him of his rank and began protracted consideration of loan facilities (from either private sources or President McKinley). In the event the Cuban Assembly, now demoralised, agreed to disband the army, to dissolve itself, and to surrender its army rolls to Brooke (to facilitate the agreed payments to army veterans). Brooke and Gómez resumed negotiations, and the plans proceeded: in effect, the US government paid the Cuban soldiers to disarm. All the signs were – by the late summer of 1899 – that the Cuban army, without any real alternative, had accepted the authority of the United States. Now the pressure was mounting for an active US *commercial* colonisation of the island.

On 20 December 1899 General Wood, still believing that the Cubans would ask for annexation, replaced Brooke as the American proconsul in Cuba. Máximo Gómez had refused to be bribed into friendship, and now the matter of suffrage for forthcoming local elections had to be considered: the Cuban leaders demanded universal suffrage while Wood commented that people without property were 'a social element unworthy to be counted upon for collective purposes'; and in the same spirit he suggested that the 'great mass of public opinion is perfectly inert. . . . The people here, Mr President, know that they are not ready for self-government and those who are honest make no attempt to disguise the fact . . . *we are dealing with a race that has been steadily going downhill for a hundred years . . .*' (original italics).[69] A fortnight later (5 May) Wood was obliged to report massive financial fraud in the US administration on the island. Charles Neely, head of the financial section of the Post Office, had disappeared with $100,000 (Wood: 'We can find no records at all for the finance department of the post office for the past year'). Eventually, the absconding Neely and another official, Estes Rathbone, were jailed for embezzlement.

Wood worked hard to extend the number of schools on the island, though he was soon accusing Alexis Frye, his agent and 'an educational eccentric of great brilliance' (Thomas), of spreading the 'most intense radicalism as to the future relations between Cuba and the United States'.[70] And on 16 June 1900 municipal elections, the first in Cuba, were

held with three contesting parties (the Republicans, who wanted immediate independence; the Nationalists, who also wanted independence; and
the conservative Unión Democrática, who favoured annexation). On
25 July Wood proposed that delegates be elected to frame a constitution,
'and as part thereof *to provide for and agree with the government of the
US . . . the relations to exist between that government and the government
of Cuba*' (my italics). This proviso outraged the mostly pro-independence
elected delegates. Nine separate political groupings protested to Wood that
relations between Cuba and the United States fell outside the framing of a
constitution. Again the American intentions were transparent: no Cuban
constitution would be allowed that provided the island with real independence. The scene was set for the drafting of the infamous Platt
Amendment, the imposed legalistic mechanism whereby the Cuban people
would be kept in thrall to the colossus from the north.

THE PLATT AMENDMENT

By late 1900 it was becoming clear that the United States would have to
resolve the troubling question of regional hegemony. The pacification of
Cuba had been more or less accomplished – by dint of bribery and military
pressure – and now the US government was forced to contemplate the
prospect of evacuation. In military terms the occupation could have been
indefinitely prolonged, but there were various reasons why this was not the
preferred option to Washington policy makers. This had nothing to do
with the Teller Amendment, disclaiming any US intention to annex the
island: the terms of the original joint resolution in Congress were now
deemed to have been overtaken by events. Instead there was reluctance in
Washington to assume Cuba's financial burdens, and in any case there
were divided opinions in racist America at the prospect of absorbing a
black recalcitrant people into the Union. Many Americans, including
influential figures in the US government, shared the anxieties expressed by
Carl Schurz. The Cuban people were mostly Spanish creoles and people of
negro blood. It was unlikely that such an uncongenial population could be
submerged in a wave of white immigration to the island – for the simple
reason that Anglo-Saxons were reluctant to settle in the tropics in
sufficiently large numbers. The consequence, according to Schurz, would
be that 'another lot of . . . Spanish-Americans and negroes' would expect
representation in Congress. The worthy Americans who had discovered
the Cubans to be a 'sorry lot' should at least have the wisdom not to
'permit those same Cubans to take part in governing us'. So a military

occupation leading to annexation was out. How much better to protect American hegemony in other ways.

It did not help that the Cubans had persisted in their stubborn attitudes by electing pro-independence delegates: a member of the McKinley administration commented that the United States could not be expected to turn the island 'over to the insurgents'. In his 1899 message to Congress McKinley made the position plain: 'The new Cuba yet to arise from the ashes of the past must be bound to us by ties of singular intimacy and strength if its enduring welfare is to be assured. . . . Our mission . . . is not to be fulfilled by turning adrift any loosely framed commonwealth to face the vicissitudes which too often attend weaker states.' The option of annexation might prove to be Cuba's ultimate destiny but now other options should be sought.

The dilemma facing the US government was well revealed in the correspondence of Secretary of War Elihu Root. In a letter (9 January 1901) to General Wood he observed that if the United States were simply to withdraw from Cuba and make a treaty with the new government, 'no foreign government would recognise any longer a right on our part to interfere in any quarrel which she might have with Cuba'. It might not be helpful to invoke the Monroe Doctrine since it was 'not a part of international law' and had 'never been recognised by European nations'.* The US occupation of the island would have to be brought to an end – a policy that Root favoured – but in such a way that American control over Cuba would not be eroded. On 11 January, in a letter to Secretary of State John Hay, Root proposed a policy framework:

Will you turn over in your mind . . . the advisability of requiring the incorporation into the fundamental law of Cuba of provisions to the following effect:

1. That in transferring the control of Cuba to the Government established under the new Constitution the United States reserves and retains the right of intervention for the preservation of Cuban independence and the maintenance of a stable government . . .

2. That no government organised under the Constitution shall be deemed to have authority to enter into any treaty or engagement with

---

*Hugh Thomas (*Cuba or The Pursuit of Freedom* (London: Eyre and Spottiswoode, 1971) p. 449) points out that in any case the Monroe Doctrine did not apply to Cuba since it focused on the *status quo* of 1823.

any foreign power which may tend to impair or interfere with the independence of Cuba, or to confer upon such foreign power any special
right or privilege without the consent of the United States, and that the
United States will be entitled to be a party . . . to any negotiations
having in view any such provision.

3. . . . for her own defence the United States may acquire and hold the
title to land, and maintain naval stations at certain specified points.

4. That all acts of the Military Governor, and all rights acquired thereunder, shall be valid and be maintained and protected.

The example of Britain in Egypt, recalled Root, suggested a fruitful
approach to US–Cuban relations: of Britain's withdrawal policy, retaining
the right of military intervention, 'some good authorities were of the
opinion that it would enable England to retire and still maintain her moral
control'.

On 8 February General Wood, sensitive to the need to resolve the
matter of Cuban relations with the United States, commented in a letter to
Root that it was his opinion 'that at the next municipal elections we shall
get hold of a better class of people' – that is, Cuban representatives less
wedded to the unsettling notion of *Cuba Libre*. 'If we do not,' wrote
Wood, 'we must choose between establishing a central American republic
or retaining some sort of control for the time necessary. . . . The time has
been very short to convert a people into a Republic, who have always
existed as a military colony, 60% of whom are illiterate, and many sons
and daughters of Africans . . .'. The next day Root wrote to Wood,
conveying largely the essence of his earlier letter (11 January) to Hay –
which Wood applauded, reaffirming the idea that it was 'very probable
that we shall have to exercise directly the intervention provided for . . .'.

The representatives of the Cuban Constitutional Convention, when they
were told of such proposals were horrified: some – including the
influential Juan Gualberto Gómez, supported by the pro-independent
Patria journal – called for Wood's immediate recall. But by now such
Cuban protests had no effect on the US administration. In February
Senator Orville Platt of the Foreign Relations Committee drafted a bill to
incorporate Root's proposals and to be introduced as an amendment to the
Army Appropriations Bill: hence the Platt Amendment (Appendix 5).
When, on 25 February, the amendment went to the Senate, Senator
Morgan declared that it was 'a legislative ultimatum to Cuba'; and Senator
Foraker noted that adoption of the amendment 'would seem to invite inter-

vention' – a defeated party in Cuban elections might believe that 'by making trouble and creating difficulties they would make a condition that would lead to an intervention by the US to put the successful party out'. But such objections did not sway congressional opinion. On 27 February 1901 the Senate passed the amendment, despite some opposition: 43 (all Republicans) voted for and 20 (17 Democrats and Populists, 3 Republicans) voted against; Foraker (having opposed the amendment) voted for it, and Teller (who had supported it) voted against. In the House of Representatives the amendment was passed by a vote of 161 to 137, largely along party lines. On the next day, 2 March, McKinley signed the bill and it became law.

Cubans were horrified at this development, even though the course of events had been largely predictable. On the evening of 2 March a torch-light demonstration was staged outside Wood's residence in Havana in protest against the Platt Amendment. Speakers at public meetings in Santiago urged a return to arms to redeem national honour and to secure Cuban independence from the United States. Municipalities, civic associations and veterans' groups across the island cabled protests to Havana.[71] Washington responded by threatening an indefinite continuation of the military occupation: if the Cubans refused to accept the Platt Amendment the island would remain in effect an American colony with a military governor. Said Root: 'No constitution can be put into effect in Cuba, and no government can be elected under it, no electoral law by the Convention can be put into effect, and no election held under it until they have acted upon this question of relations *in conformity with this act of Congress*' (my italics). And he declared that if the Cubans persisted with their 'ingratitude and entire lack of appreciation . . . the public sentiment of this country will be more unfavourable to them'.

On 12 April (Good Friday) a cartoon in the Cuban newspaper *La Discusión* showed a crucified Cuba between two thieves, Wood and McKinley, with a spear-holding Senator Platt standing nearby. Wood sent soldiers to arrest the editor, but released him the next day. The protests and press criticisms continued, suggesting that the Cubans would never accept the Platt Amendment. Then, in late April, five members of the Convention went to Washington; and – by dint of much flattery and implicit threat – came to declare that they were 'now looking for a way of accepting the Amendment with dignity'. On 28 May, after much deliberation, the Cuban Convention accepted the imposed addition of the Platt Amendment to the Constitution: the vote was 15 to 14. Wood noted the 'general feeling of relief'; but because the Convention had added various interpretative qualifications Root quickly objected that the acceptance of the Platt Amendment 'is surrounded by such a cloud of words, by way of recitals and explanations, that it is difficult to tell what the real meaning is'. The US military authorities maintained the pressure (Wood: 'no-one can interpret the scope of the Platt amendment except Congress'), and eventually the Cubans succumbed to the threat that unless they accepted the American demands, without qualification, the military occupation would continue. On 12 June the delegates adopted the unqualified Platt Amendment by a vote of 16 to 11 (with 4 not voting). Four months later (28 October 1901), Wood summarised the situation in a letter to Theodore Roosevelt: 'There is, of course, little or no independence left Cuba under the Platt Amendment.'[72] This was of course the deliberate American intention.

The Cuban leaders were in no doubt what had transpired. Thus Juan Gualberto Gómez, one of the most distinguished fighters in the long war against Spain, observed bitterly that the Platt Amendment had 'reduced the independence and sovereignty of the Cuban republic to a myth'. But perhaps the departure of the Americans, the end of the military occupation, would be the first step towards genuine Cuban independence. Said General Máximo Gómez: 'The Americans are going to leave. It is our primary duty to avoid any stumbling which could bring them back.' But in this the Cubans failed: there was enough 'stumbling' in the years that followed to provoke further American invasions.

As provided in the new Cuban constitution, presidential elections were held in December 1901. In an attempt to ensure that General Wood's 'better class of people' were elected, the franchise was designed to exclude Afro-Cubans, women and those with less than $250-worth of assets. The strategy worked. Tomás Estrada Palma was elected president. His credentials, from a Cuban perspective, seemed admirable: he was in fact José Martí's successor as the head of the Revolutionary Party. But he had lived most of his life outside Cuba, and had a deep admiration for the United States. To Estrada Palma a dependent but stable Cuba was quite acceptable: the Platt Amendment did not trouble him. On 20 May 1902 Estrada Palma took over the command of the Cuban administration from General Wood. The American military occupation was at an end, for now; and a new phase of Cuban political subservience was about to begin.

In March 1903, seemingly satisfied with the pliant Cuban government, the United States signed a so-called 'commercial reciprocity' treaty which in fact gave the US control of Cuban markets. This was followed on 22 May by a further treaty with Cuba, incorporating the Platt Amendment and so further strengthening the American control over the island. On 2 July, citing Paragraph VII of the Platt Amendment (Appendix 5), the

United States compelled Cuba to cede Bahía Honda and Guantánamo (this latter a superb deep-water port in eastern Cuba). Six months later, control of the Cuban territory at Guantánamo Bay was officially handed over to the United States in a ceremony on the American *Kearsage* battleship, the flagship of the Atlantic Fleet. The Cuban government had requested that the ceremony be kept low-key because of Cuban protests against the indefinite lease of Cuban land; with only one Cuban present, the Cuban flag was lowered to a 21-gun salute, while the US flag was raised in its stead. At last a partial annexation had taken place: the United States had secured a strategic base in the Caribbean, facilitating the rapid deployment of forces anywhere within the region.[73] The same year the administration of President Theodore Roosevelt contrived the separation of Panama from Columbia, and launched the Panama Canal project. In such a fashion the United States consolidated its hegemony in the Caribbean and beyond.

It is useful to note that the US base at Guantánamo, secured through unequal treaties, represented – as it continues to represent today (mid-1995) – an illegal occupation of sovereign territory. The legality of the base can be questioned on several grounds,[74] but in particular because international law demands consent as the basis for any legal obligation deriving from a treaty between two or more countries. The treaty ceding Guantánamo to the United States derived directly and unambiguously from the Platt Amendment (Paragraph VII), which was imposed on the Cuban people through the coercion of a military occupation. In this connection it is essential to recall provisions in the *Vienna Convention on the Law of Treaties*; in particular, two Articles in Section 2 on 'Invalidity of Treaties':

ARTICLE 51   Coercion of a representative of a State
The expression of a State's consent to be bound by a treaty which has been procured by the coercion of its representative through acts or threats directed against him shall be without any legal effect.

ARTICLE 52   Coercion of a State by the threat or use of force
A treaty is void if its conclusion has been procured by the threat or use of force in violation of the principles of international law . . .

It is clear that the imposition of the Platt Amendment involved coercion. Hence, insofar as the Platt Amendment was forced on the Cuban constitution or was cited to inform subsequent treaties between Cuba and the United States, such manifestations of the Amendment are 'without any legal effect', 'void', in international law. It should also be remembered that the US and Cuban governments together abrogated the Platt Amendment in 1934. The continued US occupation of sovereign Cuban territory is a flagrant violation of international law.

FURTHER US INVASIONS

The new Republic of Cuba, virtually a US protectorate, lasted little more than four years before the next American invasion. President Estrada Palma, increasingly inclined to assume his indispensability, resolved to stay in power by the characteristic means that successive US administrations were happy to tolerate in their client authoritarian regimes: namely, by manipulating 'democratic' elections. When Estrada perceived that many Cubans, unlike the ideologically sympathetic Americans, did not share his view of his competence and rectitude, 'he did not curb the measures which were taken in the name of his government to control the elections'.[75] An initial step was the 'thorough cleansing' of government offices of all those who did not share Estrada's political objectives, followed by the 'wholesale eviction' of his opponents in the municipalities. Having planted his own people in useful parts of the administration, Estrada then set about contriving a favourable election result, a political tactic to which earlier American administrators were far from averse. (Thus the sugar baron Edwin Atkins recalled that General Wood had asked him to fix the election of the mayor of Cienfuegos: 'I sent for one of the *alcaldes de barrio* and told him my wishes. He told me to have no anxiety: it was a simple matter; they would take possession of the ballot boxes and destroy the ballots of the opposition candidates. I told him it was a magnificent idea and worthy of Tammany Hall.'[76])

The election of November 1905 was widely perceived as fraudulent. Estrada had secured the dismissal of unsympathetic employees (even schoolteachers); he had amassed a surplus in the Treasury, which his running mate, Alfredo Zayas, was prepared to deploy to best advantage; and in the run-up to the election it was evident that General Freyre de Andrade, the Secretary of the Interior, was ready to use the police and rural guards to achieve an Estrada victory. Immediately after Estrada's second inaugural ceremony (20 May 1906), a revolutionary committee was formed to depose the US-favoured autocrat. The fresh insurrection began on 16 August, with the rebels well aware that they faced the risk of a new American invasion under the imposed terms of the Platt Amendment.

The veteran Liberal, General Pino Guerra, declaring that the Cubans 'must seek justice somewhere else', headed the revolt. Before long such rebel leaders as Eduardo Guzmán and Orestes Ferrara in Santa Clara, and Colonel Asbert and General Loynaz del Castillo in Havana province, were organising military contingents. The rebels numbered around 24,000, set against a mere 600 artillerymen and some 3000 thinly spread rural guards. The government responded by arresting Juan Gualberto Gómez (Martí's chosen heir) and the popular opposition politician, José Miguel Gómez, as well as the military leaders Monteagudo and Castillo Duany. Then the rich sugar baron General Mario Menocal arrived in Havana to urge President Estrada to hold honest elections, and so resolve the crisis. While Estrada procrastinated the crisis deepened: the rebels began taking over government properties and issuing proclamations, and sporadic fighting broke out in various regions.[77]

Estrada deliberated for three weeks and then authorised Consul-General Frank Steinhart to send a telegram to Washington (8 September 1906). This requested immediate American intervention. President Theodore Roosevelt was asked to send 'two vessels; one to Habana, other to Cienfuegos; they must come at once'. The situation was desperate: 'Government forces are unable to quell rebellion. The Government is unable to protect life and property. President Estrada will convene Congress next Friday, and Congress will ask for our forcible intervention. It must be kept secret and confidential . . .'. (When the content of the despatch became known in Havana in October there was a fresh upsurge of anger against Estrada.) Roosevelt did not respond immediately, despite daily telegrams from Steinhart: at the time Secretary of State Elihu Root was touring South America to persuade the republics of the US's pacific intentions. Then Roosevelt ordered two ships, the *Denver* and the *Marietta*, to sail to Cuba. On 12 September they anchored in the harbours of Havana and Cienfuegos, with orders to protect American lives and property. The *Denver*'s commander landed 125 men the following day and the American flag was raised over the Fuerza fortress; this earned a speedy rebuke from Washington, and the men were quickly re-embarked. On 14 September Roosevelt informed Gonzalo de Quesada, the Cuban representative in Washington, that the United States would intervene only 'if Cuba herself shows that she has fallen into the revolutionary habit, that she lacks the self-restraint necessary to ensure peaceful self-government and that her contending factions have plunged the country into anarchy'. Five days later, on 19 September, William Howard Taft, the Secretary for War, and Robert Bacon, the Under-Secretary of State of Havana, arrived in Cuba to assess the situation for themselves. The next day Taft wrote to Roosevelt declaring that the best solution was 'to permit Palma (sic) to resign and select an impartial Cuban for temporary chief executive'.

On 21 September Taft was declaring that if the United States tried to maintain the present government in Havana, 'we would be fighting the whole Cuban people'. But what was the alternative? Washington could scarcely sanction insurrectionists as the new Cuban government. To Taft, as he reported in a further letter to Roosevelt, the rebel force 'is not a government . . . only an undisciplined horde of men under partisan leaders'; he acknowledged that the movement was 'large and formidable and *commands the sympathy of a majority of the people of Cuba*', but pointed out that '*they are the poorer classes and uneducated*' (my italics).[78] It was now obvious that the government would have to be abolished, that an American invasion was inevitable, and that fresh elections would have to be held. On 28 September Estrada submitted his resignation, along with the resignations of his entire cabinet. The next day Taft appointed himself Provisional Governor of the Republic of Cuba, under the authority of the US president and by virtue of the relevant imposed feature (appendix, third Article) of the Cuban constitution. He took pains to emphasise, by proclamation, that the Provisional Government 'in the name of the President of the United States will be maintained only long enough to restore order and peace and public confidence, and then to hold such elections as may be necessary to determine those persons upon whom the permanent government of the Republic should be devolved. While Taft was proclaiming himself Governor of Cuba, some 2000 US marines landed and set up camp outside Havana.

On 12 October 1906 Taft relinquished his governorship to General Charles E. Magoon, a lawyer from Nebraska who had served as Governor of the Canal Zone in Panama. Now the United States was set to rule an 'independent' Cuba for more than two years. In one reckoning the Magoon occupation was 'the most disastrous in the island's history';[79] at the start of the second US occupation Cuba had accumulated $13 million in the Treasury, but when Magoon departed in 1909 the national debt amounted to more than $12 million. The new administration perceived its main task as one of patronage: 'It was out to divide the spoils.'[80] Cuban writers have had no doubts about Magoon's character: he was 'greedy for despoilment', he fell 'like a buzzard on the treasury of Cuba', he was 'a Jew who fondles gold like a sweetheart', he 'profoundly corrupted the Cuban nation and on account of his venality was looked upon with contempt . . .'.[81] It has been suggested that Magoon was not corrupt, merely 'very wasteful' and incompetent. In any event it appears that the Cuban people were not unambiguously blessed by his administration.

Magoon, perhaps inadvertently, encouraged a proliferation of patronage claims. Individuals and groups complained that they had not been fairly treated in the matter of spoils, and new positions were created on an ad hoc basis for those judged to be deserving – so laying 'an excellent basis . . . for corrupting administrative discipline'.[82] Roads were built and other public works undertaken, so running the Cuban budget into massive debt. The infrastructure of many interior towns was improved, and Magoon won good-will among the workers by urging the payment of wages in American currency to increase the general level of purchasing power. An Advisory Law Commission under Colonel Crowder led to the enactment by decree of a substantial corpus of administrative law, and to various changes in the Cuban constitution. Changes to electoral law were intended to produce a 'perfect electoral instrument or at least proof against frauds and electoral abuses' and to provide Cuba with 'government machinery that would not go wrong'. Crowder and his team studied the Australian governmental system, which impressed him; and also 'proportional representation as it existed in Belgium and Switzerland'. The resulting electoral scheme was introduced on 1 April 1908 for testing in provincial and municipal elections in August of that year.

The local elections (270,000 votes, i.e. 60 per cent) were followed by national elections on 14 November: José Miguel Gómez, with Alfredo Zayas standing as his vice-president, won by about 200,000 votes to 130,000 (to General Mario García Menocal and Rafael Montoro). On 28 January 1909 General Magoon handed over the Cuban administration to Gómez, who was soon initiating scrutiny of the host of illicit Magoon contracts. An American company, the Havana Electric Railway, Light and Power Company, was allowed to extend its activities under the terms of a Magoon concession; the president of the company was Consul-General Frank Steinhart, who had pressed hard for US intervention. Steinhart had various other interests, not least serving as the financial representative of Speyer and Company; it was Speyer who provided the $16.5 million loan for the paving and sewerage concession awarded by Magoon to another US company, the McGivney and Rokeby Construction Company. American corporations were beginning to derive substantial benefits from the fresh US intervention.[83] But the Gómez cabinet was now taking account of 'certain favouritisms and certain privileges and irregularities' and working to rescind them, since they were 'based on profound immoralities'. The weekly newspaper *La Opinión Cubana* (August 1909) commented:

Other contracts made by the Provisional Administration to all appearances just as profoundly immoral . . . have been recognised by the

Cuban government. . . . But the American public should know that this is the sort of contract which is creating embarrassments of a political and financial nature to the new Cuban Administration, and that the best energies of the Government at Washington are at present devoted to sustaining these questionable contracts.

The second American occupation of Cuba was at an end, though American commercial interests were now well entrenched in the island. But President Theodore Roosevelt, impressed with the effectiveness of military adventurism, was prepared to observe that intervention might become a habit.[84] And so it proved.

On 17 January 1912, US Secretary of State Philander Chase Knox, noting a spasm of racial unrest in Cuba, expressed his 'grave concern' in a note to the Cuban government, urging prompt action so that the US government would not have to decide 'what measures it must take'. Here, under the terms of the Platt Amendment, was a further threat of military intervention. The veterans of the War of Independence, who had been agitating against pro-Spanish elements in the government, heeded the veiled threat and resolved to work 'for the benefit of all Cubans'. But this was not enough. On 25 May the battleship *Nebraska* sailed for Cuba, while reinforcements were sent to Key West in Florida. In addition a gunboat was sent to Nipe Bay, where the US corporation, the United Fruit Company, had large sugar plantations, and where the Spanish-American Iron Company, a Bethlehem Steel subsidiary, owned mills and mining interests.[85] On 31 May US marines landed (again) at Daiquiri (not a principal sugar area), with the declared intention of protecting the sugar estates. It was not clear whom the American forces were intended to confront.

The internal unrest was quickly brought to an end, but at the cost of several thousand lives. Monteagudo's rural guard and soldiers crushed the forces of Evaristo Estenoz in a pitched battle, and then set about hunting down the survivors; Monteagudo later claimed to have killed 3000 rebels. The US government suggested that it had intervened to prevent the need for 'real intervention'; President Taft maintained that the preventive intervention did not constitute intervention. The signals had been sent; the US flag had again been shown in Cuba; no-one now doubted that the United States would intervene – under the legalistic cloak of the Platt Amendment – whenever, rightly or wrongly, it judged American interests to be under threat. Thus President Woodrow Wilson, following the imperialistic examples of his predecessors, launched a fourth invasion of Cuba in February 1917. The circumstances were grimly familiar.

General Mario García Menocal, the Conservative president of Cuba, had staged a fraudulent election in 1916. The inevitable protests flared up, and quickly escalated into military confrontations. On 19 February the US government declared its predictable support for the reactionary Menocal and further announced that it would hold the rebels responsible for any damage to property. At the same time, having declared that it only 'gave confidence and support' to constitutional governments (including presumably those that come to power through fraud), the United States provided Menocal with 10,000 rifles and 2 million cartridges. On 8 March 1916 Commodore Belknep landed 500 US marines, who then dispersed to occupy various locations: including Guantánamo, El Cobre, Manzanillo and Nuevitas. The American deployments enabled Colonel Miguel Varona to enter Santiago and to thereby consolidate the position of President Menocal.

Again Cuba had been rendered secure for US proxies and American capital. On 7 April, to show his gratitude, Menocal brought Cuba into the First World War, only one day after the United States had made its own war declaration. The island was opened up as a training base for US marines, some of whom were to remain until 1922.

THE AMERICAN INTEREST

American business interests in Cuba escalated after the 1898 intervention. Said General Wood: 'One of the hardest features of my work was to prevent the looting of Cuba by men who were presumed respectable. Men came down there apparently with the best recommendations and wanted me to further the most infamous of schemes. They expected to profit by sharp business practices at the expense of the people of the island . . .'. The Foraker Amendment, designed to prevent the granting of contracts to US citizens, had limited effect: by the time it was first invoked in 1900 many of the most powerful commercial interests had already begun operations in Cuba, and business initiatives were often launched in the absence of formal concessions from the government. The substantial capitalist penetration of Cuba that had developed through the nineteenth century was set to gather pace in the twentieth.

The Quaker financier Perceval Farquhar, who arrived in Havana in 1898, was one of the most successful of the early entrepreneurs. He and the Cuban-Spanish financier Tiburico Castañeda browbeat shareholders to gain company control, an outcome accomplished by such methods as 'hiring a strong-voiced man to shout down disaffected stockholders'.[86] Farquhar, in vicious rivalry with other business interests, was involved in the electrification of Havana's tramways; in the purchase, with Henry O. Havemeyer (of the Sugar Trust), of the Maranzas–Sabanilla railway; and in various other enterprises in Cuba and elsewhere. With William Van Horne, the founder of the Canadian-Pacific Railway, Farquhar bought sugar mills in Oriente, purchased the Guantánamo–San Luis railway, founded lumber mills, drafted a Cuban Railway law, and cajoled Wood into letting them import Canary Island workers in preference to North American labourers (who allegedly drank too much rum). Juan Gualberto Gómez bitterly attacked Farquhar's railway initiatives as giving the United States excessive economic power in the island. At the same time other entrepreneurs, using bribes and bullying tactics, were penetrating the Cuban economy.

In 1902, by the time of Wood's departure, the US capital investment in Cuba amounted to around $100 million ($45 million in tobacco and $25 million in sugar). The Havana Commercial Company, promoted by the entrepreneur H. B. Hollins of New York, had bought twelve cigar factories and a cigarette factory in 1899. Soon afterwards the American Tobacco Company, controlled by a group of railway stockholders, created the American Cigar Company out of twenty US-owned Cuban tobacco factories. In addition the new corporation absorbed the Havana Commercial Company (which had already swallowed Henry Clay and Block) and forced British tobacco interests to enter into commercial deals. By May 1902 North American control had been established over 90 per cent of Havana cigar exports and over half of the entire production of Cuban cigars and cigarettes.[87]

There was also growing American interest in Cuba's mineral resources. Following a report from US geologists, Wood granted 218 mining concessions to foreign (mostly US) companies who were at the same time exempted from property taxation. Now the United Fruit Company, a prodigious conglomerate with American interests throughout the region, owned the massive *Boston* sugar mill in Oriente; while the Cuban American Company, formed with the help of the Texas congressman R. B. Hawley, owned the huge *Chaparra* mill in the same province. The United Fruit Company had run banana and citrus plantations in the 1890s;

purchased 200,000 acres on Nipe Bay; and brought cheap foreign labourers, mostly British West Indians, into Cuba, just as the slavers had done a few years before.[88]

American politicians, most with substantial commercial interests, were quick to see the advantage of the tightening US grip on the Cuban economy. Thus President Theodore Roosevelt, in his annual message to Congress (2 December 1902), urged the need for a treaty with Cuba *'because it is enormously in our interest to control the Cuban market and by every means to foster our supremacy in the tropical lands and waters south of us'*. The resulting 'commercial reciprocity' treaty (March 1903) helped to consolidate US control of the Cuban economy; with a subsequent treaty (May 1903), incorporating the insidious Platt Amendment, stipulating the 'legal' right of the United States to intervene if political developments in Cuba were not to American taste (that is, were such as to threaten US business interests). The reciprocity treaty, reinforced by the subsequent Platt provisions, further boosted American penetration of the Cuban economy, mostly in the sugar industry. US investment in Cuban sugar production became 'the symbol of a North American penetration of the last Spanish dominion in the New World'.[89]

The 1898 intervention laid the basis for American control of the Cuban economy that would last until 1959. And with this control came the usual concomitant of commercial enterprise – corruption. The character of public administration in Cuba, under a US client regime increasingly geared to financial opportunism, increased the likelihood of bribery and the theft of state assets. Entrepreneurs worked hard to suborn officials into offering public concessions, such as public contracts for the building of roads, bridges and government offices. One estimate suggests that through the decade of the 1910s as much as 25 per cent of customs revenue, around $8 million, was lost annually through corrupt practices, with 'graft, bribery and embezzlement' serving 'as the medium of political exchange'.[90] Thus during the terms of office of José Miguel Gómez (1908–12) and Mario García Menocal (1912–20) nearly four hundred indictments were brought against public officials – mainly by their political opponents – involving charges of 'embezzlement, fraud, homocide (sic), infraction of postal regulations, violations of lottery law, misappropriation of funds, and violation of electoral laws. By 1923, the number of indictments had increased to 483.'[91] Cuban officeholders were commonly under criminal investigation,* though sentences were rarely served. Pardons were the rule (Palma and Zayas issued hundreds; Gómez and Menocal, thousands): since their own time might come, partisan political campaigners were often reluctant to press for sentences to be served.

1898 had been depicted as 'a year of destiny in American foreign relations; it signalled the involvement of the United States in the dialectic of imperialism'.[92] The United States, which had already accomplished its imperial expansion across a continent, had now seized Puerto Rico, Guam, the Mariana Islands, and the Philippines, annexed the Hawaiian republic, and converted Cuba into a protectorate. In Cuba, as elsewhere, the United States had imposed a manifestly exploitative capitalist regime in which financial corruption and political fraud were symbiotically linked. The election of President Mario García Menocal in 1916 was typical of the genre: 'the President was reelected but by a slight oversight there were more votes cast than there were voters'.[93] Such minor matters did not trouble the US administration: Menocal continued to enjoy American support. The US intervention had set the scene for the commercial and political elements that would shape the evolution of Cuba until 1959: capitalist exploitation, bloody dictatorship, and gangsterism.

---

*It is interesting to compare this situation with the scale of political corruption in the administration of Ronald Reagan. In 1988 the House Subcommittee on Civil Service had noted more than 225 Reagan appointees facing 'allegations of ethical or criminal wrongdoing' (Shelley Ross, *Washington Babylon*, W. H. Allen, London, 1989, p. 269). Said then Vice President George Bush: 'Our administration has been the victim of individuals who haven't had the judgement or integrity to put the public's business above their own selfish interest.'

Part III
The Modern Transformation

6 Towards Revolution

As Cuba moved through the twentieth century the political tensions mounted, heralding further social dislocations, yet more bouts of US involvement, and an ultimate seismic shift in the ideological orientation of the island. Many factors contributed to the climax that would bring the decisive rupture from the past. The First World War, the subsequent vicissitudes of the Cuban economy, the Bolshevik revolution in Russia, the ongoing American interference in Cuban affairs, the failure of successive US puppet governments to reflect the popular will, the evolving Cuban tradition of resistance to oppression, the endemic political corruption, gangsterism, the Cold War – all helped to shape the course of events that led to the first successful Cuban revolution in more than four centuries of struggle.

One particular event was signally influential in what it would come to mean for the course of Cuban history in the second half of the twentieth century. On 13 August 1926 the one-time maid Lina Ruz Gonzáles, the second wife of the small land-owner Ángel Castro y Argiz, gave birth to Fidel in Oriente province at two in the morning. Said Fidel Alejandro Castro Ruz, many years later: 'I was born a guerrilla because I was born in the night.' Fidel Castro was destined to succeed where all the other Cuban patriots – Hatuey, Céspedes, Maceo, Gómez, Martí and all the rest – had failed.

THE ECONOMIC FACTOR

In 1913 Cuban sugar production reached two million tons, amounting to 12 per cent of the total world supply. Cuban sugar, as a result of the reciprocity treaty with the United States, was now monopolising the US market and seeking other markets abroad. At the same time the peculiarities of the market had reduced the price of sugar, forcing it down to the lowest level since 1902. Then came the First World War, impacting with dramatic effect on the world economy. In 1913, in circumstances of mounting crisis, Britain had taken two-thirds of her total sugar from Germany (at that time a larger sugar producer than Cuba) and Austria–Hungary. But in 1914 this supply of beet-sugar to England was cut off, and the devastation of Belgium and France wrecked the production of sugar in those countries.

Thus in 1914–15 England imported 450,000 tons of Cuban sugar, and 550,000, 780,000 and 883,000 tons in the succeeding years.[1] This development stimulated the planting of virgin land in Cuba, the founding of three new *centrales*, and the building of twelve new mills (eight of which were American) in 1915; by the start of 1918 some 39 mills were being built, were undergoing reconstruction, or had been newly founded.[2]

Most of the new mills were funded by Cubans with wealthy friends and useful commercial connections, while substantial US investments were being made at the same time. Edwin F. Atkins, president also of the American Sugar Refining Company, combined two of the new mills (Florida and Punta Alegre) with Trinidad to create the Punta Alegre Sugar Company in 1916. In January of that year the New York-based Cuba Cane Sugar Corporation bought fourteen Cuban mills, enabling the company to emerge by 1918 as the largest sugar enterprise in the world. The Warner Sugar Refining Company built the Central Miranda mill in Oriente; the West India Sugar Finance Corporation funded and managed the mills at Alto Cedro, Cupey and Palma (this latter with Cuban proprietorship that passed to the American backers in 1922); and in 1916 the Cuban Bureau of Statistics listed some 72 mills as 'American' (reduced to 55 by 1920). The Rionda family (Manuel Rionda and Miguel Arango had promoted Cuba Cane) were involved with the McCahan Sugar Refining Company of Philadelphia, substantial sugar estates in Cuba, shipping enterprises, a coal-dock in Havana, and various stock market ventures. Rionda himself, though Cuban in origin, increasingly identified with US commercial interests[3] – a common posture among Cuban entrepreneurs. One estimate suggested that in 1919 almost a half of all Cuban mills were owned by Americans, with another proposing a lower proportion (about a third of the 209 total).[4]

The war had stimulated the Cuban economy, and others. Entrepreneurs in the United States and elsewhere seized their chance, and considerable fortunes were amassed. But the boom was not set to last: in the immediate aftermath of the armistice (11 November 1918) the commercial scramble – the so-called 'dance of the millions' – escalated to its (1919–20) height; but the trading situation, inherently unstable as it was, now ran into severe dislocation. By 1920 there was a world abundance of sugar, a circumstance that would soon impact on prices: after the price peak (of 22½ cents per pound) in May, the slide began (to hit 3¾ cents in December). In July, traders hit by falling prices refused to accept ordered goods; and a US commission was despatched to Havana to assess the situation. Sugar producers struggled to restrain the slide, but to no avail: the banks were hit as the large depositors withdrew their accounts. The vast expansion in sugar production had involved the provision of massive credit facilities, and now the producers were unable to service their debts: unclaimed imports piled up in the Havana shipyards, commerce ran into terminal collapse, the over-extended bankers faced ruin, and the Banco Nacional (the government's fiscal agent) struggled to avoid bankruptcy. Unemployment spread and consumer prices rapidly escalated; strikes occurred throughout the island and protesters took to the streets. All the signs were that the commercial and economic chaos would be soon followed by political collapse. The United States, perceiving this new threat to its expanded commercial interests, invoked the Platt Amendment as justification for a fresh bout of political intervention.

FROM ZAYAS TO MACHADO

On 1 November 1920, as the financial crisis deepened, Alfredo Zayas stood in the presidential elections against ex-President José Miguel Gómez, his old Liberal chief. It is significant that the Gómez faction included Miguel Arango, a senior executive of the Cuba Cane Sugar Corporation, promoted as candidate for the vice-presidency. The election was widely perceived to be fraudulent. In some 112 municipalities the government instructed 'military advisors', hired thugs, to ensure that the appropriate candidates were elected. In areas where it was judged that government opponents might do well the polls failed to open on time and often closed early; in some well-documented cases Liberal victories were avoided by the simple expedient of burning the ballot papers. In some areas the total votes cast – invariably favouring the government candidates – far exceeded the number of voters on the electoral list; elsewhere, where a Gómez victory over Zayas seemed certain, the polls never opened. The Menocal regime had secured, by whatever means, the election of its favoured candidate.

The scale and character of the corruption was dismally typical for the political scene in Cuba. The mayors of Liberal towns 'were shorn of their executive rights and military supervisors responsible to the Secretary of the Interior and having at their beck and call the intimidating forces of the army were put in charge throughout Cuba';[5] some 335 criminals, including 44 murderers, had been amnested to serve as Menocal gunmen; election booths in Liberal areas were set up in deliberately inaccessible places; and the government used treasury resources to bribe electors and to fund its thugs. Despite all this, despite all the ballot rigging and intimidation, Zayas managed an overall majority of only 10,585 votes in 312,765 but so distributed as to provide an overwhelming result.

The Liberals, suspecting the likely election fraud, had appealed to the US government in August. In response the Chargé d'Affaires Francis D. White published a note (30 August) to the Cuban government, stating that because of the 'exceptionally intimate relations which exist between Cuba and the United States' the US government had the duty 'to use all available means to follow the course of the elections in Cuba . . .'. It was emphasised that the US government did not propose 'to exercise supervision over the elections . . .', but since it was '*bound by treaty* to maintain a government in Cuba which is adequate for the protection of lives and property and of individual liberty' it was 'opposed unalterably' to any violence or revolution against the process of government (original italics). The note added for good measure that the US government was 'no less opposed' to election intimidation and fraud.

In the event, Zayas was duly 'elected', in circumstances of massive intimidation and fraud; and at first the US government, interested above all in the security of the American economic interest, showed no inclination to dispute the result. But now the protests were mounting. Liberal publications declared that Gómez was the rightful president; electoral disputes brought before the Central Election Board showed no sign of abating; and, with the election unresolved, Liberals and other government opponents were calling for Menocal's immediate resignation. Boaz Long, the US minister in Havana, reported that the Board seemed incapable of resolving the contentious issues, and that Menocal could not be relied upon to run fresh elections. On 4 January 1921 Norman Davis, the US Treasury under-secretary (with financial interests in Cuba), urged Long to 'take immediate and forceful steps' to prevent further Cuban press attacks on the National City Bank and the Royal Bank of Canada, the two main foreign banks operating in Cuba. But by then Robert Lansing, the US Secretary of State, had decided on a fresh American intervention in Cuba. General Enoch Crowder was despatched to organise new elections: on 6 January 1921, conveyed appropriately enough on the battleship *Minnesota*, Crowder arrived in Havana.

He resolved, however, to maintain his headquarters on the ship, from which he issued 'in effect orders' to Menocal. It was decided that the election results in a fifth of the electoral districts would be annulled, and that fresh elections would be held in March. The three most powerful political figures in Cuba – Zayas, Gómez and Menocal – met with Crowder on 26 February to resolve how the revamped elections would be held: Menocal, for instance, agreed that he would dispense with his hired thugs, the so-called 'military advisors'. And on 1 March the young Sumner Welles, a new future proconsul, offered a pertinent memorandum in the US State Department. In this document, the first of many, Welles elaborated the desirable qualities that a future Cuban president should possess. Two of these (the first and sixth) were: a 'thorough acquaintance with the desires' of the US government, and an 'amenability to suggestion of advice which might be made to him by the American legation'.[6] Thus it was made plain to Zayas and Gómez that, whatever the result of the new elections, the Cuban president would be expected to follow American orders.

Crowder found it impossible to win the compliance of the various Liberal and Conservative groups: the protests continued, and on 9 March the demonstrations erupted into violence. Crowder, undaunted, pressed ahead with the new elections, arguing that if the Cubans did not comply the United States would be compelled to intervene formally and set up its own administration.[7] The aggrieved Liberals, suspecting that the elections would be rigged to suit US interests, stayed away from the polls on 15 March. Again the corrupt government candidate Alfredo Zayas won the election, and again it was made plain that 'no one could become President of Cuba without the endorsement of the United States'.[8]

President Zayas, a manifest US puppet, inherited an empty treasury. Economic dislocation and the collapse of sugar prices had drastically reduced government receipts. At the same time, while perhaps as much as $24 million of government money was tied up in the insolvent Banco Nacional, there was pressure to service past debts: a previous loan agreement meant that the Zayas administration was now forced to make payments to New York bankers at the rate of $200,000 a month. The government, resolving not to default (and to thereby antagonise its American political backers), decided to accept mounting arrears: in the fiscal year 1920–21 the expenditures of the Zayas administration reached more than $182 million with receipts amounting to around $108 million.[9] Some of the debts had arisen through sheer Menocal profligacy: there were hundreds of unpaid bills for food and drink consumed at the palace (one, for $20,000, was for 'pheasants and roses'). In these dire economic circumstances Zayas had no option but to implement radical policies: ones moreover that would be congenial to the United States.

Unemployment would have to rise, salaries would have to be reduced, investment in public works would have to be slashed, and fresh loans would have to be negotiated – all at the effective behest of the US administration. While avoiding the burden of direct fiscal administration, the American government established 'a detailed financial censorship' over Cuban affairs.[10] And that was not all. Soon Crowder was demanding that US officials be allowed to investigate the operations of any department of the Cuban government. One month after the election, US representatives were active throughout Cuba, scrutinising the tax system, the banking laws, public investment, and anything else of interest to US financiers.[11] In response to such interference and to the resulting strictures, the entire Cuban cabinet resigned; whereupon a new cabinet, popularly known as 'Crowder's Cabinet', was appointed.[12] In June 1922, with Washington now claiming the right to hire and fire Cuban public servants, the new cabinet (what Crowder chose to regard as the 'honest cabinet') included Ricardo Lancis, Carlos Miguel de Céspedes, Demetrio Castillo, Arístides Agramonte and Manuel Despaigne. This meant that Washington was now appointing the key ministers (for the Treasury, Foreign Relations, Public Works, and so on) in the Cuban government. The spirit of the Platt Amendment was alive and well. In such circumstances, necessarily congenial to the US administration, Zayas was permitted to request a loan of $50 million from J. P. Morgan and Company. Washington was prepared to prop up the Cuban government, provided it was prepared to play by American rules.

Not all Cuban politicians were eager to acquiesce in this fresh phase of Cuban subservience to US financial strategy. Thus in June 1922 the Cuban Senate, while acknowledging that it would be unrealistic to demand total abrogation of the offensive Platt Amendment, urged the United States to adhere to what was judged to be the moderate Root interpretation of the relevant provisions. Platt, in some version or other, was deemed inescapable, but perhaps its worst meddlesome aspects could be avoided:

> The Platt Amendment . . . was accepted in virtue of the interpretation which the Military Governor of the Island stated in writing in the name of the President of the United States . . . that it was not synonymous with intermeddling or interference in the affairs of the government of Cuba.
>
> The Senate declares that it is the vehement desire of the people of Cuba that the action of the government of the United States in our internal affairs should be fitted to the spirit and letter of the Platt Amendment as such appeared from the referred interpretation.[13]

If Washington noticed this declaration it ignored it, so further fuelling Cuban resentment. Reflecting the popular mood, the Cuban newspaper *La Nación* (21 June 1922) declared that 'the day will have to arrive when we will consider it the most sacred duty of our life to walk along the street and eliminate the first American we encounter and if at a ball to leave the side of our companion to annihilate the intruder who has for years and years annoyed us'. Sometimes the resentment spilled over into violence, and US government officials were assaulted in Havana.[14]

President Zayas, unconcerned at the mounting Cuban resentment and as befitting a US puppet, had 'embarked on an unrestrained crusade of personal enrichment'.[15] One Havana deal alone netted him around $1 million. Then, with the growing arrogance to which US proxies are sometimes prone,* Zayas contrived a political crisis and sacked Crowder's entire 'honest cabinet'. Crowder, by now the US ambassador to Cuba, fumed but seemed impotent. Zayas, temporarily aided by reviving sugar prices, continued to prosper, skimming government contracts and awarding a dozen or so of his family members lucrative sinecures. This was not a situation that could long endure.

At first it seemed that Zayas would be able to survive in the new regime. Crowder's initial anger abated somewhat when it was realised that Zayas did not pose any immediate threat to US commercial interests in the island. A new round of government spending was begun, with fresh budget allocations, new franchises, salary increments, and a new lottery run by the president's son. The awarding of the coveted Morgan loan had signalled US approval of Zayas, and his high-handed dismissal of Crowder appointees did not pose an immediate threat to the stability of the regime. The important consideration was whether American business interests would be protected, and in this regard observers saw no problem. Charles E. Mitchell of the National City Bank spoke for much of US business when he declared at a New York banquet that Cuba was 'a solvent nation enjoying an excellent administration'. In August 1923 the Cuban government settled the debt to the United States run up during the First World War, the first US ally to do so; the business community, interested above all in returns on investment, was impressed by such punctilious behaviour. Washington was happy to note what it perceived as a suitably congenial situation: '. . . the State Department . . . did not make a policy change. Conditions in Cuba improved, American business interests were satisfied, so there was no occasion for further action.'[16]

At the same time, as befitted the character of a US proxy state, the bulk of the Cuban people were excluded from the successes of the capitalist entrepreneurs. Bribery and corruption were the common means to political influence, a practice where powerful foreign investors – usually American – had an advantage over the smaller local businessmen. The US

---

* We need only recall the respective fates of Panama's Manuel Noriega and Iraq's Saddam Hussein – both one-time beneficiaries of American largesse. Washington has never been perturbed by the manifest brutalities perpetrated by its proxies: all that has ever mattered is when the puppet decides to challenge the sway of the puppet master.

government, content to note how (business) conditions in Cuba had improved, was largely indiferrent to how this had been accomplished: by such familiar practices as 'widespread corruption and coercion against the electorate, a growing trend of political violence and assassination, and the wholesale practice of electoral fraud, ballot stuffing, and falsification of returns . . .'.[17] Again, amid mounting resentment of the enduring implications of the Platt Amendment, the Cuban people began a fresh wave of protest against the scale of political corruption, the behaviour of mercenary officials at all levels where the protection of the American interest seemed the prime consideration.

In business terms, 1923 was good for the Zayas administration: the Morgan loan ($50 million) had been secured, and a substantial sugar harvest had been achieved at a time of good sugar prices. Such relative commercial success did nothing to allay the mounting resentment of political and financial corruption. Thus in the famous 'protest of the 13' a group of students headed by the poet Rubén Martínez Villena demonstrated against the corrupt practices of the Zayas government. Wrote Martínez Villena, perceiving well the ubiquitous American influence:

Nuestra Cuba bien sabes cuan procipia a la caza
De naciones y cómo soporta la amenaza
Permanente del Norte que su ambición incuba
La Florida es un índice que señala hacia Cuba.

[Our Cuba, how well you know when the hunting
Of nations is in season and how
The menace of the North is prepared
Florida is a finger which points to Cuba.]

Other protest factions were the Grupo Minorista, the Liga Anticlerical, and the Cuban Committee of National and Civil Renovation (for this last, Fernando Ortiz wrote a manifesto in which he denounced the Zayas administration as 'inefficient from lack of culture, rotten in character, ready to compromise with every sort of delinquency . . . an unbridled pilferer from the public treasury . . .'.[18] On 12 August 1923 the powerful Veterans' and Patriots' Association came out in support of the protests against corrupt government, in particular to oppose rumoured pension cuts. The prestigious organisation, an acknowledged repository of civic virtue and patriotic devotion, called for the regeneration of Cuba and presented a 12-point declaration, including demands for the repeal of the corrupt lottery law, the honest collection of taxes, genuine elections, competitive open bidding for government contracts, the creation of an independent judiciary, legal accountability in the management of public funds, an end to congressional immunity to criminal prosecution, political rights for women, and a renewed focus on the national commercial interest. Scores of organisations rushed to endorse the Association's stand.[19] Zayas responded with a fresh wave of repression. The leaders of the movement were harassed, meetings were disrupted, printing shops were closed down, and in October 1923 the Zayas government issued an order prohibiting the Association from holding public meetings. Protest grew throughout Cuba, stimulating fresh repression. Martínez Villena was gaoled for supposed gun-running, while a group of patriots under Colonel Laredo Brú marched on Santa Clara.

Despite the widespread agitations, Zayas managed to retain power, though by now it was clear that his administration was running to a close. He continued to accumulate wealth, much as his corrupt predecessors had done; but the Conservatives, seeing that Zayas was becoming increasingly threatened by national revolt, rejected him as their candidate in the forthcoming elections. Vested economic interest, with all the financial corruption that this implied, would still have to be protected – but by a fresh US proxy. The Conservatives again decided to back Menocal; Zayas was content to support the rising figure of General Gerard Machado. Now the discredited Conservatives realised that the election of Machado, the Liberal candidate, seemed inevitable.

General Gerardo Machado Morales was highly regarded by the US business community. From the beginning he had enjoyed 'intimate connexations with United States corporate interests';[20] he had managed a small electric light company in Santa Clara, and later became vice-president of Cuban Electric, the Havana subsidiary of the vast American Electric Bond and Share Company (by 1924 Cuban Electric had acquired most of the electric supply businesses in Havana). In 1922 Machado had been well prepared to discount the Platt Amendment, against the agitations of most Cuban patriots. The Amendment 'does not', declared Machado, 'either by historical precedent, or by the interpretation of its North American authors, or by its literal rendering, or in the light of international law, or in the opinion of commentators, entail a limitation upon our independence or upon our sovereignty . . .'. In the past, he argued, too much attention had been given to the matter. Machado, seemingly not having noticed the repeated US invocations of the Platt Amendment to justify every sort of intervention, was able to comment:

. . . we have been adverse judges in our own cause; we have talked too much of the horrible sword of Damocles hanging over our nationality. . . . Political quarrels, governmental errors, . . . particularistic passions, and a thousand other factors have put the problem upon a plane entirely alien to its juridical reality. We have spoken among ourselves with endless frequency and unpatriotic readiness of foreign interventions, with the same calmness with which we spoke of a police event . . .

The Platt Amendment could be rendered 'an organ without functions, a dead-letter law that can be laid away in the tomb, a relic among the annals of our sovereignty and independence'. It was a mistake, declared Machado, against all the evidence, to assume that the Platt Amendment gave the United States any right to intermeddle in 'our domestic affairs'.[21] In such a fashion, by seeking to defuse the issue of the Amendment (at the same time consolidating his US business interests), Machado sought to attract patriotic Cuban support without alienating his American backers.

Machado campaigned against the perceived corruptions of the Zayas administration, pledging an end to such practices and promising substantial social investment. The army would be improved, the social services modernised, and Cuba's national integrity would be protected. International events now seemingly underwrote the idea of genuine Cuban independence, a final emancipation from US client status: Cuba, unlike the United States (despite all the efforts of President Woodrow Wilson), had joined the League of Nations; in 1922 a Havana jurist, A. S. de Bustamante, became a World Court judge; in 1923 the Cuban lawyer Cosmé de la Torriente served a term as League president; and Cuba was elected (for 1927–28) to a seat on the League Council.[22] To some observers such developments suggested that with Cuba at last moving onto the international stage the island would be able to escape the baleful impact of foreign strategies. The hope was forlorn.

The election was a surprisingly peaceful affair: the widespread resentment at earlier corruptions had made it less necessary for Machado to buy votes in the time-honoured tradition. Duly elected, he was inaugurated in May 1925, whereupon his supporters looked for serious reform. Machado moved quickly to reassure the US business community, his first priority. As soon as the election result was clear, he travelled to the United States, giving every sign that he would protect the American interest in Cuba. Machado praised President Calvin Coolidge, that keen advocate of the US capitalist ethic, as 'this great man who knows how to love liberty and practises the civil virtues'. At a banquet staged by Charles E. Mitchell, president of the National City Bank, Machado declared that in his administration 'there will be absolute guarantees for all businesses . . . there are sufficient forces to repress all disorder'. Speaking to workers, he defended the right to strike ('when the worker finds his daily wage is inadequate to live on'), but took pains to assure businessmen that there would be 'no more strikes'.[23]

Machado's initial proposals, after inauguration, pleased many people. He declared that there would be reforms in the judiciary, education and elsewhere; that the hated Platt Amendment would be abrogated (US business would be protected by other means); the reviled lottery would be abolished; and there would be new commercial deals with the United States. At the same time Machado was talking of the need to 'discipline these Cubans', these 'Italians of America'[24] – suggesting to some observers an unwholesome empathy with the fascism of Benito Mussolini. There were complaints also about Machado's evident puritanism: bars and gambling houses were closed, and prostitutes were encouraged to take up a new profession. A film censorship board was created, street vendors were fined, an American expert – August Vollmer from Berkeley, California – was invited to advise on police methods, and the *vil garrote* (the disgusting Spanish execution device) was reintroduced.[25]

It soon became clear that Machado had little stomach for extensive reform. The promises had served their purpose: in circumstances of widespread political disillusion he had secured power, to general US approval, and was now in control of effective repressive machinery. Little attempt was made to curtail the endemic corruption, and many of the detested practices of the Zayas administration were allowed to continue. In August 1925, three months after Machado's inauguration, the leading newspaper proprietor Armando André, known to have offended Machado in a published article, was shot dead outside his house. Conservative politicians passed a mild resolution regretting the incident, and such influential ex-presidents as Menocal and Zayas (both discredited but still commanding a certain following) did not choose to comment.

Machado, with ebbing public support, was now increasingly relying on terror to preserve his administration – an approach that would only alarm the US business interest if it became counterproductive. In 1927 William Green, the president of the Pan American Federation of Labour, commented that in Cuba 'a condition of virtual terrorism existed . . . the stories of extreme cruelty, assassination, and inhuman treatment were so amazing that they seemed incredible'[26] – a state of affairs that some may have judged incompatible with the political stability that US entrepreneurs would have wished. But to American commercial interest the situation seemed not merely acceptable but highly desirable. Thus in testimony before the US Senate an executive of the Cuba Company declared that the company supported the Machado government since they deemed it 'the best they have ever had down there'.[27]

One of Machado's immediate post-inauguration pledges was that he would not seek re-election; in 1927 he repeated the pledge, and then sought re-election in November 1928. By now Machado had bought off the other political parties – to the point that he was able to stand for re-election unopposed. To secure his rule he imprisoned or deported thousands of political opponents, suppressed free speech, extended his presidential term from four to six years, and closed down the University of Havana (having promised to protect its autonomy). Machado had bribed the Liberal, Conservative and Popular parties into mercenary acquiescence, under the terms of the so-called *Cooperativismo* policy, and persecuted his remaining opponents until they were politically impotent. Those who dared to protest were incarcerated, tortured, deported, murdered: the threat to 'life . . . and individual liberty' (Paragraph 3 of the Platt Amendment) was manifest to all. Would the United States intervene – under its much-cited Amendment rights – to protect the lives and liberties of the Cuban people? It would not. During his visit to Cuba, President Coolidge declared:

> Today Cuba is her own sovereign. Her people are independent, free, prosperous, peaceful, and enjoying all the advantages of self-government. . . . They have reached a position in the stability of their government, in the genuine expression of their public opinion at the ballot box and in the recognised soundness of their public credit that has commanded universal respect and admiration.[28]

The US administration made no secret of the fact that its primary concern was with the protection of 'foreign [i.e. US] interests and local finance rather than Cuban liberties'; and the American business community remained enthusiastic about Machado's endeavours.

In February 1927 General Crowder, US ambassador in Havana until the summer of that year, reported to Secretary of State Frank Billings Kellogg that 'most Cubans favoured a second term for Machado' and proposed that the State Department give him an 'informal' (i.e. covert) assurance that the United States would favour his re-election; after all, Machado had made it plain that he wanted the 'closest possible co-operation' with the US.[29] At the same time Chester Wright, the editor of *International Labour News*, was informing his readers that Machado had by then arranged the assassinations of some 147 people, many of them prominent Cuban labour leaders murdered in 'a condition of virtual terrorism'.[30] Such minor matters did not trouble Machado's US backers; and when, prior to the November (1928) election he introduced the Emergency Law (20 July) to prevent presidential nominations by parties he had not already suborned or intimidated, the US government made no comment. Machado was their man; the important consideration was that he remain in power, by whatever means.

The repression continued. Immediately after the Coolidge visit to Havana, four students (Claudio Brouzón, Noske Yalob, Puerto Reyes and Manuel Cotoño) were tied to weights and then dropped out of the Morro castle into the sea.[31] Machado, who had by now dubbed himself 'Illustrious and Exemplary Citizen', was duly inaugurated for the second time (20 May 1928). The US ambassador R. Judah had been happy to report that Machado was 'in complete political control of all the parties because all the constituted political parties support him and his policies'; there was no mention that the 'complete control' had been established by the expedient of banning all opposition organisations. Machado had portrayed the fragmented opposition as 'insignificant groups formed by ambitious and unscrupulous persons' – which did not mean that he felt disposed to ignore them. Thus José I. Rivero, the director of *Diario de la Marina*, observed in his 'Impresiones' (20 May 1928) that a dictator is recognisable 'not so much for what he does, but for what he forbids others to do'; and it was abundantly obvious to all that Machado was not about to allow any hint of real opposition to his authoritarian rule. By 1929 he had effectively suppressed all opposition groups, but soon his administration would be threatened by forces far beyond his control – economic slump in the United States and worldwide recession.

Soon after his second inauguration Machado initiated a propaganda campaign urging all sections of the Cuban population to support him. In the prevailing circumstances of military intimidation most of the Cuban city councils rushed to offer their support, declaring that the government had, above all, 'opened new roads for Cuban economic development and progressive prosperity'.[32] Such optimistic acclaim was short lived: at the time these words were being published the New York stock market collapsed, bringing an abrupt end to Cuban prosperity. Now the (largely suppressed) struggle against the Machado tyranny 'began to develop into a revolutionary movement'.[33] In conditions of mounting economic disarray the Machado dictatorship limped into the 1930s. Now it was becoming clear that yet another Cuban favourite of the US business community had served his purpose. Soon the United States would be moved yet again to intervene in Cuban affairs, under the convenient terms of the Platt

Amendment, to safeguard the American business interest. Yet again the revolutionary will of the Cuban people was starting to impact on the course of Cuban history. The Machado terror was running to a close. But what then would be set in its place?

THE RADICAL FRAME

The long struggle of the Cuban people against slavery, colonialism and oppression did not occur in an ideological vacuum. There were many contributing elements in political philosophy, with disparate roots in Spanish radicalism, the work of indigenous Cuban theorists (notably José Martí), and the eruption of international Marxist theory after the Bolshevik revolution in Russia. The impact of this rich historical tradition is still manifest in Cuban communism at the end of the twentieth century.

One of the main radical themes in Cuban political thought (and action) in the late nineteenth and early twentieth century was *anarcho-syndicalism*, the revolutionary socialist doctrine in which it is proposed that workers take over the factories and other places of employment. Cuban anarchism was closely associated with Spanish anarcho-syndicalism, which in turn drew inspiration from the work of the Russian anarchist Mikhail Bakunin (1814–1876) and his principal disciple, Prince Peter Alekseyevich Kropotkin (1842–1921). The philosophy of anarcho-syndicalism, first formulated by Bakunin and the libertarian factions of the 'First' International Workingmen's Association (IWMA) set up in 1864, came to have a significant impact on Cuban radicalism. Thus Francisco Tomás, active in the IWMA's Spanish Region, commented that 'relations with the Cuban sections were frequent after 1881'.[34] Bakunin's Declaration of Principles, drafted in 1868, declares that his International Alliance of Social Democracy 'seeks the complete and definite abolition of classes and the political, economic, and social equality of both sexes . . .', and 'wants the land and the instruments of labour like all other property [not personal possessions] to be converted into the collective property of the whole society for utilisation by workers: that is, by agricultural and industrial societies [unions] and federations'. In this framework the state would be reduced to 'simple and administrative functions dealing with public utilities', which in turn would be replaced by a worldwide union of free (agricultural and industrial) associations.

These were the sorts of notions that were influencing Cuban political thought towards the end of the nineteenth century. Anarcho-syndicalist activists, well acquainted with the main themes of radical Spanish politics, constituted the main faction in the Cuban labour movement at that time. Under Menocal the anarchists had organised sporadic strike activity, and long before the US intervention in 1898 the anarchists had a powerful voice in the maritime, railway, restaurant and tobacco industries. They argued that the working class must strive to build a new world without the structural imperfections that served to consolidate traditional exploitation and injustice. A federal structure would be constructed on a global basis to facilitate the local, regional, national and international coordination through free agreement of voluntary workers' alliances covering the whole of social life. Thus it was that 'on the ruins of capitalism, the State and the Church' the workers 'will build an anarchist society; the free association of free workers' associations . . .'. In this context governments were perceived as necessarily evil, as exemplified so clearly by the United States: 'To ask a worker what kind of government he prefers is to ask him what executioner he prefers . . . the great United States Republic is an example. There is no king nor emperor, but there are the giant trusts: the kings of Gold, of Steel, of Cotton.'[35]

The Spanish anarcho-syndicalists who came to Cuba as exiles in the 1880s found fertile soil: here was a people who had struggled for decades, centuries even, against exploitation and oppression. Various labour organisations predated the arrival of the Spanish activists. For example, one of the earliest was the Sociedades Económicos de Amigos del País (Economic Society of the Friends of the Country); and the Association of Tobacco Workers of Havana, created in 1866, anticipated many of the syndicalist aims and principles. In 1885 the Circular de Trabajadores de la Habana (an informal federation of workers' unions) was created as an effective free association on the anarchist model (two years later running into heated dispute between 'reformists' and 'radicals'); and in 1886 a Workers' Centre, opposed to the Marxist idea of exploiting parliamentary social-democratic parties, was created to spread anarchist principles through its organ *El Productor* (The Producer). José Martí himself frequently cited anarchist groups and, in his paper *La Patria*, printed articles by the anarchist Elisée Reclus and others. With them, via the mechanism of the Cuban Revolutionary Party, Martí envisaged an end to traditional exploitation and oppression; and like them he knew that a mere multiparty system, such as that in the United States where political corruption was rife, was no guarantee of democratic justice. But Martí was, it seems, prepared to tolerate the need for a free-enterprise economic system in a post-revolutionary Cuba – a doctrine that was offensive to many Cuban radicals. Capitalist excesses would be curbed through legislation; and, as befitted Martí's reputation as the so-called 'Apostle', by exhortation. Martí noted that he was living 'in a period of struggle between capitalists and workers', and that 'a militant alliance of workers will be a tremendous event. They are now creating it . . .'. But, as was inevitable, the activists disagreed amongst themselves about how the revolution should be directed, and about the shape of the new society, once the old order had been abolished.

In 1892 the Spanish authorities in Cuba closed down the first Workers' Congress when demonstrations for Cuban independence were staged on 1 May. The Congress had approved independence resolutions drafted by the anarchists Enrique Cresci, Enrique Suárez and Eduardo González; one such resolution included the words: 'the working class will not be emancipated until it embraces revolutionary socialism, which cannot be an obstacle for the triumph of the independence of our country'. The Liga General de Trabajadores, an anarchist group established in the 1890s, organised strikes and demonstrations, and disseminated propaganda supporting the rights of workers; when the Liga organised the first general strike in Cuba for an eight-hour day the Spanish authorities launched a fresh wave of brutal suppression. At the same time the anarchists struggled to combat the racism that was endemic in post-slavery Cuba. Thus the anarchist Pedro Estévez commented that 'not even the exemplary conduct of the anarchists who unfailingly welcomed the negroes on equal terms at meetings, schools and all other functions on a person to person basis, sufficed for a long time to shake the belief that all whites were their natural enemies'. Here, as elsewhere, the activists struggled to adapt anarchist and Marxist doctrine to the peculiar circumstances of Cuban society.

In early 1900, during the US occupation of Cuba, the activists publishing *El Mundo Ideal* (The Ideal World) invited the anarchist Enrico Malatesta to visit Cuba and to speak to workers and peasants; but upon arrival he was quickly expelled by the authorities. His farewell letter to his Cuban comrades included the following words:

> . . . I have, for a very long time, admired the self-sacrifice and heroism with which you have fought for the freedom of your country. Now I have learned to appreciate your clear intelligence, your spirit of progress and your truly remarkable culture, so rare in people who have been so cruelly oppressed. And I leave with the conviction that you will soon take your place among the most advanced elements in all countries fighting for the real emancipation of humanity . . .
> . . . I assume that the libertarians fighting against the existing government will not put another government in its place; but each one will understand that in the war for independence this spirit of hostility to all

governments incarnated in every libertarian, will now make it impossible to impose upon the Cuban people the same Spanish laws, which
martyrs like Martí, Cresci, Maceo, and thousands of other Cubans died
to abolish.[36]

After the emancipation of Cuba from Spanish colonialism, anarchists and
other activists continued the struggle against US neocolonialism, and the
inevitable economic exploitation and political oppression that this implied.
The famous tobacco workers' strike in 1902, the so-called 'strike of the
apprentices', was organised by the anarchist Gonzáles Lozana and others.
Havana port workers joined the strike, whereupon the government used
force, killing twenty workers and making threats about the possibility of
US military intervention. The anarchists Casanas and Montero y Sarria
were assassinated under orders from José Miguel Gómez, then Governor
of Las Villas and later a Cuban president, during the 1903 strike of sugar
workers. Other significant strikes took place in 1907 (tobacco workers,
striking for 145 days, joined by maritime, construction and other workers);
in 1910 (Havana and Cienfuegos sewer workers), in 1912 (restaurant
workers), and in subsequent years strikes by bricklayers, railway workers,
tunnel workers and others. In many of these strikes the anarchists were
prominent.[37]
    The end of the First World War (in which Cuba was nominally involved
as a sop to the United States) and the Bolshevik revolution in Russia gave
an immense boost to political radicalism throughout the world. In 1919 a
group of Cuban anarchists, swept along in the revolutionary fervour,
issued a declaration in support of membership of the Bolshevik-dominated
Third International.* But traditional anarchist distrust of Marxism prevailed: Bolshevik excesses became apparent, and soon many of the
leading anarchists – Kropotkin, Voline, Berkman and others – were publishing critical comments on the new Russian government. The Cuban
government continued to suppress legitimate worker protest; strike leaders
were imprisoned, and on occasions the police fired into crowds of
unarmed demonstrators. Protests were organised against the rapacious
exploitation of workers and peasants, against police brutality, and against
government corruption (in 1921 Alfredo Zayas, then nicknamed 'the
Peseta Snatcher', was elected president). The anarchists continued to
organise and to agitate (in 1924 all the anarchist groups joined together in
the Federación de Grupos Anarquistas de Cuba); but following the success

---

* The Russian Third (Communist) International, or 'Comintern'.

of the Russian Bolsheviks there was mounting pressure for the creation of a fully-fledged Cuban communist party.

In the early 1920s a quantity of revolutionary literature in Spanish was brought into Cuba, not least by communist sympathisers among seamen. Moreover, some leading anarchists were attracted to the idea of a new disciplined socialist party, and imagined that they would gain invaluable support from the Russian communists. The Cuban anarchist groups had been severely damaged, not only by deportation and repression but also by *colaboracionismo* on the part of some anarchist leaders. It seemed clear that a fresh organisation, tightly organised and benefiting from the evident successes of revolutionaries in Russia, should be created to address the peculiar circumstances of the Cuban struggle.

Cuban socialists were now agitating for the creation of a communist party that would affiliate to the Third International (the Comintern). Carlos Baliño, the veteran president of the Agrupación Socialista of Havana, began a series of debates in his organisation; and then, with four of his followers, founded the Agrupación Comunista in March 1923. More Agrupaciónes Comunistas were formed, notably in Havana and Oriente; and another communist group, mostly comprising Jewish immigrants from Poland, was established in Havana. The international political climate was now encouraging independence movements, workers' groups, and hostility to what was perceived as capitalist imperialism. By 1920 the Cuban workers' organisations, now bolstered by international radicalism, were again challenging the traditional US interference in Cuban affairs. Thus the Second National Workers' Congress, held in Havana under the aegis of the Federación Obrera de la Habana (newly formed by Alfredo López and Enrique Varona), demanded better conditions for workers and condemned the 'Yankee intrusionism' represented by Enoch Crowder.[38]

In 1924 the charismatic student leader Julio Antonio Mella joined the Havana communists, bringing a number of students with him. Then, instructed by the Agrupación Comunista, he travelled to greet the first Soviet ship to arrive in Havana; but there the port authorities, nervous of the propaganda significance of such an arrival, refused the vessel permission to dock and sent it instead to Cárdenas. Mella, avoiding the police and managing to find a convenient boat, spent 'four hours under the Red Flag'.[39] Soon the mounting revolutionary fervour would lead to the founding of the Cuban Communist Party. In 1925 the anarcho-syndicalists, realising the limitations of the Federación Obrera de la Habana, established the first national organisation of its type, the National Confederation of Cuban Workers (CNOC). But by now the anarchists were being challenged for control of the workers' movement by the growing power of the communists. In early August, communist representatives attended the founding CNOC Congress in Camagüey; and on 16 August the six Agrupaciones Comunistas combined to form the Cuban Communist Party. This was a modest affair: in one account (Aguilar) only ten people witnessed the founding of the party, and at first there were no more than eighty members (Thomas: 'There could then have been hardly a hundred members . . .'). Enrique Flores Magón, a representative of the Communist Party of Mexico, explained to the Cuban representatives what a 'cell' was; how to organise in unions, clubs and other groups; the details of party democracy, and so on.[40] The authority of the Comintern was accepted, workers' conditions were discussed, a youth group and a journal were founded, and officers were elected. A fortnight later, on 31 August 1925, the party's first Secretary-General, José Miguel Pérez, was arrested by the authorities and transported to Spain; ten years later he fought in the Spanish Civil War, was captured by General Franco's Nationalists, and then shot. Thus José Peña Vilaboa emerged as the party's first effective secretary-general. In 1927, after the death of the veteran Carlos Baliño, Rubén Martínez Villena became the most prominent figure in the organisation.

The Cuban Communist Party was at that time small and ineffectual, afforded by some an unreal significance by dint of international political developments. Links were established between the Moscow Comintern and the Cuban party, but the party was not offered full Comintern membership until 1928. The CNOC, in the late 1920s comprising thirty-five unions, became affiliated to the Profintern (the so-called 'Red Union') organisation in Moscow, but the anarchists were facing crisis: 'the revolution cannot be made by proclamations . . . strikes cannot be made every twenty-four hours and . . . to combat the *bourgeousie*, it was not sufficient to have a weekly paper and a few hundred members . . .'. In particular, the recognition had dawned that 'it was necessary to have a sufficiently strong organisation eventually to combat and finally to overthrow the capitalist state'.[41] It now seemed unrealistic to expect the workers to take control of their factories on a local basis, prior to union in voluntary organisations: the utopian idealism had to be matched by realistic practical politics. And the brutal depredations of the Machado dictatorship continued to ravage radical political movements in Cuba.

In the spring of 1927, following the staging of a tribute (under Martínez Villena's initiative) to the expelled Peruvian writer Serafín Delmar, the Peruvian Chargé d'Affaires lodged a formal protest. He charged that Delmar and Cuban radicals were plotting to overthrow the Machado regime, whereupon the Cuban authorities arrested all those who had taken part in the 'conspiracy'. The foreigners were deported, and, following 'the Communist trial of 1927', the Cuban Communist Party was declared illegal. Now the party was 'without leadership or organization. . . . Everything had to be rebuilt';[42] the circulation of the party newspaper *El Comunista* slumped to less than a thousand copies; and for a time the Communist influence seemed to have waned irretrievably. But the Marxist message continued to spread throughout the island. Small groups (for example, the Liga Anti-Imperialista, the Liga Anticlerical, the Defensa Internacional Obrera, and others), linked to the Communists and seemingly impervious to financial blandishment, sprang up and continued to agitate for revolutionary change. Such groups remained committed to eliminating from Cuba what Martínez Villena had dubbed '*la castra tenaz del coloniaje*' (the tenacious scab of the colonial heritage). By 1930 the Machado regime seemed relatively secure, but his rule was moving to its end. At that time Cuba was in the grip of corrupt politicians who conspired with gangsters; and Fidel Castro Ruz was three years old.

FROM CÉSPEDES TO BATISTA

The early 1930s saw increasing instability in the Machado administration: the dictatorship had blocked any chance of parliamentary reform, so laying the basis for a revolutionary upheaval. On 30 June 1931 the Supreme Court dismissed the arguments against new taxation provisions (as embodied in the Emergency Tax Law) aimed at increasing government revenues. This development served only to increase the unpopularity of the Machado regime, and now the prospect of revolution could not be ignored. Machado himself doubted 'the force and the success of the revolution if it ever breaks'; and he declared: 'The peasants do not want or support it, and the Negro, whom I have done so much to dignify, would side with me. The loyalty, discipline and courage of the army are in my opinion beyond doubt. I am ready for any event.'[43]

In August 1931 a revolt – the so-called Río Verde episode – was staged; but generated only fiasco. The exiled Mario Menocal, speaking to student activists in Miami, had promised that soon he, with Carlos Mendieta and other veteran leaders of the War of Independence would be fighting in Cuba to defeat tyranny. Plans were laid for a coordinated revolt involving certain army groups, a landing in Oriente, and a rebellion in the navy. In the event the Machado forces crushed the ineffectual invasion at Gibara, and the navy remained loyal (or indifferent). Menocal and Mendieta, offering little resistance, were captured in Pinar del Río, and the pro-government *El Heraldo de Cuba* rejoiced at what it saw as 'the inglorious finale' to the illegal action. Soon Machado, boosted by this outcome, was announcing that he intended to remain in office until May 1935. The active opposition, as represented by the old *caudillos*, had been crushed; but that was not an end of the matter. The growing hostility to the Machado regime was scarcely affected by the failure of the desultory military adventure at Gibara.

Student militancy was increasing, stimulated by gaol sentences against some of their leaders; and growing sections of the population sympathised with student opposition to the bloody record of the Machado regime. In October 1931 a group led by Joaquín Martínez Sáenz and Juan Andrés Lliteras formulated plans for the creation of a secret terrorist society structured on a cellular basis (to prevent the collapse of the organisation in the event of police penetration). The top cell was known as A, the second as B, and so on; with the entire organisation referred to as the ABC. The new society spread quickly throughout Cuba, attracting activists who were unsympathetic to the ineffectual Student Directory and who rejected the ideological assumptions of the Communists and other leftist factions. The Program Manifesto of the ABC, issued in 1932, emphasised that the purpose was 'not only to get rid of the present tyrannical regime but also of the causes that had determined its existence'; there would now be a battle for new ideas, land reform, political liberty, and social justice. The ABC was prepared to acknowledge that Cuba 'is a young American republic, without an economy of her own, placed in the economic orbit of the United States . . . it does not pretend to go beyond the real possibilities of Cuba. It does not encourage easy illusions, nor does it try to incite one social class against another in a nation where all classes are needy, and where it is urgent to create national union . . . it does not speak of socializing an economy which is still to be conquered.'[44] In such a fashion the ABC chose to address the Cuban predicament in a realist way, divorced from the utopian visions of most other activist groups. Critics portrayed the seeming acknowledgement of US hegemony, and the rejection of a socialist solution, as a needless betrayal of the radical agenda.

In conditions of mounting terrorist activity, Menocal and Mendieta, released in early 1932, urged the United States to 'settle the chaotic conditions in Cuba'. Machado responded to the growing turmoil by intensifying the repression. A special unit, the 'Porra' – an effective death squad – was formed to crush street protests and to murder opponents of the dictatorship. The press was increasingly censored, the military courts were given extended powers, and Congress authorised Machado to suspend constitutional guarantees. Mendieta was again arrested and imprisoned, while

Menocal was exiled. The terrorist opposition responded in kind to the new level of repression: in May a lieutenant was blown up by a letter bomb, and in July the infamous Captain Calvo, the head of the death squad, was killed by a shot from a passing automobile. Bombs were exploding in Havana, bursts of machine-gun fire were common, the police raided homes and arrested protesters, the jails were filled with students and other demonstrators (many suffered the so-called *ley de fuga*, 'shot while trying to escape'). In September Clemente Vázquez, a close friend of Machado and President of the Senate, was shot dead in his car.[45]

The United States was watching such events with mounting concern. Machado, so friendly to the American business interest, was now a spent force. It was time, Washington judged, for a fresh intervention under the Platt provisions. Military action might not be needed, but the recent election of Franklin D. Roosevelt as the new US president would do nothing to erode the traditional American commitment to intervention in Cuba to protect the business interest. Roosevelt himself was no doubt much moved to receive a letter from a self-dubbed 'old Yank', Caldwell Pérez, urging US action: 'Cuba is dying with hunger. . . . I beg you Mr President to do something for her. Pay attention to the voice of common sense . . .'. Perhaps, thought Pérez, 'some friend' might be sent to Cuba to address the problems, whereupon money would 'cease to flow out . . . and there will be peace and the American government, recognizing the new government, will save Cuba's soul, and, like in fairy tales, everything will be all right'.[46]

Roosevelt, perhaps less inclined to intervention than were his predecessors, now faced a dilemma. Sumner Welles, soon to be a significant player in Cuban affairs, later commented on the problem. Two facts were clear: the 'existing treaty with Cuba' gave the United States the right to intervene, but this would be contrary to Roosevelt's 'general line of inter-American policy'; and 'a state of affairs where government murder and clandestine assassination had become matters of daily occurrence must be ended'.[47] And inevitably, above all, the US business pressures for a stabilisation of the Cuban turmoil were mounting. All the American business interests on the island had been affected by the political chaos, and many of these had useful connections with the new US government: for example, key executives in the American Molasses Company, which in turn controlled the Sucrest Corporation, that relied on Cuban sugar, had contacts in the Roosevelt administration. A new US intervention in Cuban affairs was inevitable.

As the bloodshed in Cuba continued, and Machado showed no signs of being able to resolve the crisis, Roosevelt proposed that his old friend

Sumner Welles be sent as a 'special envoy' to the island. The activities of Machado's *La Porra* (the Big Stick) against the ABC and the students continued to escalate the levels of violence: the *porristas* were unable to stabilise the situation and did no more than stimulate a countervailing terror. On 6 April a police lieutenant was wounded by gunmen in an auto-mobile; and on the same day the police arrested the student leader Carlos María Fuertes (later shot), for his alleged role in the murder of Clemente Vázquez. A week later the police shot two students, the Valdés Daussá brothers, José Antonio and Solano, in full sight of James Doyle Phillips, a *New York Times* correspondent. When this event was duly reported, Phillips and his wife (who described the incident in her diary) were threatened by *porristas*. This was the lawless scene that was to confront Sumner Welles when he arrived in Havana.

Welles himself had received a long instruction (issued on 1 May 1933) from Cordell Hull, the new US Secretary of State. This covered four main areas: Welles was expected to offer friendly advice and expressions of concern; the Cuban government must avoid terrorism and other excesses; the US government would offer mediation between Machado and the opposition (with the aim of creating 'a truce in the present dangerous political agitation . . . until such time as national elections can be held . . .'); and the US government would help 'to ameliorate the distressing econ-omic situation' in Cuba (this last of course was Washington's prime concern). Hull made plain Machado's constitutional derelictions, reaffirmed the Platt Amendment, noted that the murders in Cuba had out-raged American public opinion, and emphasised to Welles that the nature of his mediation 'must necessarily be left to your discretion'. For good measure Hull commented that US–Cuban relations were 'those of sovereign independent powers', a notion that was not expected to constrain the endeavours of the 'special envoy'.

On 8 May 1933 Welles arrived in Havana and soon decided that the United States would not be able to breathe fresh life into the Machado administration. After a mere three days' deliberation Welles communi-cated to Washington that if 'the present acute bitterness of feeling persists or becomes intensified . . . it would in all probability be highly desirable' to replace Machado, 'at least during the electoral period'. Welles met with opposition leaders, and held unfruitful interviews with Machado himself. Again the radicals were uniting to denounce the fresh US intervention, the pro-government *Heraldo de Cuba* (10 May 1933) even going so far as to print the arguments of the Communist Martínez Villena, condemning the 'false opposition and the lackeys of Wall Street'. The 'realistic' ABC found itself unable to preserve unity in the face of the fresh US intervention: a splinter group, the ABC Radical, denounced the interference of Ambassador Welles.

The diplomatic discussions continued, against a background of violence and social dislocation. In late July protesting bus drivers in Havana clashed with police, leading to a spate of sympathy strikes – until Havana was paralysed; on 7 August the police fired on protesters, causing scores of deaths and injuries; and soon what had emerged as a general strike was acquiring all the momentum of a revolutionary upheaval. In a belated and vain attempt to defuse the crisis Machada released students and workers' leaders from gaol, in exchange for pledges from the Communists and other radicals. But now there was nothing – bar Machado's resignation – that could halt the swelling revolt. The *New York Times* described the 'race between mediation by the United States Ambassador and open revolution'; and of these events Welles later wrote: 'The ominous signs provided by a paralyzing general strike, wholly political in character, made it doubly clear that only some radical solution could forestall the cataclysm which otherwise was inevitable.'

The solution, Welles now perceived, was for the United States to force Machado to resign. To this end the American Ambassador issued the appropriate threats, so spreading disaffection among the pro-government factions. In this atmosphere the formerly pro-Machado politicians, unwilling to remain tethered to a collapsing administration, decided to adjust to the changing circumstances. In early August, the leaders of the Conservative, Liberal and Popular parties – the people whom Machado had previously bribed and intimidated into acquiescence – endorsed plans for the early retirement of Machado; his fate was sealed when, on 12 August, the army rose up against his continued rule. Welles had never sought to discourage fears of a possible US armed intervention, and the Cuban army had become increasingly concerned at the growing rift between Machado and Welles. When Machado, in mounting desperation, urged the Cuban people to unite to resist a fresh US military invasion, the army leaders were horrified. By dint of persistent diplomatic effort and veiled threat, Welles had encouraged the Cuban army to stage a military coup. A Cuban military representative later commented that the 'sole purpose' of the army uprising 'was the avoidance of American intervention'.[48]

Ambassador Welles then proposed that Carlos Miguel de Céspedes, whom he reckoned 'a most sincere friend of the United States' (and who had been Cuban Ambassador in Washington), be appointed to act as the provisional President. Representatives of the army and the political opposition agreed to the proposal; the entire Cuban cabinet resigned (apart from Céspedes who had been hurriedly designated Secretary of State); and Machado boarded a plane and departed for Nassau in the Bahamas.[49] The erstwhile president, one-time darling of US business and one of a number of US proxies who won the accolade 'Butcher', flew out of history appropriately equipped with five revolvers and seven bags of gold. He arrived in Nassau at dawn on 13 August 1933, and later in the same day his family sailed from Havana.[50] Cuba, courtesy of the United States, now had a new president.

The appointment of Céspedes as president reduced the political tensions and the level of armed conflict, but did not end the crisis. Céspedes himself, despite the marginal advantage of a famous Cuban name, was 'without popularity, without a party, and without a program, and all at once he inherited a cabinet, a constituency, and a country in collapse'.[51] The political and economic difficulties that had plunged Cuba into crisis remained substantially unchanged. The *machadato*, to general relief had been brought to an end; the level of repression was reduced; and the atmosphere of terror abated to a degree. But many workers remained on strike, and an escalation of worker militancy was threatened. In some areas sugar mills were seized, workers' *soviets* were set up, and there were still widespread calls for revolution. Céspedes had prudently appointed members of leading opposition organisations (including the ABC) to his new cabinet, but it was very significant that many of the new ministers were devoted admirers of the United States. Céspedes himself had been born and educated there – a common pattern for US proxies; the wealthy engineer Eduardo Chibás had served General Ludlow during the US invasion of Cuba in 1898; Demetrio Castillo Pokorny, an aide and friend to Crowder and Wood, was 'almost more North American than Cuban'; and the ABC men, long sympathetic to the United States, were well prepared to support American strategic and commercial policies. There was little in Céspedes, or in the instincts of his US-approved cabinet, to meet the prevailing revolutionary aspirations of the Cuban people.

Soon there were rumours of fresh radical plots against Céspedes and the army; more and more sugar mills were being taken over by the workers; and various factions – the Communists, the ABC Radical, the Student Left Wing, supporters of General Menocal, and others – began spreading black propaganda about likely wage reductions in the army and new blocks on promotions. Sumner Welles, having rejoiced at his despatch of Machado, now viewed the situation with mounting despair; on 24 August, having asked Washington to recall him, he commented on the 'general process of integration' in the island. At the same time the Student Directory issued a radical Manifesto to the Cuban people: denouncing the US-contrived government, the compliant ABC, and the entire political structure that had been foisted on Cuba. Those in power, declaimed the Manifesto, had betrayed the Revolution, the Cuban people, and Latin America – by (respectively) agreeing the pre-revolutionary political structure, by suggesting that the Cuban people could not determine their own destiny, and by approving the characteristic Yankee meddling and penetration. The Cuban people were then exhorted to fight for the Student Directory's revolutionary programme.

On 29 August some thirty prominent American businessmen in Cuba visited Sumner Welles to discuss what might be done; they were of course firmly of the opinion that all the troubles were caused by communist agitators 'in the pay of Russia'. Welles, perhaps underestimating the degree of communist support among the Cuban workers, declared that he saw little evidence of the 'red menace'. But, whatever the reasons, the Céspedes administration, rootless construct that it was, could not long survive. The government moved tardily to introduce minor reforms, and then called general elections for 24 February 1934; but it was all too little and too late.

The so-called 'Junta de los Ocho', comprising disgruntled sergeants in the Cuban army, began meeting on 26 August 1933 and subsequently established the Columbia Military Union. A principal aim was to prevent any purge of (formerly) pro-Machado men, and it was hoped also that means might be devised to promote the sergeants to officer rank without the need for examinations. These relatively modest objectives were converted into a more ambitious agenda, once the disarray among the high-ranking officers was realised. On 3 September a group of dissatisfied sergeants, corporals and enlisted men at Camp Columbia in Havana met to consider their various grievances. The officers on duty refused to discuss the grievances and then departed from the regimental headquarters, whereupon the disgruntled soldiers found themselves in control of the camp. The army protesters, under Sergeant Fulgencio Batista, urged the troops to hold fast until the officers agreed to address the grievances. So began the escalating mutiny, the so-called 'Sergeants' Revolt', that was to herald the emergence of what many commentators have depicted as a revolutionary government.

On hearing of the revolt, students and other radicals rushed to Camp Columbia in a desperate attempt to transform the limited insubordination into a fully-fledged military *coup* able to serve revolutionary ends. The sergeant leaders, by now facing disciplinary action and probable imprisonment, were soon persuaded into expanding the mutiny. By 5 September a five-man revolutionary junta (Ramón Grau San Martín, Porfirio Franca,

Guillermo Portela, José María Irisarri, and Sergio Carbó) was in place; a proclamation was issued to the nation; and President Céspedes, notified that he had been deposed, at once abandoned the presidential palace. The provisional government, so carefully contrived by Sumner Welles, had lasted all of three weeks.

Now there again loomed the prospect of US military intervention. Welles, in despair that his plans had so quickly melted away, was soon identifying the supposed 'Communist influence' in the Pentarquía. As a characteristic intimidatory move a fleet of US naval vessels was ordered to sail towards Cuba, so that within days all the large Cuban ports harboured at least one American destroyer.[52] By 6 September Welles was ambivalent about the possibility of a US invasion, commenting to Cordell Hull that 'if we go in . . . we will never be able to come out'. The next day Welles was reporting that if the Céspedes government was to be resurrected the United States would have to offer military assistance: 'Such policy on our part would presumably entail the landing of a considerable force at Havana and lesser forces in certain of the more important ports of the Republic.' Both Hull and Roosevelt, considering the likely reaction through Latin America, now inclined strongly against US military intervention.

With the revolutionary government composed of various civil and military factions, it soon gave the appearance of disorganisation and lack of central direction. The government, the first in Cuban history not to be shaped by foreigners, had managed to create a new feeling of dignity and independence; but, in view of the general chaos, *El Mundo* (23 September 1933) could still ask: 'Who is ruling Cuba?' Now the scene was set for the dissolution of the Pentarquía.

On 9 September the radical students learned that the Pentarchs intended to nominate Gustavo Cuervo Rubio as president, whereupon a commission from the Student Directory contacted the Pentarchs to inform them that they no longer had any authority. Now the United States was growing increasingly alarmed: for the first time in decades events in Cuba had drifted beyond the control of Washington. It was seeming increasingly likely that the US would not be able to resist the option of a further phase of military intervention in the island. Roosevelt, despite the promotion of his Good Neighbour Policy toward Latin America and his doubts about the wisdom of a fresh invasion of Cuba, had by now ordered more than two dozen warships to the island, alerted the US Marines, and prepared bombers for use if necessary. The US Secretary of the Navy sailed to Havana on the *Indianapolis* but did not venture onto land. The American flag was being shown, but the Roosevelt administration seemed uncertain how to proceed. One possibility – much-favoured among traditional

Washington strategists – was to identity some likely player in the Cuban political scene and to convert him into a US proxy.

A confrontational situation at the Hotel Nacional, where a commission of sergeants had arrived to search for weapons, revealed that Fulgencio Batista y Zaldívar – a power behind the Sergeants Revolt and now a self-appointed colonel – was not acting in concert with the Pentarquía. The authority of the Pentarchs, already being undermined by student opposition, was now being further eroded by military disaffection. By now the idea was being floated that Batista, if made chief of staff, would even support a resurrected Céspedes administration. The students, prevailing against the Pentarquía, acclaimed Ramón Grau San Martín as president; whereupon Washington, refusing to recognise the Grau government, redoubled its efforts to promote a useful proxy: the ambitious Batista was now being encouraged to make a final break with the radicals.

At 2.30 a.m. on 10 September Grau became president of Cuba; quickly nominated four men to his cabinet (Eduardo Chibás as Secretary of Public Works, Carlos Finlay as Secretary of Sanitation, José Barquín as Secretary of the Treasury, and Antonio Guiteras as Secretary of the Interior); and then began a radical programme of reform. On the very day of his appointment Grau announced the abrogation of the Platt Amendment, a momentous and symbolic act, even if Washington at that time refused to agree the abrogation. On 20 September (via Decree No. 1693) the new government established the eight-hour day for workers, and (Decree 1703) stipulated that all professionals join their respective professional organisations; a Department of Labour was set up on 2 October, and on 9 October the autonomy of Havana University was proclaimed; a week later, the importation of workers from Haiti and Jamaica was prohibited, and workers already brought in illegally faced deportation; and on 18 November a Decree (2583) specified that at least 50 per cent of workers in industry and commerce should be Cubans. Further decrees gave land rights to the peasants, reduced loan interest rates, dissolved the formerly pro-Machado political parties, enfranchised women, and cut electrical rates.[53] For the first time in Cuban history a real effort was being made – in the unprecedented absence of US political manipulation – to legislate for the benefit of the Cuban people. President Grau himself defined the task of the government as to 'liquidate the colonial structure that has survived in Cuba since independence'.[54] It was not a scheme that could long survive.

Washington remained bitterly opposed to these political developments, and did what it could to spread disaffection among the Cuban radicals. Cuban workers were now parading with red banners, and speaking of the establishment of Russian-style *soviets* (workers' councils) in Cuba. In such an atmosphere it was easy for Sumner Welles to conclude that the Grau government was committed to the elimination of the US commercial interest in Cuba: 'It is . . . within the bounds of possibility that the social revolution that is under way cannot be checked. American properties and interests are being gravely prejudiced and the material damage to such properties will in all probability be very great.' He protested at the 'confiscatory' government decrees, and declared that the US commercial interests in Cuba 'cannot be revived under this government'. With Grau an 'extreme radical' and the new government 'frankly communistic', Welles concluded that Cuba was now intent on minimising US power and influence in the island. But still Washington declined to take the step of a fresh military intervention: it was possible to destabilise the Cuban government in other ways.

The US refusal to recognise the Grau government was in itself a destabilising factor, causing many of the radicals to hesitate and making it more difficult for the new administration to establish order throughout the country. In fact the United States now favoured a policy that would promote 'conditions of continued instability and disorder . . . stability and order were now inimical to US interests in Cuba'.[55] Despite Grau's optimistic unilateral abrogation of the Platt Amendment the United States still reserved to itself the right to intervene in Cuban affairs when and how it chose. One ploy was to encourage the activities of the anti-Grau opposition as a means of stimulating social disorder and so deny the new regime the chance of consolidating its power. In short, Washington resolved to encourage political subversion. It was not long before the policy bore fruit.

In November Grau San Martín suspended repayment of the unpopular loans from the Chase Manhattan Bank; and then seized two sugar mills of the Cuban–American Sugar Company in order to resolve labour disputes. In December the government introduced a scheme to facilitate the state acquisition of land; and in January 1934, after a workers' strike had hit the Cuban Electric Company (a subsidiary of the American Electric Bond and Share Company), the government took control of the company. Such developments served to convince opposition activists that the government was running to extremes; and, reinforced by the US posture, they refused to negotiate constructively with the Grau administration. Washington continuing to encourage disunity among government supporters, paid crucial attention to the role of the army – and to the cultivation of Colonel Fulgencio Batista y Zaldívar in particular.

For some time Batista had seemingly supported the Grau government, prepared to suppress rebel initiatives and apparently disinclined to stage a *coup d'état* of his own. But the ambitious self-proclaimed colonel was not immune to US blandishments. On 4 October 1933 Sumner Welles reported his 'protracted and very frank discussion' with Batista, during which the US Ambassador took pains to inform the ambitious army chief that he was the 'only individual in Cuba today who represented authority'. Batista's leadership of the army, Welles assured him, had brought him the support of 'the very great majority of the commercial and financial interests in Cuba who are looking for protection and who could only find such protection in himself'. Furthermore, former Batista opponents were now willing to support him 'as the only possible solution'. And the flattery and cajolery were mixed with threat. If, declared Welles, Batista were to retain his affiliation with the Grau government and the government were to fall, 'that disaster would necessarily inextricably involve not only himself [Batista] but the safety of the Republic, which he has publicly pledged himself to maintain'.[56] Put plainly, the ambitious Batista would only be fulfilling his national duty if he were to decide to stage a *coup* against the Grau government. Batista drew the obvious conclusion: at the end of October he announced that 'a change in government is imperative'.

Sumner Welles had succeeded in uniting some of the anti-Grau factions, in stimulating divisions among nominal Grau supporters, in forging links between important political factions and US investors, and in advancing the ambitions of a powerful army chief who could be relied upon to support US policy requirements. On 15 January 1934 Colonel Fulgencio Batista staged a successful *coup d'état* against the revolutionary government of President Grau San Martín. Batista then installed Carlos Hevia as president (for three days) and, on 18 January, Manuel Márquez Sterling y Guiral as president (for less than a day), before installing Colonel Carlos Mendieta Montefur as president (as a more permanent arrangement). Within five days of the Batista *coup* the United States recognised the Mendieta government as the only legitimate authority in the island. Perhaps now Cuba had at last been made safe for American capitalism.

President Mendieta, sixty when appointed, was widely regarded as ineffectual: Batista ruled as the strong man behind the scenes, an effective dictator in the US-contrived Cuban tradition. On 29 May 1934 the United States and Cuba signed a new treaty finally abrogating the hated Platt Amendment, but with the US retaining the illegal Guantánamo provisions that it continued to regard as strategically vital. Washington saw enough in the new Mendieta–Batista regime to agree the sacrifice of Platt, but few observers imagined that the United States was about to curtail its dominant influence over Cuban politics and the Cuban economy: the word *plattista* continued to be used by the Cuban Left as a term of abuse.

For the rest of the decade Batista ran Cuban affairs, working through the easy mechanisms of puppet presidents and supine administrations: José A. Barnet (1935–36), Miguel Mariano Gómez (1936), and Féderico Laredo Brú (1936–40). The Cuban Communist Party redefined its role in 1937, struck up an accord with Batista, and in return for legal status agreed to support the regime. The party convened its Third National Congress in 1939, with 350 delegates representing some 24,000 members: resolutions were passed, the national labour federation (CNOC) was reorganised, and the Confederación de Trabajadores de Cuba (CTC) was established – but the heady revolutionary fervour of 1933 was no more. Strikes and protests continued, though Batista – via military repression and palliative reforms – seemed able to contain the situation. Thus in 1934 the government introduced a minimum wage law (never fully enforced) and worker employment protection (rarely effective); in January 1935 *habeas corpus* was suspended, with life imprisonment and the death sentence imposed to discourage cane burning and other terrorist acts; in 1937 many political prisoners were released and a range of social provisions (a workers' health insurance scheme, state-funded health programmes, etc.) was proposed; and by the late 1930s the army-run Civic–Military Institute was running various popular social enterprises. It now appeared that Batista, in collaboration with the Communists, was implementing many of the reforms proposed by the radicals.

In 1939 a constituent assembly, representing a wide range of political opinion, convened to draft a new constitution. The resulting document emerged as essentially an agenda of goals: universal suffrage, free elections, political and civil liberties – all in the absence of mechanisms for enforcement. Moreover the constitution explicitly allowed the suspension of all political rights for a period of forty-five days whenever the government judged that 'security' was at risk; no fixed arrangement for elections was defined; and political movements based on sex, class or race were prohibited. Specified entitlements would require enabling legislation, and there was no guarantee that such would ever be introduced. Nonetheless the 1940 constitution represented a significant advance, a clear move in the direction of social democracy, an attempt to shape a new political climate. The Communists were prepared to regard the constitution as 'progressive and in some cases as really advanced', an assessment that clearly served to undermine the efforts of 'extremists' working for more radical change.

Now Batista was ready to step out of uniform and contend the 1940 election with Grau San Martín, recently returned from exile. In the event Batista was elected president – in what were conceived to be, by Cuban standards, relatively fair elections: Batista won more than 800,000 votes, Grau 575,000, and the Communists 73,000. There now followed the seismic global upheavals of the Second World War. Batista had promptly announced that the United States 'can count on us as a factor in their plans for the defence of the Caribbean'; whereupon two American officers, Colonels P. A. del Valle and Archibald Randolph, discussed with Batista how Cuba might be expected to support the US war effort: the United States would, for example, build 'adequate airfields' on the island, and have access to Cuban ports 'in time of need'. Such demands seemingly presented no problems, but the war years had a mixed impact on Cuban fortunes: some industries were boosted but Cuba's European markets were either lost or heavily curtailed, and the formerly lucrative tourist industry all but collapsed. The war did serve to reinforce the favourable attitude of US business to Batista: trade deals were struck and US military forces were given unprecedented rights over Cuban territory. American aviation detachments were stationed at Cuban airfields; US army contingents were given expanded access to Cuban bases; and 'armed and uniformed' US personnel were allowed to go anywhere in Cuba and to photograph the territory. The belligerent Axis powers had conferred the United States with rights over Cuba that Americans had not enjoyed since the US occupation of the island some four decades before.

Batista had emerged as a new American darling. The Cuban Communists had been induced to abandon most of their revolutionary ideals, the other traditional radical groups had been tamed, and as the Second World War drew to a close it was even possible to stage celebrations in Cuba on 4 July, US Independence Day: in 1944 '80,000 Cubans paraded in the streets, and Batista, his breast clinking with North American medals, visited the *Maine* memorial'.[57] The previous year it had been possible for Batista to legalise the (reformist) Communist Party and to establish diplomatic relations with the Soviet Union, then an ally of the United States. In 1944 Batista faced the prospect of a new presidential election with confidence, but this time he had miscalculated. In June Grau San Martín, now almost sixty years old, was swept to power, winning more than one million votes and sweeping five of the six provinces. Batista, having pulled all the strings for more than a decade, was forced to step down. Now Cuba was emerging into the Cold War, soon to join the United Nations on the day (24 October 1945) the UN Charter took effect, and soon to experience the impact of organised crime on the course of Cuban politics.

The Grau presidency (1944–48) quickly ran into the problem of political corruption, seemingly endemic in Cuban society and far from dormant in the war years. The past enthusiasm for reform had now largely evaporated; and now a new generation of politicians were looking to enhancing their own positions by whatever means possible. Soon all branches of municipal, provincial and national government were experiencing embezzlement, graft and the corruption of public office. With hired thugs running much of politics and official activities, the word *gangsterismo* now came to symbolise the unprincipled character of the Grau administration. Officials looted the pension funds, robbed the national treasury, and deliberately misdirected public funds. Grau, while president, was formally charged with the misappropriation of $174 million, while the outgoing Minister of Education was charged with embezzling $20 million. Nor did the situation improve under the administration of Carlos Prío, formerly a colleague of Grau San Martín. One international observer noted in 1950: 'Many . . . inspectors who . . . visit factories expect to be paid for not making bad reports. The factories pay them, moreover, and so they do not even make the inspections.'[58] The scandals connected with Grau's Auténtico (Authentic Revolutionary Party) leadership continued to mount during his term of office.

In 1948, partly as a response to the Grau corruption, Carlos Prío Socarrás was elected president. Again violence was increasing throughout the island, the law against *gangsterismo* having had no effect. The early revolutionary gains were now seen to be largely ephemeral, and the baleful impact of the Cold War was starting to erode any residual impulse to reform. The 1948 election saw a further reduction in Communist influence, with the refashioned Communist Party, the Partido Socialista Popular (PSP), losing control over key labour organisations. Radical labour activists were killed, including Jesús Menéndez, the leader of the sugar workers, and Aracelio Iglesias Díaz, an organiser of the Maritime Workers Union. Such developments were congenial to Washington, keen to combat what it perceived as the growing communist menace throughout the world.

The Auténtico administrations of Grau (1944–48) and Prío (1948–52) had failed to curb the political corruption and the associated gangster violence; more importantly they had failed to satisfy popular aspirations for independence and social progress. There were still disruptive protests against US control and exploitation of the Cuban economy; and when Prío agreed to send Cuban troops to support the US invasion of Korea in 1950, the offer was blocked by a successful campaign around the slogan, 'No cannon fodder for Yankee imperialists'. The general political instability, the growing unpopularity of the Auténticos, the rampant corruption and violence – all were again setting the scene for political upheaval.

A presidential election had been scheduled for June 1952, but it would not take place. Batista, who had robbed the Cuban treasury and then fled to Florida, was planning his return. By dint of intimidation, bribery and use of his army connections, he contrived to get himself elected Senator of Las Villas Province. Then, spending huge sums that he had amassed through embezzlement from the Cuban people, he planted his supporters in the mass organisations, cultivated his support in the armed forces, developed his residual influence in the government bureaucracy, and cajoled the bankers, industrialists and land-owners. Further funds were used to spread propaganda about the venality and corruption of the Auténtico administration; and to promise democratic reforms.

On 8 March 1952 Batista laid his plans for a seizure of power: reliable officers were instructed, and new commands were drawn up in the police and army. The next day Batista's young officers moved to their positions, surrounding strategic sites and arresting the principal Cuban generals (Ruperto Cabrera, the chief of staff, Quirino Uría, inspector-general of the army, Rogelio Soca Llanes, adjutant-general, and others). On 10 March Batista (now a self-appointed General) sent tanks to surround the presidential palace. President Prío, now under no illusions about what was happening, contemplated both resistance and suicide. Soon it was clear to all that General Fulgencio Batista had staged a successful *coup d'état*. On 13 March 1952 Carlos Prío Socarrás flew to Mexico under safe conduct. With Batista's seizure of power, and the imminent creation of a new Cuban dictatorship, constitutional rule had been crushed.

THE MAFIA CONNECTION – I

The geographical position of Cuba attracted Spanish colonialists, American entrepreneurs, US strategists, and gangsters. The criminal exploitation of the island began early: with the handling of contraband, the shipping of slaves and other goods. Cuba was well sited to take produce from Europe, Africa and elsewhere and then to re-export it to the lucrative US market: smugglers plied the sea routes to Florida and beyond, seeking out unpoliced coves and so avoiding tariffs and other unwelcome government impositions. The nineteenth-century American Prohibitionists – blaming alcohol for increased sexual desire, poverty, insanity, racial suicide and crime – resolved on a course of action that would serve to immeasurably boost criminal activity, and to position Cuba as one of the strategic centres of international crime.

The American Prohibition Party, founded in 1869, sought the direct election of its own candidates; but was overtaken in the 1890s by the Anti-Saloon League, then prepared to support pro-Prohibition candidates from the major parties. The success of the Prohibition movement was such that in 1917 Congress passed the Eighteenth Amendment to the Constitution (in the Senate by 65 votes to 20, in the House by 282 to 128), declaring (Section 1) that: '*After one year from the ratification of this article the manufacture, sale, or transportation of intoxicating liquors within, the importation thereof into, or the exportation thereof from the United States and all territory subject to the jurisdiction thereof for beverage purposes is hereby prohibited.*' The required ratification (specified in Section 3) was achieved, and in 1919 Andrew Volstead sponsored the law (specified in Section 2) enforcing the Amendment. On 16 January 1920 Prohibition began in the United States, so laying the basis for a massive expansion of organised crime that would come to affect every sector of American commercial enterprise.

The prodigious demand of the American people for alcohol stimulated the growth of a vast criminal empire. Al Capone, Prohibition's most notorious gangster, was later to comment: 'I make my money by supplying a public demand. If I break the law my customers, who number hundreds of the best people in Chicago, are as guilty as I am. . . . Everybody calls me a racketeer. I call myself a businessman. When I sell liquor it's bootlegging. When my patrons serve it on a silver tray it's hospitality.'[59] And the 'best people' were not always content to leave the hard end of the trade to the racketeers: for example, the respectable businessman Joseph Kennedy, father of a future US president, was a bootlegger.

Soon after the imposition of Prohibition the 'rum-runners' began supplying alcoholic beverages from around the world: Scotch whisky, London gin, French champagne and cognac, Jamaica rum. Well-laden ships hovered on 'Rum Row', just outside America's 12-mile limit, with fast boats used to speed the alcohol ashore. Ports in Cuba and the Bahamas, only a day's sail from Florida, profited enormously from this trade; and the resulting revenues were deployed to fund further criminal enterprises and to buy politicians in Cuba and elsewhere. By the early 1930s Meyer Lansky, one of the most powerful mafia figures, was working to cultivate a friendship with Fulgencio Batista. Soon Lansky was paying Batista millions of dollars a year from mafia casinos in Cuba in return for a monopoly of the business. Thus in 1937 Lansky established a luxurious casino at the Hotel Nacional in Havana, at the same time leasing a lucrative race track near Havana from the New York National City Bank. The pattern was for Lansky to hand the cash to link-man Joseph 'Doc' Stacher, who then conveyed the substantial bribes to Batista himself. Stacher, close to the Cuban government, also helped Meyer Lansky in other ways, supervising the couriers who carried the mafia cash (and Batista's loot) to Switzerland for safe deposit.[60]

The mafia interest in Cuban (and US) politics had an obvious commercial justification: political leaders were in the best position, along with the captains of industry (often themselves with mafia connections), to ensure the security and growth of mob profits. Thus Lansky discussed political matters with Batista, keen to discourage government policies that might adversely affect mafia revenues: for example, Lansky argued against Batista's growing collaboration with the communists in the late 1930s, on the ground that cooperation with the 'reds' might provoke an unhelpful US response. Lansky himself claimed that President Roosevelt had wanted Batista to understand that if he shifted further to the left he would not be allowed to win the 1944 elections (in fact he lost them), and that US 'intelligence people' had asked him [Lansky] to convey this information to Batista.[61] Two decades later the United States government would again work to exploit the mafia's political interests in a (futile) attempt to destroy a Cuban government.

It is significant also that Meyer Lansky saw Cuba as a likely sanctuary for the exiled Charles 'Lucky' Luciano, one-time mafia *Il Capo di Tutti Capi* (boss of bosses). The mafia had cooperated with the US government during the Second World War (by keeping the dockyards peaceful and by aiding the Allied invasion of Sicily), and so a Luciano sojourn in Havana was judged unlikely to upset the Truman administration. Said Lansky to Luciano: '. . . why not Cuba? There's no reason why you shouldn't come and live in Havana. You could operate from the island the way you did in the old days. You'll be warmly welcomed there, I'll make sure of that. And there shouldn't be any flak from the American government, since I did exactly what Naval Intelligence asked me to in Cuba. . . . We don't want war or revolution there. All we need is peace, so that we can get on with the business that we set up together . . . '.[62]

The mafia enterprises developed by Lansky and Luciano in Cuba had thrived in the late 1930s. In January 1937 most of Cuba's gambling operations were transferred by decree from civil to military control; but when Batista became dissatisfied with the gambling revenues he asked Lou Smith, a New England operator of horse and dog tracks, to improve the performance of the Oriental Park racetrack, one of the main destinations of gambling visitors to Havana. Smith in turn invited Meyer Lansky to run the track's two casinos. Lansky's own staff were brought in to replace the

Cubans at the Oriental Park casino room; and Al Levy, a Lansky crony, was invited to run the crap tables. Once the casino had been reformed Levy and Lansky devised a ceremony, the presentation of the 'Golden Ticket', to mark the new opening; and at a special reception Colonel Batista was presented with his own complimentary 'key' to the casino room.[63] Under Lansky's management the gambling revenues rapidly increased; and Lansky, like Al Capone, was sometimes inclined to philosophise: 'If Socrates and Plato had trouble defining what morality was, how can people come along, just like that, and lay down that gambling is immoral?'[64] In such a climate it was natural that Lucky Luciano should regard Havana as a natural refuge.

In 1946 Meyer Lansky was preparing for Luciano's imminent arrival in Cuba: he arrived by plane via Mexico City, Cuban officials rushed him through VIP facilities with no customs control, and then he was driven to meet Lansky at the Hotel Nacional. From there, with the permission of the Minister of the Interior, Alfredo Pequeño, for Luciano to stay in Cuba as long as he wished, the erstwhile 'Boss of Bosses' was driven to the elegant Miramar suburb. Luciano rejoiced to be back in the Americas. At the Hotel Nacional he had savoured the moment: 'I think it was the palm trees that got me. Everyplace you looked there was palm trees and it made me feel like I was back in Miami. . . . When I looked down over the Caribbean from my window, I realised somethin' else; the water was just as pretty as the Bay of Naples, but it was only ninety miles from the United States. That meant I was practically back in America.'[65] Now Lansky and Luciano were planning for the future. 'Doc' Stacher recalled their calculations: 'Both men were banking on the fact that Tom Dewey would run for president in 1948. . . . Meyer and Charlie were certain that Dewey would accept financial support from them – and in return they would be allowed to operate their gambling without much interference.'[66]

With Luciano ensconced in Havana, and with the rackets producing the revenues, Cuba became a focus for mafia intrigue. In late 1946 Lansky travelled round the United States inviting mafia bosses to meet with Luciano in Havana for discussions about future business opportunities. It proved to be a famous gathering. In early 1947 mafia chieftains from all over American flew to Havana where some thirty-six suites had been reserved. Every underworld boss of any importance attended: Albert 'The Executioner' Anastasia, Joe Adonis, Frank Costello, Carlo Gambino, Willie Moretti, Joe Profaci, Mike Miranda, Vito Genovese, Augie Pisano, Joe 'The Fat Man' Magliocco, Carlos Marcello, 'Dandy Phil' Kastel, Tony Accardo, Charlie and Rocco Fischetti (Al Capone's heirs), Santos Trafficante, Joe Bonanno, Tommy 'Three-Fingers Brown' Lucchese, and

Meyer Lansky himself. On 31 January Frank Sinatra requested a gun permit, saying that he sometimes carried large sums of money. After spending time at Luciano's mansion on Allison Island, and visiting the Colonial Inn in Hallendale, a casino jointly owned by Adonis and Lansky, Sinatra flew to Havana on 11 February. There he consorted with the mafia chieftains. 'Doc' Stacher later commented, recalling the 1947 conference: 'The Italians among us were very proud of Frank . . . they had spent a lot of money helping him with his career . . .'.[67] The Havana conclave lasted a week, and everyone brought envelopes of cash for Luciano. Cuba had hosted one of the most remarkable business conferences that the world had seen.

Plans had been laid to buy land on the Isle of Pines, off Cuba and belonging to it, for conversion into a vast gambling centre, a Caribbean Monte Carlo. But now trouble was brewing for the mafia conspiracy. Ray Olivera, an agent of the US Narcotics Bureau, had succeeded in tapping Luciano's telephone in Havana. The Bureau chief, Harry Ansliger, then complained to the Cuban ambassador in Washington that Luciano's presence in Havana was a danger to the United States. Batista, reminded by Lansky of the massive bribes he had received, struggled to prevent any upset to the mafia schemes. The Cuban police chief, Benito Herrera, and Interior Minister Pequeño, as well as various other officials and a Cuban congressman, had all been on the mafia payroll; and so Cuba continued to resist US demands to expel Luciano. Then Washington threatened to embargo the shipment of medical supplies to Cuba. President Grau San Martín complained of US bullying, but Cuba could not resist the mounting American pressure for ever. Despite all the millions of dollars poured into the pockets of Batista and his cronies, Luciano was first arrested and then (February 1947) put aboard a Turkish vessel and sent back to Italy.

The mafia plans for Cuba had suffered a setback, but they were far from at an end. In the early 1950s, following the Batista *coup d'état*, Meyer Lansky was developing the gambling empire in Cuba that he had started before the war. Lansky was not involved in the planning of the *coup* but, warned by Batista that there might be 'problems' in March 1952 (and having discussed Batista's political options with him), it is likely that he knew what was about to happen. Once Batista was again securely in power, Lansky persuaded him to invest government money in the development of the mafia-run gambling empire. Hotels sprang up along the sea front in Havana, and Lansky rejoiced that he was helping the unemployment problem: 'I got Sammy Bratt, who worked for me in the United States, to open a casino school in our Montmartre Club in Havana. It was a functioning casino, but hundreds of Cuban youngsters were trained there to become efficient operators at blackjack, roulette, and the other games. We taught them something about running a hotel properly. It was hard work because they were uneducated, and it would have been easier to import Americans. But I ran it as a kind of social experiment.'[68] By now Lansky had a monopoly of the casino business in Cuba. When the mafia boss Santos Trafficante, from Florida, wanted to set up a casino on the island Batista told him that he would have to get approval from the 'Little Man' 'before you can get a licence . . .'. The Lansky organisation was now running a substantial part of the Cuban economy.

The massive explosion of gambling in Cuba after the 1952 Batista *coup* led to the paradoxical situation that many of the gambling houses were fraudulent: this was not good for Batista or Lansky since the high rollers had little interest in visiting crooked houses (as opposed to 'honest' houses run by the mafia). This led to the nice irony of Meyer Lansky being invited by Batista to advise on gambling reform. Lansky took on his new job for the winter season of 1953–54, agreeing an annual retainer of around $25,000.[69] The subsequent reforms included blackjack dealt from a box, rather than the hand, 'ladder men' expected to spot sharp practice from their seats on stepladders, and the banning of razzle-dazzle, cubolo, and other 'come-on' games.[70] In such a fashion the mafia chieftain Meyer Lansky, the much feared 'Little Man', cleaned up Cuba's gambling houses.

In 1955 the Nacional was taken over by International Hotels Inc., a subsidiary of Pan Am; and a luxurious complex of public rooms was sublet to Lansky. His new casino, one of the public rooms, opened the winter season of 1955–56 with Lansky's brother Jacob ('Jack' or 'Jake') in charge of the casino floor and Eartha Kitt as the star of the show. Jacob's younger daughter, Linda, gambled in the casino, as did various Lansky friends and associates; but Batista, despite his commitment to the business relationship, rarely visited the casinos. He was happy to grant the required tax exemptions (as with Hotel Law 2074 in 1955), and to take his rake-off, but he left Lansky to run the business. In 1956 Lansky began construction of his own Riviera Hotel, 21 stories and 440 rooms, the biggest casino-hotel in the world, outside Las Vegas. Soon the biggest gamblers in America were flocking to Lansky's Cuba establishments: in particular, the Riviera, a gambling palace, was an immense success, attracting men who thought nothing of writing a cheque for $30,000 at the end of an evening's entertainment.

By 1958 Meyer Lansky and Fulgencio Batista were enjoying annual revenues of many millions of dollars. There were frequent political disruptions as unkempt but highly motivated guerrilla groups made inroads into the mafia–government symbiosis, but the situation seemed to be containable. The army remained loyal to Batista, and he had no compunction about using traditional terror and repression to maintain his brutal and mercenary grip over Cuban society. The Batista who had once been associated with reform, and who had at one time alarmed Washington with his leftist leanings, was now rich and corrupt – and thus well regarded by US policy makers. But it was all drawing to a close. Lansky and Batista – and their assorted tribe of relatives, cronies, corrupt officials, sadistic police officers and mafia fixers – had one view about Cuba's future. Fidel Castro Ruz had another.

THE CASTRO FACTOR

Fidel Castro's father, Ángel María Bautista Castro Arguiz, had left Galicia in north-west Spain to sail to Cuba with the Spanish army at the time of the Spanish–American War. In 1898 he fought against both the Cuban rebels and the US army: to Ángel Castro it was essential that Cuba remain a Spanish colony. After the defeat of the Spanish forces Ángel worked as a labourer for the Nipe Bay Company, a subsidiary of the powerful United Fruit Company.[71] Many years later the columnist Drew Pearson published a story (7 February 1960) suggesting that Fidel's abiding hostility to the United States derived in part from his knowledge of how his father was treated at a United Fruit warehouse (Fidel himself has always been reluctant to talk about his family roots). Pearson's claim that Ángel Castro was fired for stealing refined sugar was subsequently denied by United Fruit. The company stated that Ángel had worked on one of their railroads in 1904, had eventually bought his own land, and in 1919 or 1920 sold United Fruit two or three houses that he then owned.[72] It seems surprising that a pick and shovel labourer hired to dig ditches could have achieved this degree of economic success.[73]

The Castro *hacienda*, Manacas, comprised about 10,000 acres and employed 500 men.[74] The estate lay in a region that came to be dominated by four large American companies: United Fruit, the Dumois-Nipe Company (producing bananas, oranges, grapefruit and sugar cane), the Spanish-American Iron Company, and the Cuba Railroad Company. By the 1950s the Castro *hacienda* was supplying an annual quota of some 18,000 tons of sugar cane a year to the *Central Miranda*.[75] Ángel Castro was sufficiently well established to send Fidel (and Fidel's brother Ramón and Raúl) to the La Salle school in Santiago de Cuba, attended by many upper-class boys from the region. Fidel had entered the public grammar school in Marcané at the age of four, but after a year he was transferred to Santiago, going first to the Colegio La Salle, then to the Colegio Dolores, and finally to the Belén school run by Jesuits in Havana. Fidel is said to have been tormented at school by two circumstances of his background: that his father was not married to his mother, Lina Ruz, when Fidel was born; and by the fact that Ángel had arrived in Cuba as a 'soldier of Spain'. Thus Fidel was mocked as 'doubly illegitimate – politically as well as personally'[76] – though he was probably not physically bullied: tall and strong, he won a prize (1943–4) as Cuba's best all-round school athlete. Of Fidel's school life, his brother Raúl commented: 'He succeeded in everything. In sport, in study. And every day he fought. He had a very explosive nature. He defied the most powerful and the strongest and when he was beaten he began again the next day. He never gave up.'[77] Castro himself was later to comment: 'I spent most of my time being fresh . . . whenever I disagreed with something the teacher said to me, or whenever I got mad, I would swear at her and immediately leave school, running as fast as I could. . . . One day, I had just sworn at the teacher, and was racing down the rear corridor. I took a leap and landed on a board from a guava-jelly box with a nail in it. As I fell, the nail somehow stuck in my tongue. When I got back home my mother said to me: "God punished you for swearing at the teacher." I didn't have the slightest doubt that it was really true.'[78] At the same time he enjoyed school trips to the mountains: to such places as El Cobre, Gran Piedra, and the foothills of Sierra Maestra ('I did not imagine that mountains would one day play such an important role in my life').

There is little evidence that Castro was political before his graduation from Belén. In 1940, aged thirteen, he apparently tried to organise a sugar workers' strike against his father, but his sister Juana said (*Life*, 28 August 1964) that Fidel showed no interest in the *guajiros* on the estate. Perhaps Belén, concerned with the education of Cuba's future right-wing leaders, had discouraged any commitment to social justice. But when, in October 1945, Castro went to the University of Havana to study law, all this was to change. He had no particular interest in law *per se*. Thus in 1961 he commented: 'I ask myself why I studied law. I don't know. I attribute it partly to those who said "He talks a lot, he ought to be a lawyer". Because I had the habit of debating and discussing, I was persuaded I was qualified to be a lawyer.'[79] But, on his own admission, he never attended lectures, never read a book except just before examinations, and often regretted that he had not been made to study something else.[80] While a teenager, Castro had written to President Roosevelt, applauding his 1940 re-election, praising democracy, condemning Nazism, and requesting a $20 bill (the State

Department expressed regrets that the money could not be sent – the first occasion on which a Castro request for US aid was refused). Now, in the heady atmosphere of university debate (and violence), Castro would soon develop a sterner approach to political thought and activity.

From the very start of his time at Havana University Castro was involved in political discussion and agitation. The University Students' Federation (FEU) was a principal focus of student political activity and exerted an influence far beyond the university. The FEU president and other officials were elected by the presidents of the thirteen schools that together constituted the university. In his first year Castro was elected a 'class delegate' in the Law School, the lowest elective position in the FEU organisation. His friends at that time included Alfredo Guevara (no relation to Ernesto 'Che' Guevara), FEU secretary in 1948 and later the Cuban ambassador to UNESCO in Paris, Leonel Soto, with Guevara already a member of the Communist youth organisation, Justo Fuentes, Alfred 'Chino' Esquivel, Raúl 'El Flaco' Granados, Rafael del Pino and Baudilio 'Bilito' Castellanos. Already it was clear that Castro was a leader rather than a 'team player' in politics as in sport – which is probably why he failed to be elected to any important university post. He thrived in the turbulent atmosphere of the university, which, traditionally autonomous, provided a sanctuary not only for extremist politicians of all types but also for assorted gangsters and criminals who often saw advantage in dubbing themselves 'revolutionary'. The police and the army were constitutionally barred from the campus but the university was not immune to the turmoil and violence of Cuban society. Brutal beatings and shoot-outs were common on campus, and few of Castro's biographers have doubted that 'he joined in the extraordinary gang warfare in which against his better judgement he excelled'.[81]

Of the various violent revolutionary groups active in the university and outside, Castro has been associated with Rolando Masferrer's Socialist Revolutionary Movement (MSR), founded in 1945; and the Insurrectional Revolutionary Union (UIR), headed by Emilio Tró (until he was murdered), who fought alongside the anarchists in the Spanish–American War and served with the US Army in the Guadalcanal campaign in the Second World War. Castro took part in the abortive invasion of the Dominican Republic, organised by the MSR and other groups, in 1947 (which led to Castro's famed and well-attested swim across the shark-infested Bay of Nipe). The MSR was opposed to what it saw as Communist 'revolutionary socialism' (the Communists at that time found Castro too unreliable), and campaigned against US imperialism and Grau's *Auténtico* party. One of Castro's first political acts was to organise a protest against bus-fare increases introduced by Grau: after the police had stopped and beaten the demonstrators, Castro (his head heavily bandaged) and Raúl visited the radio station and newspaper offices to spread word of what had happened. The threat of a second demonstration won the students, including Castro (his head 'still wound up like a mummy's'), a meeting with Grau. Here Castro reportedly whispered to his friends: 'I have the formula to take power and once and for all get rid of this son-of-a-bitch . . . when the old guy [Grau] returns, let's pick him up, the four of us, and throw him off the balcony. Once the president is dead, we'll proclaim the triumph of the student revolution and speak to the people from the radio'; and Esquivel reportedly replied: '*Vamos, guajiro, tu estás "chiflado"*' ('Listen, redneck, you're nuts').[82] Grau, it is worth remembering, was a constitutional president in the period between the two phases of Batista dictatorship.

On 27 November 1946, aged twenty and in his second year at law school, Castro delivered a public speech that won front-page coverage in the next day's newspapers. The occasion was the ceremony organised by the university for the seventy-fifth anniversary of the execution of the eight medical students by the Spanish authorities for their activities in the independence struggle. At the martyrs' grave in the Colón cemetery in Vedado Castro paid the expected tribute, and then launched into a bitter denunciation of the Grau government. He accused the regime of exploitation, denounced Grau's plans for re-election, and urged Cubans to rise up and bring down the government. In particular he condemned 'the presidential tolerance for some ministers who steal public funds and for the gangs that invade the inner circles of the government'; proclaiming that 'if Machado and Batista assassinated and persecuted decent persons and honourable revolutionaries, Doctor Grau has now killed all the hopes of the Cuban people, transforming himself into a scourge for the entire nation'.[83] Two months later, on 20 January 1947, Castro was one of thirty-four signatories of an FEU declaration against Grau's possible re-election; and, as a law school delegate, he helped to draft the document, asserting that 'the ideas of re-election, extension of the period in power, or even the imposition of candidates can be found only in the sick minds of traitors, opportunists and the consistently insincere'. The declaration (signed also by FEU president Enrique Ovares, Law School president Castellanos, and Castro's future brother-in-law Rafael Díaz-Balart) pledged 'to fight against re-election even if the price we have to pay in the struggle is our own death – it is better to die on your feet than to live on your knees'.[84]

Castro had denounced the 'betrayed revolution': the peasants were still without land, and Cuba's wealth remained in foreign hands. Also, five years before Batista's *coup d'état* (1952), Castro was warning about the growing power of the military; in 1947, he and the other student revolutionaries, following in the footsteps of José Martí, were passionately denouncing the corrupt and exploitative role of 'Yankee Imperialism'. Cuban resentment of the northern 'monster' was not a Castro invention.

The protests continued. On 22 January 1948 an army captain shot dead Jesús Menéndez Larrondo, a black union leader who was also a Communist member of the Chamber of Deputies. General Pérez, the army chief of staff, promptly commended the captain, declaring that 'every time a similar situation [i.e. a refusal to submit to arrest] occurs, similar action is to be taken'. On 11 February Commander José Caramés, the police chief of the university district, pistol-whipped a student, on the ('autonomous') university campus, who had been protesting against police brutality. Castro organised a demonstration for the following day: a huge Cuban flag was carried, signs proclaimed 'We protest against the violation of university autonomy!', and the students shouted 'Out with Caramés, Down with Grau – The Assassins!' The police moved in and began clubbing the protestors. Later reports stated that Fidel Castro (headlined for the first time) had 'suffered a grave contusion' on the head. In fact the wound was superficial – but of immense symbolic value. Now Castro's blood had been shed for the revolution!

A few days later, on 22 February, Manolo Castro (no relation), an earlier FEU president and now State Secretary of Sports and friend of various *Auténtico* leaders, was lured out of a cinema and shot dead. Fidel Castro was accused of implication in the murder. He was arrested, brought to court, and had his passport confiscated; but the evidence was inconclusive. Castro has been accused also of other murders,[85] and was doubtlessly capable of such acts (Castro: '*When the worst is enthroned, a pistol at his belt, it is necessary to carry pistols oneself in order to fight for the best*'); though, even if proved guilty, he would always have claimed revolutionary justification.

On 29 March 1948 Castro and Rafael del Pino, then both members of UIR, arrived in Bogotá, the capital of Columbia, to attend a Pan-American Conference arranged to convert the old Pan-American Union of American states into a more closely knit body, the Organisation of American States (OAS). On 3 April Castro and del Pino were dropping anti-US leaflets from balconies in the Teatro Colono, where Columbian notables were attending a public ceremony. The two students were arrested and interrogated, more Communist leaflets were found in their hotel rooms, and they were ordered to cease such hostile acts ('*actos hostiles*'). Six days later the great Columbian reformer Jorge Eliécer Gaitán was murdered by Juan Roa Sierra (quickly lynched), while on a demonstration. Bogotá erupted: in what was later dubbed the 'Bogotazo', riots broke out, shops were looted, police stations blown up, and Bogotá collapsed into violent chaos. Estimates of the number killed reached 3000, and someone had to be blamed.[86]

The US representatives at the Pan-American Conference were quick to blame the Communists in general and one individual in particular. Thus William Pawley, the US ambassador to the United Nations, a veteran anti-Communist in Bogotá at the time, later declared: 'We had information that there was a Cuban there, a very young man who appeared to us not to be the real threat'; but then Pawley remembered hearing a voice on the radio immediately after Gaitán's assassination: 'This is Fidel Castro from Cuba. This is a Communist revolution. The President has been killed, all the military establishments in Columbia are now in our hands, the Navy has capitulated to us and this Revolution has been a success.' Few commentators think this makes much sense, though other items of evidence support the idea of Castro's involvement in the *Bogotazo*: Alberto Niño, Columbian police chief, claimed that Castro and del Pino had been sent in to organise the riots; a guest at the Hotel Claridge claimed to have heard the two students rejoicing in their success, and one report tells how they brought in 'a large quantity of arms'.[87] Castro himself admits he was active in the riots after the Gaitán murder,[88] but this is a far cry from being involved in the original assassination. Perhaps, as 'Gloria Gaitán and most historians believe . . . logically and in terms of the evidence, Gaitán was killed by the Columbian far Right, by some conspiracy of oligarchic conservatives.'[89]

In any event the *Bogotazo* had a profound effect on Castro, stimulating his efforts 'to create political conscience in Cuba'. He was appalled by the total lack of organisation in the popular uprising, and saw also the need for public discipline in the triumph of the revolution. There would have to be no anarchy, looting or disorders; the people would not be allowed to take the law into their own hands: 'Bogotá's greatest influence was on the Cuban revolutionary strategy, on the idea of educating the people during our struggle.'[90] Castro may also have heeded Gaitán's own words: *No soy un hombre, soy un pueblo* (I am not a man, I am a people). It had to be essential that the revolution survive the death of any one individual. But when Gaitán died, it seemed his own people, the Columbian poor, were without direction. In the early days of the Cuban revolution that particular question was not asked of the Cuban people.

Castro's return to Cuba was widely reported in Havana newspapers: aged twenty-one, he was now beginning to acquire an international significance. At once he plunged into the presidential election campaign, maintaining his strong support for the candidacy of Senator Eduardo 'Eddy' Chibás, who had created the Ortodoxos (or Orthodox) party. Castro at that time, despite all his revolutionary rhetoric, was still prepared to operate within constitutional politics. On the eve of the elections Castro described the event as 'a decisive battle' between Chibás's idealism and the 'vested interest' of the Grau *Auténticos*. In the event Chibás was defeated, whereupon Castro continued to agitate for radical change – and then ran into a fresh crisis. On 6 June Oscar Fernández Cabral, a university police sergeant, was fatally shot outside his house; before he died he reportedly named Castro as the assassin, and the charge was corroborated by an unnamed witness (who later retracted, saying that he had been bribed by the police). Castro denied any involvement in the murder, and declared before a judge that the police were looking for an excuse to assassinate him. The matter was dropped.

On 10 October 1948 President Carlos Prío Socarrás was inaugurated, and Cuba began a new phase of corruption, mismanagement and civil violence. Castro continued with his political activities, at the same time cramming for his law degrees. In September 1950 he graduated as Doctor of Law, Doctor of Social Sciences and Doctor of Diplomatic Law, claiming to have completed forty-eight of the fifty required courses on his own, a record in the elapsed time. Then another event took place that was to have a deep impact on Castro's passionate political nature. On 5 August 1951 Senator Chibás, in whom Castro had at one time invested much hope for a Cuban political renewal, shot himself in the abdomen while giving his weekly radio broadcast. The reason remains a mystery, though perhaps Chibás's final words should be taken at face value. At the end of the speech he gave an exhortation: 'Comrades of the Orthodoxy, forward! To economic independence, to political liberty, to social justice! Take a broom and sweep away the thieves in the government! People of Cuba, rise up and move! People of Cuba, awaken! . . . This is my last knock to awaken the civic conscience of the Cuban people . . .'. And then, aged forty-three, he discharged a powerful .38 Colt Special revolver into his stomach. On his way to the hospital, in a car driven by Castro, Chibás whispered, 'I am dying for the revolution . . . I am dying for Cuba . . .'. In fact he took eleven days to die.

If the suicide of Chibás had damaged the possibility of democracy in Cuba, a more powerful blow came with Batista's *coup d'état* on 10 March 1952. The two events were not unrelated: Chibás's death had prepared the ground for the *coup* the following year. Castro, according to some accounts, had suggested that the funeral procession be diverted with the aim of placing Chibás's corpse in the presidential chair at the palace, so proclaiming a symbolic victory for the people. The officer commanding the escort of the gun carriage transporting the body rejected the idea, and an imaginative political opportunity was lost! Soon, as the inevitable alternative, Castro would be waging a revolutionary struggle against General Fulgencio Batista, by now the darling of the United States and the political fixer for the Mafia.

Castro had run his own campaign against Prío, not least by representing thousands of the poor in Havana whose homes the government was planning to raze for the building of a huge civic square. In this slum district, La Pelusa, Castro told the people what to say to the government inspectors, and demanded in court that the Public Works Ministry indemnify the owners of the properties (mostly shacks) to be removed. Under pressure from Castro, the government agreed to pay compensation in every case; but then Batista staged the *coup*, cancelled the agreement, evicted the urban dwellers of La Pelusa, and built the civic square.

The scale of corruption under the Prío administration was also exposed, at least in part, by Castro. On 28 January 1952, the anniversary of José Martí's birth, he presented an indictment of Prío to the Court of Accounts, a federal tribunal, charging that Prío had taken bribes, freed a friend imprisoned for child molestation (then making him nominal owner of presidential farms, violated labour laws, forcing soldiers into 'slave labour', replaced paid workers by soldiers, and sold farm produce at prices below its market value. Prío, Castro declared, had built 'ostentatious palaces, swimming pools, airports, and a whole series of luxuries', and had acquired 'a chain of the best farms and most valuable lands' in the Havana region. On 19 February Castro issued a further indictment, charging that Prío was funding political gangs, employing 2000 gangsters in public jobs, and corruptly increasing his personal land holdings.[91]

At the same time Castro was also campaigning for the forthcoming congressional elections. Roberto Agramonte had taken Chibás's place as the *Ortodoxo* presidential candidate; and now it was widely assumed that the *Ortodoxo* Castro, enthusiastically supported by the urban and rural proletariat, would win a congressional seat for his Radical Orthodox Action (ARO) faction. Castro, by all accounts, had run a *blitzkrieg* of a campaign, inaugurating a new radio programme, sending stencilled personal messages to all the 100,000 *Ortodoxo* party members in Havana, and electrifying the crowds that flocked to his rallies (Conchita Fernández, who had been Chibás's secretary, recalled that Castro 'had such magnetism and people simply had to listen to him').

All the efforts were in vain. Batista overthrew the Prío government, and the elections never took place. Had they done so, it is likely that Castro would have won a seat in the Congress, stood later for the Senate, and then campaigned for the presidency. Until 10 March 1952 Castro had been well prepared to work through constitutional politics. Now that route had been blocked, and another way would have to be found: Batista, inadvertently, had launched the Castro revolution and secured his own ultimate political demise. After the *coup* the United States at once recognised the military dictatorship.

Castro had suspected that Batista was planning a *coup*. Raúl Chibás, Eduardo's brother, later recalled that Castro had told him that Batista was thinking of a *coup d'état*; and some commentators suggest that Castro was told of unusual military and civilian activity at Batista's estate. The *coup*, when it came, met little resistance. Castro's first response was to continue working ('simply as one more soldier') within the *Ortodoxo* movement, but it soon became clear that more was needed: *'I began to organise the first action cells, hoping to work alongside those leaders . . . who might be ready to fulfil the elemental duty of fighting against Batista. . . . But when none of these leaders showed that they had the ability, the resolution, the seriousness of purpose or the means to overthrow Batista it was then that I finally worked out a strategy on my own.'*[92]

There was no alternative to the abandonment of traditional methods; Batista had seen to that. The moment was 'revolutionary, not political. . . . Revolution opens the way to true merit – to those who have valour and sincere ideals, to those who carry their breast uncovered, and who take up the battle standard in their hands. To a revolutionary party there must correspond a young and revolutionary leadership, of popular origin, which will save Cuba.'[93] Without consulting the *Ortodoxo* leadership, relying instead on his own following within the movement, Castro developed his desperate plan: for an attack on the Santiago and Bayamo barracks in Oriente province. If successful, he would win weapons and recruits, and possibly spark off a general uprising.

The attacks – on the Moncada barracks (Santiago) and the Bayamo barracks – were planned with care. Most of Castro's guerrilla band, some 134 men, would attack Moncada, with a mere 28 left to assault Bayamo. The 26 July (1953) was chosen since officers were reportedly attending a carnival celebration the previous night: they would not, it was thought, be ready for fighting at dawn the following day. With Moncada holding about 1000 soldiers, Castro's meagre force was massively outnumbered, but he was relying on the element of surprise: he would capture the barracks and then invite disenchanted soldiers to come over to his side. The guerrillas were able to muster a grand total of three US army rifles, six ancient Winchesters, an old machine gun and various game rifles. Juan Almeida, one of Castro's supporters, later said that he awaited his rifle 'as if it had been a Messiah', and then 'froze' when he saw it was only a 0.22.[94] *Fidelista* women had sewn *Batistiano* uniforms for the guerrillas, to disguise them and so to spread confusion in the ranks of the defending soldiers.

The omens were not good. Castro himself reportedly forgot to bring his glasses, and so was hampered by poor sight in the heroic exploit. Perhaps more importantly, the morale of some of the guerrillas began to crack: ten suddenly declared that they would be unable to take part in the attack on Moncada. At 5.00 a.m. on the 26 July twenty-six cars carrying 111 men, all dressed as *Batistiano* sergeants, and two women drove into Santiago to launch the Castro revolution. The poet of the group, Raúl Gómez García, had included apposite words from the Cuba national anthem into a hymn he had written for the occasion: '*Morir por la Patria es Vivir*' (To die for the Fatherland is to live). And die they did.

By all accounts the *Fidelista* attacks were a military disaster. After some initial inconsequential successes – Raúl Castro captured the Palace of Justice in Santiago, and Abel Santamaría the Civil Hospital – the guerrilla groups were completely routed by Batista's well-armed soldiers. Castro's forces were poorly armed, unfamiliar with the Santiago terrain, and poorly coordinated; Castro himself was later to admit that the better armed half of his forces had gone astray at the entrance to Santiago, 'and were not on hand to help us at the decisive moment'. The battle for Moncada lasted about one hour, yielding at that time many wounded but few fatalities. The attack at Bayamo also collapsed, with some dispute about Castro's leadership, many wounded and six guerrilla fatalities.

About a half of the original force of around 160 guerrillas were captured, and most of those taken in the first day or two were murdered, usually after extensive torture. The prisoners were beaten with rifle butts and tortured in other ways; at Bayamo three men were dragged behind a jeep for miles. At his subsequent trial Castro charged that Moncada had been turned into a place of death and torture: 'the walls were splattered with parts and particles of human bodies: skin, brains, human hair – not the marks of honourable death, but of bullets fired only a few inches from human bodies.'[95] Judge Manuel Urrutía, later Castro's President of Cuba (subsequently deposed), commented that the killings were 'savage and barbaric' and vainly demanded that Batista punished the guilty soldiers.[96] The guerrillas not immediately captured, including Castro, were subsequently rounded up and taken before the courts; a number of Communists, including Lázaro Peña, Blas Roca and Carlos Rafael Rodríguez, were also arrested. Castro was sentenced to fifteen years imprisonment, Raúl to thirteen, and others to shorter terms; the charges against the Communists were dropped.

The attack on the Moncada barracks had proved a total military failure: Castro had lost many of his staunchest supporters, either through death or incarceration, and there seemed no way of resurrecting the revolution. But to all this there was another side. The revolution had its glorious martyrs, the Batista regime had been shaken and shown signs of panic,[97] and at his trial on 16 October Castro had given a brilliant speech, *History Will Absolve Me* (Appendix 6), that was to form the basis of the Moncada programme for the Cuban Revolution.[98] In Carlos Franquí's work *The Book of the Twelve*, Celia Sánchez, one of Castro's closest associates, is quoted as saying that Moncada was 'the commencement of the struggle . . . Moncada – it was the mother of the Revolution'.[99] Similarly the Cuban revolutionary Faustino Pérez commented that the combatants of Moncada 'did not achieve their military objectives, but they did achieve their revolutionary objectives'. Haydée Santamaría recalled later that it was at Moncada 'that we were forged, where we got used to the sight of blood, to men suffering, to the struggle'. And in the same vein the Cuban writer Guillermo Cabrera Infante wrote: 'The Moncada attack . . . was a failure from the military point of view. But it was a resounding political success. After July 26, 1953, everything in Cuba became of vast historical moment – brutal, bloody, and inevitable.' It was at Moncada that the *July 26 Movement* was born.

On 15 May 1955 General Batista, responding to public pressure and assuming that Castro was no longer a threat, offered an amnesty to Fidel and his fellow-prisoners. Cuba remained racked by strikes, demonstrations and general disruption; and it is unlikely that Batista would have freed Castro in this atmosphere if he had judged him to be of much consequence. On 11 August Prío, covered by the same amnesty, returned to his farm, *La Chata*, and resolved to oppose Batista only through the ballot box. Castro, perceiving that constitutional means were no longer a way to power, issued a fresh manifesto pledging that the fight would continue: 'Our freedom will not be a fiesta or a rest, but a struggle and a duty, fighting ardently from the first day without respite for a country free of despotism and misery, whose better destiny nothing and nobody will be able to change.' Back in Havana, having been released from the Isle of Pines, Castro began fresh agitations against Batista, but made no inroads into the US-supported police state. Soon he was resolving that a fresh violent struggle would have to be launched, and that this could not be done from within the confines of the Cuban dictatorship. Castro concluded that it would be necessary to leave Cuba, to prepare elsewhere for a new invasion of the island: 'We will return when we can bring to our people the liberty and the right to live decently without despotism and without hungers. . . . Since all doors to a civic struggle are closed to the people, no other solution remains but that of '68 and '95' [1868 and 1895, see Chapter 4]. On 7 July 1955 Castro left Havana en route for Mexico. Here it was that he met Ernesto 'Che' Guevara, an asthmatic medical graduate from Argentina, with whom he was to plan the next phase of the Cuban Revolution.

On 19 March 1956 Castro finally broke his links with the *Ortodoxo* party; no longer would he present his efforts and ideas as a part of *Chibasismo*. The July 26 Movement had been defined as 'the revolutionary apparatus of *Chibasismo*', but now the radical social revolution that Castro wanted for Cuba would have to be achieved via a different route.

The planning continued, though at first with desultory progress in the unsympathetic climate of Mexican politics. When Castro and his followers struggled to accumulate arms they were invariably seized by the Mexican authorities; some of the group – Cándido González, Jesús Montané and Máximo Celaya – were arrested, jailed and brutally treated; and there was at least one attempt, probably by a Batista agent, to kill Castro. Throughout 1956, despite the police harassment and limited funds, the plans were laid for an invasion of Cuba. A farm, *Rancho La Rosa*, was bought outside Mexico City, where the guerrillas received training at the hands of Colonel Alberto Bayo, a former Spanish officer who had served General Franco in Spanish Morocco; and the weapons, some smuggled in from Cuba, began to accumulate. In November word about what was transpiring reached the Mexican police: three caches of arms were seized, and two of the group were arrested and imprisoned. Now it seemed that Castro's plans would be frustrated. He resolved to act without further delay.

It was decided that the 'invasion' force, a pitifully ill-prepared band, would sail from the small port of Tuxpán on the Gulf of Mexico. A shabby 38-foot wooden boat, the *Granma*, propelled by two small diesel engines, was located at Tuxpán; and the American owner agreed to sell the vessel to the Cuban 'fool' for twenty thousand dollars.[100] The *Granma*, ill-equipped for the enterprise, was in a poor state of repair, and in any case was only designed to carry twenty or so people. Eighty-two men were packed into the little vessel: twenty of whom had been involved in the attacks at Moncada and Bayamo, and four of whom were non-Cubans (Guevara, the Italian Gino Doné, the Mexican Guillén, and the Dominican Ramón Mejías de Castillo). Castro, designated a major, commanded three platoons captained by Raúl Castro, Juan Almeida and José Smith; with Guevara the medical officer. Castro was necessarily the supreme commander but Onelio Pino, an ex-captain in the Cuban navy, was ship's captain.

On the wet night of 26 November 1956 the rebel force set sail in *Granma* to begin the next stage in the planned overthrow of the Batista dictatorship. The boat was so overloaded that water was almost coming over the sides. The 82 men had slim provisions and meagre weapons: two anti-tank guns, 35 rifles with telescopic sights, 55 Mendoza rifles, three Thompson machine guns and 40 machine gun pistols. The crowded men sat with their legs doubled up; many became nauseous and vomited. There were rough seas and bad weather all the way across, and the vessel began to ship water. Then it became clear that the engine was in a sorry state, that there was a contrary wind, and that the navigation of the boat left much to be desired. The voyage took seven days: the men were exhausted, hungry, thirsty, sick and less than enthusiastic about invading anywhere. Another military disaster was in the offing.

The *Granma* reached Cuba on 2 December, finally reaching a marshy part of the western coast of Oriente between Niquero and Cabo Cruz. The ex-Lieutenant Roberto Roque had fallen overboard (then been rescued), the good landing point had been missed and the vessel could not be beached. So the men, weak and dispirited, were forced to flounder ashore as best they could, losing much of their equipment and remaining supplies in the process. It took the group three hours to reach solid ground, having battled through swamp and thick undergrowth. The becalmed *Granma* was spotted from the air, and a frigate moved in to start shooting at the abandoned vessel. A scheduled attack in Santiago had been suppressed. Now Batista would be able to devote all his attention to the bedraggled bunch of revolutionaries who had struggled ashore at Las Coloradas de Belic. Castro remarked, a decade later, that 'our revolution began under incredible conditions'.

The force, dispersed in the landing, gradually came together and moved inland to Alegría de Pío. There, on 5 December, the guerrillas came under attack by Batista's aircraft and troops. The cane field where the rebels had paused was set alight, possibly by incendiary bombing, and a number of the men were forced to surrender; some were immediately shot, others maltreated. Some twenty-four rebels were killed in the first encounter and soon afterwards, leaving a few bedraggled groups to struggle in the direction of the Sierra Maestra. Guevara had been wounded, and Raúl Castro was accompanied by only three other men. Fidel was now isolated with only two others, Universo Sánchez and Faustino Pérez. Some of the survivors were now giving themselves up, to be shot; and some eventually made their way back to Havana.

Castro remained hidden for some days in a cane field, sucking cane stalks and eating food supplied by a peasant. The lorry driver Cresencio Pérez, a Castro supporter, helped to bring together the rebel survivors. On 17 December Raúl was reunited with Fidel, and some time later they were joined by Almeida's group. So the *Granma* remnants were brought together, a dozen or so men still committed to the Cuban Revolution.[101] According to Universo Sánchez, one of the survivors, Castro then addressed his men: 'With the same vehemence which he would have done before a large political audience in the Central Park in Havana. He assured them that they had triumphed in the first stage of this adventure. He communicated to them that he did not have the least doubt that in the long run victory would be theirs . . . all left convinced of the strength of their position and the confidence of obtaining victory in a long run or the short . . .'.[102]

General Fulgencio Batista was rejoicing at his conclusive victory over the rebel *Fidelistas*, but yet again he had grossly underestimated his enemy. The military disaster of Moncada had been transformed into a political victory. Now Castro was intent on converting the fiasco of the *Granma* landing into a political triumph. A mere two months after the routing of the rebel group by Batista's troops and aircraft Castro despatched Faustino Pérez to Havana to 'bring back a foreign journalist'. Soon Herbert Matthews, the respected *New York Times* foreign correspondent, would be reporting to the world that Fidel Castro was still alive and intent upon the overthrow of the Batista regime. In his first article (24 February 1957) Matthews wrote, of Castro: 'He has strong ideas of liberty, democracy, social justice, the need to restore the Constitution, to hold elections. . . . The 26th July Movement talks of nationalism, anti-colonialism, anti-imperialism. I asked Señor Castro about that. He answered, "You can be sure we have no animosity towards the United States and the American people. Above all, we are fighting for a democratic Cuba and an end to the dictatorship."'[103] Batista continued to maintain that Castro was dead (until Matthews produced a dated photograph), and the Cuban Communists continued to express their 'radical disagreement with the tactics and plans' of Fidel Castro.

To many observers, who had not yet noticed the swelling tide, it seemed reasonable to dismiss the words and antics of twelve or so isolated guerrillas in the distant reaches of the Sierra Maestra. It must have seemed very unlikely that a dozen dishevelled rebels, albeit led by a tireless and charismatic man, would be able to bring a revolution that would topple the well-armed Batista dictatorship – and to accomplish, as inevitable corollaries, the expulsion of the Mafia from their favourite Caribbean territory, and the humiliation of the regionally omnipotent United States.

7 A New Era

> We refused to help Cuba meet its desperate need for economic progress. . . .
> We used the influence of our government to advance the interests and
> increase the profits of the private American companies which dominated
> the island's economy. . . . Administration spokesmen publicly hailed
> Batista, hailing him as a staunch ally and a good friend at a time when
> Batista was murdering thousands, destroying the last vestiges of freedom
> and stealing hundreds of millions of dollars from the Cuban people. . . .
> Thus it was our own policies, not those of Castro, that first began to turn
> our former neighbour against us.
>
> John F. Kennedy[1]

VICTORY

On 3 January 1957 Fidel Castro and his small group of guerrillas reached
the Tatequieto heights in the Sierra Maestra. To the east, five miles away,
he could see the triple Caracas peaks: 'If we can get there, neither Batista
nor anybody else can defeat us in this war.' Now peasants had begun
joining the rebel force, though their commitment was sometimes uncertain: on 11 January, five of perhaps two dozen new recruits decided to
return home and Castro made no effort to stop them. Two days later, government troops, suspecting that the local peasants were aiding Castro,
arrested eleven local people and murdered them all. On 14 January, having
decided to attack La Plata barracks at the river estuary of that name,
Castro reached the banks of the river Magdalena.

At this time, when Batista was announcing that the United States had
recently agreed to supply his regime with sixteen brand-new B-26
bombers, the guerillas in the Sierra Maestra had eighteen rifles, two
Thompson machine guns, two pistols and a 16-bore air gun.[2] The barracks
at La Plata contained five Rural Guard soldiers and five sailors commanded by an army sergeant; for once, Castro, with some twenty-two
men, enjoyed a numerical superiority. The night attack on 17 January was
brief: the Batista force lost two dead and five wounded, and there were no
rebel losses. With this initiative, the first rebel attack on government
troops since Moncada, the guerrillas won nine Springfield rifles, a
Thompson machine gun, ammunition, food and other supplies. Castro told
his prisoners that they had behaved like men and were free to leave whenever they chose. Then he left medicine for the enemy wounded, before

leading his guerrillas back into the Sierra Maestra. This showed what would be Castro's consistent policy towards the enemy throughout the war: prisoners would be allowed to live, whereas traitors and 'exploiters' would be executed.[3]

Che Guevara later recalled the importance of the victory at La Plata: 'It came to everyone's attention, proving that the Rebel Army existed and was ready to fight. For us, it was the reaffirmation of the possibility of our final triumph.'[4] But then, even after the victory at La Plata, the poor morale among the rebel fighters was clear: 'The column lacked cohesion. It had neither the spirit which comes from the experience of war nor a clear ideological consciousness. Now one comrade would leave us, now another; many requested assignments in the city, which were sometimes much more dangerous but which meant an escape from the rugged conditions in the countryside. Nevertheless, our campaign continued on its course.'[5]

Already the peasants in the Sierra Maestra were feeling the impact of the war. Government troops increased the level of repression of those suspected of aiding the rebels, and overseers and rural guards used the pretext of likely bombing raids to evict the *pecaristas* from their homes. At the same time the rebels were spreading propaganda to win recruits and logistical support. In the cities the pro-Batista press continued its campaign to portray the guerrilla force as a minor irritation. No longer able to deny the existence of Castro and his guerrillas, events were misrepresented. Thus at La Plata, 'eight rebels and two members of the armed forces had been killed';[6] and six weeks later the army announced that the encounter had involved the deaths of 'forty rebels', with twenty prisoners taken.[7] The July 26 Movement, now increasingly active in Havana, had issued its manifesto and programme in November 1956 (Appendix 7); and this was followed, on 12 July 1957, by the 'Declaration of the Sierra Maestra'.

The Declaration, announced by Castro, demanded an end to foreign interference in Cuban affairs, the repudiation of any type of military junta, the separation of the army from politics, and the holding of general elections under the terms of the 1940 constitution. Specific measures were to be implemented immediately:

1. Immediate freedom for all political, civil, and military prisoners.

2. Absolute guarantee of freedom of information, of the spoken word and written press and of all the individual and political rights guaranteed by the constitution.

3. Designation of provisional mayors in all the municipalities prior to consultation with the civic institutions of the locality.

4. Suppression of speculation in all its forms and adoption of measures that tend to increase the efficiency of all organisms of the state.

5. Establishment of a civil service.

6. Democratisation of labour policy, promoting free elections in all unions and federations in industries.

7. Immediate start of an intensive campaign against illiteracy and for civic education, exalting the duties and rights which the citizen has in relation to society and the fatherland.

8. Establishment of the foundations for agrarian reform that tends to the distribution of barren lands and to convert into proprietors all the lessees – planters, partners, and squatters who possess small parcels of land, be it property of the state or of private persons, with prior indemnification to the former owners.

9. Adoption of a sound financial policy that safeguards the stability of our money and tends to use the credit of the nation in productive works.

10. Acceleration of the process of industrialisation and the creation of new jobs.[8]

Castro did not allow the practical affairs of the war to prevent his characteristic issuing of statements, plans and declarations.

On 30 January 1957 the guerrilla camp in the Sierra Maestra was attacked by B-26 bombers and government troops: the aircraft machine-gunned the forest close to the rebel base, and a bomb exploded on top of the kitchen stove. The precision of the raid was made possible by the traitor Eutimio Guerra, who had housed the rebels prior to the assault on La Plata and acted as a guide through the mountains. The small group of Batistianos, part of a contingent commanded by Lieutenant Sánchez Mosquera, had been successfully repelled by the guerrillas, but the unexpected air attack had demoralised the rebels. The force had been dispersed by the attack, and it took three days for them to regroup. On 1 February word came that at least three army columns were advancing on the Caracas mountains; whereupon Castro ordered the rebels, now increasingly beset by hunger and thirst, to resume their westward march. One of the rebels collapsed from thirst, whereupon Castro offered him a dry lemon to suck; another drank putrid water from a bottle he found. Guevara recorded how 'particularly painful' the march was for him, since he was suffering from an attack of malaria. The size of the force had to be reduced, because 'there was a group of men with very low morale, and one or two seriously wounded . . . those who stayed and passed the first tests grew accustomed to dirt, to lack of water, food, shelter and security, and to continually relying only on a rifle and the cohesion and resistance of the small guerrilla nucleus'.[9] On 7 February the Caracas mountains were again bombed and strafed by Batista aircraft, whereupon the traitor Eutimio urged Castro to set up camp in a deep canyon; the next day, more bombs fell on the area. Castro, increasingly preoccupied with Eutimio's comings and goings, eventually uncovered his treachery: Eutimio was executed during a thunderstorm.

On 8 February, in a battle that lasted for several hours, the guerrillas were again dispersed, struggling in several groups to retreat into the terrain. Again the peasants rallied to their support. Castro, now with an army of less than two dozen men, still felt confident: 'We had practically no political connections there, but we established good relations with the population. . . . Batista was carrying on a fiercely repressive campaign, and there were many burned houses, and many murdered peasants. We dealt with the peasants in a very different manner from that of the Batista soldiers, and we slowly gained the support of the rural population – until that support became absolute.' There were brief pauses to allow reinforcements to reach the rebel army, and then the group would move off again, conscious that the only chance of survival lay in mobility. Guevara, afflicted by asthma, was sometimes left behind until able to rejoin the guerrillas. On 16 February Castro met the woman who was to play such a central part in his life: Celia Sánchez Manduley, wholly dedicated to the July 26 movement (as interpreted by Castro), and one of the daughters of the radically-minded Oriente physician Dr Manuel Sánchez Silveira. Celia became the principal organiser of the peasant network through which arms, ammunition, supplies and volunteers reached the rebel army. It was on 16 March 1957 that Castro received his first batch of substantial reinforcements: fifty Santiago men headed by Jorge Sotús.

Batista, still prepared to assert that Castro was not in the Sierra Maestra, was now continuing to receive substantial support from the United States. Arthur Gardner, the US ambassador to Cuba, was suggesting as a representative of President Eisenhower that the Central Intelligence Agency (CIA) should assassinate Castro; while the Eisenhower administration continued to heap munitions and awards on Batista and his cronies. Thus US Air Force Major-General Truman Landon took the trouble to fly to Havana to award the United States Legion of Merit to Colonel Carlos M. Tabernilla y Palmero, responsible for organising the bombing and strafing of the rebels and Sierra peasants. Landon paid due tribute to 'the furtherance of amicable relations between the Cuban Air Force and the United States Air Force . . .'; while the US Congress was being told that from 1955 to 1957 the US had donated to Batista equipment amounting to seven tanks, a battery of howitzer artillery, 4000 rockets, 40 heavy machine guns, 3000 M-1 semi-automatic rifles, 15,000 hand grenades, 5000 mortar grenades, and 100,000 armour-piercing cartridges for machine guns.[10]

On 20 February Castro launched an 'Appeal to the people of Cuba' for a violent uprising against the dictatorship; and some weeks later Batista, yet again declaring that Castro was not in the Sierra, arranged to fly eighty journalists over the region to prove the point. Paradoxically, Batista's troops increasingly found themselves engaged in military exercises against rebel forces that 'did not exist'. Through 1957 the Rebel Army continued to expand, as activists (from the July 26 Movement, the Communists and other factions) organised strikes and other disruptions in Havana, and as other groups – now increasingly aware of the impact of Castro's survival in the Sierra – tried to create parallel factions in the mountains.[11]

Now Castro decided that a fresh military initiative was needed. On 28 May a three-hour battle at Uvero resulted in six rebel deaths and nine wounded, against some fourteen Batista troops killed and nineteen wounded (with 14 taken prisoner). The rebels won two machine guns and forty-six rifles, and Castro declared 'a new phase' in the Sierra. Che tended the wounded of both sides; Castro later commented that because the enemy wounded had been left 'in the care of their own doctor, so that the army might pick them up and move them to their own hospitals', none of them had died. The Cuban historian Pedro Alvarez Tabío subsequently observed that the battle of Uvero had shown for the first time that the rebels 'could defeat the army of the tyranny, and that the seizure of power through a military defeat was therefore possible'. Guevara recorded that the battle at El Uvero 'was one of the bloodiest of the revolutionary war'.

Gradually the Rebel Army began to expand and consolidate its area of control, progressively enlarging the liberated territory to the east. Batista, beset by mounting problems in Havana, seemed uncertain how to respond. It seemed clear that some government initiative would have to be taken, but a vast military campaign in the Sierra would belie the claim that the rebels were an inconsequential faction. The United States too seemed confused, still keen to support Batista but by now increasingly alarmed that he could not last. US confusion even extended to the provision of CIA funds to leading members of the July 26 Movement,[12] presumably on the assumption that if Batista were to fall, enough of the rebel leaders could be bought off in the usual way. At the same time Batista continued to receive US honours of various kinds; on 18 May even becoming an honorary citizen of Texas. He reciprocated in kind, indulgently distributing Cuban honours to a motley assortment of US officers and government officials. Ambassador Gardner, who had recommended that the CIA assassinate Castro, remarked of Batista: 'I don't think we ever had a better friend. . . . It was regrettable . . . that he was known . . . to be getting a cut . . . in almost all the things that were done. But . . . he was doing an amazing job.'[13]

Earl E. T. Smith, Gardner's successor, proved to be less pliant. When he witnessed Batista's police attacking 200 black-clad women protesters in Santiago, soon after the funeral of Frank País (tortured to death for supporting the July 26 Movement), he protested against the 'excessive use of force'. Still Ambassador Smith was not prepared to countenance a Castro victory. The Communists, by contrast, began to see how things were moving: now certain party members would be allowed to join the Rebel Army, but there would be few other accommodations.

On 24 May, in a desperate attempt to inflict a final defeat on the Rebel Army, Batista launched *operación verano*, his 'big push', the only major offensive of the war. By now the United States, sensing that Batista was doomed to failure, had reversed their earlier policy and imposed an arms embargo. In Havana, in circumstances of mounting civil disorder, Batista was losing authority; throughout Cuba the rebel activists, heartened by the course of events, were urging worker strikes and spreading propaganda. The Rebel Army, now comprising around 300 men (against Batista's 20,000 demoralised troops), prepared to repel Batista's final effort.

In the event the Batista forces, nominally vastly superior to Castro's, were defeated. *Operación verano* ended in humiliation for the government. Batista lost a thousand men (dead and wounded), with the added humiliation that Castro kept returning prisoners – many of whom refused to continue fighting – as he captured them. It has been estimated that some 321 *Fidelistas* threw back the huge Batista offensive.[14] Then it was only a matter of time before the final collapse of the Batista regime.

On 26 July Raúl Castro, at the head of 200 rebel soldiers, came down from the Sierra Cristal to Moa Bay and captured ten US citizens and two

Canadians. Over the next few days Raúl captured Richard Sargent, the Canadian manager of the *Isabel* sugar mill, two executives of the Nicaro Company, and 27 US sailors and marines. Then he informed Ambassador Smith that the men would be released once the United States stopped supplying *all* equipment to the Batista regime, aircraft fuel from the Guantánamo base, and other forms of assistance to the discredited regime. In early July the rebels kidnapped two US officials and four United Fruit Company officials. Batista, increasingly impotent, could offer no help to Washington; and soon the US Navy was urging 'an immediate intervention in Cuba of divisional size'. The State Department was reluctant to begin an open-ended action that in any case would be unlikely to save the lives of the hostages.[15]

Castro, having gained substantial publicity from this incident, released the men; at the same time issuing a formal statement that 'the presence of North American forces . . . is illegal and constitutes aggression against Cuban national territory . . .'. As through all the years that followed, Castro had no wish to pick a quarrel with the United States, but Cuban sovereignty must be regarded as inviolate. The incident served to convey what would become the policy of the new Cuban government. It also demonstrated that it was now the *Fidelistas* rather than the corrupt Batista regime who had to be considered.

On 9 December 1958 a secret envoy from President Eisenhower, William D. Pawley, visited Batista to urge him to accept exile at Daytona Beach, Florida. Ambassador Smith was now acknowledging that the rigged election to plant another US puppet, Andrés Rivero Agüero, would not deliver the needed political stability. Batista, still full of pride and absurd hopes, declined the Pawley offer. On 1 January troops under the command of Che Guevara captured Santa Clara, and in final desperation Batista fled in the dead of night to the Dominican Republic. Fidel Castro and his victorious rebels entered Santiago, and for the second time confronted the Moncada barracks: 5000 Batista soldiers surrendered without firing a shot, and Castro called a general strike to prevent a counter-revolutionary *coup*. The pro-Batista elements – the corrupt officials, the gangster cronies, the sadistic police chiefs – began leaving Cuba; hundreds of exiles started to return. And in Washington the *Fidelistas*, surveyed by the perplexed US administration, took over the Cuban embassy.

On 2 January 1959 the formerly clandestine pro-rebel newspaper *Revolución* was paraded and distributed openly; while Castro named the exiled judge Manuel Urrutía Lleó the Provisional President of Cuba, and Santiago the provisional capital. That evening Fidel Castro gave his first speech as the victorious revolutionary:

The revolution begins now. The revolutionary will not have an easy task. The revolution will be a very difficult undertaking, full of danger. This time it will not be like 1898, when the North Americans came and made themselves masters of our country. This time, fortunately, the revolution will truly come to power. At this moment we must consolidate our position before anything else. . . . The revolution will not be made in two days, but now I am sure that the revolution *will* be made, that for the first time the republic will really be entirely free, and that the people will have what they deserve. . . . The war has been won by the people!

From Santiago Castro moved slowly towards Havana, frequently delayed by cheering crowds eager to set eyes on their national hero for the first time. At Camagüey, at Holguín, wherever he stopped, there were more deliriously happy people, more speeches. *Revolución* (4 January) published a photograph of Castro, with the caption 'The Hero–Guide of Cuban Reform. May God continue to illuminate him'; and in *Revolución*, on radio and on television, the heroes of the Revolution – all referred to by their first names – were celebrated.

Fidel Castro entered Havana on 8 January – moving slowly in a column of cars, lorries and tanks past journalists, television cameras, placards inscribed with the words *Gracias Fidel*, and the endless crowds of cheering people. In one account, a dove released by someone in the crowd alighted on Castro's shoulder.[16] In January 1959 few observers doubted that a powerful new force had entered the world of Latin American politics; but few imagined the extent to which this seismic shift would come to vibrate around the globe.

INTO AMERICA

Castro moved quickly to consolidate his power – exploiting his immense popularity and adopting the harshest measures against the henchmen of the old regime. For the first time full exposure was given to the atrocities committed by Batista's torturers against the Cuban people. While Castro was celebrating his triumph before a liberated people, trials and executions were taking place all over the island (the chief executioner being Captain Herman Marks, an erstwhile criminal from Milwaukee).[17] On 7 February Castro approved measures whereby legislative power would be vested in the cabinet, an autocratic move that upset the liberals and encouraged the prime minister, Miró Cardona, to resign. A week later, Castro assumed the premiership, announcing to his pliant cabinet that it was necessary to 'begin . . . the revolution'.

At a subsequent cabinet meeting in February, Castro announced that he had been invited by the American Society of Newspaper Editors (ASNE) to visit the United States. Should he go? Philipe Pazos, Castro's Bank Director, urged him to make the trip, but Castro hesitated. There must be no impression created that he was journeying to Washington to win acceptance and financial aid: the Cuban leader did not belong in the tradition that required a suitably humble pilgrimage to the United States. Castro decided to accept the invitation – not only because he would be able to underscore Cuban sovereignty but also because the trip would provide him with a wider platform. The Castro revolution, he perceived, should not be confined to Cuba: it had deep relevance to the entire hemisphere and to the wider world.

Castro arrived in Washington on 15 April 1959. More than a thousand Cubans greeted him at the airport with banners and shouts of '*Viva Fidel!*'. Rejoicing in the passionate welcome, Castro broke away from the waiting US Under-Secretary Roy Rubottom and his guards and went over to greet the cheering Cubans. It soon transpired that wherever Castro went he would be followed by crowds; whatever he said was taken seriously. To different audiences in Washington and New York he gave characteristically long and charismatic speeches. And Castro himself was to some extent seduced by the attention. To his group he said repeatedly: 'We have never met Americans like these. We only knew the colonialists.'[18] But it did not stop him sleeping with a loaded pistol next to the bed.

A number of personal encounters were arranged: with Henry Luce of *Time* magazine, Frank Bartholomew of United Press International, and Acting Secretary of State Christian Herter. Perhaps most significantly, Castro also met Vice-President Richard Nixon at his office (after refusing to go to the vice-presidential home). It was ironic that the revolutionary who had deposed one crony of gangsters should now be consorting with another,* but here there was no useful dialogue, no useful meeting of minds (Castro later complained ruefully in a filmed interview that he had not even been offered a cup of coffee). Nixon seemed intent on producing files to demonstrate that there were Communists among Castro's supporters; and on objecting to Castro's harsh treatment of Batista supporters in Cuba. For his part, Castro confined himself 'to . . . explaining the realities of our country, which I believe were similar to those of the rest of Latin America, and to demonstrating that the measures we were going to take, some of which affected North American interests, were just'.[19]

President Eisenhower had refused to see Castro: as a deliberate slight to the Cuban leader, he had absented himself from Washington for a week,

---

* See pp. 308–9.

playing golf in Carolina. Nixon was advised that an informal meeting might be useful: it was useful, Nixon later recorded in his *Memoirs*, to find out whether Castro was 'an unwitting front man for the Communists, or perhaps even a Communist himself'. After the meeting, Nixon dictated a memorandum for Eisenhower, Herter, and Foster and Allen Dulles, in which he noted Castro's 'almost slavish subservience to prevailing majority opinion – the voice of the mob'; and commented: 'He is either incredibly naïve about communism or under Communist discipline – my guess is the former . . .'. This was the shape of things to come. Eisenhower came to share Nixon's analysis, and 'authorized the CIA to organize and train Cuban exiles for the eventual purpose of freeing their homeland from the Communists'. After all, Nixon recalled, 'Batista at least was friendly; Castro turned out to be an implacable and dangerous enemy.'[20]

Aid had not been discussed, either by Castro or his ministers and advisors. The revolutionaries had survived their encounter with the *Yanquis* with their integrity intact. When officials from the State Department had enquired about the Cuban economy, Castro's Finance Minister Rufo López Fresquet had replied that it was magnificent. No, Castro had repeatedly asserted, we are not Communists; and even if there were Communists in the Cuban government 'their influence is nothing'. And he emphasised that the time was not ripe for elections, which Nixon had demanded. The Cuban people had bad memories of elections, where US and mafia money could buy corrupt politicians. 'Revolution First, Elections Afterwards!'

In New York Castro had addressed a rapturous night-time crowd of 30,000 in Central Park; he gave speeches to publishers and businessmen; and visited City Hall. In Boston he gave a long and successful speech at Harvard University; and then travelled to Montreal where he announced that he would be attending the inter-American economic conference in Buenos Aires. Before long there would be another opportunity to visit the United States.

On 13 September 1960 Havana announced that Castro was to attend the General Assembly of the United Nations. An ad hoc commission set up by the Cuban foreign ministry produced a report which Castro would subsequently use as the basis of his address to the United Nations. Cuba would be represented as a non-aligned nation, but its revolutionary sympathies would be plain. Thus a headline in *Revolución* (14 September) read: 'Topics to be treated at the U.N.: ALGERIA, CHINA, CONGO and CUBA. Fidel Will Speak to the General Assembly.' Now, already an international figure, Castro was about to address the world.

The vast Cuban delegation, its movement restricted to Manhattan, arrived at the luxurious Shelbourne Hotel where a hostile management immediately demanded that the Cubans pay in advance. This, and the posture of the American press – 'that portrayed the Cuban premier and his men as orgiastic primitives, plucking chickens in their luxurious suites, throwing lit cigars on expensive carpets, and cooking their own food on camp stoves in the bathrooms of their suites'[21] – made it plain that a concerted campaign was under way to humiliate and discredit Castro and his delegation. On 19 September Castro protested about such discriminatory treatment to UN Secretary-General Dag Hammarskjöld, who offered official UN accommodation facilities. Castro had other ideas. How about pitching tents in Central Park? What could bring greater embarrassment to Washington? Better still, suggested Robert Taber and Richard Gibson of the Fair Play for Cuba Committee (FPCC), how about Castro and his Cubans moving to America's largest black ghetto – Harlem?[22] The US State Department, now in a panic, rushed to stop the scheme. Suddenly the luxurious Commodore Hotel was offering free lodging to Castro's entire delegation, but it was too late. The Cubans were off to Harlem.

Castro had turned the situation to immense propaganda advantage. With him and the Cuban delegation ensconced in the Hotel Theresa in Harlem, hundreds of people thronged the area, delighted to celebrate what they took to be a strong blow against American racism. The events had turned the Cuban leader into a hero 'to much larger numbers of Negroes ready to cheer any challenger of white American power. Great crowds turned out to greet the white Cuban Castro when, in pursuit of his own shrewd exploitation of the racial tensions in the United States, he came to Harlem.'[23] At the same time mass rallies were organised throughout Cuba to denounce American racism; in Havana one million Cubans assembled to condemn US discrimination 'against Fidel'.

The Harlem crowds blocked the traffic, cheering and marching in unprecedented scenes of protest. The shouted slogans were plain: 'Fidel, free American Negroes too!', 'Fidel, turn Harlem into another Sierra Maestra!', 'Fidel, *si*, Ku Klux Klan, *no!*'. Now, stimulated by such events, Castro was moving to broaden his foreign policy in acknowledgement of the perceived ethno-political links between Afro-Cuba, the US's Harlem ('little Africa'), and the African continent itself. Washington too began to estimate the power of the new revolutionary force that was breaking on the world stage.

Castro then took another shrewd propaganda initiative, requesting that Major Juan Almeida – the black chief of the Cuban army and a Castro devotee since the first attack on Moncada – be sent at once from Cuba to New York. On 21 September, before a vast crowd chanting 'FI-DEL, FI-DEL, FI-DEL!', Castro appeared at his hotel window, his right arm over Almeida's shoulders. The next day, Almeida, to the delight of the crowds, walked in the streets of Harlem and mixed with the people. On 20 September, in front of the Theresa Hotel, Castro first met Nikita Khrushchev, who was soon to impact so dramatically on Cuban affairs (Egypt's Abdul Nasser and India's Jawaharlal Nehru later came to Harlem to meet Castro). Two days later, Castro met various African leaders, and Marshall Tito and Ahmed Sukarno (as well as other leaders of non-aligned countries), in the UN building. Then Castro invited the entire black staff of the Theresa Hotel to share a luncheon with him; and, as a final gesture, presented Love B. Woods, the hotel manager, with a bust of José Martí bearing the inscription, 'He who incites and propagates racial hatred and opposition is sinning against mankind'; whereupon, to thunderous applause, Richard Gibson, the black FPCC leader, offered the Cuban revolutionary a bust of Abraham Lincoln with the words 'From one liberator to another liberator'.[24]

Castro had met American radicals (such as Robert Williams and the Black Muslim leader Malcolm X), and a host of world leaders. Already the visit to New York had proved a propaganda triumph. Now, on 26 September 1960, Castro was set to address the UN General Assembly. Speaking in Spanish, he began this epic speech[25] by saying: '*Although we have been given the reputation of speaking at great length, the Assembly need not worry. We shall do our best to be brief, saying only what we regard it as our duty to say here.*' The speech – occupying (in large page, 2-column format) twenty pages – took five hours to deliver. Full of rhetoric and passion, it ranged over Cuban and American history, the historical plight of the Cuban people, US policy, the character of the Batista tyranny, the reforms being introduced by the revolutionary Cuban government, economic policies, the role of the Organisation of American States (OAS), capitalist exploitation, US subversion in Cuba, the imbalance of economic power around the world, the oppression of Africa, the question of disarmament, US opposition to the sovereignty of other nations, and other topics. Castro concluded the speech by quoting the Havana Declaration* (see Appendix 8) and with the comment: '*Some people wanted to know what the line of the Revolutionary Government of Cuba was. Well then, there you have our line.*'

The tone and the policy were unambiguous. Fidel Castro and his revolutionary government were implacably opposed to US imperialism around the world, and to the arrogant assumption that national peoples, mainly in the Third World, should be maintained in unending poverty and suffering

---

* Subsequently known as the First Havana Declaration after a Second Havana Declaration (1962) renewed the call for worldwide revolution.

in order to swell the coffers of the capitalist monopolies. If Eisenhower, Nixon, the Dulles brothers, and the rest were in any doubt, their worst fears were now confirmed: Castro was a Communist or a Communist dupe. On 24 February 1948 the US Policy Planning Staff in Washington had emphasised the essential task facing the United States:

> We have about 60% of the world's wealth but only 6.3% of its population. Our world task in this position is to devise a pattern of relationships which will permit us to maintain this position of disparity. We should cease to talk about such vague and unreal objectives as human rights, the raising of living standards, and democratisation.

This was (and remains) the principal strategic theme in US foreign policy. By 1960 the decision had already been taken that the revolutionary government of Cuba should not be allowed to interfere with the profiteering impulses of American corporations. Already plans were being laid in Washington for the military overthrow of the Castro regime.

BAY OF PIGS

Throughout the nineteenth century and the first half of the twentieth there were frequent US military invasions of the Caribbean states. Costa Rica, Honduras, Haiti, the Dominican Republic, El Salvador, Nicaragua, Mexico and Cuba – all experienced invasions by American troops sent to protect US commercial interests. Thus the famous American historian Henry Steele Commager commented: 'It was the West – not Communist countries – that invented imperialism and colonialism. . . . We should remember that in the eyes of the 19th century world it was the United States that was pre-eminently an expansionist and aggressive nation.' At that time 'this new nation' had 'an ideology as pernicious in the eyes of legitimist governments as Communism is in our eyes'.[26] The Monroe Doctrine and the Polk Doctrine proclaimed American hegemony in the western hemisphere, the convention whereby US strategists reserved their God-given right to intervene where and when they chose in the interests of American capital. And the policy laid down so unambiguously in the nineteenth century was consolidated and expanded in the twentieth: military force was the means whereby smaller states would be kept subservient to the expanding needs of US capitalism. Major-General Smedly D. Butler of the United States Marine Corps summarises the prevailing American ethic:

I spent thirty-three years and four months in active military service . . . during that period I spent most of my time being a high-class muscle man for Big Business, for Wall Street and for the bankers. . . . I was a racketeer, a gangster for capitalism. . . . I helped make Mexico and especially Tampico safe for American oil interests in 1914. I helped make Haiti and Cuba a decent place for the National City Bank boys to collect revenues in. I helped in the raping of half a dozen Central American republics for the benefit of Wall Street. . . . I helped purify Nicaragua for the international banking house of Brown brothers in 1902–12. I brought light to the Dominican Republic for the American sugar interests in 1916. In China in 1927 I helped to see to it that Standard Oil went its way unmolested.[27]

For his efforts Butler was 'rewarded with honors, medals and promotion'; but in his eyes he had been no more than a racketeer: 'I feel I might have given Al Capone a few hints. The best *he* could do was to operate his racket in three city districts. I operated on three continents.'[28]

This is the traditional US framework, particularly relevant to the Caribbean, within which a fresh invasion of Cuba was being contemplated in the late 1950s (see also 'Towards Isolation' below). It is important to remember that what was to emerge as the Bay of Pigs fiasco was not an isolated aberration of Washington strategists but derived from a principal theme in traditional US foreign policy.

A few months after the collapse of the Batista dictatorship in Cuba, the United States moved to address the new situation. In May 1959 Vice-President Richard Nixon met with mafia representatives and with the directors of Pepsi Cola International, Standard Oil, Ford Motor Company and the United Fruit Company to do a deal. Nixon pledged that the US government would overthrow the Castro regime if the Mafia and the capitalists would agree to fund his candidacy for president of the United States.[29] Some months later, on 11 December, Colonel J. C. King, chief of the CIA's western hemisphere division, sent a memorandum to CIA director Allen Dulles proposing the assassination of Fidel Castro, to 'discourage similar activities against US possessions in other Latin American countries' and to encourage the collapse of the Cuban regime.[30]

President Eisenhower, having refused to meet Castro, came to share Nixon's assessment of the Cuban leader. Eisenhower noted that Che Guevara had been associated with the leftist Jacobo Arbenz* in Guatemala, that Castro had welcomed the support of the Communists, that

---

* Head of a democratically-elected government overthrown by CIA-sponsored subversion and invasion in 1954.

Mao Tse-tung and other Communist leaders had begun praising Castro, and that Guevara had told Indian Communists that Castro had ambitions to remove the US naval base at Guantánamo.[31] With Communist newspapers sprouting up in Cuba, and CIA claims that the Soviet Union had sent an expert to Havana to help guide the revolution, Eisenhower was in no doubt that Communism 'had penetrated this hemisphere'.[32] In these alarming circumstances it was clear that something would have to be done.

Now the plans were being laid. Richard Mervin Bissell, the CIA deputy director for plans (euphemism for chief of covert operations) and second only to Dulles, focused on the possibility of killing Castro ('assassinations are as old as history'). Bissell, responding to King's memo, wondered whether the proposed 'elimination' of Castro meant in fact mere incapacitation; but Bissell wanted it to be made clear that an assassination might be arranged. By early March 1960 the CIA had produced a top-secret policy document, 'A Program of Covert Action Against the Castro Regime', which was promptly approved in Washington: in particular by the special 5412 Committee, involved in covert operations under the authority of the National Security Council Directive NSC 5412/2. Eisenhower had been unimpressed with the Dulles suggestion of merely sabotaging a Cuban sugar refinery; a more ambitious scheme was needed. Now the CIA policy paper proposed: creating a 'responsible and unified' Cuban government in exile; 'a powerful propaganda offensive'; 'a covert intelligence and action organisation' within Cuba; and 'a paramilitary force' outside Cuba 'for future guerrilla action'. On 10 March the full National Security Council discussed ways of bringing 'another government to power in Cuba'; and four days later the special committee considered what would happen if Fidel, Raúl Castro and Che Guevara were to 'disappear simultaneously'. On 17 March Eisenhower ordered the CIA to begin the training of Cuban exiles, mainly in Guatemala, 'against a possible future day when they might return to their homeland'.[33]

Castro now represented a growing problem to the Washington strategic planners. In April Cuba's foreign minister Raúl Roa García declared that plans were being prepared in Guatemala for an invasion of Cuba, and that the United Fruit Company was involved in the preparations; at the same time Castro initiated a scheme for the expropriation of the remainder of the land occupied by United Fruit. In May Cuba re-established diplomatic relations with the Soviet Union, so healing the rift that had occurred after the Batista *coup* in 1952; and the non-aligned President Ahmed Sukarno of Indonesia (later to suffer CIA attention) made a state visit to Havana. Then, in June and July, Castro moved to nationalise all US business and commercial property in Cuba, and to take over the oil refineries owned by Texaco, Esso and Shell. On 6 July President Eisenhower acted to cancel

Cuba's sugar quota, declaring: 'This action amounts to economic sanctions against Cuba. Now we must look ahead to other moves – economic, diplomatic and strategic.' So began the trade and other commercial sanctions that were set to intensify over the decades that followed.

By October 1960 the United States was preparing to close the government-owned Nicaro nickel-processing plant in Cuba and to end all preferential tariffs for Cuban exports to the United States. There were also moves to block the bulk of exports to Cuba, partly on the ground that Cuba had failed to pay for imports from the United States. Washington was now urging its citizens not to travel to Cuba; and Raúl Roa García, now ambassador to the United Nations, was informing the UN that the CIA was training exiles and mercenaries for an invasion of Cuba. On 14 October Castro moved to nationalise further American companies (all large industrial, commercial and transportation companies, 20 of which were US-owned, were nationalised; about 200 small US firms were allowed to remain in private hands); four days later, Cuba withdrew from the International Bank for Reconstruction and Development (the World Bank). At the United Nations Raúl Roa García commented that Richard Nixon and John F. Kennedy, in their televised debate (21 October), discussed Cuba as if it were a 'piece of real estate owned by the United States'.

On 1 November the UN General Assembly rejected (by 45 votes to 29, with 18 abstentions) Cuban and Soviet-bloc demands for a debate of Havana's claim that Washington was preparing an invasion of Cuba. James Wadsworth, US ambassador to the United Nations, declared that Cuba's claims were 'monstrous distortions and downright falsehoods' and asserted that 'there is no threat from the United States of aggression against Cuba'. Cuba, declared Luis Coronada Lira, the Guatemalan representative, was the one guilty of aggression, as shown by Havana's granting of asylum to deposed Guatemalan president Jacobo Arbenz. Now the US plans, consistently denied by Washington, were moving into their final phase. Towards the end of 1960, the National Security Council approved what had been dubbed Operation Pluto: the organisation of 2000 men (in land, naval and air contingents) available for action when the US-sponsored invasion of Trinidad (on Cuba's southern coast) began. Here, it was hoped, CIA-controlled groups would be able to repel any initiative from Cuban troops and prepare the way for the establishment of a US puppet government in Havana. Washington duly severed diplomatic relations with Cuba on 3 January 1961, 'clearing the way' for the invasion (planned for April). On 25 January President Kennedy, holding his first news conference after his defeat of Nixon (and by now well briefed on the invasion plans), declared that the United States had no plans to resume diplomatic relations with Cuba. Five days later, in his State of the Union address, Kennedy asserted that 'Communist agents' had 'established a base in Cuba'; and declared that 'Communist domination in this hemisphere can never be negotiated.'

In a meeting with the CIA and the Chiefs of Staff on 28 January, Kennedy and his National Security Advisor McGeorge Bundy were presented with an outline of Operation Pluto. Some weeks later, having evaluated the plans, Kennedy argued that US forces should not play a part in the forthcoming invasion, not least because it would be difficult to disguise American involvement in the flat area around the town of Trinidad. The Joint Chiefs then suggested that the Bay of Pigs,* on the Zapata Peninsula, be substituted for Trinidad and that a US military contingent be held as a backup force. President Kennedy approved what was now called Operation Zapata. Still he did not want a plan that was 'too spectacular': a 'quiet' landing, preferably at night would be best; and he emphasised that to avoid an international anti-American reaction the US sponsorship of the invasion must be thoroughly concealed.[34]

Castro had no doubt that an invasion was coming. Ramiro Valdés, the architect of Cuba's security services (an Interior Minister until 1986), commented that Cuban Intelligence was able to monitor the invasion plans and preparations step by step: 'It was an open secret.' Valdés managed to frustrate a principal element in the CIA scheme, that the invasion would stimulate a general anti-Castro uprising through the island: 'We knew who everybody was, what weapons they carried, how much ammunition they had, where they were going to be, how many of them, at what time, and what they proposed to do. . . . We were very successfully infiltrated into the counter-revolutionary bands.'[35] And so CIA contacts, and others involved in clandestine anti-Castro activities, were efficiently rounded up: the inadequate invasion force, a motley band of exiles and mercenaries, would receive no support from within the island. Against the 1400-man brigade of counter-revolutionary exiles soon to arrive at Playa Girón, Castro had a regular army of some 25,000 well-trained men plus around 200,000 militia fighters stationed throughout Cuba. Castro had overall command of three tactical regional forces: those under Raúl in the east (Oriente and Camagüey), Che Guevara in the west (western Havana province and Pinar del Río), and Juan Almeida in the centre. Castro had

---

* The 'Bay of Pigs' (from the Spanish name of the inlet, *Bahía de Cochinos*) is largely the American designation of the invasion site. The Cubans refer to the event by the name of the beach, *Playa Girón*, where the main body of the invaders landed. Another beach, *Playa Larga*, was less important in the invasion. Beyond *Playa Larga* lies the *Ciénaga de Zapata* swamp.

emphasised that no main-force units would depart from their assigned areas unless absolutely necessary: the Cubans would not be trapped by any CIA-planned deceptions.[36]

On 15 April, two days before the launch of the invasion, B-26 bombers flying from Nicaragua with CIA-paid pilots began 'softening-up' raids against Cuban airfields. Castro was well prepared. To one million Cubans massing in Havana he proclaimed:

> This is not a country whose ruling system allows the greater majority of people . . . to toil for an exploitative and privileged minority of millionaires, this is not a country whose ruling system allows a sizable segment of its population to be discriminated against and relegated to oblivion as is the case with the Negro masses in the United States. What they cannot forgive is that right here under the very noses of the United States, we have made a Socialist revolution! A Socialist revolution to be defended with our rifles. . . . Comrades, workers and peasants, this is the Socialist and democratic revolution of the humble and for the humble. . . . Yesterday's attack was the prelude to aggression by mercenaries. All units must now go to their battalions.[37]

The following day, on 17 April 1961, the CIA released to the press a CIA-drafted message supposedly from the US puppet José Miró Cardona, a former Cuban premier (now in exile in Miami), the designated head of the so-called Revolutionary Council designed to constitute a US-friendly Cuban provisional government. The message, actually written by the CIA's E. Howard Hunt, announced that 'Cuban patriots' had begun 'to liberate' Cuba. At the same time the CIA's Radio Swan urged the Cuban people to rise up against the Castro regime.

In the early morning of the same day, an invasion force – commanded by the CIA's Grayston Lynch and William Robertson – landed at Playa Girón. After Kennedy's clear instructions that US forces were not to take part, it is ironic that one of the first men to reach the beach was an American frogman.[38] The invaders were at once intercepted by a militia patrol, rifle fire broke out, and the possibility of tactical surprise was lost. Some of the incoming small boats hit coral reefs, not mentioned in the briefings, and foundered. As the men reached the beach and began moving inland, paratroops dropped from the skies and managed to seize a few interior points; they would not hold them for long.

Castro's forces, by all accounts, reacted with immense vigour and operated under highly competent command. In one of the various operations of the tiny Cuban air force, a Sea Fury sank the vessel carrying the invaders' ammunition reserve for the next ten days and also most of the communication equipment. When other ships were hit, the rest of the flotilla put out to sea. A few B-26s attempted to fly defensive missions along the beach, but Castro's T-33 jet trainers managed to shoot four of them down. As the fighting on the beachhead continued, and the invaders struggled to dig in behind their tanks and mortars, the Cuban troops closed in. Some of the invaders managed to press some miles inland, but they were doomed. Castro, having set up his headquarters just north of the battle area, called in tanks and artillery, held in readiness near Havana. In desperation Richard Bissell, the CIA director of covert operations, ordered six US pilots to attack with three bombers loaded with napalm and high explosives. Four of the pilots were killed, and when Castro recovered one of the bodies he was able to demonstrate to the world that the United States had been actively involved in the invasion.

The invading forces at Playa Girón, having exhausted their ammunition and with no hope of reinforcement, surrendered at 5.30 on the afternoon of 19 April 1961. It had taken Castro about seventy-two hours to defeat an invasion force upon which had been lavished some of the CIA's best brains and millions of dollars. Arthur M. Schlesinger, Special Assistant to President Kennedy, later admitted: 'For the reality was that Fidel Castro turned out to be a far more formidable foe and in command of a far better organized regime then anyone had supposed. His patrols spotted the invasion at almost the first possible moment. His planes reacted with speed and vigor. His police eliminated any chance of sabotage or rebellion behind the lines. His soldiers stayed loyal and fought hard. He himself never panicked. . . . His performance was impressive.'[39]

President Kennedy, massively bruised by the débâcle, began to reflect on the role of Allen Dulles in particular and the CIA in general. Then he moved towards decisions – regarding the CIA, Cuba, Vietnam, the Soviet Union – which, in some analyses, were to determine his own assassination. Castro, despite all the CIA machinations, had survived. On 1 May more than a million Cubans massed in the Plaza de la Revolución to celebrate Castro's abiding humiliation of the imperialist United States. Before he spoke a word, the Cubans laid on a ten-hour parade before him. Then, after powerful floodlights had been switched on, Fidel Castro began his speech with the characteristic words, 'I'm going to be brief' – and then held the attention of an enraptured crowd for three hours.

The situation was plain. Castro had now defined the Cuban revolution as 'Socialist'; and inflicted a devastating humiliation on the United States. Later the same year, on 2 December 1961, Castro detailed on Cuban television his development as a fully-fledged Marxist–Leninist. The

United States, smarting under the Bay of Pigs fiasco, had now imposed a complete embargo on trade with Cuba; and in February 1962 secured her expulsion from the Organisation of American States (OAS). The battle was now joined: the Cuban people, daring to thumb their nose at an oppressive and arrogant superpower, would have to face many crises and tribulations in the years ahead. But for the moment, buoyed by a remarkable triumph, they rejoiced in a fresh confidence. One fruit was the Second Declaration of Havana, urging violent revolution as the only realistic answer to the problems of exploitation and oppression.

US TERRORISM

The Bay of Pigs fiasco did not mean that Washington would abandon its efforts to overthrow the Castro regime. Quite the contrary: the US government was now set to initiate a programme of terror, sabotage and economic embargo, specifically designed to make it impossible for the Cuban government to continue in power. As Carl von Clausewitz, soldier and war theorist, might have said: 'Terrorism is the continuation of war by other means.' In fact the perpetration of US-supported terrorist acts against the Castro regime predated the Bay of Pigs invasion, as well as continuing long after it.

In October 1959 aircraft based in the United States had bombed and strafed targets in Cuba.[40] In the period 11 to 21 October planes flying from US territory carried out bombing raids in Camagüey and Pinar del Río. On 21 October a bombing raid on Havana resulted in 45 people wounded and two killed in the streets: a former Cuban Air Force chief, Pedro Luis Díaz Lanz, who had fled to Miami, later admitted to the Federal Bureau of Investigation (FBI) that he had flown over Havana on the day in question. And on 22 October a train packed with passengers in Las Villas was machine-gunned by an aircraft flying from US territory. Through 1960 and early 1961 further raids, acts of sabotage and assassinations were carried out as part of the escalating campaign intended to climax with a successful invasion of Cuba.

In early 1960 US pilots took part in incendiary bombing raids on Cuban cane fields and sugar mills: at least three American pilots died in crashes and others were captured. The US State Department admitted that one aircraft that had crashed, killing two US servicemen, had flown against the wishes of the US authorities.[41] One of the incendiary bombing raids resulted in the destruction of ten tons of sugar cane in Havana province; another raid (21 January) involved the dropping of four 100-pound bombs on Havana; and another (28 January), involving several aircraft, caused damage to three sugar cane fields in Oriente province and five in Camagüey. On 7 February a further attack in Camagüey resulted in the destruction of 30 tons of sugar cane at various mills. And on 18 February a US pilot, Robert Ellis Frost, was killed while bombing a sugar mill in Matanzas province. In this case documents recovered from the aircraft established that he had bombed Cuba on three previous occasions: the US State Department later admitted that the bomber had flown from US territory.

On 4 March a French freighter, the *Coubre*, unloading arms and ammunition from Belgium, exploded in Havana harbour; some 100 Cuban workers and soldiers were killed in the explosion, with 200 wounded. Sabotage was suspected but never proved, with the United States disclaiming any involvement but acknowledging that it had taken steps to stop the Belgian shipment. Further bombing raids had taken place in Matanzas province and Las Villas; and four days after the *Coubre* disaster incendiary devices resulted in the destruction of more cane in Pinar del Río province. On 4 April a plane flying out of the illegally-occupied US base at Guantánamo dropped incendiary bombs in Oriente province. And so it continued . . . up to the time of the abortive US-orchestrated invasion. Here four Americans flying for the CIA, as well as more than 100 Cuban exiles, were killed in the attack: 1200 captured exiles were later returned to the United States in exchange for $62 million worth of medical supplies.

In the summer of 1961 the Kennedy administration, smarting under the Bay of Pigs humiliation, resolved to expand the terrorist campaign against Cuba. A new political strategy – involving propaganda, surveillance, sabotage, guerrilla strikes, and assassination – was devised with the aim of overthrowing the Castro regime. The new plan was called *Operation Mongoose*: a carnivorous snake-killing mammal would be let loose to exterminate the Castro cobra. On 30 May 1961 CIA-armed dissidents had assassinated the Dominican Republic's Rafael Trujillo; and what had worked here might be expected to work with Castro. The US government was well prepared to contrive the assassination of foreign leaders, as signalled in the *Interim Report* of the 1975 Senate Committee on Intelligence: 'There is no indication or suggestion contained in the record of those post-assassination meetings, or in Robert Kennedy's notes, of concern as to the propriety of the known United States involvement in the assassination.' There was no record of any 'reprimand or censure' of any of the involved American officials: 'Later the Agency [CIA] described the project as a "success".'

President Kennedy's Cuba Study Group had concluded that 'there can be no long-term living with Castro as a neighbor'; Kennedy himself declared that he wanted 'massive Mongoose activity'; and Robert Kennedy urged that 'the terrors of the earth' be invoked against Castro.[42] On 30 November 1961, as recommended by the National Security Council and approved by President Kennedy, the Special Amplified Group (SAG) was created under Attorney-General Robert Kennedy and General Maxwell Taylor, as the effective instrument for the implementation of Operation Mongoose. All the concerned US government agencies and departments were represented: the State Department, the Defence Department, the Commerce Department, the Pentagon, the United States Information Agency (USIA), and the CIA (who referred to its Mongoose unit as Task Force W). On 19 January, at a top-secret Mongoose meeting, Robert Kennedy urged that 'no time, money, effort, or manpower, be spared' in the campaign to overthrow Castro,

The CIA's Task Force W, under William K. Harvey, established its nerve centre (code-named JM/WAVE) at the University of Miami. By now the CIA organisation dedicated to the overthrow of the Castro regime had around 400 men in Washington and Miami, some fifty business front operations in Florida, a navy comprising hundreds of high-speed vessels and yachts, an airforce, 3000 Cuban agents, and an annual budget of $100 million. The JM/WAVE installation, the largest CIA station in the world after the CIA headquarters (Langley, Virginia), was now one of the main employers in Florida. The CIA front organisations included: 'press, travel, publicity and detective agencies; arms warehouses, bars, banks, hotels, stores, print shops, real estate agencies, shipping and air lines, equipment maintenance and repair shops, research centres and other "ghost societies" to employ officials and collaborators . . .'.[43]

In August and September 1962, in the preamble to the 'missile crisis' (see below), the CIA began to organise a secret 'parallel' structure for the organisation of terrorist activity against Cuba. Now CIA-directed terrorist factions were being trained in fourteen bases spread throughout the Caribbean (in Guatemala, Nicaragua, Panama, Haiti and the Dominican Republic). Soon there was a significant expansion in the scope of terrorist activities being carried out against Cuba. Sea and air raids were carried out by Cuban exiles, often accompanied by their CIA trainers and supervisors; extensive damage was inflicted on oil refineries, chemical installations, bridges, cane fields, sugar mills and warehouses; Cuban fishing boats and merchant vessels were attacked; Soviet ships docked in Cuban harbours were bombarded; and spies, saboteurs and assassins were infiltrated into Cuba.[44]

The US-sponsored terrorist activities included the bombing of hotels as well as industrial installations, the poisoning of crops and livestock, and the chemical contamination of sugar exports. In August 1962 a British freighter, under lease to the Soviet Union for the transportation of Cuban sugar, docked in Puerto Rico for repairs. CIA agents broke into the dry-dock warehouse and successfully contaminated the sugar with an unpalatable chemical substance.[45] On another occasion a speedboat strafing attack on a Cuban hotel near Havana succeeded in killing a score of Russians and Cubans.[46] In 1964 an East German cargo ship carrying forty-two British Leyland buses to Cuba (after US protests to Leyland) collided in thick fog with a Japanese vessel in the Thames river, London. The event was written off as an accident: a decade later the American columnist Jack Anderson confirmed that the CIA, with the cooperation of British intelligence, had caused the accident;[47] at the same time a CIA officer admitted that 'we were sabotaging the Leyland buses going to Cuba from England . . .'.[48]

It was acknowledged also that CIA efforts to contaminate Cuban sugar were not isolated events: 'There was lots of sugar being sent out from Cuba, and we were putting a lot of contaminants in it.'[49] In 1962 a Canadian technician working for the Cuban government was paid $5000 by the CIA to infect Cuban turkeys with the virus that causes the fatal Newcastle disease: 8000 turkeys died.[50] Terrorist acts were now taking place long after the official termination of the Mongoose programme. For example, two researchers have described how during 1969 and 1970 the CIA sent aircraft from the China Lake Naval Weapons Center in the California desert to overfly Cuba and seed rain clouds with crystals to cause torrential rains 'to ravage Cuba's sugar crop and undermine the economy'.[51] And in 1971, according to participants in the plan, the CIA provided Cuban subversives with a virus responsible for African swine fever: six weeks later Cuban farmers were forced to slaughter 500,000 infected pigs to prevent a nationwide epidemic. The UN-linked Food and Agriculture Organisation (FAO) called this event the 'most alarming' of the year.[52] The Castro government has claimed that Washington has maintained chemical and biological warfare against Cuba over the years: a charge that gains credence from released CIA documents. It was revealed in 1977 that the CIA 'maintained a clandestine "anti-crop warfare" research program targeted during the 1960s at a number of countries throughout the world'.[53] Who could doubt that one of these countries was Cuba?

The terrorist activities against Cuba continued long after Mongoose, long after the Kennedys: many of such acts, not all, were (are?) US-sponsored. Typically, Cuban exiles in Miami, dreaming about the fall of Castro and with access to covert funding, have embarked upon acts of sabotage against the Cuban regime.* For example, in April 1976 two Cuban fishing vessels were attacked by high-speed boats sailing out of Miami, 'the main center of anti-Cuban terrorism worldwide'.[54] A few weeks later two people were killed when the Cuban embassy in Portugal was bombed. In July there were bombings of various Cuban targets in Columbia and the Caribbean, in addition to a bombing of the Cuban mission to the UN in New York and the attempted bombing of a pro-Cuban meeting being held at the Academy of Music in New York. A month later terrorists kidnapped two officials from the Cuban embassy in Argentina, and in Panama the Cubana airline offices were bombed. In October CIA-trained Cuban terrorists, working out of Miami, blew up a Cubana civil airliner: all the 73 people on board, including Cuba's entire gold medal-winning international fencing team, were killed. One of the terrorists, Luis Posada Carriles, was mysteriously sprung from jail, whereupon he arrived in El Salvador to help the CIA-sponsored terrorist operations in Nicaragua.[55]

In 1980 Ronald Reagan declared: 'I do not believe relations can be normalized until Cuba is out from under Soviet domination. . . . My policy would be based on my longtime view that captive nations must once again know freedom.'[56] And, in the same spirit, the American conservative William Buckley, Jr reflected a powerful element in US politics when he proclaimed: 'We have got to get at Cuba. . . . A declaration of war could possibly be framed'[57] – so echoing Richard Nixon's advice to President Kennedy, immediately after the Bay of Pigs débâcle: 'I would find a proper legal cover and I would go in. There are several justifications that could be used, like protecting American citizens living in Cuba and defending our base at Guantánamo.'[58] There was no threat to Guantánamo, but Nixon well knew that the lie would serve as effectively as any other. In fact the Guantánamo base has served not only as an illegal provocation but also as a base for US terrorism in Cuba. Thus US marines shooting from the base killed Ramón López Peña (in 1964) and Luis Ramírez López (in 1966), as well as wounding a number of Cuban soldiers (including Luis Ramírez Reyes, Antonio Campos and Andrés Noel Larduet). In addition, known murderers and Batista henchmen were given sanctuary and training at Guantánamo, prior to being sent to carry out terrorist activity in Cuba.[59]

---

* OMEGA 7, founded in 1974 by Eduardo Arocena and others to carry out terrorist acts against Cuba, has been identified by the FBI as one of the most dangerous Cuban-exile terrorist groups.

From the time of the overthrow of the Batista dictatorship in 1959, the United States and its Miami proxies* have launched countless terrorist acts against Cuba – all in the interest of restoring 'freedom'. US terrorism against Cuba has been largely ignored in the academic literature; as has the corollary that the United States is one of the world's leading terrorist states. The example of Cuba is plain enough: in order to first protect and then to restore the American stake on the island Washington has been prepared to sponsor a wide range of terrorist activities, including arson, bombings, biological and chemical warfare, and assassination. Successive US administrations have found it useful, over the period of this long campaign, to enlist the skills of murderers and other criminals. Just as Batista organised a congenial accommodation with the Mafia, so did successive US administrations.

THE MAFIA CONNECTION – II

American capitalism – like the burgeoning capitalism of the states that were once Soviet republics – is rooted in crime. From the debauching and genocide of the indigenous Americans, through the era of the 'robber barons', to the massive growth of the Mafia in the twentieth century, there has always been a congenial symbiosis between entrepreneurial activity and the culture of the criminal underworld. Researchers such as Gustavus Myers have demonstrated that the great American capitalists (Rockefeller, Morgan, Vanderbilt, Carnegie, Guggenheim, Rosenwald, Mellon, etc.) built up their empires through levels of corruption that amounted to formal criminality, buying legislators to enact laws sympathetic to corporate wealth, bribing officials to offer land and water grants, extorting public funds, ignoring taxes, and abusing and exploiting working people.[60] In the twentieth century many substantial fortunes derived at least in part from criminal activity. For example, Ambassador Joseph Kennedy, destined to be father of a US president and a US attorney-general, made money by

---

* The mind-set of the anti-Castro Miami community was well demonstrated when in April 1994 Magda Montiel Davis, a Cuban-born immigration lawyer, brushed her lips lightly against Castro's cheek at a reception for Cuban exiles and thanked him for what he had done 'for my people'. She was deluged in a torrent of abuse, much of it obscene. She was sent faxes depicting her agonising death; pornographic pictures showing her copulating with Castro were pushed through her door; she received obscene telephone calls and death threats (160 in one day) (*The Sunday Times*, 5 March 1995).

importing illegal whiskey from Ireland during Prohibition. In 1927 one of Kennedy's paid gangs came into conflict with a mob hired by the Lansky/Luciano organisation. The Mafia bungled the operation and there were fatalities on both sides. Kennedy lost a fortune in the hijack and thereafter held a grudge against his criminal business competitors. This was the reason, according to mafia sources, that the next generation of Kennedys were so keen to crack down on organised crime ('They were out to get us. They had a personal grudge'[61]).

The criminal activities of various capitalist factions were paralleled by the political involvement of the Mafia. The underworld chieftains knew well the value of buying political influence. Thus Lucky Luciano, one-time mafia *Il Capo di Tutti Capi* ('Boss of all Bosses'), recalled: 'There was [sic] people on the streets with muscle to make things go the way I wanted, and I had them. Then there was the other kind of muscle, to get the law passed the right way, to get things done smooth and legal. I had that kind of muscle, too. I personally helped elect more than eighty guys over a short time, all votin' my way, aldermen, councilmen, mayors, congressman, even senators. They was [sic] mine. I picked 'em. I elected 'em. They belonged to me, lock, stock and barrel.'[62] In the post-Luciano political world the reach of the Mafia extended into the White House.

In this *realpolitik* culture it was inevitable that American politicians (presidents even) and high officials should on occasions ask favours from well-placed mafia figures. It is now common knowledge that elements of the US government enlisted top mafia people in a vein attempt to assassinate Fidel Castro. It is of interest also that J. Edgar Hoover, FBI chief from 1924 to 1972, hired his own mafia assassins (the 'Squad') to kill selected people.[63] There has always been a strong connection between the criminal underworld and particular reaches of high officialdom in the United States.

The US government and the Mafia had a shared interest in the elimination of Fidel Castro. With the collapse of the Batista dictatorship the gangster fraternity stood to lose millions of dollars.[64] Castro had been quoted: 'I'm going to run all these fascist mobsters, all these American gangsters, out of Cuba.' At least one mafia chieftain, Santos Trafficante, doubted the pledge: 'You think he's going to close up a hundred million dollars' worth of business that we got? We generate over ten thousand people working. He's going to put all those Cubans out of work? He'll never do it.'[65] Then Castro started closing down the casinos; and Trafficante and others found themselves in jail. Now the anxieties of the Mafia were shared by the US government.

In top-secret meetings with CIA chief Allen Dulles there was mounting pressure for a strategy of having Castro, his brother Raúl, and Che Guevara 'eliminated in one package . . .'.[66] Already the CIA had been trying to send an LSD-like chemical for use against Castro; and plans were discussed to douse him with a substance that would make his beard fall out, so destroying Castro's charisma.[67] Now, it seemed, more drastic measures were called for. In the summer of 1960, in parallel with discussions about a possible invasion of Cuba, the US government was giving serious thought to the 'elimination' of Fidel Castro. In August 1960, according to the CIA's Robert Aime Maheu, his case officer, Jim O'Connell, was offering $150,000 to anyone 'tough enough' to assassinate Castro.[68] In another account, the CIA was contemplating paying $1 million for a successful 'hit' against Castro.[69] What was now clear was that Richard Bissell, the CIA's director of covert operations, had decided that mafia personnel could be employed for the planned assassination.[70]

In early September Maheu met with the Chicago gangster John Rosselli at a restaurant in Beverly Hills, with the aim of discussing how Castro might be killed. Maheu later testified that he explained to Rosselli that it was 'natural' for the Mafia to cooperate with the CIA in this plan: 'There were legitimate business reasons for them to participate, considering what they'd lost in Cuba.' In fact the CIA had learned of how various underworld figures had been hit by the Castro revolution, and had worked to exploit this knowledge. For example, when Castro closed down the business interests (a race track and casino near Havana) of the mafia figure Russell Bufalino and his associates, these crime leaders were forced to place $450,000 with friends for safekeeping, with Bufalino's partners Salvatore Granello and James Plumeri driven to burying $300,000 'in a field outside Havana'.[71] The CIA contacted these mafia figures to assure them that if they cooperated with the anti-Castro plans they would be helped to recover their money.

The CIA had already been floating various plots for the assassination of the Cuban leader. In early 1960 a box of Castro's favourite cigars was impregnated by botulism toxin by the CIA's Technical Services Division (TSD). In addition to the 'super-acid' (LSD-like) plan, there were plots to contaminate Castro's skin-diver wet suit with a virulent strain of tuberculosis, to provide him with a poisoned ball-point pen, and to explode a conch shell in his vicinity. Perhaps most bizarre of all, General Edward Lansdale proposed that an American submarine emit star-shell flares into the sky: to convince religious Cubans that the Second Coming was nigh, whereupon they would rush to overthrow the Castro Anti-Christ. Perhaps, the CIA began to consider, it might be more practical to arrange Castro's death through a typical gangland killing: perhaps he could be ambushed and shot dead. One problem was that Castro tended to be surrounded by machine gun-toting bodyguards who were notoriously unsympathetic to the idea of their leader's early demise.

Rosselli, the CIA knew, had been responsible, with others, for managing mafia investments in Cuba: in particular, operations owned by Meyer Lansky, a crony of Batista (see Chapter 6), and Santos Trafficante. In addition, the powerful gangland figures Carlos Marcello and Sam 'Momo' Giancana, with involvement in Cuban 'business', had lost out when Castro came to power. It was obvious to the CIA that Rosselli had useful contacts in any scheme to subvert the Cuban government or, in particular, to assassinate Fidel Castro. After a second meeting with Rosselli, Bissell and Colonel Sheffield Edwards, the director of the CIA Office of Security, informed Allen Dulles that 'contact had been made with the Mafia'.[72] But soon Rosselli was complaining that the job was too big for him to handle: it was then that Sam Giancana (later widely known to have links with John Kennedy) and Santos Trafficante were brought in on the act. Giancana, then the mafia boss of Chicago, became Trafficante's backup in the plot to kill Castro, required at that time to find a likely assassin from among his Cuban contacts. Before long it seemed that the plot was on course, as signalled by a memorandum sent by J. Edgar Hoover to Bissell: 'During recent conversation with several friends, Giancana stated that Fidel Castro was to be done away with very shortly. . . . Moreover, he allegedly indicated that he had already met with the assassin-to-be on three occasions. . . . Giancana claimed that everything had been perfected for the killing of Castro, and that the "assassin" had arranged with a girl . . . to drop a "pill" in some drink or food of Castro's.'[73]

There were complications, not least sexual: Giancana shared a mistress, Judith Exner, with John Kennedy. And when Kennedy and the FBI learned of the full extent of the CIA–Mafia connection, there was general outrage: Robert Kennedy, by now the new Attorney-General, perceived that any leaks about the tie-in between the US government and organised crime would damage his anti-Mafia campaign. Later there was much debate about how much the Kennedys knew about the CIA–Mafia conspiracy to assassinate the Cuban leader.

By the end of 1961, Rolando Cubela, a Cuban army major recruited by Trafficante, was exploring ways of 'eliminating' Castro. Cubela had qualifications for the job in hand: in 1956 he had shot Blanco Rico, Batista's head of military intelligence. Cubela, much valued by the CIA, was duly assigned a case officer and given the code name AM/LASH. In September 1963 Cubela, meeting with a CIA agent in São Paulo, Brazil, indicated that he was prepared to attempt the assassination of Castro. The CIA's Desmond Fitzgerald, an author of many plots against Castro (and

also a personal acquaintance of Robert Kennedy), then agreed to meet
Cubela 'as Robert Kennedy's personal representative'; Cubela was
assured that President Kennedy and the US government fully supported
his efforts.[74] Despite the efforts of the Kennedys to distance themselves
from the murder plots there is evidence that they were fully aware of what
was happening. Thomas Hughes, then the State Department director of the
Bureau of Intelligence and Research (later president of the Carnegie
Endowment for International Peace), subsequently commented that Robert
Kennedy had fully supported the AM/LASH plot.[75]

Following the missile crisis (see below), President Kennedy terminated
Operation Mongoose in 1963, not because he disapproved of terrorists acts
against the Cuban regime but because the campaign was ineffective and
out of control: many of the Mongoose operatives were seemingly less
interested in attacking Castro than in running drugs, a common CIA
practice.[76] Mongoose was then replaced with the Special Group (SG) of
the National Security Council, which in April 1963 discussed contingency
options in the event of Castro's death. On 19 June Kennedy ordered the
Special Group to launch a fresh campaign of terror and sabotage against
Cuba; and on 3 October nine specific sabotage operations were approved.
According to the *Interim Report* of the Senate Committee on Intelligence
(the Church Committee), thirteen major terrorist operations were approved
in the period from November 1963 to January 1964: these included the
sabotage of a sugar mill, an oil refinery, and an electric power plant. The
question of whether President Kennedy had initiated further assassination
attempts against Fidel Castro has remained open. The administration had
already established an 'executive action capability', designed to allow
political murders, including the assassination of foreign heads of state.[77]
So subsequent attempts on Castro's life, as with the escalating genocide in
Vietnam, may well have been set in train by Kennedy.

The CIA–Mafia connection, despite the common interests of the US
government and the criminal underworld (and despite the prodigious
resources at their joint disposal), had failed to secure the elimination of
Fidel Castro. The collaboration between high officials of the American
state and known gangsters has been passed off as a brief episode, an
aberration that was uncharacteristic of normal political behaviour. In particular, we are encouraged to believe that US presidents do not make a
habit of consorting with criminals. It is useful to remind ourselves of some
of the connections that developed in the post-Kennedy political environment. Such a consideration is highly relevant to current (1995) US policy
towards Cuba. The United States found it perfectly acceptable for Batista
to run Cuba as a vast brothel and gambling den, provided that US business

interests were protected. We need to remind ourselves that ambitious criminal elements, able to reach inside the White House, are likely to have similar objectives.

It has been suggested that John F. Kennedy himself relied upon mafia connections to win the presidency. Thus Chicago Mayor Richard J. Daley was quoted as telling Jack that 'with a bit of luck and the help of a few close friends, you're going to carry Illinois', a state that was essential for a Democrat victory. In fact Kennedy did win Illinois, after the mob-dominated 'West-Side Bloc' had indulged in eleventh-hour vote stealing in Cook County wards. The gangster Mickey Cohen commented: 'Certain people in the Chicago organisation knew that they had to get John Kennedy in. . . John Kennedy was the best of the selection . . .'. In the same spirit Vincent Teresa, a mob defector, reiterated Lucky Luciano's claim when he declared that the Mafia 'reach congressmen just as quickly as they reach state houses and police precincts . . .'. Mafia support for Kennedy may have been poor judgement: he was to embark upon an unprecedented campaign against organised crime. Richard Nixon was an entirely different case.

The mobster Mickey Cohen recorded in his memoirs that he had contributed $5000 to Murray Chotiner for Nixon's first congressional campaign in 1946.[78] To fund his senatorial race against Helen Gahagan Douglas in 1950, Nixon raised $75,000 from gamblers in Las Vegas; the $500,000 funnelled through Jimmy Hoffa for the 1960 presidential campaign came from mafia chief Carlos Marcello, one of the many gangland bosses with commercial interests in Havana. The criminal investigator Russell Bintliff was later to observe that there were 'strong indications of a history of Nixon connections with money from organised crime'. And a Justice Department official commented that Nixon, when president, 'pardoned organised crime figures after millions were spent by the government putting them away, a guy whose had these connections since he was a congressman in the 1940s'.

When Nixon won the presidency he made Peter Brennan, boss of the Mafia-linked Building and Trades Council in New York, his Secretary of Labour. Bebe Rebozo, a close business friend of Nixon, was linked to the Cleveland drug trafficker 'Big Al' Polizza. And a lender for a Nixon property in Key Biscayne was Arthur Desser, a colleague of Meyer Lansky. James Crosby, chairman of the Mafia-linked company Resorts International, contributed $100,000 to Nixon's presidential primary campaign; and a suspected mafia figure, John Alession, a business contact of C. Arnold Smith (jailed for grand theft and tax evasion), contributed $26,000 to Nixon's 1968 presidential campaign. Nixon gave Murray

Chotiner, who with his brother had defended mafia figures in 221 prosecutions, a private office in the White House.

One of the White House tapes (5 May 1971), after Watergate, revealed that Nixon had considered the use of criminals to attack anti-war protesters:

> *Haldeman*: . . . do it with the Teamsters. Just ask them to dig up those, their eight thugs.
> *Nixon*: Yeah . . . they've got guys who'll go in and knock their heads off.
> *Haldeman*: Sure. Murderers . . . it's the regular strikebuster types . . . and then they're gonna beat the [expletive deleted] out of some of these people.

Arthur M. Schlesinger, Jr noted that even before the various investigations into Watergate had been completed it seemed likely that Nixon staff's, some of whom had links with the Bay of Pigs fiasco, had engaged 'in a multitude of indictable activities'. At the least there had been involvement

> in burglary; in forgery; in illegal wiretapping; in illegal electronic surveillance; in perjury; in subornation of perjury; in obstruction of justice; in destruction of evidence; in tampering with witnesses; in misprision of felony; in bribery . . .; in acceptance of bribes . . .; in conspiracy to involve government agencies (the FBI, the CIA, the Secret Service, the Internal Revenue Service, the Securities and Exchange Commission) in illegal action.[79]

The Nixon years, after a brief hiatus, gave way to the Reagan years. The mafia-linked Teamster's Union helped to fund Ronald Reagan's 1980 presidential bid; and he was quick to appoint men with mafia connections. Paul Laxalt, Reagan's 'closest friend and most trusted adviser' (*Wall Street Journal*, 20 June 1983), was his campaign manager in 1976, 1980 and 1984. Laxalt also had a long association with the convicted extortionist Allen Dorfman who had drained Teamster pension funds into mafia enterprises; and was friendly also with the Las Vegas gangster Moe Dalitz who, when Laxalt was elected to the Senate, claimed – in the style of the 1920s Lucky Luciano – 'Laxalt is my boy. I put him there.' In fact, in his two Senate campaigns Laxalt received $50,000 from organised crime; once elected, he was dubbed the 'First Friend' of Ronald Reagan, his 'eyes and ears' in the Senate.

Other Reagan appointees were Jackie Presser, a 'well known corrupt union leader' (according to an internal Justice Department file), who was later prosecuted for allegedly draining $700,000 from union funds; Roy Brewer, one-time boss of another mafia-controlled union; and CIA director William Casey, partner of a crime figure in an agribusiness firm that went bust in 1971 after deceiving investors. In June 1984 – in the tradition of Richard Nixon – Reagan commuted the 18-year sentence of Gilbert Dozier, an official convicted of extortion and racketeering who had enquired about contracting to kill an individual associated with the case.

More than two hundred Reagan appointees have faced allegations of ethical or criminal wrongdoing. The then Vice-President George Bush explained: 'Our administration has been the victim of individuals who haven't had the judgement or integrity to put the public's business above their own selfish interest.' So Reagan and Bush were hapless victims of natural disasters, with no responsibility for the teams they headed. Through the 1980s the Reagan–Bush administrations witnessed resignations, dismissals, indictments and convictions – for theft, misusing government funds, favouring business cronies, falsifying records, lying about earnings from interested companies, tax evasion, and so on.

This was the US superpower keen to moralise about the iniquities of smaller states, keen to proclaim the abiding virtue of the American political framework, intent upon organising terrorist acts in unsympathetic countries around the world, committed implacably to the economic embargo and ultimate overthrow of the Castro regime in Cuba. When President Bill Clinton assumed the presidency the embargo against Cuba was tightened (see Chapter 1): there would be no slackening of US efforts – against mounting world opinion – to force the Cuban people into economic collapse and destitution. The days of the old transparent CIA–Mafia connection had passed, but the political attitude signalled by that important conspiracy survived. The priority remained the same: the overthrow, by whatever convenient means, of a sociopolitical system unsympathetic to US capitalism. This circumstance has informed American policy on Cuba for almost four decades. It should be borne in mind when considering the peculiar circumstances of the Cuban missile crisis.

THE MISSILE CRISIS

Following the failure of the United States to overthrow the Castro regime by means of a CIA-directed invasion, the political situation again began to move into crisis. The launch of Operation Mongoose and the laying of plans for the assassination of Fidel Castro made it abundantly clear that the Kennedy administration remained committed to the escalating use of terror and murder against Cuba. Washington had at first claimed to have had no responsibility for the Bay of Pigs invasion, but soon the truth was out. On 3 May 1961 Manuel Artime Buesa, one of the principal leaders of the CIA-trained Brigade 2506 that had come ashore at Playa Girón, admitted that the CIA had planned and directed the invasion. (Artime, recommended by Howard Hunt to be the Brigade's overall political and military leader, later embarked upon terrorist attacks against Cuba from Florida.) Now, through Mongoose and other initiatives, the terrorist activities against the Castro regime began to escalate.

One American plan, denounced by Guevara at the Inter-American Economic and Social Council conference (held in Punte del Este, Uruguay, in 1961), was for US forces to fire six mortar shells into the American base at Guantánamo.[80] This plan (called 'Immediate Action') would, the US strategists reasoned, give adequate justification for an American military 'response' against Cuba. (Humberto Rosales Torres, one of the participants in the plan, later admitted the scheme during an International Tribunal in Havana.) Other attacks included strafing shore targets from high-speed boats, and assassinations within Cuba. Thus on 3 October a volunteer teacher in the Literacy Campaign, Delfínsen Cedré, was assassinated, one of a number of such workers to be murdered as a means of subverting Castro's social programmes. On 15 October a Cuban worker at Guantánamo, Rubén López Sabariego, was tortured to death, an event that led to the secret dismissal of US Marine Captain A. J. Jackson. On 26 November another volunteer teacher, Manuel Ascunce Domenech, and one of his students, Pedro Lantigua, were both assassinated.

On 3 January 1962 the Cuban government lodged a protest with Washington concerning 119 further violations of its territory, including 76 incidents involving aircraft flying from Guantánamo. Four days later, arms dropped from a plane flying over Pinar del Río and Las Villas, and intended for insurgents, were seized by the Cubans. The US policy was plain. On 18 January General Edward Lansdale described current plans in a top-secret report to President Kennedy: they included, wrote Lansdale, the preparation of 'a political action organization . . . in key localities inside Cuba, with . . . its own voice for psychological operations, and its own action arm (small guerrilla bands, sabotage squads, etc.). . . . The popular movement will capitalize . . . by initiating an open revolt. . . . *The United States, if possible in concert with other Western Hemisphere nations, will then give open support. . . Such support will include military force, as necessary*' (my italics).[81]

At a meeting of the Organisation of American States (OAS), held in Punte del Este (22 to 31 January), 14 of the 21 members, under heavy pressure from Washington, voted to expel Cuba from the organisation. Six states (Argentina, Bolivia, Brazil, Chile, Ecuador and Mexico) abstained on the ground that such a measure would violate a key provision in the OAS Charter, namely the Principle of Nonintervention in the Internal Affairs of another member state. On 28 January the Cuban authorities uncovered further evidence of a sabotage campaign against the Cuban economy: a group of saboteurs planning to use chemicals and magnetic mines against motors used in urban transportation were arrested. Six days later, the Kennedy administration announced that a total embargo of trade with Cuba would begin on 7 February. Then Washington demonstrated its effective manipulation of the UN membership: despite the naked aggression at the Bay of Pigs and all the subsequent US-sponsored acts of terrorism against Cuba, a General Assembly resolution calling on the US government to stop interfering in Cuban affairs was defeated (by a vote of 50 to 11 with 39 abstentions). Now it was clear that Cuba could not rely on the international community for protection: it would have to seek friends where it could.

On 20 February General Lansdale presented to the Special Group (Augmented) (SGA) a top-secret report detailing the programme for the overthrow of the Castro government. Here it was stipulated that CIA agents ('pathfinders') would be infiltrated to carry out sabotage activities and to spread propaganda. In Florida, Jacqueline Kennedy, given United States Information Agency (USIA) coverage, 'would be especially effective in visiting children refugees'; and pressure would be put on the OAS, the North Atlantic Treaty Organisation (NATO), and the United Nations to provide political support.[82] At the same time Cuba's efforts to bring the worsening situation to the attention of the UN Security Council were dismissed by Washington and London as a 'propaganda exercise'.

And so the crisis continued to escalate: a heavily armed ship attacked a Cuban patrol boat, killing three and wounding five (12 May); two saboteurs were killed in Oriente province (7 June); an entire peasant family was slaughtered by terrorists in Las Villas, while on the same day (5 July) shots were fired for several hours from Guantánamo, planes flew over Cuban territory, and another boat violated Cuban territorial waters; and more CIA agents were arrested in Cuba (17 July, 11 August, 15 August, and so on). This was the context – involving extensive US-orchestrated acts of terrorism and unambiguous evidence of plans for a further invasion of Cuba (this time probably by US forces) – in which the Cuban government, in its US-contrived isolation from most of the world community, continued to acquire Soviet weapons and agreed ultimately to accept Soviet missiles on its soil.

On 2 July 1962 Raúl Castro, then Minister of the Armed Forces, arrived in Moscow. Then, or soon afterwards, the Cuban and Soviet governments agreed that Soviet missiles would be installed in Cuba. Some weeks later, the Cuban government again (18 September) denounced the increasing US violations of Cuban air space; and an NBC television broadcast (19 September) showed Cuban exiles being trained by US servicemen in Florida and Guatemala in preparation for a further invasion of Cuba. And on 26 September *the US Congress passed a joint resolution giving the president the right to intervene militarily in Cuba.*

By late July 1962 an unprecedented range of Soviet shipments were beginning to arrive in Cuba; the CIA reported to President Kennedy that 'something new and different' was taking place. Some 5000 Soviet 'specialists' were now working in the island, clearly indicating unusual developments. In August a U-2 flight gave clear evidence of what were taken to be surface-to-air missile (SAM) sites in preparation; and subsequent flights (on 5, 17, 26 and 29 September, and 5 and 7 October) revealed a continuing military build-up on the island.[83] At the end of September a House Republican caucus dubbed the Cuba issue 'the biggest Republican asset'; and Clare Boothe Luce wrote in *Life* (5 October): 'What is now at stake in the decision for intervention or nonintervention in Cuba is the question not only of American prestige but of American survival.' Now the pressure was mounting on President Kennedy for action.

On 10 October the Republican Kenneth Keating claimed '100 per cent reliable' evidence from Cuban exiles that nuclear missile bases were being constructed in Cuba; and the columnist Richard Rovere wrote in the *New Yorker* that there was now a war party in Washington as active as the party that had produced the 1898 war over Cuba.[84] And President Kennedy was soon thinking in the same terms; with his brother, Attorney-General Robert Kennedy, even going so far as to remember the *Maine*: 'We should also think of, uh, whether there is some other way we can get involved in this through, uh, Guantánamo Bay, or something, or whether there's some ship that, you know, sink the *Maine* again or something.'[85] Still the pretext was being sought for a US invasion of Cuba.

Now the crisis was moving to its climax.* On 14 October a U-2 aircraft detected a site near San Cristobal which was clearly being prepared for

---

* Scott Sagan, a political researcher at Stanford University, claimed in 1995 that US officers at the Malmstrom Air Force Base in Montana had 'jerry-rigged their Minutemen missiles' to allow a launch without authorisation from Washington; then altered the evidence to hide what they had done. In addition the North American Air Defence Command was told on 28 October 1962 that a nuclear missile from Cuba was about to hit Tampa in Florida: 'Only when the expected detonation failed to occur was it discovered that a radar operator had inserted a test tape simulating an attack from Cuba . . .' (*The Independent*, London, 20 February 1995).

Soviet missiles. Four days later, Washington came to the conclusion that the first of the Soviet missiles (presumed to be nuclear) installed in Cuba could be made ready for launching within 24 hours. After considering the options – an invasion, massive air strikes, a blockade of Cuba – President Kennedy resolved to place Cuba in effective quarantine: US ships were ordered to blockade the island to prevent further deliveries of Soviet nuclear weaponry. On 22 October, in a national television broadcast, Kennedy declared to the American people: 'My fellow citizens: let no one doubt that this is a difficult and dangerous effort. . . . No one can foresee precisely what course it will take or what costs or casualties will be incurred. . . . But the greatest danger of all would be to do nothing. . . . Our goal is not the victory of might, but the vindication of right – not peace at the expense of freedom, but both peace *and* freedom, here in this hemisphere, and, we hope, around the world. God willing, that goal will be achieved.'[86]

At first the Soviet Union, in conditions of mounting crisis, refused to accede to US demands that it halt its approaching ships and dismantle the nuclear missile sites in Cuba. The OAS met in emergency session and a majority of its members agreed that if the US demands were not met an invasion of Cuba should result. On 23 October Castro reaffirmed the point to which any nation state would give its nominal support: that any sovereign government has the right to strengthen its defences with any weapons it chooses. Now the arguments of the pro-nuclear factions in the West were coming home to roost. If nuclear weapons were justified as an effective deterrent, why was it that only certain 'approved' countries were allowed to deter aggression against their territory. The answer of course was a simple matter of *realpolitik* connivance: Washington was well prepared to impose a blockade on the high seas – in itself an act of war in international law – to protect perceived American interests.

At an emergency meeting of the UN Security Council the United States presented the other permanent members with the decision to impose a US blockade of Cuba. Kennedy had already rejected Adlai Stevenson's suggestion that consideration might be given to abandonment of the illegal US base at Guantánamo, and to dismantling of the Jupiter missiles sited close to the Soviet borders. It was legitimate, in Washington's perceptions, that the Soviet Union should be forced to tolerate US missiles on its borders; but the United States refused to tolerate any analogous threat to its own territory. It was announced that the US navy would stop any ships carrying 'offensive weapons' from reaching Cuba; and that premier Khrushchev should 'move the world back from the abyss of destruction' by removing the missiles from Cuba.

On 26 October the Soviet Union sent a message to UN Secretary-General U Thant, declaring that Soviet merchant ships would not enter the zone of the US naval blockade. Now the crisis was largely at an end. On 25 October 1962 the Security Council held its final meeting on the issue. At this meeting, immediately prior to the Soviet statement, the Soviet representative Valerian Zorin, seemingly very badly briefed, recklessly challenged Stevenson to produce the evidence of a Soviet military build-up in Cuba – which Stevenson was happy to do. Three days later, Vasily Kuznetsov replaced Zorin on the Cuba issue, and Nikolai Fedorenko became the new Soviet ambassador at the United Nations. An accommodation, much of it secret, was reached between Washington and Moscow; and Castro, fuming on the sidelines, was forced to acknowledge that he had been little more than a pawn in the *realpolitik* moves of the superpowers.

The Cuban missile crisis has been depicted as the most serious hazard the world faced through the period of the Cold War. This may well be true: it is hard to think of any other international crisis that brought the prospect of nuclear war so close. It was easy in these circumstances for the West to portray the event as a reckless Soviet–Cuban gamble against peace. Yet the crisis would never have occurred if Washington had been prepared to tolerate the Castro regime in Cuba. US-sponsored terrorism, Bay of Pigs, Operation Mongoose, the economic blockade of Cuba, the mounting threat of a new invasion – these were the elements that drove the Castro regime into taking arms from the Soviet Union, into accepting the development of missile sites on Cuban territory. Many observers have judged that Castro's decision to accommodate Soviet missiles was his worst miscalculation: he should have known how Washington would react. It is equally true that the Kennedy administration should have more accurately judged the consequences of pushing Castro into the arms of the Soviet Union.

Castro himself was outraged at what he perceived was a political betrayal by the Soviet Union. In an interview with the French journalist Claude Julien he said:

Cuba does not intend to be a pawn on the global chessboard. Cuban sovereignty is a reality; that is what we fought for. I cannot accept that Khrushchev should have promised Kennedy to withdraw his missiles without the slightest reference to an indispensable accord with the Cuban Government. To be sure, it was a case of Soviet missiles which were out of our direct control. But they were on Cuban territory and nothing should have been decided without consulting us. We are not a satellite. . . . Nobody has the right to dispose of Cuban sovereignty.[87]

Then Castro made reference to the 5-point programme 'which, alone, can guarantee peace in the Caribbean'. It is hard to imagine anyone who wanted peace not agreeing to Fidel Castro's five points:

1. an end to the economic embargo and all commercial pressures;

2. an end to all subversive activities by the United States against Cuba;

3. an end to 'pirate attacks' from bases in the US and Puerto Rico;

4. an end to violations of Cuba air and naval space;

5. a United States withdrawal from the Guantánamo naval base.

The United States made it quite clear that any such programme was unacceptable; Washington would reserve the right to promote acts of terrorism, assassination and economic sabotage as it saw fit.

One incident in particular revealed the traditional mind-set of Washington. The English anti-nuclear campaigner (Lord) Bertrand Russell had intervened in the missile crisis, communicating with both Khrushchev and Kennedy to urge sanity.[88] Russell's intervention probably had little effect, bearing in mind the vast *realpolitik* forces at work, but a cable that he received from President Kennedy was highly significant. This telegram (26 October 1962) included the words: 'While your messages are critical of the United States, they make no mention of your concern for the introduction of secret Soviet missiles into Cuba. *I think your attention might well be directed to the burglars rather than to those who have caught the burglars*' (my italics).[89] Here it was – the transparent admission by Kennedy of the tacit assumption that he regarded Cuba as US property!

The ending of the missile crisis had many consequences. The principal participants learned much about the dynamics of power politics; and communication – at least between the United States and the Soviet Union – was thereafter conducted on a different basis. The US, having expelled the nuclear missiles from Cuba, quietly removed various batches of its own nuclear missiles from close to the Soviet border some months later (a probable element in the secret deal). And Fidel Castro, forced to acknowledge that he was far from an equal partner in the Cuban–Soviet relationship, could at least rejoice in the fact that the likelihood of a direct US invasion of Cuba had been much reduced.

THE INTERNATIONAL STAGE

The US–Cuba confrontation – in particular, the Bay of Pigs invasion and the missile crisis – served to give the Cuban revolution an international significance. In addition, there was much in Castroism that would not be limited to the confines of a Caribbean island. In the words of one biographer: 'From Mexico to Moscow to Managua, and from the universities of Minnesota, Mainz, and Minsk, Fidel Castro remained the single modern revolutionary of epicentral consequence.'[90] The overthrow of the dictator Batista had consequences that reverberated around the world, not only because of the romantic drama that the event represented for many people but also because Castro himself was determined to influence political affairs far beyond the shores of Cuba. Through the early decades of the revolution, the Castro regime exported fresh ideas and revolutionary optimism – and also teachers, engineers, doctors and troops: at one time there were nearly 60,000 Cubans in Angola, perhaps as many as 7000 in Ethiopia, and hundreds of thousands more in South Yemen, Libya, Nicaragua, Mozambique, Syria, Equatorial Guinea, Tanzania, Guinea Bissau, North Korea, São Tomé, Algeria, Uganda, Laos, Afghanistan, and Sierra Leone.[91] Here was a vital revolutionary influence that dismayed capitalists and heartened countless millions of oppressed and exploited people around the world. The influence of Castroism, like any human construct, was not unsullied by dogma, error and injustice – much of it admitted by Castro himself – but the main thrust of the revolution was that powerful plutocratic élites, backed by state military force, have no inherent right to exploit the peoples of the earth.

In Havana, Castro met with Ahmed Ben Bella, who had resolved to transform Algeria into the springboard of the 'African revolution' (Ben Bella himself described his ideology as 'Castro-style socialism'); and Algiers was one of the first foreign cities to welcome Cubans as successful revolutionaries. And soon the Cuban impact was being felt throughout the continent. Thus the Columbian novelist Gabriel García Márquez observed, of the early 1960s: 'at that epoch there were no African liberation movements which did not rely on Cuban solidarity either by way of civilian or military hardware, or by way of technical training'.[92] Radical African groups (the PAI of Senegal, the UMMA of Zanzibar, and others) began sending their people to Cuba for military training; and Cuban 'specialists' began arriving in Africa in growing numbers. In July 1963 Che Guevara arrived in Algiers; with Colonel Houari Boumédienne, Algeria's defence chief, visiting Cuba in August. Soon, according to Carlos Franqui, Castro's contact in Algiers, Cuba was sending 'tanks, heavy equipment and a complete military detachment of about 2000 men . . .'.[93] Three ships transported 40 Soviet T-34 tanks, 4 jet fighters, trucks, more than 800 tons of light arms, ammunition and artillery, and troops.[94] In 1964 Cuba was supporting revolutionary struggles in Mali, Niger and Senegal; while at the same time a Castroite 'big push' was being attempted in Latin America, with Cuban soldiers infiltrating Venezuela and Columbia at a rate to cause the governments of these countries to complain that Castro was conducting an undeclared war against them.[95]

On 11 December 1964 Che Guevara attended the UN General Assembly and delivered an historic address (subsequently titled 'Cuba's example shows that the peoples of the world can liberate themselves').[96] Here, in a wide-ranging analysis of the world situation, Guevara reaffirmed Cuban solidarity with oppressed peoples, in particular 'with the colonial peoples of so-called Portuguese Guinea, Angola and Mozambique, who have been massacred for the crime of demanding their freedom'; and he emphasised that the Cuban people were prepared to help the colonised African peoples 'to the extent of our ability'. Furthermore, noting the intervention in the Congo by white mercenaries and Cuban exiles, Guevara deplored how, 'with absolute impunity, with the most insolent cynicism, the rights of peoples can be flouted'. The reason was plain: 'the enormous wealth of the Congo, which the imperialist countries want to keep under their control. In the speech he made during his first visit to the United Nations, Compañero Castro observed that the whole problem of coexistence among peoples boils down to the wrongful appropriation of other peoples' wealth. He made the following statement: "End the philosophy of plunder and the philosophy of war will be ended as well."'

Guevara's performance at the United Nations, like Castro's before him, was a triumph: again the Cuban commitment to the oppressed people of the world had been dramatically affirmed. On 18 December Guevara arrived in Algeria for the start of what would be his first tour of black Africa. From Algiers he travelled to Mali, where he spent a week with President Modibo Keita. Then Guevara travelled to Congo-Brazzaville to meet with the Cuban ally, President Alphonse Massemba-Debat, with their attention now focused on the general insurrection in progress in neighbouring Zaire. On 8 January 1965 Guevara arrived in Guinea; a week later, moving on to Accra, Ghana, for discussions with Kwame Nkrumah, known to be jealous of Ben Bella's revolutionary ambitions. Nkrumah, Ghana's self-proclaimed *Osagyefo* (redeemer), was now depicting himself as the likely leader of what would emerge as a Pan-African union of states. It was not difficult for Guevara to play on Nkrumah's detestation of the reactionary Tschombé to justify Cuban intervention in the Congo. Then Guevara travelled to Dahomey for a 2-day visit; then back to Algiers for talks with Ben Bella. On 12 February Guevara met Abdul Nasser in Egypt, before travelling to Dar es Salaam in Tanzania, where two Cuban battalions had been welcomed before crossing the border into Zaire. A week later, Guevara returned to Cairo and invited Nasser to contribute to the Cuban effort in Zaire: Nasser refused, so confirming Guevara's doubts about the revolutionary credentials of the United Arab Republic (UAR). On 21 February Malcolm X, by then broadly sympathetic to Castro's ambitions in Africa, was assassinated in New York – inviting comparison with the murder of Patrice Lumumba four years earlier, and widespread suspicions of CIA involvement.[97]

On 18 March, with Guevara having reported on his African tour, Havana Radio broadcast a summary of his impressions. With China's Chou En-lai, who visited Africa in 1963, Guevara had no doubt in proclaiming that Africa was ripe for revolution: the continent was usefully distant from the United States and so might be judged to have a revolutionary advantage over Latin America. It was decided that Guevara himself would become involved in the Zairean civil war: the death of Malcolm X had reduced the number of forces that Guevara planned to command, but it was still judged that the gamble was worthwhile. Then Cuba received the news that Boumédienne had staged a successful *coup* against Ben Bella, Castro's principal African ally. Now there was no prospect of Algerian forces being sent to support Cuban military initiatives in Africa; moreover, other African states that had formerly promised support to the Cubans were now cooling on the idea – Cuba would have to go it alone. Again Guevara set out for Zaire. Soon there were other powerful players on the scene. By the end of 1965 the Chinese, with a dominant influence over the Zairean rebels, were increasingly alarmed by the growing Cuban involvement in the region. Thus Zaire became the focus of a struggle between the 'anti-"revisionist" China and messianic Communist Cuba',[98] with the Soviet Union watching from the sidelines and hoping for a Castro victory.

In the event, regional *realpolitik* forced the withdrawal of the Cuban forces. A *coup d'état* staged by Colonel Joseph Mobutu, with help from the CIA, helped the reactionary factions to consolidate their grip on the region. Guevara himself, with the *nom de guerre* of 'Tatu' ('number two', in Swahili), was almost killed in ambushes on more than one occasion. Furthermore, the Chinese were putting growing pressure on Cuba by imposing an effective rice blockade, not dissimilar to the hated US embargo. On 3 October 1965 Fidel Castro, announcing the transformation of the United Party of the Cuban Socialist Revolution into the Communist Party of Cuba, gave a coded criticism of China and for the first time revealed why Che Guevara had disappeared from the Cuban political scene. In the words of Guevara's farewell letter, read out by Castro: 'Other nations of the world call for my modest efforts. I can do that which is denied you because of your responsibility at the head of Cuba. . . . I have always been identified with the foreign policy of our Revolution and I will continue to be.' Now it was public knowledge that Guevara was trying to foment revolutions elsewhere. China, with its own regional ambitions, increasingly resented Cuban efforts.

By this time Havana had been chosen as the headquarters of the Organisation for the Solidarity of the Peoples of Africa, Asia and Latin America (OSPAAAL), with the *Fidelista* Captain Camilo Cienfuegos elected as its secretary-general. OSPAAAL eventually merged with the Afro-Asian Peoples Solidarity Organisation (AAPSO), so helping to consolidate Cuban influence in the world revolutionary movement. But it was now clear that Castro's efforts in Zaire had accomplished little, just as the African revolutionary movement suffered a dramatic set-back: in February 1966 General Ankrah toppled the *Osagyefo* Kwame Nkrumah in a bloody *coup*. Now, with the overthrow of the Ben Bella and Nkrumah, Castro had lost two of his staunchest African allies. Guevara, seen as a mere adventurer by some African revolutionaries, was now forced to withdraw from Zaire, but the Castroites had no intention of withdrawing from Africa: now the Portuguese colonies became the target.

In Angola, under the Marxist government of the MPLA (*Movimento Popular de Libertacão de Angola*), some 9000 Cuban teachers, doctors and other professionals provided training and technical support; until early 1988 the Cubans did not normally take part in battles against insurgents trying to overthrow the regime. Nonetheless a Cuban defector, Air Force General Rafaél del Piño, claimed in May 1987 that there had been 10,000 Cuban casualties in Angola, including several thousand dead. In 1988 there were serious clashes between Cuban and South African forces encroaching on Angolan territory; for example, on 27 June 1988 a fight between Angolans and Cubans on the one side with South Africans on the other resulted in twelve South African deaths and a greater number of wounded, with the Cubans also suffering casualties. Soon the Cubans, having prevented the forcible overthrow of the MPLA government by pro-

West factions, were preparing to withdraw. A ceasefire agreed between Cuba and South Africa stipulated a process (to begin on 1 April 1989) that would lead to Namibian independence: some 3000 Cuban troops were required to leave Angola, with all the remaining Cuban troops to move 300 km (190 miles) north of the border. Then the Cubans, according to the negotiated agreement, made further staged withdrawals from Angola. Another Cuban involvement in Africa was gradually brought to an end.

The impact of *Castroism* around the world – for good or ill – has been out of all proportion to the size of Cuba. At a time when the total population of the island was around ten million people, 'Castro had more troops around the world than all the other Communist leaders put together.'[99] This state of affairs, in the second half of the 1980s, did not endure for long. Not for the first time in Castro's political experience, the vast seismic forces unleashed by the Cold War were about to leave him stranded on the sidelines.

In Asia, perennially shaped by the rivalries of the great powers (China, Japan, Russia, the United States), Castro has had little enduring influence. In Africa, where more may have been expected of *Afro-Cuba*, the gains were significant but limited to only a few countries. (In 1977, following Che, Castro made his own widely-publicised tour of Africa: Libya, South Yemen, Somalia, Ethiopia, Tanzania, Mozambique, and Angola. At that time he spoke of future days when 'feelings will go beyond the narrow horizons of a country's boundaries'.) Most of continental Africa felt the Castro factor, but in the hard world of *realpolitik* the Cuban influence was mostly brief and inconsequential. In southern Africa there were significant gains. It can be argued that the Cuban presence contributed substantially to the survival of the MPLA government in Angola, to the independence of Namibia, and to the collapse of South African apartheid. In Latin America, close to home but close also to the United States, there were few successes. Che Guevara was captured in Bolivia on 7 October 1967, and quickly brought before a US-trained officer, Captain Gary Prado Salmón. Two days later, the wounded Che was shot nine times by an officer named Mario Tenán. Few doubted the hand of the CIA in both the capture of Guevara and the decision that the Argentine-born revolutionary had to be killed. Bolivia became a symbol for the failure of Castroism in Latin America.

The years of revolutionary struggle led to inevitable tensions between Cuba and the great powers: not only (inevitably) with the United States. The proud and independent Castro had his ideological differences with the Soviet Union, and resented his obvious dependence on Soviet aid; and China saw Cuba as a Soviet proxy in the enduring Sino-Soviet confrontation that had consequences around the world. There were tensions too between Castro and other revolutionary leaders, jealous of his ascendancy on the world stage: many of them, as well as Cuba's revolutionary allies, were forced to struggle for survival against US-sponsored terrorism and economic sabotage.

In Central America, closest of all to Cuba, Castro was forced to witness the crushing of allies and potential allies by US-trained death squads, torturers and military juntas (see 'Towards Isolation', below). But at another level, despite all the failures, the spirit and vision of the Cuban revolution continues to inspire hope in oppressed peoples around the world. To this extent, whatever happens now, Fidel Castro has won.

THE POLITICS OF SOCIAL CHANGE

The dramatic events of the early years of the Cuban revolution have tended to obscure what the turmoil was all about: while the world's media are keen to report military invasions and nuclear threats, the lives of ordinary people generally attract less interest. We need to remember the simple fact, uncongenial to many Western observers, that Fidel Castro's principal objective was to bring the Cuban people out of oppression and exploitation. Cuba had been run as a milch-cow for US business, a brothel and gambling-den for wealthy tourists, the haunt of racketeers and their political cronies. In this world, highly congenial to Washington, the bulk of the ordinary Cuban people lived wretched lives, with no expectation that their basic needs would be met and little hope of improvements to come. It is the abiding contribution of the *Fidelistas* that they demonstrated that a different sort of society was possible.

In the years leading up to the Cuban revolution, at a time when General Fulgencio Batista was being fêted in Washington, and Havana was the 'Paris of the Caribbean', the lot of many ordinary Cubans was actually deteriorating. In the mid-1950s, with a decline in labour's share of net income, wages were being reduced. Thus a worker who earned $5 daily in 1951 was being paid $4.35 in 1955; during these years, employees in transportation, tobacco, henequen, manufacturing and other economic sectors experienced a 20 per cent cut in wages.[100] A steady growth in the Cuban population was outstripping the creation of new jobs, so helping to fuel industrial and other social tensions. Labour agitation discouraged foreign investment, further exacerbating the problems and inducing the International Bank for Reconstruction and Development (the World Bank) to observe: 'Unless this vicious cycle can be broken, all efforts at economic betterment in Cuba will be severely handicapped. Then Cubans of all classes will suffer by lower incomes, by few and inferior job opportunities, and perhaps even by internal dangers to their cherished political freedoms.' The regime responded in characteristic fashion – by blocking any hope of industrial democracy, by imprisoning and torturing workers' leaders, by intensifying the level of police repression.

The bulk of the productive land (8 per cent of the total) was owned by large farmers, with a fifth of the agricultural land owned by 22 large sugar companies. In the rural areas fewer than a tenth of all homes had electricity, while between 40 and 50 per cent of the people were illiterate. There were vast disparities between the urban and rural areas: 80 per cent of urban residents possessed running water, compared with fifteen per cent in rural areas; and in most rural areas there were no health and educational services. Social deterioration was exacerbated by prevailing economic trends, not least Cuba's diminishing share of the vital US sugar market.[101]

In the years before the revolution the bulk of the Cuban population, rural and urban, lived in poverty. Absentee landlords, mostly with US business connections, derived huge profits from sugar cane crops, while the farm workers on whom they depended were paid subsistence wages; in these areas, sick and dying children, denied all forms of medical attention and mostly suffering severe malnutrition, were commonplace. And while in the cities the government, the army and the police, in full cooperation with the Mafia, raked in their profits, most urban dwellers lived in overcrowded slums, with many people – men, women and children – struggling to survive through crime, prostitution and begging.

By late 1958 unemployment in Cuba was almost 20 per cent, and rising. Many employed people were scarcely able to survive; and many – about 150,000 in a total labour force of 2.7 million – were offered food and shelter in lieu of wages. In Havana the effects of widespread destitution were obvious everywhere; in such neighbourhoods as Luyano, Jesús del Monte and Las Yaguas tens of thousands of unemployed poor lived in squalor, 'eight to a room in hovels of tin sheeting and cardboard without sanitary facilities, garbage collection, sidewalks, or street lighting, and increasingly without hope'.[102] In all the urban centres, beggars were commonplace – more than 5000 on the streets of Havana alone. Illegal drug pedlars, protected by the Mafia and Batista's police, plied their trade in every neighbourhood; the casinos, catering largely for wealthy foreign tourists, had developed as a major industry; and by the late 1950s, with 11,500 women living as prostitutes in Havana, some 270 brothels were in operation. Some years later, Arthur Schlesinger, Jr commented: *'I was enchanted by Havana – and appalled by the way that lovely city was being debased into a great casino and brothel for American businessmen over for a big weekend from Miami. My fellow countrymen reeled through the streets, picking up fourteen-year-old Cuban girls and tossing coins to make men scramble in the gutter. One wondered how any Cuban – on the basis of this evidence – could regard the United States with anything but hatred.*'[103]

A population of about 6 million – more than half living in hovels and huts, more than 600,000 permanently unemployed, half with no access to electricity, 95 per cent of rural children infested with parasites. On 26 May 1957 the weekly magazine *Carteles* reported that twenty members of the Batista government owned Swiss bank accounts, each with deposits in excess of $1 million. This was the state of affairs that Washington preferred to a Castro victory. This was the state of affairs that Castro resolved to change – in the teeth of US-sponsored terrorism, assassination attempts, military invasion and economic embargo.

As soon as the Castro regime had consolidated its power in 1959, despite all the attempts at subversion and sabotage, a radical programme of social reform was begun: a total transformation of Cuban society was the result. The entire rural population, historically forced to suffer massive exploitation, saw enormous benefits. One authority (in other respects critical of the Revolution) commented in 1969: 'Only the most stubborn and emotional critics of the Castro regime would argue that the Cuban peasants, taken as a whole and considering the "fringe benefits" in food, medical care, education and housing, are not better off today then ever before.'[104] For the first time in Cuban history there was massive investment in all forms of social provision, not only in such primary areas as health and education but also in such cultural sectors as sport, music and dance, film-making, and literature. A 1963 report of the United Nations Economic, Social and Cultural Organisation (UNESCO) noted that the increased budgetary expenditures for education in Cuba far exceeded any educational budget in Latin America. By the end of the 1960s the expenditure on education was running at three times the pre-revolutionary levels: 'Engineers, doctors, nurses, teachers, military officers – technicians and professionals of all kinds – are pouring out of schools and universities now.'[105] And Cuban medical practice – not only social provision (far outstripping the rest of Latin America) but also fundamental scientific research – developed to the point that in many respects it is now a world leader (see Chapter 1). For the first time in Cuban (or Latin American) history, pre-cradle-to-grave health care was available free of charge to all citizens; and hi-technology medical products,* developed for domestic

---

* A principal purpose of the US Cuban Democracy Act, introduced by Bush and later agreed by Clinton, is to prevent Cuba's successful export of medical products (see Chapter 1 and Appendix 1).

purposes, were offered as exports to earn foreign revenue and to meet specific health requirements in other countries.

One of the Castro regime's most important early initiatives was the creation of a Ministry of Health – established on the principle that health care is a human right and a responsibility of government, that all medical services are free, and that these must be integral (dealing with the relationship of cure to prevention, treatment to environment, and physical problems to social ones). In 1976 the Ministry divided the country into 358 health districts, in each of which polyclinics were established to deal with health care, hygiene, dentistry, social assistance and daycare nurseries. By the early 1980s there were nearly 400 polyclinics throughout the country, and three different types of hospital: for children, for pregnancy, and for clinical and surgical care. In Havana alone, some 44 hospitals had been built, some of which specialised in psychiatric, orthopaedic and oncological care. Before the Revolution there were no clinics or institutions for dentistry; by 1983 there were 137. Infant mortality was brought down as low as 14.2 per 1000 live births in the first six months of that year (compared with 47 in Mexico, 49 in Bolivia, 60 in El Salvador, and 96 in the Dominican Republic). Today, despite the crippling US embargo, infant mortality per 1000 live births in Cuba is less than 10 (see Chapter 1), better than any other country in Latin America and better than some regions of the United States.

The basic theme in the Revolution is that of the *communal approach* to problems: the idea that people working together, often on an unpaid basis, can accomplish important social objectives. Thus in 1961 (the 'Year of Education') some 271,000 people were organised in a national crusade to eliminate illiteracy. Almost 100,000 student volunteers in the 'Conrado Benítez' brigade received intensive training before being sent into the countryside as part of the nationwide literacy campaign. In addition, about 121,000 *alfabetizadores populares*, part-time volunteers, worked in the towns. At the same time about 15,000 workers were granted leave of absence to participate in the campaign, with 35,000 professional teachers serving as administrators and advisors. Further campaigns were launched in subsequent years.

In virtually all social areas – nutrition, ante-natal care, eradication of endemic diseases, life expectancy, child mortality, nursery care, primary and secondary education, professional training, higher academic research, housing, and so on – the Revolution has claimed significant gains. In the 1990s, as a consequence of the Soviet collapse and the US embargo, there has been marked deterioration in many social spheres (see Chapter 1), though it is highly significant that Cuba has so far managed to avoid the mass starvation and social collapse that would have afflicted any other Latin American country in a similar plight.

It is spurious in this context to dwell on the failures and mistakes of the Revolution, not least because the Cuban leadership has always been the first to advertise them. No reader of Castro's marathon speeches can fail to notice the extent to which he openly shares Cuba's problems with his audience. In the same spirit, Guevara was always keen to publicise problems as part of the process of searching for a communal solution. Thus in an article in *International Affairs* (October 1964), dealing with agricultural policy, Che wrote: 'Our first error was the way in which we carried out diversification. . . . The second mistake was, in our opinion, that of dispersing our resources over a great number of agricultural products. . . . I have spoken of certain achievements in the industrial field during the first years, but it is only just that I should also mention the errors made.' It is an easy matter – at a comfortable distance and with hindsight – to list the hasty decisions and tactical blunders, and what some observers have been quick to see as the abrogation of human rights (Chapter 1): the unforeseen consequences of sweeping nationalisations, the failure to achieve real economic diversification, the stultifying (and ultimately catastrophic) dependence on Soviet aid. Such issues can be endlessly debated, but at the same time there are people in the real world struggling to solve the basic problems of survival.

What Cuba managed to achieve in the social sphere (much of which is today being gradually eroded through US ideological bigotry) will always serve to illustrate what even relatively poor countries can accomplish, when they are allowed to do so. Above all, the Castroite reforms[106] give the lie to the worn cliché, so frequently on the lips of Western politicians, to the effect that 'we must *first* get the economic growth and *then* we will be able to pay for the social services that we all want'. Economic growth has never guaranteed social justice; and that a country is relatively poor does not mean that much cannot be done – in the spirit of a fair and cooperative philosophy – to meet the broad spectrum of human needs.

TOWARDS ISOLATION

The Cuban Revolution has by now (late-1995) lasted for almost 37 years. It has brought the transformation of an entire nation: the reform of agriculture, industry, banking, defence, health, education, cultural investment, and other social provisions. The situation – in particular, the continuous confrontation with the United States – has stimulated *Fidelista* fervour as much as *Yanqui* bigotry. In a world where the Devil has all the best tabloids it is easy to find critics of the Castro regime; but few can dispute that many of the changes – for example, in health and education – represent impressive advances that cannot be ignored. We also need to remember that revolutionary Cuba has always had to cope with US-sponsored terrorism, assassinations (and unsuccessful assassination attempts), military invasion (and threat of further invasions), and economic embargo.

The Cuban gains have been accomplished in the teeth of one of the most prolonged campaigns of hostility and sabotage in modern times: most Cubans alive today have known nothing else. It is one of the signal triumphs of the Castro regime even to have survived in these oppressive circumstances. Many other popular groups, movements and governments in the region have not been so successful. The campaign of US terror, subversion and economic sabotage has not been confined to Cuba.

In Guatemala, for example, the people elected the progressive leader Jacobo Arbenz in 1951. A principal element in his programme was land reform, a break with the landowner-dominated culture of the past, in which 'farm labourers had been roped together by the army for delivery to the low-land farms where they were kept in debt slavery. . .'.[107] Arbenz proceeded to expropriate large tracts of uncultivated land for distribution to 100,000 landless peasants, to improve workers' rights, and to introduce other social reforms. The Arbenz regime was not Communist: the Guatemalan Labour Party, the Communists, held four of the 51 seats in Arbenz's ruling coalition in the 1953–54 legislature. However, Washington decided that the popular reforms represented a threat to American interests. It was necessary therefore for the CIA to stimulate a campaign of terror and subversion, terminating in the US-sponsored invasion of Guatemala that succeeded in overthrowing the Arbenz government in 1954.

The sustained campaign of terror against the Guatemalan people represents one of the most appalling phases of political repression in the modern world: 'Indians tell harrowing stories of village raids in which their homes have been burned, men tortured hideously and killed, women raped, and scarce crops destroyed. It is Guatemala's final solution to insurgency: only mass slaughter of the Indians will prevent them joining a mass uprising.'[108] One witness to a military massacre of Indians in 1982 remembers: 'Children, two years, four years old, they just grabbed them and tore them in two.' Another victim recalled a more recent assault on an Indian camp: 'With tourniquets they killed the children, of two years, of nine months, of six months. They killed and burned them all. . . . What they did [to my father] was put a machete in here [pointing to his chest] and they cut open his heart, and they left him all burned up. This is the pain we shall never forget. . . . Better to die here with a bullet and not die in that way, like my father did.'[109] In another account: 'the soldiers began to fire at the women inside the small church. The majority did not die there, but were separated from their children, taken to their homes in groups, and killed, the majority apparently with machetes. . . . Then they returned to kill the children. . . . The soldiers cut open the children's stomachs with knives or they grapped the children's little legs and smashed their heads with heavy sticks'.[110]

This is the regime that grew directly out of the CIA-sponsored *coup d'état* against President Jacobo Arbenz. This is the regime that Washington finds more congenial than a government committed to land reform and workers' rights. The United States funded the Guatemalan army, trained its officers, supplied its weapons. In 1986 the Commission on Human Rights of the Organisation of American States (OAS) reported that more than 40,000 people had simply 'disappeared' over the preceding fifteen years.* This is one of the many brutal regimes in the region that Washington has supported while running an unremitting economic embargo to punish Cuba for its so-called human rights violations.

In Chile in 1970 the Marxist Salvador Allende was democratically elected to power: he, like Arbenz before him, had a programme designed to benefit the broad mass of the people, particularly the poorest. On 8 September Washington's principal strategist, Henry Kissinger, ordered a 'cold-blooded assessment' of the situation, including consideration of whether a Chilean military *coup* should be organised with US assistance. Soon CIA agents were despatched to Chile to provide money and weapons to right-wing officers planning the overthrow of Allende. Washington authorised $250,000 to bribe members of the Chilean parliament to vote against Allende; and various *coup* and assassination options were explored.[111]

Financial institutions under the control of the United States (the World Bank, the Export–Import Bank, and the Inter-American Development Bank) acted to exclude Chile from the international credit markets. US

---

* In March 1995 it was acknowledged that the bloody civil war had claimed more than 120,000 victims in the 1980s, with the 'bodies of suspected guerrillas . . . frequently found dumped on roadsides, left by government death squads as a warning to others'. In early 1995 mutilated corpses, 'most showing signs of torture, with gunshot wounds to the head and hands bound behind the back' (*Time*, 27 March 1995), were being found along the highways. Furthermore there was now mounting evidence that the CIA had worked with the death squads and had been implicated 'in numerous political crimes and assassinations' (*The Nation*, 31 March 1995; *The Guardian*, 1 April 1995).

companies were prevented from sending supplies to Chile: there were no spare parts for buses and taxis, and now frequent breakdowns were experienced in the copper, steel, oil and electricity industries. International Telephone and Telegraph (ITT), which had a massive stake in the Chilean telephone industry and which had enthusiastically funded Allende's opponents, expressed its hope 'that a swiftly-deteriorating economy will touch off a wave of violence leading to a military *coup*'. The CIA funded long strikes in the Chilean trucking industry and other economic sectors; and trained members of the fascist group *Patria y Libertad* in bombing and other terror tactics. At the same time the CIA funded the right-wing newspaper *El Mercurio* to spread false rumours and other forms of disinformation. Comprehensive files were compiled of Chilean citizens who were to be targeted after a *coup*.

The *coup* duly took place in September 1973. US military attachés supported the Chilean army, a US Navy commando team penetrated the country, US ships were off the coast, and US fighter planes were held in a state of readiness at an Argentine base just across the border. The democrat Salvador Allende was murdered, and there then began the repressive rule of the military dictator General Augusto Pinochet. The ensuing pattern was grimly familiar: arrests, torture, disappearances, and executions – of politicians, trade unionists, teachers, social workers, priests . . . Washington was well satisfied with the outcome. Financial credits and supplies were restored, and training and equipment was offered to the Chilean army and the other forces of repression. Well into the 1990s, after the election of President Patricio Aylwin and the discovery (in 1990) of mass graves of torture victims, General Pinochet remained commander-in-chief of the army. The dictator that Washington installed in 1973 remained the effective power centre in the 'new Chile'.

In Jamaica in 1972 the democratic socialist Michael Manley was elected prime minister – and US action was immediately taken to destabilise his government. Kissinger acted to withdraw American aid and to pressure other countries into blocking assistance. CIA-trained Cuban exiles were sent to the island to carry out terrorist acts, while the CIA induced labour leaders to organise anti-Manley strikes. As with Chile, Jamaica was frozen out of private lending markets, so preventing the Jamaican government from seeking aid to salvage the nation's sabotaged economy. The US-dominated International Monetary Fund (IMF) offered aid, on conditions that would ensure the unpopularity of the Manley administration. Manley managed to win re-election in 1976, despite all the US-sponsored terrorism and economic sabotage; but was finally defeated in 1980.

In 1994 fresh evidence emerged to show that President Kennedy had ordered the CIA to overthrow the democratically elected government of

Cheddi Jagan in British Guiana (now Guyana).[112] No states in the region escaped the attention of Washington.

Throughout the 1970s and 1980s the United States sustained a procession of right-wing governments in El Salvador, for the transparent purpose of protecting the economic interests of wealthy Salvador families and US corporations. This resulted in the prolonged repression of a poverty-stricken people in total violation of all human-rights considerations. Washington pursued its task by means of massive injections of military aid, by training torturers and repressive army factions, and by sanctioning the use of death squads. From 1980 to 1986 the United States supplied El Salvador with more than $2 billion in aid, most of which was used to procure military hardware: planes, small arms, machine guns, napalm bombs, oxygen reduction bombs, cluster bombs, etc. Death squads flourished, and the role of particular death-squad leaders (for example, Roberto d'Aubuisson) has been acknowledged by US personnel and other observers. Thus Robert White, former US observer to El Salvador, testified before the House Subcommittee on Western Hemispheric Affairs: 'From the first day in office, the Reagan White House knew – beyond any reasonable doubt – that Roberto d'Aubuisson planned and ordered the assassination of Archbishop Arnulfo Romero. . . . The administration of President Carter classified ex-Major Roberto d'Aubuisson, accurately, as a terrorist, a murderer, and a leader of death squads.' The US Right has hailed this man as a hero.

In March 1993, UN Secretary-General Boutros Boutros-Ghali issued a statement welcoming the 600-page report of the UN Commission on the Truth, set up to expose the human-rights abuses perpetrated by the US-backed Salvadorean army. Individuals and factions responsible for repression, murder and massacre are named in the report, but there was never any likelihood that the guilty would be brought to justice. Nor, as the playwright and political activist Harold Pinter pointed out, was the report brave enough to name many of the guilty people: 'there is another and quite substantial body of people which also walks free. . . . This body includes the American "military advisors", the CIA, Elliot Abrams, former head of the US Latin American Desk, Jeane Kirkpatrick, former US ambassador to the United Nations, former Secretary of State Al Haig, and ex-Presidents Reagan and Bush.'[113]

In the Dominican Republic the liberal Juan Bosch, democratically elected president in December 1962 (with 60 per cent of the popular vote), began to implement a modest land reform programme and minor nationalisations. Washington, appropriately alarmed, immediately set in train all the familiar measures to achieve the destabilisation of the Bosch administration: US aid came to a halt; the CIA and the US military began discussions with anti-Bosch army officers; and suitable lies about Bosch's intentions were spread around. In September 1963 a CIA-orchestrated *coup* installed Colonel Wessin y Wessin as a new US-friendly dictator – but he proved unable to stabilise the situation. Pro-Bosch factions in the army, acting in concert with the people, managed to return Bosch to power. It was now time for Washington to take sterner measures.

Hired thugs were sent onto the streets to foment violence and disruption, CIA-supported anti-Bosch factions began a series of bombing outrages, and on 28 April 1965 President Johnson sent in the Marines, later followed by the US Army's 82nd Division: a combined force of about 23,000 troops. Johnson, with unconscious risibility, tried to justify the US invasion: 'People trained outside the Dominican Republic are seeking to gain control.' To support what this statement was meant to convey, the US embassy in Santo Domingo issued – in the style of Joseph McCarthy – a list of fifty-eight 'identified and prominent Communist and Castroite leaders' in the pro-Bosch forces. Bosch himself commented: 'This was a democratic revolution smashed by the leading democracy in the world.' Some 2500 civilians were killed in the fighting, the pro-Bosch forces were crushed by US troops, and in due course Washington installed a suitable puppet government.

Nicaragua was first invaded by US troops in 1854 to avenge an alleged insult to the millionaire Cornelius Vanderbilt. Another US invasion took place in 1909, and from 1912 to 1933 (apart from one year) Nicaragua was under American military occupation. For decades the pattern was dismally familiar. A series of repressive regimes enjoyed US support in return for the protection of US business interests – until a popular revolution overthrew the military dictator General Anastasio Somoza in 1979. Washington again promptly set about reversing this blow to its fortunes.

In March 1981 the CIA Director William Casey proposed a detailed campaign of covert actions against Nicaragua (as well as Afghanistan, Laos, Cambodia, Grenada, Iran, Libya and Cuba). On 9 March 1981, weeks after taking office, President Reagan authorised covert military action and terrorism against Nicaragua, still a ravaged land and one of the poorest countries in the world. The CIA embarked upon the creation of an anti-Nicaraguan commando force (counter-revolutionaries, or 'contras'), constructed largely out of the remnants of Somoza's torturers and thugs. Again the multi-strand campaign of terror, propaganda and economic pressure was set in motion to destabilise the Sandinista government.

On 4 November 1984, in the teeth of US-sponsored terrorism and economic sabotage, Nicaragua went to the polls – so giving the lie to US propaganda that the regime lacked a democratic mandate (such as Somoza had enjoyed!): in what the international observers agreed were fair elections the Sandinistas were resoundingly supported at the polls. The Sandinista presidential candidate won 67 per cent of the vote, with nearly two-thirds of the National Assembly seats going to the Sandinistas. Washington, having tried to sabotage the elections, now called them a sham. Again the US strategists judged that it was time to escalate the tried and tested methods of terror, assassination, propaganda and economic sabotage.[114] Countless examples of contra terror have been documented: mutilations and murders of teachers, farmers, officials, ordinary people – men, women and children. The US-backed forces, operating from sanctuaries in US-backed Honduras, managed to slaughter some 30,000 people through the 1980s.*

Fresh elections were held on 25 February 1990, and even after all the terror and economic dislocation the Sandinistas managed to win almost half of the popular votes (proportionately more than Thatcher or Reagan). Ronald Reagan's 'freedom fighters' had achieved their purpose in the approved way: eyes gouged out, breasts cut off, castrations, lips sliced, tongues torn out, throats slashed, disembowellings. . . . The suffering Nicaraguan people, desperate for another way, voted a majority for the ramshackle coalition headed by the US-supported Violeta Chamorro. The 1990 victory was not for democracy but for torture and violence.

In 1983 Ronald Reagan decided to send 6000 élite US troops to invade the small Caribbean island of Grenada, where some 800 soldiers, workers and militia had to be overcome. A principal task was to overthrow the government of General Hudson Austin, a radical leader who had upset Washington by distributing land to impoverished peasants and by inviting Cuban construction workers to build an airfield. The American fighting men managed to win 8700 medals for their courage in an operation that was widely judged to have been a military fiasco. The US Navy's Special Forces men failed to enter the island on two attempts; they were subsequently beaten off by a counter attack; and troops sent to protect the Governor-General found themselves embarrassingly besieged for 24 hours inside Government House. In addition, the largest artillery bombardment of the operation missed its target; when Camp Calivigny, the home depot of the Grenadian People's Revolutionary Army, was attacked by a helicopter battalion it was found to be empty; and the US forces lost three helicopters and three men when crashes occurred through navigational errors. On one occasion an American aircraft strafed a house sheltering US

---

* In an important ruling the International Court of Justice at The Hague (the World Court) in 1986 condemned the United States for its terrorist acts against Nicaragua, demanded a cessation, and ruled that Washington pay compensation. In its response the United States declared that the World Court was incompetent to judge the matter.

troops. Five élite infantry battalions took three days to defeat one untried battalion of Grenadians. The Americans admitted to 18 US dead, with ten of these killed by 'accidents' or by 'friendly fire'.

The operation, named 'Urgent Fury', was a gross violation of International law. At the United Nations the General Assembly approved a resolution that 'deeply deplored' the American invasion. Washington, having succeeded in conquering a nation of 120,000 people, then set up the puppet government headed by Governor-General Sir Paul Scoon. The Cuban construction workers were ordered off the island, the Soviet embassy was closed, and the regime's policy of distributing land to the most impoverished islanders was quickly scrapped.

In Panama in the late 1980s the United States began having problems with one of its erstwhile puppet dictators. (This sometimes happens: as with Diem in Vietnam, Trujillo in the Dominican Republic, and Saddam Hussein in Iraq.) It was becoming apparent that General Manuel Noriega was increasingly unreliable: he had turned against the US stooge Barletta in Panama, was supporting the Contadora plan for a negotiated peace in Nicaragua, and was even making various popular concessions to the Panamanian people. Noriega, on the CIA payroll, had met CIA Director George Bush in 1976; some time later, Noriega left the payroll, but was then reinstated by President Reagan at a reported $185,000 a year. As late as 1987 Noriega was being applauded by Washington for his supposed opposition to drug trafficking. Thus John C. Lawn of the Drug Enforcement Administration (DEA), noting the DEA's links with Noriega, wrote that the organisation 'has long welcomed our close association and we stand ready to proceed jointly'; in May 1987 Ed Meese, Reagan's Attorney-General, praised Noriega for his efforts. But then the Washington strategists judged that Noriega could not be trusted to safeguard US interests when the Panama Canal reverted to Panamanian control in 1999.

The usual measures were put in train. When the CIA funding of anti-Noriega political factions and two CIA-sponsored *coup* attempts failed to overthrow the Noriega government, Washington decided on the option of last recourse – military invasion. The scene was set for further blatant violations of international law.*

In December 1989 President George Bush, one-time CIA friend of Noriega, launched Operation Just Cause for the overthrow of the Panamanian regime. An initial force of 24,000 troops, tanks, aircraft and

---

* The US invasion of Panama was a gross violation of many treaties to which Washington is a signatory, including the United Nations Charter, the Charter of the Organisation of American States (OAS), the Rio Treaty (Interamerican Treaty of Reciprocal Assistance) of 1947, the Declaration of Montevideo (1933), and the Panama Canal Treaties (1977–78).

helicopter gunships, later supplemented by a further 12,000 troops, quickly overcame Panamanian resistance. Washington then installed Guillermo, suspected of links with drug traffickers and money launderers, as the new Panamanian puppet.

There had been 347 US military casualties, 23 killed and some 200 wounded by 'friendly fire'. Washington refused to give figures for the enemy dead and wounded, though estimates quickly emerged from various sources. The journalist Martha Gellhorn, citing abundant evidence, claimed that 7000 Panamanian civilians had been killed, with labour leaders and other undesirables rounded up, and the working-class district of Chorrillo comprehensively shelled and finally flattened by US army bulldozers.[115] Again a small regional state had been rendered safe for US strategic objectives and American business interests.

In Haiti a similar pattern had been established: for decades the United States had used the familiar mix of terror, invasion and occupation to ensure that the country remained sympathetic to capitalist enterprise. Between 1867 and 1900 the US invaded the supposedly independent Haitian republic eight times, the last such incursion leading to a military occupation that lasted for nineteen years. Even President Woodrow Wilson, the celebrated propagandist for non-intervention, sent in the troops. The principle, maintained to the present day, was simple: the United States reserved the right to intervene in any regional country to protect the perceived American interest. Thus in August 1959 a rebel force struggling to overthrow the tyrannical Duvalier dictatorship was repelled by American forces. The US intervention in Haiti in 1993 was part of a well-established pattern.

On 30 October 1990 Jean-Bertrand Aristide was brought to power through supposedly democratic elections: Aristide, a radical Catholic priest, had won 67 per cent of the popular vote. But the new government, facing the hostility of the traditionally corrupt and self-serving armed forces, collapsed in September 1991 when General Raoul Cédras staged a successful *coup d'état*. It is useful in this context to remember that Aristide was not the favoured US choice in the 1990 election. Washington's preferred candidate was Marc Bazin, a one-time senior World Bank official and finance minister under the Duvalier dictatorship. It is significant also that the CIA had long-standing links with the Haitian armed forces; and that the Cédras *coup* occurred with the knowledge, if not the connivance, of the CIA (*Time*, 17 October 1994). When Cédras proved unable to protect the US interest, not least by staunching the flow of Haitian refugees, Washington resolved on more direct action.

The popular Aristide had been deposed, Cédras had failed to deliver, and now the US had the excuse it needed to instal a puppet administration directly run from Washington under nominal UN auspices. After comprehensive sanctions against Haiti – which by mid-1994 were killing several thousand infants through starvation every month – and the subsequent peaceful US invasion, Aristide was returned to Haiti. But now the radical democratically-elected leader was an emasculated figure, surrounded by US troops and having no option but to accede to IMF/World Bank schemes for the exploitation of his country. Again Washington had contrived an outcome congenial to US business.

The above examples of US intervention – involving terror, subversion, lies and military invasion – indicate the regional context in which Cuba has struggled to survive over nearly four decades. Washington has been well prepared to sanction torture,* sabotage, military aggression, economic strangulation, and the use of starvation and disease (as with today's *de facto* food and medical sanctions on Cuba and Iraq) as strategic weapons. Much of Latin America, lying inevitably under the US shadow, is characterised by poverty, violence and social dislocation. In El Salvador the death squads still operate;[116] the terror persists in Guatemala, as children are executed or traded on the streets, and as the former dictator, General Efraín Ríos Montt, runs for the presidency in 1995;[117] and Nicaragua, destabilised by US-sponsored terrorism and economic embargo, today has 40 per cent unemployment, the highest infant mortality rates in the continent, a quarter of all its children malnourished, and mounting violence.[118]

This is the political framework that Washington prefers to social reform; this is the regional environment in which Cuba struggles to protect its social gains. Today, through US policies, Cuba is ideologically isolated. Washington has worked hard to ensure that the popular leaders (Arbenz, Allende, Manley, Bosch, Ortega, Aristide and others) who might have been naturally sympathetic to Cuban reform have all been assassinated, tamed or marginalised.

---

* It is now generally acknowledged that the United States has funded and trained torturers throughout Latin America, as well as in Vietnam and elsewhere. Thus in her copiously researched *Cry of the People* (Penguin, London, 1980, p. xxiii) Penny Lernoux comments: 'The other integral part of the story of the human rights struggle in Latin America is the verified role of the US Defense Department, the CIA and corporate industry . . . on many occasions Catholic bishops and priests, including US citizens, have been tortured or murdered by organisations funded or trained by the US government, sometimes with the direct connivance of US agencies.' She declares (p. 157): 'The sickness that has engulfed Latin America, that endorses torture and assassination as routine . . . was to a significant extent bred in the board-rooms and military institutes of the United States.'

In the wider world the biggest blow to Cuban security came with the collapse of the Socialist bloc in general and the Soviet Union in particular: before 1989 some 83 per cent of Cuba's trade was with the Socialist bloc, 70 per cent of which was with the Soviet Union. On 5 December 1988 Fidel Castro, commenting on the Soviet reforms, declared that if they were successful 'it will be good for socialism and for everyone else', but 'if they have serious difficulties, the consequences will be especially hard for us'. It soon became apparent that the reforms introduced by President Gorbachev would not succeed; and that in consequence there would be grave implications for the Cuban economy. In August 1990 Castro announced that Soviet oil shipments to Cuba were only one fifth of what had been expected. Cuba would now be forced to adapt to a dramatically changed world situation.

The US government and the anti-Castro Cuban-American National Foundation, perceiving the nature of Gorbachev's 'new thinking', were now pressuring the Soviet Union to sever its links with Cuba. In this shifting atmosphere Gorbachev soon calculated that Washington's support was more valuable than a continuing association with the Cuban regime. In September 1991 he announced that the Soviet Union would be ending its military support for Cuba, at the same time hinting that the close economic relationship would be terminated. This announcement, greeted with glee in Washington, had been anticipated in Cuba: a year before, Castro had declared that the new economic crisis caused by the unreliability of the Eastern-bloc trading partners was forcing Cuba to enter '*a special period during peacetime*'. A new phase had begun. Soon Cuba would have to cope with the extinction of the Socialist bloc, regional isolation, and mounting US hostility.

Cuba, despite all US efforts, survives. Washington – with no justification in law or natural justice – had used its CIA-trained proxies in direct aggression with the aim of overthrowing the Castro regime: and failed. Next, to the same end, Washington tried terror and assassination: and failed. Then, in the interest of economic strangulation, Washington intensified its decades-long trade embargo and pressured other countries not to do business with the Castro regime: again failure. Cuba survives, but the Cubans are the first to admit their dire predicament – hard hit by the loss of the Socialist bloc, in regional ideological isolation (but winning growing political support for an end to the US embargo), and beset as they are by the psychopathic malevolence of the monster on their doorstep. The Castro regime is not without friends, and a remarkable reservoir of optimism and resilience. But the future is uncertain. The ramparts have held, but the long siege continues.

Appendix 1
The Cuban Democracy Act of 1992

SEC. 1702. FINDINGS

The Congress makes the following findings:

(1) The government of Fidel Castro has demonstrated consistent disregard for internationally accepted standards of human rights and for democratic values. It restricts the Cuban people's exercise of freedom of speech, press, assembly, and other rights recognized by the Universal Declaration of Human Rights adopted by the General Assembly of the United Nations on December 10, 1948. It has refused to admit into Cuba the representative of the United Nations Human Rights Commission appointed to investigate human rights violations on the island.

(2) The Cuban people have demonstrated their yearning for freedom and their increasing opposition to the Castro government by risking their lives in organizing independent democratic activities on the island and by undertaking hazardous flights for freedom to the United States and other countries.

(3) The Castro government maintains a military-dominated economy that has decreased the well-being of the Cuban people in order to enable the government to engage in military interventions and subversive activities throughout the world and, especially, in the Western Hemisphere. These have included involvement in narcotics trafficking and support for the FMLN guerrillas in El Salvador.

(4) There is no sign that the Castro regime is prepared to make any significant concessions to democracy or to undertake any form of democratic opening. Efforts to suppress dissent through intimidation, imprisonment, and exile have accelerated since the political changes that have occurred in the former Soviet Union and Eastern Europe.

(5) Events in the former Soviet Union and Eastern Europe have dramatically reduced Cuba's external support and threaten Cuba's food and oil supplies.

(6) The fall of communism in the former Soviet Union and Eastern Europe, the now universal recognition in Latin America and the Caribbean that Cuba provides a failed model of government and development, and the evident inability of Cuba's economy to survive current trends, provide the United States and the international democratic community with an unprecedented opportunity to promote a peaceful transition to democracy in Cuba.

(7) However, Castro's intransigence increases the likelihood that there could be a collapse of the Cuban economy, social upheaval, or widespread suffering. The recently concluded Cuban Communist Party Congress has underscored Castro's unwillingness to respond positively to increasing pressures for reform either from within the party or without.

(8) The United States cooperated with its European and other allies to assist the difficult transitions from Communist regimes in Eastern Europe. Therefore, it is appropriate for those allies to cooperate with the United States policy to promote a peaceful transition in Cuba.

SEC. 1703. STATEMENT OF POLICY

It should be the policy of the United States –

(1) to seek a peaceful transition to democracy and a resumption of economic growth in Cuba through the careful application of sanctions directed at the Castro government and support for the Cuban people;

(2) to seek the cooperation of other democratic countries in this policy;

(3) to make clear to other countries that, in determining its relations with them, the United States will take into account their willingness to cooperate in such a policy;

(4) to seek the speedy termination of any remaining military or technical assistance, subsidies, or other forms of assistance to the Government of Cuba from any of the independent states of the former Soviet Union;

(5) to continue vigorously to oppose the human rights violations of the Castro regime;

(6) to maintain sanctions on the Castro regime so long as it continues to refuse to move toward democratization and greater respect for human rights;

(7) to be prepared to reduce the sanctions in carefully calibrated ways in response to positive developments in Cuba;

(8) to encourage free and fair elections to determine Cuba's political future;

(9) to request the speedy termination of any military or technical assistance, subsidies, or other forms of assistance to the Government of Cuba from the government of any other country; and

(10) to initiate immediately the development of a comprehensive United States policy toward Cuba in a post-Castro era.

SEC. 1704. INTERNATIONAL COOPERATION

(a) CUBAN TRADING PARTNERS – The President should encourage the governments of countries that conduct trade with Cuba to restrict their trade and credit relations with Cuba in a manner consistent with the purposes of this title.

(b) SANCTIONS AGAINST COUNTRIES ASSISTING CUBA –

(1) SANCTIONS – The President may apply the following sanctions to any country that provides assistance to Cuba:

(A) The government of such country shall not be eligible for assistance under the Foreign Assistance Act of 1961 or assistance or sales under the Arms Export Control Act.

(B) Such country shall not be eligible, under any program, for forgiveness or reduction of debt owed to the United States Government.

(2) DEFINITION OF ASSISTANCE – For purposes of paragraph (1), the term 'assistance to Cuba' –

(A)   means assistance to or for the benefit of the Government of Cuba that is provided by grant, concessional sale, guaranty, or insurance, or by any other means on terms more favorable than that generally available in the applicable market, whether in the form of a loan, lease, credit, or otherwise, and such term includes subsidies for exports to Cuba and favorable tariff treatment of articles that are the growth, product, or manufacture of Cuba; and

(B)   does not include –

(i)   donations of food to nongovernmental organizations or individuals in Cuba, or

(ii)   exports of medicines or medical supplies, instruments, or equipment that would be permitted under section 1705(c).

(3) APPLICABILITY OF SECTION – This section, and any sanctions imposed pursuant to this section, shall cease to apply at such time as the President makes and reports to the Congress a determination under section 1708(a).

SEC. 1705. SUPPORT FOR THE CUBAN PEOPLE

(a)   PROVISIONS OF LAW AFFECTED – The provisions of this section apply notwithstanding any other provision of law, including section 620(a) of the Foreign Assistance Act of 1961, and notwithstanding the exercise of authorities, before the enactment of this Act, under section 5(b) of the Trading With the Enemy Act, the International Emergency Economic Powers Act, or the Export Administration Act of 1979.

(b)   DONATIONS OF FOOD – Nothing in this or any other Act shall prohibit donations of food to nongovernmental organizations or individuals in Cuba.

(c)   EXPORTS OF MEDICINES AND MEDICAL SUPPLIES – Exports of medicines or medical supplies, instruments, or equipment to Cuba shall not be restricted –

(1)   except to the extent such restrictions would be permitted under section 5(m) of the Export Administration Act of 1979 or section 203(b)(2) of the International Emergency Economic Powers Act;

(2)   except in a case in which there is a reasonable likelihood that the item to be exported will be used for purposes of torture or other human rights abuses;

(3)   except in a case in which there is a reasonable likelihood that the item to be exported will be reexported; and

(4)   except in a case in which the item to be exported could be used in the production of any biotechnological product.

(d)   REQUIREMENTS FOR CERTAIN EXPORTS –

(1)   ONSITE VERIFICATIONS – (A) Subject to subparagraph (B), an export may be made under subsection (c) only if the President determines that the United

States Government is able to verify, by onsite inspections and other appropriate means, that the exported item is to be used for the purposes for which it was intended and only for the use and benefit of the Cuban people.

(B) Subparagraph (A) does not apply to donations to nongovernmental organizations in Cuba of medicines for humanitarian purposes.

(2) LICENSES – Exports permitted under subsection (c) shall be made pursuant to specific licenses issued by the United States Government.

(e) TELECOMMUNICATIONS SERVICES AND FACILITIES –

(1) TELECOMMUNICATIONS SERVICES – Telecommunications services between the United States and Cuba shall be permitted.

(2) TELECOMMUNICATIONS FACILITIES – Telecommunications facilities are authorized in such quantity and of such quality as may be necessary to provide efficient and adequate telecommunications services between the United States and Cuba.

(3) LICENSING OF PAYMENTS TO CUBA – (A) The President may provide for the issuance of licenses for the full or partial payment to Cuba of amounts due Cuba as a result of the provision of telecommunications services authorized by this subsection, in a manner that is consistent with the public interest and the purposes of this title, except with this paragraph shall not require any withdrawal from any account blocked pursuant to regulations issued by section 5(b) of the Trading with the Enemy Act.

(B) If only partial payments are made to Cuba under subparagraph (A), the amounts withheld from Cuba shall be deposited in an account in a banking institution in the United States. Such account shall be blocked in the same manner as any other account containing funds in which Cuba has any interest, pursuant to regulations issued under section 5(b) of the Trading With the Enemy Act.

(4) AUTHORITY OF FEDERAL COMMUNICATIONS COMMISSION – Nothing in this subsection shall be construed to supersede the authority of the Federal Communications Commission.

(f) DIRECT MAIL DELIVERY TO CUBA – The United States Postal Service shall take such actions as are necessary to provide direct mail service to and from Cuba, including, in the absence of common carrier service between the 2 countries, the use of charter service providers.

(g) ASSISTANCE TO SUPPORT DEMOCRACY IN CUBA – The United States Government may provide assistance, through appropriate nongovernmental organizations, for the support of individuals and organizations to promote nonviolent democratic change in Cuba.

SEC. 1706. SANCTIONS

(a) PROHIBITION OF CERTAIN TRANSACTIONS BETWEEN CERTAIN UNITED STATES FIRMS AND CUBA –

(1) PROHIBITION – Notwithstanding any other provision of law, no license may be issued for any transaction described in section 515.559 of title 31, Code of Federal Regulations, as in effect on July, 1989.

(2) APPLICABILITY TO EXISTING CONTRACTS – Paragraph (1) shall not affect any contract entered into before the date of the enactment of this Act.

(b) PROHIBITIONS ON VESSELS –

(1) VESSELS ENGAGING IN TRADE – Beginning on the 61st day after the date of the enactment of this Act, a vessel which enters a port or place in Cuba to engage in the trade of goods or services may not, within 180 days after departure from such port or place in Cuba, load or unload any freight at any place in the United States, except pursuant to a license issued by the Secretary of the Treasury.

(2) VESSELS CARRYING GOODS OR PASSENGERS TO OR FROM CUBA – Except as specifically authorized by the Secretary of the Treasury, a vessel carrying goods or passengers to or from Cuba or carrying goods in which Cuba or a Cuban national has any interest may not enter a United States port.

(3) INAPPLICABILITY OF SHIP STORES GENERAL LICENSE – No commodities which may be exported under a general license described in section 771.9 of title 15, Code of Federal Regulations, as in effect on May 1, 1992, may be exported under a general license to any vessel carrying goods or passengers to or from Cuba or carrying goods in which Cuba or a Cuban national has an interest.

(4) DEFINITIONS – As used in this subsection –

(A) the term 'vessel' includes every description of water craft or other contrivance used, or capable of being used, as a means of transportation in water, but does not include aircraft;

(B) the term 'United States' includes the territories and possessions of the United States and the customs waters of the United States (as defined in section 401 of the Tariff Act of 1930 (19 U.S.C. 1401)); and

(C) the term 'Cuban national' means a national of Cuba, as the term 'national' is defined in section 515.302 of title 31, Code of Federal Regulations, as of August 1, 1992.

(c) RESTRICTIONS ON REMITTANCES TO CUBA – The President shall establish strict limits on remittances to Cuba by United States persons for the purpose of financing the travel of Cubans to the United States, in order to ensure that such remittances reflect only the reasonable costs associated with such travel, and are not used by the Government of Cuba as a means of gaining access to United States currency.

(d) CLARIFICATION OF APPLICABILITY OF SANCTIONS – The prohibitions contained in subsections (a), (b), and (c) shall not apply with respect to any activity otherwise permitted by section 1705 or section 1707 of this Act or any activity which may not be regulated or prohibited under section 5(b)(4) of the Trading With the Enemy Act (50 U.S.C. App. 5(b)(4)).

SEC. 1707. POLICY TOWARD A TRANSITIONAL CUBAN GOVERNMENT

Food, medicine, and medical supplies for humanitarian purposes should be made available for Cuba under the Foreign Assistance Act of 1961 and the Agricultural

Trade Development and Assistance Act of 1954 if the President determines and certifies to the Committee on Foreign Affairs of the House of Representatives and the Committee on Foreign Relations of the Senate that the government in power in Cuba –

(1) has made a public commitment to hold free and fair elections for a new government within 6 months and is proceeding to implement that decision;

(2) has made a public commitment to respect, and is respecting, internationally recognized human rights and basic democratic freedoms; and

(3) is not providing weapons or funds to any group, in any other country, that seeks the violent overthrow of the government of that country.

SEC. 1708. POLICY TOWARD A DEMOCRATIC CUBAN GOVERNMENT

(a) WAIVER OF RESTRICTIONS – The President may waive the requirements of section 1706 if the President determines and reports to the Congress that the Government of Cuba –

(1) has held free and fair elections conducted under internationally recognized observers;

(2) has permitted opposition parties ample time to organize and campaign for such elections, and has permitted full access to the media to all candidates in the elections;

(3) is showing respect for the basic civil liberties and human rights of the citizens of Cuba;

(4) is moving toward establishing a free market economic system; and

(5) has committed itself to constitutional change that would ensure regular free and fair elections that meet the requirements of paragraph (2).

(b) POLICIES – If the President makes a determination under subsection (a), the President shall take the following actions with respect to a Cuban Government elected pursuant to elections described in subsection (a):

(1) To encourage the admission or reentry of such government to international organizations and international financial institutions.

(2) To provide emergency relief during Cuba's transition to a viable economic system.

(3) To take steps to end the United States trade embargo of Cuba.

SEC. 1709. EXISTING CLAIMS NOT AFFECTED

Except as provided in section 1705(a), nothing in this title affects the provisions of section 620(a)(2) of the Foreign Assistance Act of 1961.

SEC. 1710. ENFORCEMENT

   (a) ENFORCEMENT AUTHORITY – The authority to enforce this title shall be carried out by the Secretary of the Treasury. The Secretary of the Treasury shall exercise the authorities of the Trading With the Enemy Act in enforcing this title. In carrying out this subsection, the Secretary of the Treasury shall take the necessary steps to ensure that activities permitted under section 1705 are carried out for the purposes set forth in this title and not for purposes of the accumulation by the Cuban Government of excessive amounts of United States currency or the accumulation of excessive profits by any person or entity.

   (b) AUTHORIZATION OF APPROPRIATIONS – There are authorized to be appropriated to the Secretary of the Treasury such sums as may be necessary to carry out this title.

   (c) PENALTIES UNDER THE TRADING WITH THE ENEMY ACT – Section 16 of the Trading With the Enemy Act (50 U.S.C. App. 16) is amended –
    (1) by striking 'That whoever' and inserting '(a) Whoever'; and
    (2) by adding at the end the following:

   '(b)(1) The Secretary of the Treasury may impose a civil penalty of not more than \$50,000 on any person who violates any license, order, rule, or regulation issued under this Act.

   '(2) Any property, funds, securities, papers, or other articles or documents, or any vessel, together with its tackle, apparel, furniture and equipment, that is the subject of a violation under paragraph (1) shall, at the discretion of the Secretary of the Treasury, be forfeited to the United States Government.

   '(3) The penalties provided under this subsection may not be imposed for –
    '(A) news gathering, research, or the export or import of, or transmission of, information or informational materials; or
    '(B) clearly defined educational or religious activities, or activities of recognized human rights organizations, that are reasonably limited in frequency, duration, and number of participants.

   '(4) The penalties provided under this subsection may be imposed only on the record after opportunity for an agency hearing in accordance with sections 554 through 557 of title 5, United States Code, with the right to prehearing discovery.

   '(5) Judicial review of any penalty imposed under this subsection may be had to the extent provided in section 702 of title 5, United States Code.'

   (d) APPLICABILITY OF PENALTIES – The penalties set forth in section 16 of the Trading With the Enemy Act shall apply to violations of this title to the same extent as such penalties apply to violations under that Act.

(e) OFFICE OF FOREIGN ASSETS CONTROL – The Department of the Treasury shall establish and maintain a branch of the Office of Foreign Assets Control in Miami, Florida, in order to strengthen the enforcement of this title.

SEC. 1711. DEFINITION

As used in this title, the term 'United States person' means any United States citizen or alien admitted for permanent residence in the United States, and any corporation, partnership, or other organization organized under the laws of the United States.

SEC. 1712. EFFECTIVE DATE

This title shall take effect on the date of the enactment of this Act.

Appendix 2
US–Cuba Joint Communiqué on Migration (9 September 1994)

Following is the text of the U.S.–Cuba Joint Communiqué on migration, New York City, September 9, 1994.

Representatives of the United States of America and the Republic of Cuba today concluded talks concerning their mutual interest in normalizing migration procedures and agreed to take measures to ensure that migration between the two countries is safe, legal, and orderly.

Safety of Life at Sea

The United States and the Republic of Cuba recognize their common interest in preventing unsafe departures from Cuba which risk loss of human life. The United States underscored its recent decisions to discourage unsafe voyages. Pursuant to those decisions, migrants rescued at sea attempting to enter the United States will not be permitted to enter the United States, but instead will be taken to safe haven facilities outside the United States. Further, the United States has discontinued its practice of granting parole to all Cuban migrants who reach U.S. territory in irregular ways. The Republic of Cuba will take effective measures in every way it possibly can to prevent unsafe departures using mainly persuasive methods.

Alien Smuggling

The United States and the Republic of Cuba reaffirm their support for the recently adopted United Nations General Assembly resolution on alien smuggling. They pledged their cooperation to take prompt and effective action to prevent the transport of persons to the United States illegally. The two governments will take effective measures in every way they possibly can to oppose and prevent the use of violence by any persons seeking to reach, or who arrive in, the United States from Cuba by forcible diversions of aircraft and vessels.

Legal Migration

The United States and the Republic of Cuba are committed to directing Cuban migration into safe, legal and orderly channels consistent with strict implementation of the 1984 joint Communiqué. Accordingly, the United States will continue to issue, in conformity with United States law, immediate relative and preference immigrant visas to Cuban nationals who apply at the U.S. Interests Section and are eligible to immigrate to the United States. The United States also commits, through other provisions of United States law, to authorize and facilitate additional lawful migration to the United States from Cuba. The United States ensures that total migration to the United States from Cuba will be a minimum of 20,000 Cubans each year, not including immediate relatives of United States citizens. As an additional, extraordinary measure, the United States will facilitate in a one-year period the issuance of documentation to permit the migration to the United States of those qualified Cuban nationals in Cuba currently on the immigrant visa waiting list. To that end, both parties will work together to facilitate the procedures necessary to implement this measure. The two governments agree to authorize the necessary personnel to allow their respective interests sections to implement the provisions of this Communiqué effectively.

Voluntary Return

The United States and the Republic of Cuba agreed that the voluntary return of Cuban nationals who arrived in the United States or in safe havens outside the United States on or after August 19, 1994 will continue to be arranged through diplomatic channels.

Excludables

The United States and the Republic of Cuba agreed to continue to discuss the return of Cuban nationals excludable from the United States.

Review of Agreement

The representatives of the United States and the Republic of Cuba agree to meet no later than 45 days from today's announcement to review implementation of this Joint Communiqué. Future meetings will be scheduled by mutual agreement.

For the Government of
The United States of America:
(MICHAEL SKOL)
Principal Deputy Assistant Secretary
Inter-American Affairs

For the Government of
The Republic of Cuba:
(RICARDO ALARCON)
President
Cuban National Assembly

New York, September 9, 1994

Appendix 3
GA Resolutions 47/19 (24 November 1992), 48/16 (3 November 1993), and 49/24 (26 October 1994) on Cuba

GA Resolution 47/19

The General Assembly, intent on promoting strict adherence to the principles and aims recognised by the Charter of the United Nations, stressing among other principles, the sovereign equality of nations, non-intervention and non-interference in their internal affairs, the freedom of international trade and navigation, also recognised in other international legal documents;

Concerned for the enforcement and application by member states of laws and regulations whose extraterritoriality affects the sovereignty of other nations and the legitimate interests of entities or persons within their jurisdiction and freedom of trade and navigation;

Having full knowledge of the recent enforcement of similar measures aimed at strengthening and widening the economic, commercial and financial blockade against Cuba;

1.   Calls on all member states to abstain from enforcing or applying laws and measures of the kind referred to in the preamble of the current resolution, in compliance with their obligation to adhere to the Charter and international law and the commitments legally entered into by subscribing to international legal procedures which, among others, recognise the freedom of trade and navigation;

2.   Urges nations where these kinds of laws or measures exist to fulfil their legal duty by taking whatever measures are necessary to eliminate or annul their effect as quickly as possible;

3.   Requests that the Secretary-General draw up a report back on compliance with the current resolution for consideration at the 48th session;

4.   Decides to include this issue for discussion on the provisional agenda of its 48th session.

GA Resolution 48/16
Necessity of ending the economic, commercial and financial embargo imposed by the United States of America against Cuba

The General Assembly,

Determined to encourage strict compliance with the purposes and principles enshrined in the Charter of the United Nations,

Reaffirming, among other principles, the sovereign equality of States, non-intervention and non-interference in their internal affairs and freedom of trade and international navigation, which are also enshrined in many international legal instruments,

Taking note of the statement of the heads of State and Government at the third Ibero-American Summit, held at Salvador, Brazil, on 15 and 16 July 1993, concerning the need to eliminate the unilateral application of economic and trade measures by one State against another for political purposes,

Concerned about the continued promulgation and application by Member States of laws and regulations whose extraterritorial effects affect the sovereignty of other States and the legitimate interests of entities or persons under jurisdiction, as well as the freedom of trade and navigation,

Recalling its resolution 47/19 of 24 November 1992,

Having learned that, since the adoption of resolution 47/19, further measures of that nature aimed at strengthening and extending the economic, commercial and financial embargo against Cuba have been promulgated and applied, and concerned about the adverse effects of those measures on the Cuban population,

1.   Takes note of the report of the Secretary-General on the implementation of resolution 47/19;

2.   Reiterates its call to all States to refrain from promulgating and applying laws and measures of the kind referred to in the preamble to the present resolution in conformity with their obligations under the Charter of the United Nations and international law which, *inter alia*, reaffirm the freedom of trade and navigation;

3.   Once again urges States that have and continue to apply such laws and measures to take the necessary steps to repeal or invalidate them as soon as possible in accordance with their legal regime;

4.   Requests the Secretary-General, in consultation with the appropriate organs and agencies of the United States system, to prepare a report on the implementation of the present resolution in the light of the purposes and principles of the Charter and international law, and to submit it to the General Assembly at its forty-ninth session;

5.   Decides to include in the provisional agenda of its forty-ninth session the item entitled 'Necessity of ending the economic, commercial and financial embargo imposed by the United States of America against Cuba'.

GA Resolution 49/24
Necessity of ending the economic, commercial and financial embargo imposed by the United States of America against Cuba

The General Assembly,

Determined to encourage strict compliance with the purposes and principles enshrined in the Charter of the United Nations,

Reaffirming, among other principles, the sovereign equality of States, non-intervention and non-interference in their internal affairs and freedom of international trade and navigation, which are also enshrined in many international legal instruments,

Recalling the statements of the heads of State and Government at the third and fourth Ibero-American Summits, held respectively at Salvador, Brazil, in July 1993 and Cartagena, Colombia, in June 1994, concerning the need to eliminate the unilateral application of economic and trade measures by one State against another which affect the free flow of international trade,

Taking note of Decision 356 adopted on 3 June 1994 by the Twentieth Council of the Latin American Economic System, held at the ministerial level at Mexico city, which called for the lifting of the economic, commercial and financial embargo against Cuba,

Concerned about the continued promulgation and application by Member States of laws and regulations whose extraterritorial effects affect the sovereignty of other States and the legitimate interests of entities or persons under their jurisdiction, as well as the freedom of trade and navigation,

Recalling its resolution 47/19 of 24 November 1992 and 48/16 of 13 November 1993,

Concerned that, since the adoption of resolution 47/19 and 48/16, further measures of that nature aimed at strengthening and extending the economic, commercial and financial embargo against Cuba continue to be promulgated and applied, and *concerned also* about the adverse effects of those measures on the Cuban people and on Cuban nationals living in other countries,

1.   Takes note of the report of the Secretary-General on the implementation of resolution 48/16;

2.   Reiterates its call to all States to refrain from promulgating and applying laws and measures of the kind referred to in the preamble to the present resolution in conformity with their obligations under the Charter of the United Nations and international law which, *inter alia*, reaffirm the freedom of trade and navigation;

3.   Once again urges States that have and continue to apply such laws and measures to take the necessary steps to repeal or invalidate them as soon as possible in accordance with their legal regime;

4.   Requests the Secretary-General, in consultation with the appropriate organs and agencies of the United States system, to prepare a report on the implementation of the present resolution in the light of the purposes and principles of the Charter and international law, and to submit it to the General Assembly at its fiftieth session;

5.   Decides to include this item in the provisional agenda of its fiftieth session.

Appendix 4
William McKinley, War Message to Congress (11 April 1898) – Extract

Obedient to that precept of the Constitution which commands the President to give from time to time to the Congress information of the state of the Union and to recommend to their consideration such measures as he shall judge necessary and expedient, it becomes my duty to now address your body with regard to the grave crisis that has arisen in the relations of the United States to Spain by reason of the warfare that for more than three years has raged in the neighboring island of Cuba. . . .

The present revolution is but the successor of other similar insurrections which have occurred in Cuba against the dominion of Spain, extending over a period of nearly half a century, each of which during its progress has subjected the United States to great effort and expense in enforcing its neutrality laws, caused enormous losses to American trade and commerce, caused irritation, annoyance, and disturbance among our citizens, and, by the exercise of cruel, barbarous, and uncivilized practices of warfare, shocked the sensibilities and offended the humane sympathies of our people. . . .

Our trade has suffered, the capital invested by our citizens in Cuba has been largely lost, and the temper and forbearance of our people have been so sorely tried as to beget a perilous unrest among our own citizens, which has inevitably found its expression from time to time in the National Legislature, so that issues wholly external to our own body politic engross attention and stand in the way of that close devotion to domestic advancement that becomes a self-contained commonwealth whose primal maxim has been the avoidance of all foreign entanglements. All this must needs awaken, and has, indeed, aroused, the utmost concern on the part of this Government, as well during my predecessor's term as in my own.

In April, 1896, the evils from which our country suffered through the Cuban war became so onerous that my predecessor made an effort to bring about a peace through the mediation of this Government in any way that might tend to an honorable adjustment of the contest between Spain and her revolted colony, on the basis of some effective scheme of self-government for Cuba under the flag and sovereignty of Spain. It failed through the refusal of the Spanish government then in power to consider any form of mediation or, indeed, any plan of settlement which did not begin with the actual submission of the insurgents to the mother country, and then only on such terms as Spain herself might see fit to grant. The war continued unabated. The resistance of the insurgents was in no wise diminished. . . .

The forcible intervention of the United States as a neutral to stop the war, according to the large dictates of humanity and following many historical precedents where neighboring states have interfered to check the hopeless sacrifices of life by internecine conflicts beyond their borders, is justifiable on rational grounds. It involves, however, hostile constraint upon both the parties to the contest, as well to enforce a truce as to guide the eventual settlement.

The grounds for such intervention may be briefly summarized as follows:

First. In the cause of humanity and to put an end to the barbarities, bloodshed, starvation, and horrible miseries now existing there, and which the parties to the conflict are either unable or unwilling to stop or mitigate. It is no answer to say this is all in another country, belonging to another nation, and is therefore none of our business. It is specially our duty, for it is right at our door.

Second. We owe it to our citizens in Cuba to afford them that protection and indemnity for life and property which no government there can or will afford, and to that end to terminate the conditions that deprive them of legal protection.

Third. The right to intervene may be justified by the very serious injury to the commerce, trade, and business of our people and by the wanton destruction of property and devastation of the island.

Fourth, and which is of the utmost importance. The present condition of affairs in Cuba is a constant menace to our peace and entails upon this Government an enormous expense. With such a conflict waged for years in an island so near us and with which our people have such trade and business relations; when the lives and liberty of our citizens are in constant danger and their property destroyed and themselves ruined; where our trading vessels are liable to seizure and are seized at our very door by war ships of a foreign nation; the expeditions of filibustering that we are powerless to prevent altogether, and the irritating questions and entanglements thus arising – all these and others that I need not mention, with the resulting strained relations, are a constant menace to our peace and compel us to keep on a semi war footing with a nation with which we are at peace. . . .

The long trial has proved that the object for which Spain has waged the war can not be attained. The fire of insurrection may flame or may smolder with varying seasons, but it has not been and it is plain that it can not be extinguished by present methods. The only hope of relief and repose from a condition which can no longer be endured is the enforced pacification of Cuba. In the name of humanity, in the name of civilization, in behalf of endangered American interests which give us the right and duty to speak and to act, the war in Cuba must stop.

In view of these facts and these considerations I ask the Congress to authorize and empower the President to take measures to secure a full and final termination of hostilities between the Government of Spain and the people of Cuba, and to secure in the island the establishment of a stable government, capable of maintaining order and observing its international obligations, insuring peace and tranquility and the security of its citizens as well as our own, and to use the military and naval forces of the United States as may be necessary for these purposes. . . .

Appendix 5
The Platt Amendment (1903)

That in fulfillment of the declaration contained in the joint resolution approved April twentieth, eighteen hundred and ninety-eight, entitled 'For the recognition of the independence of the people of Cuba, demanding that the Government of Spain relinquish its authority and government in the island of Cuba, and to withdraw its land and naval reserve forces from Cuba and Cuban waters, and directing the President of the United States to carry these resolutions into effect,' the President is hereby authorized to 'leave the government and control of the island of Cuba to its people,' so soon as a government shall have been established in said island under a constitution which, either as a part thereof or in an ordinance appended thereto, shall define the future relations of the United States with Cuba, substantially as follows:

I.   That the Government of Cuba shall never enter into any treaty or other compact with any foreign power or powers which will impair or tend to impair the independence of Cuba, or in any manner authorize or permit any foreign power or powers to obtain by colonization or, for military or naval purposes or otherwise, lodgement in or control over any portion of said island.

II.   That said government shall not assume or contract any public debt, to pay the interest upon which, and to make reasonable sinking fund provision for the ultimate discharge of which, ordinary revenues of the island, after defraying the current expenses of government shall be inadequate.

III.   That the government of Cuba consents that the United States may exercise the right to intervene for the preservation of Cuban independence, the maintenance of a government adequate for the protection of life, property, and individual liberty, and for discharging the obligations with respect to Cuba imposed by the Treaty of Paris on the United States, now to be assumed and undertaken by the government of Cuba.

IV.   That all Acts of the United States in Cuba during its military occupancy thereof are ratified and validated, and all lawful rights acquired thereunder shall be maintained and protected.

V.   That the government of Cuba will execute and as far as necessary extend, the plans already devised or other plans to be mutually agreed upon, for the sanitation of the cities of the island, to the end that a recurrence of epidemic and infectious diseases may be prevented, thereby assuring protection to the people and commerce of Cuba, as well as the commerce of the southern ports of the United States and of the people residing therein.

VI.   That the Isle of Pines shall be omitted from the proposed constitutional boundaries of Cuba, the title thereto being left to future adjustment by treaty.

VII.   That to enable the United States to maintain the independence of Cuba, and to protect the people thereof, as well as for its own defense, the government of Cuba will sell or lease to the United States land necessary for coaling or naval station at certain specified points, to be agreed upon with the President of the United States.

VIII.   That by way of further assurance the government of Cuba will embody the foregoing provisions in a permanent treaty with the United States.

From U.S. Statutes at Large, xxi, 897–898; *Treaty between the United States and Cuba, signed in Havana May 22, 1903; proclaimed by President Theodore Roosevelt, July 2, 1904.*

Appendix 6
'History Will Absolve Me' (Fidel Castro) – Extract*

Why were we sure of the people's support? When we speak of the people we are not talking about those who live in comfort, the conservative elements of the nation, who welcome any oppressive regime, any dictatorship, any despotism – prostrating themselves before the masters of the moment until they grind their foreheads into the ground. When we speak of struggle and we mention the people, we mean the vast unredeemed masses, those to whom everyone makes promises and who are deceived by all; we mean the people who yearn for a better, more dignified, and more just nation; those who are moved by ancestral aspirations of justice, for they have suffered injustice and mockery generation after generation; those who long for great and wise changes in all aspects of their life; people who, to attain those changes, are ready to give even the very last breath they have, when they believe in something or in someone, especially when they believe in themselves. The first condition of sincerity and good faith in any endeavor is to do precisely what nobody else ever does, that is, to speak with absolute clarity, without fear. The demagogues and professional politicians who manage to perform the miracle of being right about everything and of pleasing everyone are, necessarily, deceiving everyone about everything. The revolutionaries must proclaim their ideas courageously, define their principles, and express their intentions so that no one is deceived, neither friend nor foe.

In terms of struggle, when we talk about people we're talking about the *six hundred thousand* Cubans without work, who want to earn their daily bread honestly without having to emigrate from their homeland in search of a livelihood; the *five hundred thousand* farm laborers who live in miserable shacks, who work four months of the year and starve the rest, sharing their misery with their children, who don't have an inch of land to till and whose existence would move any heart not made of stone; the *four hundred thousand* industrial workers and laborers whose retirement funds have been embezzled, whose benefits are being taken away, whose homes are wretched quarters, whose salaries pass from the hands of the boss to those of the moneylender, whose future is a pay reduction and dismissal, whose life is endless work and whose only rest is the tomb; the *one hundred thousand* small farmers who live and die working land that is not theirs, looking at it with the sadness of Moses gazing at the promised land, to die without ever owning it, who like feudal serfs have to pay for the use of their parcel of land by giving up a portion of its produce, who cannot love it, improve it, beautify it,

---

*Fidel Castro's entire reconstruction of his courtroom speech (16 October 1953) is published as an appendix in Marta Harnecker, *Fidel Castro's Political Strategy* © copyright 1987 by Pathfinder Press. Reprinted by permission.

nor plant a cedar or an orange tree on it because they never know when a sheriff will come with the rural guard to evict them from it; the *thirty thousand* teachers and professors who are so devoted, dedicated, and so necessary to the better destiny of future generations and who are so badly treated and paid; the *twenty thousand* small businessmen weighed down by debts, ruined by the crisis, and harangued by a plague of grafting and venal officials, the *ten thousand* young professional people: doctors, engineers, lawyers, veterinarians, school teachers, dentists, pharmacists, newspapermen, painters, sculptors, etc., who finish school with their degrees, anxious to work and full of hope, only to find themselves at the dead end, all doors closed to them, and where no ear hears their clamor or supplication. These are the people, the ones who know misfortune and, therefore, are capable of fighting with limitless courage! To these people whose desperate roads through life have been paved with the bricks of betrayal and false promises, we were not going to say: 'We will give you . . .' but rather: 'Here it is, now fight for it with everything you have, so that liberty and happiness may be yours!'

The five revolutionary laws that would have been proclaimed immediately after the capture of the Moncada garrison and would have been broadcast to the nation by radio must be included in the indictment. It is possible that Colonel Chaviano may have deliberately destroyed these documents, but even if he has I remember them.

The first revolutionary law would have returned the power to the people and proclaimed the 1940 constitution the supreme law of the state until such time as the people should decide to modify or change it. And in order to effect its implementation and punish those who violated it – there being no electoral organization to carry this out – the revolutionary movement, as the circumstantial incarnation of this sovereignty, the only source of legitimate power, would have assumed all the faculties inherent therein, except that of modifying the constitution itself: in other words, it would have assumed the legislative, executive, and judicial powers.

This attitude could not be clearer nor more free of vacillation and sterile charlatanry. A government acclaimed by the mass of rebel people would be vested with every power, everything necessary in order to proceed with the effective implementation of popular will and real justice. From that moment, the judicial power – which since March 10 had placed itself against and outside the constitution – would cease to exist and we would proceed to its immediate and total reform before it would once again assume the power granted it by the supreme law of the republic. Without these previous measures, a return to legality by putting its custody back into the hands that have crippled the system so dishonorably would constitute a fraud, a deceit, one more betrayal.

The second revolutionary law would give nonmortgageable and nontransferable ownership of the land to all tenant and subtenant farmers, lessees, sharecroppers, and squatters who hold parcels of five *caballerías** of land or less, and the state would indemnify the former owners on the basis of the rental which they would have received for these parcels over a period of ten years.

---

*A *caballería* is about 33 acres.

The third revolutionary law would have granted workers and employees the right to share 30 per cent of the profits of all large industrial, mercantile, and mining enterprises, including the sugar mills. The strictly agricultural enterprises would be exempt in consideration of other agrarian laws which would be put into effect.

The fourth revolutionary law would have granted all sugar planters the right to share 55 per cent of the sugar production and a minimum quota of forty thousand *arrobas* for all small tenant farmers who have been established for three years or more.

The fifth revolutionary law would have ordered the confiscation of all holdings and ill-gotten gains of those who had committed fraud during previous regimes, as well as the holdings and ill-gotten gains of all their legates and heirs. To implement this, special courts with full powers would gain access to all records of all corporations registered or operating in this country, in order to investigate concealed funds of illegal origin and to request that foreign governments extradite persons and attach holdings rightfully belonging to the Cuban people. Half of the property recovered would be used to subsidize retirement funds for workers and the other half would be used for hospitals, asylums, and charitable organizations.

Furthermore, it was to be declared that the Cuban policy in the Americas would be one of close solidarity with the democratic peoples of this continent, and that all those politically persecuted by bloody tyrannies oppressing our sister nations would find generous asylum, brotherhood, and bread in the land of Martí; not the persecution, hunger, and treason they find today. Cuba should be the bulwark of liberty and not a shameful link in the chain of despotism.

These laws would have been proclaimed immediately. As soon as the upheaval ended and prior to a detailed and far-reaching study, they would have been followed by another series of laws and fundamental measures, such as the agrarian reform, the integral educational reform, nationalization of the electric power trust and the telephone trust, refund to the people of the illegal excessive rates these companies have charged, and payment to the treasury of all taxes brazenly evaded in the past.

All these laws and others would be based on exact compliance with two essential articles of our constitution: one of them orders the outlawing of large estates, indicating the maximum area of land any one person or entity may own for each type of agricultural enterprise, by adopting measures which would tend to revert the land to the Cubans. The other categorically orders the state to use all means at its disposal to provide employment for all those who lack it an to insure a decent livelihood to each manual or intellectual laborer. None of these laws can be called unconstitutional. The first popularly elected government would have to respect them, not only because of moral obligations to the nation, but because when people achieve something they have yearned for throughout generations, no force in the world is capable of taking it away again.

The problem of the land, the problem of industrialization, the problem of housing, the problem of unemployment, the problem of education, and the problem of the people's health: these are the six problems we would take immediate steps to solve, along with restoration of civil liberties and political democracy.

This exposition may seem cold and theoretical if one does not know the shocking and tragic conditions of the country with regard to these six problems, along with the most humiliating political oppression.

Eighty-five percent of the small farmers in Cuba pay rent and live under the constant threat of being evicted from the land they till. More than half of our most productive land is in the hands of foreigners. In Oriente, the largest province, the lands of the United Fruit Company link the northern and southern coasts. There are *two hundred thousand peasant families* who do not have a single acre of land to till to provide food for their starving children. On the other hand, nearly *three hundred thousand caballereías* of cultivable land owned by powerful interests remain uncultivated. If Cuba is above all an agricultural state, if its population is largely rural, if the city depends on these rural areas, if the people from our countryside won our war of independence, if our nation's greatness and prosperity depend on a healthy and vigorous rural population that loves the land and knows how to work it, if this population depends on a state that protects and guides it, then how can the present state of affairs be allowed to continue?

Except for a few food, lumber, and textile industries, Cuba continues to be primarily a producer of raw materials. We export sugar to import candy, we export hides to import shoes, we export iron to import plows. Everyone agrees with the urgent need to industrialize the nation, that we need steel industries, paper and chemical industries, that we must improve our cattle and grain production, the technique and the processing in our food industry in order to defend ourselves against the ruinous competition of the Europeans in cheese products, condensed milk, liquors, and edible oils, and of the United States in canned goods; that we need cargo ships; that tourism should be an enormous source of revenue. But the capitalists insist that the workers remain under the yoke. The state sits back with its arms crossed and industrialization can wait forever.

Just as serious or even worse is the housing problem. There are *two hundred thousand* huts and hovels in Cuba; *four hundred thousand* families in the countryside and in the cities live cramped in huts and tenements without even the minimum sanitary requirements; *two million two hundred thousand* of our urban population pay rents which absorb between one fifth and one third of their incomes; and *two million eight hundred thousand* of our rural and suburban population lack electricity. We have the same situation here: if the state proposes the lowering of rents, landlords threaten to freeze all construction; if the state does not interfere, construction goes on so long as the landlords get high rents; otherwise they would not lay a single brick even though the rest of the population had to live totally exposed to the elements. The utilities monopoly is no better; they extend lines as far as it is profitable and beyond that point they don't care if people have to live in darkness for the rest of their lives. The state sits back with its arms crossed, and the people have neither homes nor electricity.

Our educational system is perfectly compatible with everything I've just mentioned. Where the peasant doesn't own the land, what need is there for agricultural schools? Where there is no industry, what need is there for technological or vocational schools? Everything follows the same absurd logic; if we don't have one thing we don't have the other. In any small European country there are more than 200 technological and vocational schools; in Cuba only six such schools exist, and the graduates have no jobs for their skills. The little rural schoolhouses are attended by a mere half of the school-age children – barefooted, half-naked, and undernourished – and frequently the teacher must buy necessary school materials from his own salary. Is this the way to make a nation great?

Only death can liberate one from so much misery. In this respect, however, the state is most helpful – in providing early death for the people. *Ninety percent* of the children in the countryside are consumed by parasites which filter through their bare feet from the ground they walk on. Society is moved to compassion when it hears of the kidnapping or murder of one child, but it is criminally indifferent to the mass murder of so many thousands of children who die every year from lack of facilities, agonizing with pain. Their innocent eyes, death already shining in them, seem to look into some vague infinity as if entreating forgiveness for human selfishness, as if asking God to stay wrath. And when the head of a family works only four months a year, with what can he purchase clothing and medicine for his children? They will grow up with rickets, with not a single good tooth in their mouths by the time they reach thirty; they will have heard ten million speeches and will finally die of misery and deception. Public hospitals, which are always full, accept only patients recommended by some powerful politician who, in turn, demands the electoral votes of the unfortunate one and his family so that Cuba may continue forever in the same or worse condition.

With this background, is it not understandable that from May to December over a million persons are jobless and that Cuba, with a population of five and a half million, has a greater number of unemployed than France or Italy with a population of forty million each?

When you try a defendant for robbery, Honorable Judges, do you ask him how long he has been unemployed? Do you ask him how many children he has, which days of the week he ate and which he didn't; do you investigate his social context at all? You just send him to jail without further thought. But those who burn warehouses and stores to collect insurance do not go to jail, even though a few human beings may have gone up in flames. The insured have money to hire lawyers and bribe judges. You imprison the poor wretch who steals because he is hungry; but none of the hundreds who steal millions from the government has ever spent a night in jail. You dine with them at the end of the year in some elegant club and they enjoy your respect. In Cuba, when a government official becomes a millionaire overnight and enters the fraternity of the rich, he could very well be greeted with the works of that opulent character out of Balzac – Taillerfer – who in his toast to the young heir to an enormous fortune, said: 'Gentlemen, let us drink to the power of gold! Mr Valentine, a millionaire six times over, has just ascended the throne. He is kind, can do everything, is above everyone, as all the rich are. Henceforth, equality before the law, established by the constitution, will be a myth for him; for he will not be subject to laws: the laws will be subject to him. There are no courts nor are there sentences for millionaires.'

The nation's future, the solutions to its problems, cannot continue to depend on the selfish interests of a dozen big businessmen nor on the cold calculations of profits that ten or twelve magnates draw up in their air-conditioned offices. The country cannot continue begging on its knees for miracles from a few golden calves, like the biblical one destroyed by the prophet's fury. Golden calves cannot perform miracles of any kind. The problems of the republic can be solved only if we dedicate ourselves to fight for it with the same energy, honesty, and patriotism our liberators had when they founded it. Statesmen like Carlos Saladrigas, whose statesmanship consists of preserving the status quo and mouthing phrases like 'absolute freedom of enterprise', 'guarantees to investment capital,' and 'the law of supply and demand,' will not solve these problems. Those ministers can chat away in a Fifth Avenue mansion until not even the dust of the bones of those whose problems require immediate solution remains. In this present-day world, social problems are not solved by spontaneous generation.

A revolutionary government backed by the people and with the respect of the nation, after cleansing the different institutions of all venal and corrupt officials, would proceed immediately to the country's industrialization mobilizing all inactive capital, currently estimated at about 1.5 billion pesos, through the National Bank and the Agricultural and Industrial Development Bank, and submitting this mammoth task to experts and men of absolute competence totally removed from all political machines, for study, direction, planning, and realization.

After settling the one hundred thousand small farmers as owners on the land which they previously rented, a revolutionary government would immediately proceed to settle the land problem. First, as set forth in the constitution, it would establish the maximum amount of land to be held by each type of agricultural enterprise and would acquire the excess acreage by expropriation, recovery of the lands stolen from the state, improvement of swampland, planting of large nurseries, and reserving of zones for reforestation. Second, it would distribute the remaining land among peasant families with priority given to the larger ones and would promote agricultural cooperatives for communal use of expensive equipment, freezing plants, and single technical, professional guidelines in farming and cattle raising. Finally, it would provide resources, equipment, protection, and useful guidance to the peasants.

A revolutionary government would solve the housing problem by cutting all rents in half, by providing tax exemptions on homes inhabited by the owners; by tripling taxes on rented homes; by tearing down hovels and replacing them with modern apartment buildings; and by financing housing all over the island on a scale heretofore unheard of, with the criterion that, just as each rural family should possess its own tract of land, each city family should own its own home or apartment. There is plenty of building material and more than enough manpower to make a decent home for every Cuban. But if we continue to wait for the golden calf, a thousand years will have gone by and the problem will remain the same. On the other hand, today possibilities of taking electricity to the most isolated areas on the island are greater than ever. The use of nuclear energy in this field is now a reality and will greatly reduce the cost of producing electricity.

With these three projects and reforms, the problem of unemployment would automatically disappear and the task of improving public health and fighting against disease would become much less difficult.

Finally, a revolutionary government would undertake the integral reform of the educational system, bringing it into line with the projects just mentioned with the idea of educating those generations which will have the privilege of living in a happier land. Do not forget the words of the Apostle.* 'A grave mistake is being made in Latin America: in countries that live almost completely from the produce of the land, men are being educated exclusively for urban life and are not trained for farm life.' The happiest country is the one which has best educated its sons, both in the instruction of thought and the direction of their feelings.' 'An educated country will always be strong and free' . . .

---

*The 'Apostle' was José Martí.

Appendix 7
Manifesto and Programme of 26 July Movement (November 1956) – Extract

The Revolution is the struggle of the Cuban nation to achieve its historic aims and realize its complete integration. This 'integration' consists . . . in the complete unity of the following elements: *political sovereignty, economic independence*, and a *differentiated culture*. . . .

The Revolution is not exactly a war or an isolated episode. It is a continuous historic process which offers distinct moments or stages. The landings of Narciso Lopez at the middle of the past century, the war of '68, of '95, the movement of the 1930s and, today, the struggle against the Batista terror are parts of the same and unique national Revolution. . . .

The 26 July Movement can be defined as guided by thinking that is *democratic, nationalist*, and dedicated to *social justice*. . . .

By *democracy*, the 26 July Movement still considers the Jeffersonian philosophy valid and fully subscribes to the formula of Lincoln of 'a government of the people, by the people, and for the people'. . . .

With respect to *nationalism*, this is the natural flow of geographic and historic circumstances that leads to the birth of a Cuba of independent status. . . . Cuba, which reached nominal independence in 1902, has not yet reached economic independence. The land, the minerals, the public services, the institutions of credit, the means of transport, in a word, the most important national properties, today revert the major percentage of their utilities to the outside. The nationalist position in this case consists in rectifying that unjust situation, making it so the country receives the benefit of its own riches and economic means. . . .

By *social justice*, the 26 July Movement understands the establishment of an order such that all inalienable rights of the *human person* – political, social, economic, and cultural – are fully satisfied and guaranteed. . . . The experience of economic development of nations in the nineteenth and twentieth centuries has demonstrated that the capitalist system of free enterprise conduces inevitably to the accumulation of riches in a few hands, with the accompanying exploitation of the others. . . .

The 26 July Movement is in favour of a system of economic planning that is capable of liberating the country from the evils of monoculture, concessions, monopolist privileges, the *latifundio*, and other expressions of the absentee economy.

Appendix 8
First Havana Declaration – Extract

The national general assembly of the Cuban people condemns large-scale landowning as a source of poverty for the peasant and a backward and inhuman system of agricultural production; it condemns starvation wages and the iniquitous exploitation of human labour by illegitimate and privileged interests; it condemns illiteracy, the lack of teachers, schools, doctors and hospitals; the lack of assistance to the aged in the American countries; it condemns discrimination against the Negro and the Indian; it condemns the inequality and the exploitation of women; it condemns political and military oligarchies which keep our peoples in poverty, impede their democratic development and the full exercise of their sovereignty; it condemns concessions of our countries' national resources to foreign monopolies as a policy sacrificing and betraying the peoples' interests; it condemns Governments which turn a deaf ear to the demands of their people so that they may obey orders from abroad; it condemns the systematic deception of the peoples by mass communication media which serve the interests of the oligarchies and the policy of imperialist oppression; it condemns the news monopoly held by monopolist agencies, which are instruments of monopolist trusts and agents of such interests; it condemns repressive laws which prevent the workers, the peasants, the students and the intellectuals, the great majorities in each country, from forming associations and fighting for their social and patriotic demands; it condemns the imperialist monopolies and enterprises which continually plunder our wealth, exploit our workers and peasants, bleed our economies and keep them backward, and subordinate Latin American politics to their designs and interests. In short, the national general assembly of the Cuban people condemns the exploitation of man by man and the exploitation of under-developed countries by imperialist capital.

Consequently, the national general assembly of the Cuban people proclaims before America, and proclaims here before the world, the right of the peasants to the land; the right of the workers to the fruits of their labour; the right of children to education; the right of the sick to medical care and hospitalization; the right of young people to work; the right of students to free vocational training and scientific education; the right of Negroes and Indians to full human dignity; the right of women to civil, social and political equality; the right of the elderly to security in their old age; the right of intellectuals, artists and scientists to fight through their works for a better world; the right of States to nationalize imperialist monopolies, thus rescuing the national wealth and resources; the right of countries to trade freely with all the peoples of the world; the right of nations to their complete sovereignty; the right of peoples to convert their military fortresses into schools and to arm their workers (because in this we have to be arms-conscious and to arm our people to defence against imperialist attacks), their peasants, their students, their intellectuals, Negroes, Indians, women, young people, old people, all the oppressed and exploited, so that they may themselves defend their rights and their destinies.

Notes

Notes to Chapter 1: New World Oppression

1. Some of these chronological details derive from Jane Franklin, *The Cuban Revolution and the United States* (Melbourne, Australia: Ocean Press, 1992).
2. *Ediciones Obra Revolucionaria* (Revolutionary Works Editions), Number 13, Imprenta Nacional de Cuba, 16 July 1960, pp. 27, 29 and 31, quoted in Nicanor León Cotayo, *Beleaguered Hope: The US Economic Blockade of Cuba* (Havana: Editorial Cultura Popular, 1991) pp. 24–5.
3. *Ibid.*
4. Martin Walker, 'Pressure in the US to hasten Cuba's slide', *The Guardian*, London, 13 September 1991.
5. Mary Murray, *Cruel and Unusual Punishment: The US Blockade against Cuba* (Melbourne, Australia: Ocean Press, 1993) pp. 15–16.
6. The submission is given in *ibid.*, pp. 98–102.
7. *Uno Más Uno*, Mexican Daily, 22 April 1992, quoted in *ibid.*, pp. 18–19.
8. David Adams, 'US marlin fishermen snared by embargo', *The Independent*, London, 13 May 1992.
9. Andrew Zimbalist, 'Dateline Cuba: hanging on in Havana', *Foreign Policy*, no. 92 (Fall 1993) pp. 151–66.
10. Roberto Robaina Gonzáles, letter (25 June 1993) to UN Secretary-General Boutros-Ghali, published in Granma, Havana, 6 October 1993.
11. Noll Scott, 'US rules out any relaxation of Cuban trade embargo', *The Guardian*, London, 28 October 1993.
12. Hugh O'Shaughnessy, 'US Cuba trade ban hits British firms', *The Observer*, London, 14 November 1993.
13. Phil Davison, 'President's paises (sic) sung down south', *The Independent*, London, 2 February 1995.
14. Noll Scott, 'Cubans struggle on with their difficult father-figure', *The Guardian*, London, 16 July 1992.
15. *Ibid.*
16. See, for example, Jean Stubbs, *Cuba: The Test of Time* (London: Latin American Bureau, 1989), pp. 29–45.
17. Quoted in Gil Green, *Cuba: The Continuing Revolution* (New York: International Publishers, 1983) pp. 28–9.
18. *Ibid.*, p. 49.
19. Andrew Zimbalist and Susan Eckstein, 'Patterns of Cuban development: the first twenty-five years', *World Development*, vol. 15, no. 1 (1987) pp. 11–12.
20. JUCEPLAN. *Segunda Plenaria Nacional de Chequeo de la Implantación del SDPE* (La Habana: Ediciones JUCEPLAN, 1981), cited by *ibid.* See also Marta Harnecker, *Cuba: Dictatorship or Democracy?* (Westport, CN: Lawrence Hill and Company, 1979); and Andrew Zimbalist, 'Worker

participation in Cuba', *Challenge: the Magazine of Economic Affairs*, November/December 1975.

21. Zimbalist and Eckstein, *op. cit.*, pp. 12–18.
22. Forrest D. Colburn, 'Exceptions to urban bias in Latin America: Cuba and Costa Rica', *The Journal of Development Studies*, vol. 29, no. 4 (July 1993) p. 69.
23. *Ibid.*, p. 70.
24. See, for example, Karen Wald, *Children of Che: Childcare and Education in Cuba* (Palo Alto, California: Ramparts Press, 1978).
25. Quoted in Vladia Rubio, 'UNICEF's goals achieved three years ahead of time', *Granma International*, Havana, 23 February 1995, p. 11.
26. José A. de la Osa, '9.9 infant mortality rate in 1994: under 10 once again', *Granma International*, Havana, 18 January 1995, p. 2.
27. Alberto J. F. Cardelle, 'The preeminence of primary care within Cuban pre-doctoral medical education', *International Journal of Health Services*, vol. 24, no. 3 (1994) p. 422.
28. Milton I. Roemer, 'Primary health care and hospitalization: California and Cuba', *American Journal of Public Health*, vol. 83, no. 3 (March 1993) p. 318.
29. *Ibid.*
30. Nancy Scheper-Hughes, 'AIDS, public health, and human rights in Cuba', *The Lancet*, vol. 342, 16 October 1993, p. 967; see also John Waller, Lee Adams, Brian Lyons, Paul Redgrave and Paul Schatzberger, *AIDS in Cuba: A Portrait of Prevention*, Cuban Solidarity Campaign, London, 1993.
31. Daniel Topolski, 'A far cry from Chernobyl', *The Independent*, London, 6 August 1991; David Adams, 'Cuba works to save Chernobyl's children', *The Independent*, London, 4 July 1990.
32. Mieke Meurs, 'Popular participation and central planning in Cuban socialism: the experience of agriculture in the 1980s', *World Development*, vol. 20, no. 2 (1992) p. 235.
33. *Ibid.*
34. Trish Meehan and Dave Willets, 'Salsa and celebrations on the day we went to the polls', *Cuba Sí*, Cuba Solidarity Campaign, London, Summer 1993, pp. 8–9.
35. An AI report (AMR 25/07/90) on the human rights situation in Cuba, published in December 1990, comments that Amnesty's concerns regarding political imprisonment 'have not changed substantially' since the publication of an earlier report (AMR 25/20/89, December 1989); though 'the number of prisoners of conscience and possible prisoners of conscience has increased over the past few months'. Most of those arrested were detained because of their activities as members of illegal 'human rights or environmental groups or political opposition groups'; and 'in the context of increasing economic and political pressures on Cuba resulting from the changes in Eastern Europe and the Soviet Union'. Amnesty also expressed concern that 'other prisoners of conscience may be detained for having tried to leave the country illegally (salid ilegal del país) or for their activities connected with their membership of the Jehovah's Witnesses'. An AI report (AMR 25/12/92, January 1992) notes a sharp rise over the past few months in the 'number of prisoners of conscience and probable prisoners of conscience',

many of them 'members of unofficial political and human rights groups . . . detained as a result of their attempts to peacefully exercise their rights to freedom of expression and association'. Known dissidents have been 'verbally or physically abused' at their homes, with the police failing to intervene. This report describes the general situation of prisoners of conscience and gives details of the cases of 30 prisoners of conscience and 26 probable prisoners of conscience. AI report AMR 25/26/92 (December 1992) notes the creation of 'Rapid Response Brigades' to confront any sign of 'counterrevolution'; and, in a detailed 62-page survey, describes cases (with many named individuals) of short-term arrest, political imprisonment, alleged instances of ill-treatment, and the operation of the death penalty ('concern that the Cuban authorities might resort to using such severe punishment more frequently to suppress all types of opposition and dissent . . . has so far appeared to have been unfounded'). AI report AMR 25/01/94 (February 1994) notes an increased use of a section of Penal Code, 'The Dangerous State and Security Measures', to combat 'an increase in delinquency and vandalism' that had occurred in August 1993 'when prolonged electricity blackouts occurred in Havana and elsewhere as a result of the economic situation'. This aspect of the Penal Code is intended to combat (a) habitual drunkenness and alcoholism; (b) drug addiction; and (c) anti-social behaviour. There is also a provision for the police to issue an 'official warning' to those having a 'special proclivity' to commit crime because of their links to people who are 'potentially dangerous for society, other people and the social, economic and political order of the socialist state'. This report, noting the 'hundreds imprisoned for "dangerousness"', considers the circumstances in which this aspect of the law is used, details the specific judicial procedures, and discusses the cases of particular (named) individuals detained or imprisoned under these legal provisions. All these AI reports are important but should be considered in the context of Cuba fighting for survival in a war situation, and against such events as the US incarceration of innocent Japanese-Americans in concentration camps in the Second World War and the arrest and imprisonment, in violation of their legal rights, of Iraqis, Palestinians and Yemenis by the British authorities at the start of the 1991 Gulf War. Neither the United States nor Britain was at that time suffering terrorist attacks, foreign attempts at social disruption or a crippling economic blockade.

36. As, for example, described by the political dissident Reinaldo Arenas in *Before Night Falls* (New York: Viking Penguin, 1993).
37. For example, AI reports: *Allegations of Police Torture in Chicago, Illinois*, AMR 51/42/90, December 1990; *Torture, Ill-treatment and Excessive Force by Police in Los Angeles, California*, AMR 51/76/92, June 1992; and *United States Supreme Court Rulings Allow Execution of Juvenile Offenders and the Mentally Retarded*, AMR 51/27/89, June 1989.
38. 'US unwittingly clears Cuba on human rights', *Cuba Sí*, Cuba Solidarity Campaign, London, Summer 1994, p. 5.
39. Jim Bradbury, *The Medieval Siege* (London: The Boydell Press, Boydell and Brewer, 1992) p. 81.
40. Susan Kaufman Purcell, 'Collapsing Cuba', *Foreign Affairs*, vol. 71, no. 1 (1992) pp. 131–2.

41.   These examples, with others, are given in Murray, *op. cit.*, pp. 59–66.
42.   Klause Fritsche, 'The crisis in Cuba continues', *Aussenpolitik*, vol. 45, no. 3 (1994) p. 300.
43.   Sinan Koont, 'Cuba: an island against the odds', *Monthly Review*, vol. 46, part 5 (October 1994) p. 2.
44.   *Ibid.*
45.   Isabel Hilton, 'Every day, Cuba dies a little', *The Independent*, London, 10 October 1991.
46.   Noll Scott, 'Lean days and sacred cows', *The Guardian*, London, 15 July 1992.
47.   Lynne Wallis, 'Cuba's hunger feeds an epidemic of pain', *The Observer*, London, 23 May 1993.
48.   *Ibid.*
49.   *Ibid.*
50.   *Geneva Convention*, Protocol 1, Article 54(3)(b).
51.   See Robaina González, *op. cit.*; Nicanor León Cotayo, 'If it's of US origin . . .', *Granma International*, Havana, 9 March 1994; Roberto Gilí Colom, 'Notes for a White Paper, *Granma International*, Havana, 23 November 1994.
52.   Quoted in Carlos Tablada, *Che Guevara: Economics and Politics in the Transition to Socialism* (New York: Pathfinder, 1990) p. 150.
53.   Phil Davison, 'Cubans get on their bikes to beat fuel shortage', *The Independent*, London, 15 September 1993.
54.   Hilton, *op. cit.*
55.   Quoted by Fritsche, *op. cit.*, p. 301.
56.   Quoted by Fritsche, *op. cit.*, p. 302.
57.   Quoted by Fritsche, *op. cit.*, p. 302.
58.   Koont, *op. cit.*, pp. 7–8.
59.   Koont, *op. cit.*, p. 10.
60.   Juanita Darling, 'Cuba wobbles on road to unsure future', *The Guardian*, London, 12 August 1993.
61.   Douglas Farah, 'Cuba crawls back from the economic brink', *The Guardian*, London, 9 February 1994.
62.   Christine Toomey, 'Young capitalists lead Cuba's new revolution', *The Sunday Times*, London, 6 March 1994.
63.   Hugh O'Shaughnessy, 'Castro is forced to abandon fallen gods', *The Observer*, London, 24 October 1993.
64.   *Time*, vol. 145, no 7, 20 February 1995, p. 36.
65.   Haroldo Dilla Alfonso (translated by John F. Uggen), 'Cuba between Utopia and world market: notes for a socialist debate', *Latin American Perspectives*, vol. 21, no. 4 (Fall 1994) p. 58.
66.   Larry Rohter, 'Florida receives rising tide of Cuban refugees', *The Guardian*, London, 8 October 1992.
67.   Phil Davison, 'US blockade keeps Cuba in the cold', *The Independent*, London, 14 September 1993.
68.   Brian Lyons and John Waller, *Victims of War: The Untold Story of the Exodus from Cuba*, Cuba Solidarity Campaign, Sheffield, England, 1994, p. 17.

69. Martin Walker, 'Clinton asks allies to house Cubans', *The Guardian*, London, 24 August 1994.
70. Hilda Cuzio, 'Washington to grant entry to some Cubans', *Militant*, New York, 19 December 1994.
71. *Ibid.*
72. Cino Colina, 'Rafter's rights', *Granma International*, Havana, 18 January 1995.
73. *Ibid.*
74. Phil Davison, 'Cuban "angel" tries to save refugees', *The Independent*, London, 8 February 1995.
75. *Ibid.*
76. Letter to *The Guardian*, London, 30 July 1992.
77. Cesar Chelala, 'US should lift its blockade on medicines for Cuba', *British Medical Journal*, 7 August 1993, pp. 384–5.
78. Letter to *The Independent*, London, 20 July 1993.
79. These and other resolutions and statements are published in Murray, *op. cit.*, pp. 88–94.
80. Julie Wolf, 'Cuba embargo angers EC', *The Guardian*, London, 9 October 1992.
81. *Necessity of Ending the Economic, Commercial and Financial Embargo Imposed by the United States of America against Cuba*, Report of the Secretary-General, United Nations, New York, A/49/398, 20 September 1994.
82. 'Trade minister ends 20-year Cuba isolation', *The Daily Telegraph*, London, 7 September 1994.
83. Fritsche, *op. cit.*, p. 305.

Notes to Chapter 2: The Imperial Impact

1. *Fidel and Religion, Castro talks on revolution and religion with Frei Betto*, Touchstone edition (New York: Simon and Schuster, 1987) p. 184.
2. Louis A. Pérez, *Cuba: Between Reform and Revolution* (New York: Oxford University Press, 1988) p. 15.
3. *Ibid.*
4. Alan Burns, *History of the British West Indies* (London: George Allen and Unwin, 1954) pp. 44–5.
5. J. Gil and C. Varela (eds), *Cartas de particulares de Colón y relaciones coetáneas* (Madrid, 1984) pp. 159–60.
6. Pérez, *op. cit.*, p. 17.
7. Philip S. Foner, *A History of Cuba and its Relations with the United States, Volume I, 1492–1845* (New York: International Publishers, 1962) p. 18.
8. Fernando Portuondo, *Curso de Historia de Cuba* (La Habana, 1941) p. 98.
9. Foner, *op. cit.*
10. The work of D. Miguel Rodriguez-Ferrer and other researchers is described in M. R. Harrington, *Cuba Before Columbus* (New York: Museum of the American Indian, Heye Foundation, 1921).

11. For a detailed description of important aspects of the Spanish Inquisition see, for example, Rossell Hope Robbins, *The Encyclopedia of Witchcraft and Demonology* (New York: Crow Publishers, 1959).

12. Quoted in Fritz Blanke, *Missionsprobleme des Mittelalters und der Neuzeit* (Zurich and Stuttgart, 1966) p. 92.

13. The original shipboard journal of Christopher Columbus has long been lost; our knowledge of it survives largely through the attention given to what might have been a copy of it by Bartolomé de las Casas. Various attempts have been made to reconstruct the journal in the fullest possible way, and various translations (for example, in English) exist. See, for example, John Cummins (Introduction and translation), *The Voyage of Christopher Columbus, Columbus' Own Journal of Discovery Newly Restored and Translated* (to which I owe this extract) (London: Weidenfeld and Nicolson, 1992); and *Christopher Columbus, Journal of the First Voyage (Diario de primer viaje), 1492*, edited and translated (with an Introduction and Notes) by B, W. Ife, together with an essay on Columbus's language by R. J. Penny (Warminster, Wiltshire, England: Aris and Phillips, 1990).

14. F. R. Augier, S. C. Gordon, D. G. Hall and M. Reckord, *The Making of the West Indies* (London: Longmans, 1961) p. 10.

15. Felipe Fernández-Arnesto, *Columbus* (Oxford, England: Oxford University Press, 1992) p. 112.

16. I owe this item to John Cummins, *op. cit.*, pp. 5–6. He comments: 'Five hundred years after Columbus his evangelistic aim is unfulfilled, and the inculcation of the civilising values of Christendom continues to be a more complicated process than he and his age, in their own naïvety, anticipated.'

17. José Martí, *The Age of Gold* (San José, Costa Rica) p. 150.

18. César Rodriguez Expósito, *Hatuey, El Primer Libertador de Cuba* (La Habana, 1944) p. 98.

19. *Ibid.*, p. 84.

20. Irene A. Wright, *The Early History of Cuba* (New York, 1916) p. 48.

21. Pérez, *op. cit.*, pp. 26–7.

22. William H. Prescott, *History of the Conquest of Mexico* (London: Routledge, 1898), pp. 108–9.

23. *Ibid.*

24. Bernal Díaz, *The Conquest of New Spain*, translated and with an Introduction by J. M. Cohen (London: Penguin Books, 1963) p. 43.

25. Prescott, *op. cit.*, p. 123.

26. Díaz, *op. cit.*, p. 77.

27. Prescott, *op. cit.*, p. 168.

28. *Ibid.*

29. There is an ongoing debate about the character of this extant material. How much is Las Casas, how much Columbus? What can be said about Las Casas's working methods? His objectivity? His use of language? See, for example, B. W. Ife, *op. cit.*, pp. vi–xi; John Cummins, *op. cit.*, pp. 67–77.

30. Ife, *op. cit.*, p. vii.

31. Foner, *op. cit.*, pp. 26–7.

32. George Edward Ellis, 'Las Casas and the Relation of the Spaniards to the Indians', *Narrative and Critical History of America*, Justin Winsor (ed.)

(Boston and New York, 1884) pp. 305, 327; Wright. *op. cit.*, pp. 32–4; Hudson Strode, *The Pageant of Cuba* (New York, 1920) Volume I, pp. 73–4.

33. Pérez, *op. cit.*, p. 29.
34. Howard Zinn, *A People's History of the United States* (London: Longman, 1980) pp. 4–5.
35. Pérez, *op. cit.*, pp. 29–30.
36. Willis Fletcher Johnson, *The History of Cuba* (New York, 1920) Volume I, pp. 73–4.

Notes to Chapter 3: The Slave Society

1. St Paul, I Corinthians 7, 20–21.
2. St Augustine, *The City of God*, Book XIX, Chapter 15.
3. Edward Westermarck, *Christianity and Morals* (London: Kegan Paul, Trench, Trubner, 1939) p. 283 (sources cited).
4. I Corinthians 7, 13.
5. Joachim Kahl, *The Misery of Christianity*, translated by N. D. Smith (London: Penguin Books, 1971) p. 33.
6. *Ibid.*
7. Quoted by John Dower, *War without Mercy: Race and Power in the Pacific War* (London: Faber and Faber, 1986) pp. 150–1.
8. Westermarck, *op. cit.*, p. 303.
9. Herbert S. Klein, *Slavery in the Americas: A comparative study of Cuba and Virginia* (London: Oxford University Press, 1967) pp. 88–9.
10. *Recopilación de leyes de los reynos de las Indias*, 3 volumes (Madrid: D. Joachin Ibarra, 1791) I, 5, Libro I, Título I, Ley XIII.
11. Klein, *op. cit.*, p. 91.
12. Klein, *op. cit.*, pp. 96–8.
13. Robert Francis Jameson, *Letters from the Havana during the Year 1820* (London: John Miller, 1821) pp. 21–2.
14. Klein, *op. cit.*, pp. 15–17.
15. Clarence Henry Haring, *The Spanish Empire in America* (New York: Oxford University Press, 1947) pp. 209–10.
16. Eric Williams, *From Columbus to Castro: The History of the Caribbean 1492–1969* (London: André Deutsch, 1970) p. 50.
17. *Ibid.*
18. Louis A. Pérez, *Cuba: Between Reform and Revolution* (New York: Oxford University Press, 1988) p. 39.
19. Irene Aloha Wright, *The Early History of Cuba, 1492–1586* (New York: Macmillan, 1916) pp. 69, 81.
20. *Ibid.*, p. 203.
21. Williams, *op. cit.*, p. 26; cites Gonzalo Fernando de Oviedo (*General and Natural History of the Indies*, 1546) for a detailed account of the early Caribbean sugar industry.
22. Williams, *op. cit.*, p. 27.
23. Quoted by Klein, *op. cit.*, p. 136.
24. John Hope Franklin, *From Slavery to Freedom: A History of Negro Americans* (New York: Alfred A. Knopf, 1947) pp. 63, 69.

25. Klein, *op. cit.*, p. 149 (citations given).
26. Pérez, *op. cit.*, pp. 73–4.
27. Quoted by Pérez, *op. cit.*, p. 74.
28. Hubert S. H. Aimes, *A History of Slavery in Cuba, 1511–1868* (New York, 1907) pp. 35–7.
29. Pérez, *op. cit.*, p. 79.
30. Pérez, *op. cit.*, pp. 83–4.
31. J. G. F. Wurdemann, *Notes on Cuba* (Boston: James Monroe & Co., 1844) p. 153.
32. Quoted by Pérez, *op. cit.*, p. 98.
33. Juan J. Reyes, *Memoria sobre las causas de la vagancia en la Isla de Cuba* (Habana, 1851), in Aimes, *op. cit.*, p. 262.
34. Leslie B. Rout, *The African Experience in Latin America* (London: Cambridge University Press, 1976) p. 81.
35. *Ibid.*, pp. 81–2.
36. Quoted by Rout, *ibid.*, pp. 83–4.
37. Pérez, *op. cit.*, p. 105.
38. David Turnbull, *Travels in the West Cuba: with Notices of Porto Rico, and the Slave Trade* (London, 1840) p. 42.
39. Mariano Torrente, *Cuestión importante sobre la esclavitud* (Madrid, 1841) pp. 4–7; cited in Philip S. Foner, *A History of Cuba and its Relations with the United States, Volume I, 1492–1845* (New York: International Publishers, 1962) p. 203.
40. Quoted by Foner, *op. cit.*, p. 204.
41. Quoted by Foner, *op. cit.*, p. 210.
42. Quoted in Philip S. Foner, *A History of Cuba and its Relations with the United States, Volume II, 1845–1895* (New York: International Publishers, 1963) p. 78.

Notes to Chapter 4: The Violent Struggle

1. Eric Williams, *From Columbus to Castro: The History of the Caribbean 1492–1969* (London: André Deutsche, 1970) p. 191.
2. James Walvin, *Black Ivory: A History of British Slavery* (London: HarperCollins, 1992) p. 48.
3. Williams, *op. cit.*, p. 192.
4. Williams, *op. cit.*, pp. 195–6.
5. Elizabeth Abbott, *Haiti, the Duvaliers and their Legacy* (London: Robert Hale, 1991) p. 11.
6. Alexander Humboldt, *The Island of Cuba*, translated by J. S. Thrasher (New York, 1856) p. 271.
7. Irene A. Wright, *The Early History of Cuba* (New York, 1916) pp. 197–8.
8. Hugh Thomas, *Cuba, or The Pursuit of Freedom* (London: Eyre and Spottiswoode, 1971) p. 176.
9. Esteban Montejo, *Autobiography of a Runaway Slave*, transcribed by Miguel Barnet (London, 1968) p. 26.
10. Louis A. Pérez, *Cuba: Between Reform and Revolution* (New York: Oxford University Press, 1988) p. 99.
11. *Ibid.*

12. Leslie B. Rout, *The African Experience in Spanish America* (London: Cambridge University Press, 1976) p. 295.
13. Quoted by Pérez, *op. cit.*, p. 100.
14. Elias Entralgo, *Los Problemas de la Esclavitud. Conspiración de Aponte* (La Habana, 1934) pp. 102–5, 227; cited by Philip S. Foner, *A History of Cuba and its Relations with the United States, Volume I, 1492–1845* (New York: International Publishers, 1962) p. 93.
15. Quoted by Foner, *ibid.*, pp. 115–18.
16. Emilio Moreau Bacardi, *Crónicas de Santiago de Cuba* (Santiago de Cuba, 1904–24) volume III, p. 38; cited by Philip S. Foner, *A History of Cuba and its Relations with the United States, Volume II, 1845–1895* (New York: International Publishers, 1963) p. 168.
17. J. J. O'Kelly, *The Mambi-Land, or, Adventures of a Herald Correspondent in Cuba* (London and Philadelphia, 1874) pp. 118–20.
18. *Accounts and Papers*, LXI, p. 687; quoted by Thomas, *op. cit.*, p. 256.
19. A. E. Phillips to Hamilton Fish, 3 January 1870, published in *New York Tribune*, 23 February 1870; quoted by Foner, Volume II, *op. cit.*, p. 196.
20. *Ibid.*
21. Reprinted in *New York Tribune*; quoted by Foner, *ibid.*, pp. 196–7.
22. Thomas, *op. cit.*, p. 260.
23. Foner, Volume II, *op. cit.*, p. 238.
24. Thomas, *op. cit.*, p. 265; Foner, Volume II, *op. cit.*, pp. 260–1.
25. Maceo to Vincente García, 5 July 1877, Archivo Nacional; quoted by Foner, Volume II, *op. cit.*, p. 261.
26. Foner, Volume II, *op. cit.*, p. 265.
27. Foner, Volume II, *op. cit.*, p. 274.
28. Thomas, *op. cit.*, p. 295. Thomas cites two of the several published lives of José Martí ('all romanticised'): Jorge Mañarch, *Martí, Apostle of Freedom*, translated by Coley Taylor (New York, 1950); and Félix Lizaso, *Martí, Místico del Deber* (Buenos Aires, 1952). See also Thomas, *op. cit.*, pp. 293–309. I am also indebted to Peter Turton, *José Martí, Architect of Cuba's Freedom* (London: Zed Books, 1986).
29. Turton, *op. cit.*, p. 1.
30. *La República Española ante la Revolución Cubana, Obras Completas*, 27 volumes (Havana, Editora Nacional de Cuba, 1963–5) volume I, pp. 93–4; quoted by Turton, *op. cit.*, p. 8.
31. Herminio C. Levya, *El movimiento insurreccional de 1879* (Habana, 1893) p. 22–39; *Proclamation*, Kingston, 5 September 1879, in *La Independencia*, 18 October 1879; quoted by Foner, Volume II, *op. cit.*, p. 282.
32. Letter to Manuel Mercado, *Obras Completas, op. cit.*, p. 124; quoted by Turton, *op. cit.*, pp. 19–20.
33. Turton, *op. cit.*, pp. 33–7.
34. Horatio Seymour Rubens, *Liberty: The Story of Cuba* (New York, 1932) pp. 72–3.
35. Thomas, *op. cit.*, p. 306.
36. Turton (*op. cit.*, p. 58) notes the engaging fact that the day of Martí's death was the day that Augusto César Sandino, the great Nicaraguan freedom fighter, was born ('It does not seem likely, however, that twentieth century historians will pay much attention to such Pythagorean observations').

37.   Pérez, *op. cit.*, p. 160.
38.   Gabriel Maura Gamazo, *Historia Crítica del Reinando de Don Alfonso XIII*, 2 volumes (Barcelona, 1919, 1925) p. 235; cited by Thomas, *op. cit.*, p. 319.
39.   Quoted by Pérez, *op. cit.*, p. 162.
40.   *Ibid.*, p. 163.
41.   *Ibid.*, p. 166.
42.   Edwin F. Atkins, *Sixty Years in Cuba* (Cambridge, Massachusetts, 1926) pp. 242–3.
43.   Pérez, *op. cit.*, p. 176.

Notes to Chapter 5: The US Involvement

1.   Anthony Merry to Mulgrave, 3 November 1805, quoted in J. F. Rippy, *Rivalry of the United States and Great Britain over Latin America, 1808–1830* (Baltimore, 1929); Jefferson to Madison, 16 August 1807, Thomas Jefferson Papers, Library of Congress, Manuscripts Division, quoted by Philip S. Foner, *A History of Cuba and its Relations with the United States, Volume I, 1492–1845* (New York: International Publishers, 1962) p. 125.
2.   Address to a Harvard graduating class, Memorial Day, 1895, quoted by Richard Severo and Lewis Milford, *The Wages of War, When America's Soldiers Came Home – From Valley Forge to Vietnam* (New York: Simon and Schuster, 1990) p. 190.
3.   Louis A. Pérez, *Cuba: Between Reform and Revolution* (New York: Oxford University Press, 1988) pp. 59–60.
4.   Foner, *op. cit.*, pp. 44–5.
5.   *Ibid.*, pp. 66–7.
6.   National Congress of Cuban Historians, 1947, reprinted in Antonio Núñez Jiménez, *La Liberación de las Islas* (La Habana, 1959) p. 458; cited by Foner, *op. cit.*, p. 125.
7.   In Jiménez, *op. cit.*, p. 461, cited by Philip S. Foner, *A History of Cuba and its Relations with the United States, Volume II, 1845–1895* (New York: International Publishers, 1963) p. 10.
8.   Foner, Volume II, *op. cit.*, p. 12.
9.   Quoted by Foner, Volume II, *op. cit.*, pp. 30–1.
10.   The debate over the role of López cannot be explored here. Herminio Portell Vilá, in *Narciso López y su Época* (Narciso López and his Epoch), 3 volumes (Havana, 1930, 1952 and 1958) argues that López was a great Cuban liberator. José Martí disagreed. See accounts in Hugh Thomas, *Cuba, or The Pursuit of Freedom* (London: Eyre and Spottiswoode, 1971) pp. 212–17; Foner, Volume II, *op. cit.*, pp. 41–65 (who argues that 'López invaded Cuba in the interests of southern slaveholders of the United States').
11.   Thomas, *op. cit.*, p. 219.
12.   Cited by Foner, Volume II, *op. cit.*, p. 69.
13.   Amos Ettinger, *The Mission to Spain of Pierre Soulé, 1853–1855* (London, 1932) pp. 245–6.

14. Peter Turton, *José Martí, Architect of Cuba's Freedom* (London: Zed Books, 1986) p. 20.
15. *US Foreign Relations*, 1989, p. 88, cited in Scott Nearing and Joseph Freeman, *Dollar Diplomacy: A Study in American Imperialism* (New York: Monthly Review Press, 1925) p. 250.
16. *US Congressional Record*, V, 31, p. 3789; cited by Nearing and Freeman *op. cit.*, p. 251.
17. Gustavus Myers, *History of the Great American Fortunes* (New York: Random House, 1937) pp. 52, 59–63.
18. Leland Hamilton Jenks, *Our Cuban Colony: A Study in Sugar* (New York: Arno Press and the New York Times, 1970) p. 18.
19. *Ibid.*, p. 19.
20. R. R. Madden, *The Island of Cuba* (London, 1851) pp. 83–4.
21. Jenks, *op. cit.*, pp. 19–21.
22. Discussed in *ibid.*, pp. 30–3.
23. Benjamin Allen, *A Story of the Growth of E. Atkins and Company and the Sugar Industry of Cuba* (New York, 1925).
24. Jenks, *op. cit.*, pp. 34–5.
25. *Ibid.*, p. 36.
26. Pérez, *op. cit.*, p. 149.
27. Howard Zinn, *A People's History of the United States* (London: Longman, 1980) pp. 297–8.
28. *Ibid.*, p. 298.
29. Anna Rochester, *Rulers of America: A Study of Finance Capital* (London: Lawrence and Wishart, 1936) p. 260.
30. As, for example, in Eric Williams, *From Columbus to Castro: The History of the Caribbean, 1492–1969* (London: André Deutsch, 1978) ch. 24.
31. This bald statement cannot be explored here. Copious evidence is available, much of it assembled (with massive documentation) in Myers, *op. cit.* See also Matthew Josephson, *The Robber Barons: The Great American Capitalists, 1861–1901* (London: Eyre and Spottiswoode, 1962).
32. Carl N. Degler, *Out of Our Past: The Forces that Shaped Modern America* (New York: Harper and Row, 1970) p. 427.
33. A. H. Allen, *Great Britain and the United States, A History of Anglo-American Relations (1783–1952)* (London: Odhams, 1954) p. 199.
34. *Ibid.*, p. 369.
35. *Ibid.*, pp. 573–4.
36. Louis Martin Sears, *A History of American Foreign Relations* (London: Macmillan, 1928) p. 436.
37. Willard Grosvenor Bleyer, *Main Currents in the History of American Journalism* (Boston, 1927) p. 342.
38. See, for example, Thomas, *op. cit.*, pp. 340–1; Joseph E. Wisan, in *The Cuban Crisis as Reflected in the New York Press 1895–1898* (New York: Octagon Books, 1977) provides a detailed, massively documented analysis of press attitudes.
39. Thomas, *op. cit.*, p. 341.
40. In a letter to Commander Kimball, quoted in H. F. Pringle, *Theodore Roosevelt* (London, 1932) pp. 175–6.
41. Jenks, *op. cit.*, p. 51.

42. J. B. Bishop, *Theodore Roosevelt and His Time*, Volume I (New York, 1920).
43. Citations in Jenks, *op. cit.*, pp. 53–4.
44. Thomas, *op. cit.*, p. 358.
45. Quoted in Edmund Morris, *The Rise of Theodore Roosevelt* (London: Collins, 1979) p. 596.
46. Detail's of the *Maine's* design are given in Stephen Howarth, *To Shining Sea: A History of the United States Navy 1775–1991* (London: Weidenfeld and Nicolson, 1991) pp. 248–9.
47. G. J. A. O'Toole, *The Spanish War: An American Epic, 1898* (New York: Norton, 1984) pp. 124–5.
48. *Ibid.*, p. 400.
49. Howarth, *op. cit.*, p. 249.
50. I owe these and the following examples to Wisan, *op. cit.*, pp. 390–3.
51. Pérez, *op. cit.*, p. 178.
52. Howarth, *op. cit.*, p. 259.
53. Morris, *op. cit.*, p. 630.
54. Captain R. D. Evans, 'The Sea Fight at Santiago, as seen from the *Iowa*' (original draft), Evans papers, Library of Congress, quoted by Howarth, *op. cit.*, p. 266.
55. Pascual Cervera y Topete, *The Spanish–American War: A Collection of Documents Relative to the Squadron Operations in the West Indies*, translated from Spanish (Office of Naval Intelligence, US Government Printing Office, 1898), quoted by Howarth, *op. cit.*, p. 266.
56. Allan Nevins and Henry Steele Commager, *A Pocket History of the United States* (New York: Washington Square Press, 1962) p. 386.
57. *Ibid.*
58. Severo and Milford, *op. cit.*, p. 193.
59. I owe much of this section to Severo and Milford, *ibid.*, pp. 192–210.
60. García to Tomás Estrada Palma, 27 June 1898, cited by David F. Healy, *The United States in Cuba, 1898–1902: Generals, Politicians and the Search for a Policy* (Madison: University of Wisconsin Press, 1963) p. 30.
61. Shafter to Adjutant General of the US Army, 23 July 1898, quoted by Healy, *op. cit.*, p. 33.
62. Healy, *op. cit.*, p. 35.
63. John Black Atkins, *The War in Cuba* (London, 1899) pp. 288–9.
64. *New York Tribune*, 7 August 1898.
65. *Literary Digest*, XVII, 30 July 1898, cited by Healy, *op. cit.*, p. 37.
66. Thomas, *op. cit.*, p. 422.
67. *Civil Report of Major-General John R. Brooke, Military Governor of Island of Cuba*, Washington, 1900, United States War Department.
68. See, for example, Thomas, *op. cit.*, pp. 439–43.
69. Herman Hagedorn, *Leonard Wood* (New York, 1931) p. 285.
70. Wood to Root, in Root papers, 8 January 1908, cited by Healy, *op. cit.*, p. 181.
71. Pérez, *op. cit.*, p. 187.
72. Leonard Wood papers, Library of Congress, quoted by Healy, *op. cit.*, p. 178.

73. Roger Ricardo, *Guantánamo, The Bay of Discord* (Melbourne: Ocean Press, 1994) p. 17.
74. *Ibid.*, pp. 19–21.
75. Jenks, *op. cit.*, p. 87.
76. Edwin Atkins, *Sixty Years in Cuba* (Cambridge, Massachusetts, 1926) p. 322.
77. Thomas, *op. cit.*, p. 475.
78. Taft–Bacon correspondence, pp. 475–7, cited by Thomas, *op. cit.*, p. 478.
79. Sociedad Cubana de Derecho Internacional, 'Anuario', 1922, p. 407, cited by Nearing and Freeman, *op. cit.*, p. 180.
80. Jenks, *op. cit.*, p. 96.
81. Quoted by Thomas, *op. cit.*, p. 483, citations given.
82. Jenks, *op. cit.*, p. 97.
83. Nearing and Freeman, *op. cit.*, pp. 180–1.
84. Sears, *op. cit.*, p. 488.
85. Moody's 'Analysis of Investments: Industrials', 1916, p. 1145; 1919, p. 916; cited by Nearing and Freeman, *op. cit.*, p. 182.
86. Thomas, *op. cit.*, p. 182.
87. Jenks, *op. cit.*, pp. 155–6.
88. Dana Munro, *Intervention and Dollar Diplomacy* (Princeton, 1964) p. 19.
89. Thomas, *op. cit.*, p. 470.
90. Pérez, *op. cit.*, pp. 216–17.
91. *Ibid.*
92. Geoffrey Barraclough, *An Introduction to Contemporary History* (London: Penguin Books, 1967) p. 63.
93. John B. Rae and Thomas H. D. Mahoney, *The United States in World History* (New York: McGraw-Hill, 1964) p. 500.

Notes to Chapter 6: Towards Revolution

1. Hugh Thomas, *Cuba, or the Pursuit of Freedom* (London: Eyre and Spottiswoode, 1971) p. 537.
2. Leland Hamilton Jenks, *Our Cuban Colony: A Study in Sugar* (New York: Arno Press and the New York Times, 1970) p. 178.
3. Thomas, *op. cit.*, p. 541.
4. Thomas, *op. cit.*, p. 541.
5. H. J. Spinden, *World's Work*, XLI, March 1921, pp. 465–83.
6. NA 837.00 (2216), quoted by Thomas, *op. cit.*, p. 549.
7. Jenks, *op. cit.*, p. 240.
8. Austin F. MacDonald, *Latin American Politics and Government* (second edition, New York, 1954) p. 560.
9. Louis A. Pérez, *Cuba: Between Reform and Revolution* (New York: Oxford University Press, 1988) pp. 226–7.
10. Jenks, *op. cit.*, p. 251.
11. Jenks, *op. cit.*, p. 258.
12. Russel H. Fitzgibbon, *Cuba and the United States: 1900–1935* (Menasha, Wisconsin, 1935) Appendix.

13. *Ibid.*, p. 177.
14. Raymond Leslie Buell, *Cuba and the Platt Amendment*, Foreign Policy Association, New York, April 1929, p. 57.
15. Thomas, *op. cit.*, p. 555.
16. Robert F. Smith, *The United States and Cuba: Business and Diplomacy, 1917–1960* (New Haven, 1960) p. 101.
17. Pérez, *op. cit.*, p. 233.
18. Fernando Ortiz, *La Decadencia Cubana*, cited by Thomas, *op. cit.*, p. 567.
19. Pérez, *op. cit.*, pp. 246–7.
20. Robert Scheer and Maurice Zeitlin, *Cuba: An American Tragedy* (London: Penguin Books, 1964) p. 45.
21. Machado, in *El Día* (Havana daily), 9 May 1922, cited by Jenks, *op. cit.*, pp. 270–1.
22. Jenks, *op. cit.*, p. 271.
23. Quoted by Thomas, *op. cit.*, p. 572.
24. Aldo Baroni, *Cuba, país de poca memoria*, Mexico, p. 26, quoted by Thomas, *op. cit.*, p. 573.
25. Thomas, *op. cit.*, pp. 573–4.
26. *Proceedings of the Fifth Congress of the Pan American Federation of Labour*, 1927, p. 43, quoted in Raymond Leslie Buell, *The Caribbean Situation* (New York: Foreign Policy Association, 21 June 1933).
27. Quoted in Buell, 1933, *op. cit.*, p. 84.
28. *Report of the Delegation of the United States of America to the Sixth International Conference of American States*, p. 64, quoted in Buell, 1929, *op. cit.*, p. 62.
29. Crowder–Kellogg, NA 837.00/2627, quoted by Thomas, *op. cit.*, p. 584.
30. Quoted by Buell, 1929, *op. cit.*, pp. 42–3.
31. *El País*, 5 March 1928, 15 March 1928, cited by Thomas, *op. cit.*, p. 587.
32. *Diario de la Marina*, 4 November 1929, p. 10.
33. Luis E. Aguilar, *Cuba 1933: Prologue to Revolution* (London: Cornell University Press, 1972) p. 97.
34. Francisco Tomás, in Max Nettlau, *Reconstruir*, 15 January 1975, cited in Sam Dolgoff, *The Cuban Revolution: A Critical Perspective* (Montreal: Black Rose Books, 1976) p. 31.
35. Anselmo Lorenzo, *El Proletariado Militante* (Mexico: Ediciones Vertice), quoted by Dolgoff, *op. cit.*, p. 33.
36. *Solidaridad Gastronómica* (organ of the anarcho-syndicalist food workers' union), 15 August 1955, quoted by Dolgoff, *op. cit.*, p. 43.
37. Dolgoff, *op. cit.*, pp. 43–4.
38. Mario Riera Hernández, *Historial obrero cubano, 1574–1965* (Miami: Rema Press, 1965) p. 50; quoted by Aguilar, *op. cit.*, p. 82.
39. Some versions of the event suggest that Mella swam to the Soviet ship. In an article reprinted in *Granma* (10 January 1970), he denies this (cited by Thomas, *op. cit.*, p. 576).
40. Thomas, *op. cit.*, p. 577.
41. Lozovsky, *El movimiento sindical Latino Americano – sus virtudes y sus defectos* (1928), quoted by R. J. Alexander, *Communism in Latin America* (New Brunswick, 1957) p. 47.
42. Fabio Grobart, 'Recuerdos sobre Rubén', *Hoy*, 16 January 1964, p. 3; cited by Aguilar, *op. cit.*, p. 86.

43. Manuel Márquez Sterling, *Las conferencias del Shoreham* (Mexico City: Ediciones Botas, 1933) p. 123.
44. *Doctrina del ABC*, Publicaciones del Partido ABC, 1942, quoted by Aguilar, *op. cit.*, p. 120.
45. Aguilar, *op. cit.*, pp. 125–6.
46. *FDR Papers*, F.159, quoted by Thomas, *op. cit.*, p. 606.
47. Sumner Welles, *The Time for Decision* (New York: Harper, 1944) p. 194.
48. Pérez, *op. cit.*, p. 264.
49. Aguilar, *op. cit.*, pp. 149–50.
50. Thomas, *op. cit.*, p. 625.
51. Pérez, *op. cit.*, p. 264.
52. Thomas, *op. cit.*, p. 644.
53. Aguilar, *op. cit.*, pp. 174–5.
54. *Diario de la Marina*, 7 December 1935, quoted by Aguilar, *op. cit.*, p. 175.
55. Pérez, *op. cit.*, p. 271.
56. Pérez, *op. cit.*, p. 275.
57. Thomas, *op. cit.*, p. 734.
58. *World Bank*, p. 90, quoted by Thomas, *op. cit.*, p. 740.
59. Quoted by Martin Short, *Crime Inc.: The Story of Organised Crime* (London: Methuen, 1984) p. 68.
60. Dennis Eisenberg, Uri Dan and Eli Landau, *Meyer Lansky, Mogul of the Mob* (London: Corgi, 1979) p. 201.
61. *Ibid.*, pp. 263–4.
62. *Ibid.*, p. 265.
63. Robert Lacey, *Little Man: Meyer Lansky and the Gangster Life* (London: Century, 1991) p. 109.
64. Quoted in *ibid.*
65. Martin A. Gosch and Richard Hammer, *The Last Testament of Lucky Luciano* (Boston: Little, Brown and Company, 1974) p. 305.
66. Quoted in Eisenberg *et al.*, *op. cit.*, p. 270.
67. Quoted in Kitty Kelly, *His Way: The Unauthorised Biography of Frank Sinatra* (London: Bantam, 1987) p. 133.
68. Quoted in Eisenberg *et al.*, *op. cit.*, p. 297.
69. Interview with Joseph Varon, Meyer's lawyer, 9 June 1989, in Lacey, *op. cit.*, p. 227.
70. Lacey, *op. cit.*, p. 228.
71. Some details of the Castro family are contained in United Fruit Company records.
72. Statement (16 May 1960) of Joseph Baker of United Fruit Company to Nathaniel Weyl (*Red Star over Cuba: The Russian Assault on the Western Hemisphere*, Devin-Adair, New York, 1962, p. 41).
73. When Angel Castro died on 21 October 1956 his estate was worth half a million dollars. There are suggestions that he stole land in various ways; there were various law suits (Weyl, *op. cit.*, p. 42).
74. Ángel's daughter Juana suggested this size of workforce. *Life*, 28 August 1964, cited by Thomas, *The Cuban Revolution** (London: Weidenfeld and Nicolson, 1986) p. 19.

*See bibliographic note (p. 390).

75. Thomas, 1986, *op. cit.*, p. 19.
76. Georgie Anne Geyer, *Guerrilla Prince: The Untold Story of Fidel Castro* (London: Little, Brown and Company, 1991) p. 25.
77. Letter, quoted by Robert Merle, *Moncada, premier combat de Fidel Castro* (Paris, 1965) p. 90.
78. Interview (1959) with Carlos Franquí, editor of *Revolución*, quoted by Tad Szulc, *Fidel: A Critical Portrait* (London: Hutchinson, 1986) p. 65.
79. *Revolución*, 10 April 1961.
80. *Ibid.*, 7 March 1964; 14 March 1964.
81. Thomas, 1986, *op. cit.*, p. 25.
82. Quoted by Geyer, *op. cit.*, pp. 49–50.
83. Szulc, *op. cit.*, p. 92.
84. Szulc, *op. cit.*, p. 94.
85. See, for example, Weyl, *op. cit.*, pp. 61–5; Geyer, *op. cit.*, pp. 54–5.
86. Thomas, 1986, *op. cit.*, pp. 28–9.
87. Sources in Thomas, 1986, *op. cit.*, p. 30.
88. See, for example, Szulc, *op. cit.*, pp. 120–3.
89. Geyer, *op. cit.*, p. 85.
90. Castro, quoted by Szulc, *op. cit.*, p. 123.
91. Szulc, *op. cit.*, pp. 141–2.
92. Lee Lockwood, *Castro's Cuba: Cuba's Fidel* (New York, 1967) p. 141.
93. From Fidel Castro's mimeographed sheet, *El Acusador*, quoted by Raúl Castro, *Fundamentos* (June 1961) pp. 8–9; Thomas, 1986, *op. cit.*, p. 41.
94. Quoted by Thomas, 1986, *op. cit.*, p. 49.
95. Ruby Hart Phillips, *Cuba: Island of Paradox* ((New York: McDowell, Oblonsky, 1959) p. 268.
96. Ray Brennan, *Castro, Cuba and Justice* (New York: Doubleday, 1959) p. 25.
97. The island was placed on alert, and anyone wounded (even through road accidents) was suspected of involvement in the Moncada attack and interrogated. One innocent Santiago citizen, his arm in plaster was taken to Moncada and beaten (Merle, *op. cit.*, p. 249).
98. An attempt was made to poison Castro to prevent him appearing in court (Thomas, *op. cit.*, p. 57). While in jail Castro reconstructed *La Historia me absolverá* ('History will absolve me') from memory and smuggled the speech out bit by bit in match-boxes.
99. Carlos Franqui, *Le Livre des Douze* (*The Book of the Twelve*) (Paris: Gallimard, 1965) p. 68.
100. Geyer, *op. cit.*, p. 156.
101. Thomas, 1986, *op. cit.*, p. 115, lists fifteen survivors, but then discusses (p. 115n) in detail the various estimates of the number of men left. Was it 8, 9, 12, 15, 16 or 17 (as variously specified in different accounts)? It was 12, however, that came to occupy the central position in Cuban mythology.
102. Quoted by Thomas, 1986, *op. cit.*, p. 115.
103. Quoted by Geyer, *op. cit.*, p. 169.

Notes to Chapter 7: A New Era

1. *New York Times*, 7 October 1960.
2. Hugh Thomas, *The Cuban Revolution* (London: Weidenfeld and Nicolson, 1986) pp. 126–7.
3. Tad Szulc, *Fidel: A Critical Portrait* (London: Hutchinson, 1986) pp. 308–9.
4. Che Guevara, *Reminiscences of the Cuban Revolutionary War* (London: George Allen and Unwin, 1968) p. 54.
5. *Ibid.*, p. 65.
6. *Havana Post*, 19 January 1957.
7. *Havana Post*, 2 March 1957.
8. The 'Declaration of the Sierra Maestra' is given in Jules Dubois, *Fidel Castro – Rebel Liberator or Dictator?* (New York, 1959) pp. 162–72. The extent to which the Declaration is a *socialist* plan is debated. In February 1958, Castro indicated in an interview with Andrew St George, a US correspondent, that he had become uncertain of the need for socialist economic policies.
9. Guevara, *op. cit.*, p. 70.
10. Szulc, *op. cit.*, p. 324.
11. Carlos Prío supported the efforts of Calixto Sánchez to establish an anti-Batista guerrilla base in Oriente. The group, trying to emulate the *Granma* 'invasion', sailed in the *Corinthia* to reach Cuba on 24 May 1957. Betrayed by a peasant, 24 men were arrested and executed.
12. Szulc, *op. cit.*, pp. 336–7.
13. Gardner to Thomas, in Thomas, *op. cit.*, p. 163.
14. Szulc, *op. cit.*, p. 355.
15. Robert Daniel Murphy, *Diplomat among Warriors* (London, 1964) p. 456.
16. Thomas, *op. cit.*, p. 252.
17. *Ibid.*, p. 415.
18. Georgie Anne Geyer, *Guerrilla Prince: The Untold Story of Fidel Castro*, (London: Little, Brown & Company, 1981) p. 231.
19. Lee Lockwood, *Castro's Cuba: Cuba's Fidel* (New York, 1967) p. 186.
20. Richard Nixon, *Memoirs* (London: Arrow Books, 1978) pp. 201–3.
21. Carlos Moore, *Castro, the Blacks and Africa* (Los Angeles: Center for Afro-American Studies, University of California, 1988) p. 78.
22. *Ibid.*, pp. 78–9.
23. Harold R. Isaacs, *The New World of Negro Americans* (New York: Viking Press, 1963) p. 337.
24. Moore, *op. cit.*, p. 82.
25. There is no space here, in text or as appendix, to include this speech (given on 26 September 1960, at the 872nd meeting, Fifteenth Session of the UN General Assembly). It can be obtained (for example, from the UN Information Centre, 18 Buckingham Gate, London SW1E 6LB), and deserves to be widely read.
26. Henry Steele Commager, *New York Times Magazine*, 12 March 1967.

27. Smedly D. Butler, article in *Common Sense*, November 1935.
28. *Ibid.*
29. Claudia Furiati, *ZR Rifle: The Plot to Kill Kennedy and Castro* (Melbourne, Australia: Ocean Press, 1994) citing article, 'The Kennedy Assassination – the Nixon–Bush Connection?' by investigative journalist Paul Kangas.
30. Report of the US Senate Committee investigation into plans to assassinate foreign leaders, 1975. The Church Committee Report (Report Number 94–465).
31. Dwight D. Eisenhower, *Waging Peace: The White House Years 1956–61* London: Heinemann, 1956) p. 523.
32. *Ibid.*
33. *Ibid.*, p. 533.
34. Peter Wyden, *Bay of Pigs* (London: Jonathan Cape, 1979) p. 100.
35. Quoted in Szulc, *op. cit.*, p. 439.
36. Szulc, *op. cit.*, pp. 440–1.
37. Quoted by Moore, *op. cit.*, pp. 111–12.
38. Herbert L. Matthews, *Castro: A Political Biography* (London: Allen Lane, 1969) p. 181.
39. Arthur M. Schlesinger, Jr, *A Thousand Days: John F. Kennedy in the White House* (Boston: Houghton Mifflin, 1965) p. 293.
40. *New York Times*, 23 October 1959.
41. Facts on File, *Cuba, the US and Russia 1960–63* (New York, 1964) pp. 7–8; *New York Times*, 19, 20 February 1960; 22 March 1960.
42. John H. Davis, *The Kennedys: Dynasty and Disaster* (New York: SPI Books/Shapolsky, 1992) p. 394.
43. Furiati, *op. cit.*, p. 42.
44. Facts on File, *op. cit.*; Taylor Branch and George Crile III, 'The Kennedy Vendetta', *Harper's Magazine*, New York, August 1975, pp. 49–63; *New York Times*, 24 August 1962; 21 March 1963; *Washington Post*, 1 June 1966; 30 September 1966.
45. Victor Marchetti and John D. Marks, *The CIA and the Cult of Intelligence* (London: Jonathan Cape, 1974) pp. 53–4.
46. Noam Chomsky, 'International Terrorism: Image and Reality', in Alexander George (ed.), *Western State Terrorism* (Cambridge, England: Polity Press, 1991) p. 22.
47. *Washington Post*, 14 February 1975.
48. Branch and Crile, *op. cit.*, p. 52.
49. *Ibid.*
50. *Washington Post*, 21 March 1977.
51. Warren Hinckle and William W. Turner, *The Fish is Red: The Story of the Secret War against Castro* (New York: Harper and Row, 1981) p. 293.
52. *San Francisco Chronicle*, 10 January 1977.
53. *Washington Post*, 16 September 1977.
54. Chomsky, *op. cit.*, p. 23.
55. *Ibid.*
56. R. Dugger, *On Reagan* (New York: McGraw-Hill, 1983) p. 360.
57. *Ibid.*
58. Nixon, *op. cit.*, p. 234.

59. Roger Ricardo, *Guantánamo: The Bay of Discord* (Melbourne, Australia: Ocean Press, 1994) pp. 25–6.
60. Gustavus Myers, *History of the Great American Fortunes* (New York: Random House, 1937).
61. Dennis Eisenberg, Uri Dan and Eli Landau, *Meyer Lansky* (London: Corgi, 1979) pp. 130–1.
62. Martin A. Gosch and Richard Hammer, *The Last Testament of Lucky Luciano* (Boston: Little, Brown and Company, 1975) pp. 82–3.
63. Michael Milan, *The Squad: The US Government's Secret Alliance with Organised Crime* (London: Prio, Multimedia Books, 1989).
64. Castro quickly closed all the mafia-run casinos, opened some for a time (following a protest by unemployed croupiers), and then closed them all for good.
65. William Scott Malone, 'The Secret Life of Jack Ruby', *New York Times*, 23 January 1978.
66. '*Alleged Assassination Plots Involving Foreign Leaders*', Report Number 94–465 (Church Committee Report), 1975, p. 93.
67. *Ibid.*, p. 72.
68. Jim Hougan, *Spooks: The Private Use of Secret Agents* (London: W. H. Allen, 1979) pp. 332–3.
69. Dan E. Moldea, *The Hoffa Wars: Teamsters, Rebels, Politicians and the Mob* (New York: Paddington Press, 1978) p. 127.
70. Church Committee Report, *op. cit.*, p. 74.
71. *Time*, 9 June 1975.
72. Church Committee Report, *op. cit.*, p. 97.
73. Hougan, *op. cit.*, p. 339.
74. Davis, *op. cit.*, p. 495.
75. *Ibid.*
76. Alfred W. McCoy, *The Politics of Heroin: CIA Complicity in the Global Drug Trade* (New York: Lawrence Hill Books, 1991).
77. Davis, *op. cit.*, p. 497.
78. See David E. Scheim, *The Mafia Killed President Kennedy* (London: W. H. Allen, 1988) chs 22 and 23 for comprehensive details of Nixon's and Reagan's Mafia connections.
79. Arthur M. Schlesinger, Jr, *The Imperial Presidency* (Boston: Houghton Mifflin, 1973) p. 379.
80. Ricardo, *op. cit.*, pp. 26–7.
81. Report partially declassified in 1989, quoted in Jane Franklin, *The Cuban Revolution and the United States* (Melbourne, Australia: Ocean Press, 1992) pp. 49–50.
82. Report partially declassified in 1989, quoted in Franklin, *ibid.*, p. 51.
83. Schlesinger, 1965, *op. cit.*, p. 799.
84. Richard Rovere, 'Washington Letter', *New Yorker*, 10 October 1962.
85. Tapes of part of the discussions made public at the John F. Kennedy Library, Boston, 1983, quoted in Franklin, *op. cit.*, p. 57.
86. Schlesinger, 1965, *op. cit.*, p. 813.
87. Fidel Castro, interview with Claude Julien, published in *Le Monde*, 22 and 23 March 1963.

88. These efforts are described in Bertrand Russel, *Unarmed Victory* (London: Penguin Books, 1963) pp. 18–63. It is of interest that Che Guevara, in 1967 desperately fighting for survival in the jungles and mountains of Bolivia, observes (21 March) that he 'must write letters to Sartre and Russell, so that they can organize an international fund to raise money for the Bolivian liberation movement'; and (29 April) decodes a message asking him to authorise the use of his signature in support of Russell's campaign against the Vietnam War (Ernesto 'Che' Guevara, *Bolivian Diary* (London: Jonathan Cape, 1968) pp. 65, 87).
89. *Ibid.*, p. 45.
90. Geyer, *op. cit.*, p. 3.
91. *Ibid.*, p. 4.
92. Gabriel García Márquez, 'Operation Charlotte', *Liberation*, 27 January 1977.
93. Franqui, interview with Moore, *op. cit.*, p. 178.
94. David Ottaway and Marina Ottaway, *Algeria: The Politics of a Socialist Revolution* (Berkeley, Los Angeles: University of California Press, 1970) p. 166.
95. Moore, *op. cit.*, p. 179.
96. Reprinted in Fidel Castro and Ernesto Che Guevara, *To Speak the Truth* (New York: Pathfinder, 1992) pp. 123–42.
97. Moore, *op. cit.*, p. 203.
98. Moore, *op. cit.*, p. 225.
99. Geyer, *op. cit.*, p. 3.
100. Louis A. Pérez, *Cuba: Between Reform and Revolution* (New York: Oxford University Press, 1988) p. 300.
101. *Ibid.*, pp. 302–3.
102. *Ibid.*, p. 304.
103. Quoted by Pérez, *op. cit.*, p. 305.
104. Matthews, *op. cit.*, p. 223.
105. Matthews, *op. cit.*, p. 234.
106. Here I cannot outline the full scope of the reforms. Interesting and accessible accounts are given in Jean Stubbs, *Cuba: The Test of Time* (London: Latin American Bureau, 1989); John Griffiths and Peter Griffiths, *Cuba: the Second Decade* (London: Writers and Readers Publishing Cooperative, 1979); Gil Green, *Cuba: The Continuing Revolution* (New York: International Publishers, 1983); Karen Wald, *Children of Che: Childcare and Education in Cuba* (Palo Alto, California: Ramparts Press, 1978).
107. The character of the pre-Arbenz dictatorship of General Jorge Ubico and the subsequent CIA-sponsored *coup* against Arbenz is well described in Stephen Schlesinger and Stephen Kinzer, *Bitter Fruit: The Untold Story of the American Coup in Guatemala* (London: Sinclair Browne, 1982).
108. See, for example, the account in William Blum, *The CIA: A Forgotten History* (London: Zed Books, 1986) pp. 260–72.
109. Duncan M. Earle, 'Mayas aiding Mayas: Guatemalan refugees in Chiapas, Mexico', in Robert M. Carmack (ed.), *Harvest of Violence: The Maya Indians and the Guatemalan Crisis* (Norman: University of Oklahoma Press, 1988) pp. 263, 269.

110. Quoted in David E. Stannard, *American Holocaust: Columbus and the Conquest of the New World* (New York: Oxford University Press, 1992) p. xiv.

111. See, for example, Robinson Rojas Sandford, *The Murder of Allende, and the End of the Chilean Way to Socialism* (New York: Harper and Row, 1976).

112. Jonathan Freedland, 'CIA "toppled PM of British Guiana"', *The Guardian*, London, 31 October 1994.

113. Harold Pinter, 'Archbishop Romero's ghost can be avenged', *The Observer*, London, 28 March 1993.

114. A CIA manual, *Psychological Operations in Guerrilla War*, made available to the contras, included a section headed 'implicit and explicit terror'.

115. Martha Gellhorn, 'The Invasion of Panama', *Granta 32* (London: Penguin Books, 1990); see also John Weeks and Phil Gunson, *Panama: Made in the USA* (London: Latin American Bureau, 1981).

116. Phil Davison, 'Death squads in El Salvador on prowl again', *The Independent*, London, 11 November 1993; Phil Gunson, 'Death squads still cast shadow over El Salvador', *The Guardian*, London, 2 June 1994.

117. Christine Toomey, 'Panic sweeps Sewer City', *The Sunday Times*, London, 31 July 1994; Tracey Wilkinson, 'Guatemalans bury the dead, but not the fear', *The Guardian*, London, 6 January 1995.

118. Hugh O'Shaughnessy, 'Nicaragua vies with Haiti as West's nightmare', *The Observer*, London, 12 September 1993; Michael Reid, 'Nicaraguan troops quell uprising', *The Guardian*, London, 23 July 1993.

Bibliography

Abbot, Elizabeth, *Haiti: The Duvaliers and their Legacy* (London: Robert Hale, 1991).

Aguilar, Luis E., *Cuba 1933: Prologue to Revolution* (London: Cornell University Press, 1972).

Aimes, Hubert S. H., *A History of Slavery in Cuba, 1511–1868* (New York: 1907).

Alexander, R. J., *Communism in Latin America* (New Brunswick, 1957).

Allen, A. H., *Great Britain and the United States: A History of Anglo-American Relations (1783–1952)* (London: Odhams, 1954).

Allen, Benjamin, *A Story of the Growth of E. Atkins and Company and the Sugar Industry of Cuba* (New York, 1925).

Andrew Kenneth R., *The Spanish Caribbean: Trade and Plunder 1530–1630* (New Haven: Yale University Press, 1978).

Atkins, Edwin F., *Sixty Years in Cuba* (Cambridge, Mass., 1926).

Atkins, John Black, *The War in Cuba* (London, 1899).

Augier, F. R., Gordon, S. C., Hall, D. G, and Reckord, M., *The Making of the West Indies* (London: Longman, 1961).

Barraclough, Geoffrey, *An Introduction to Contemporary History* (London: Penguin Books, 1967).

Beckles, Hilary and Shepherd, Verene (eds), *Caribbean Slave Society and Economy* (New York: New Press, 1991).

Bishop, J. B., *Theodore Roosevelt and His Time* (New York, 1920).

Bleyer, Willard Grosvenor, *Main Current in the History of American Journalism* (Boston, 1927).

Blum, William, *The CIA: A Forgotten History* (London: Zed Books, 1986).

Brennan, Ray, *Castro, Cuba and Justice* (New York: Doubleday, 1959).

Buell, R. Leslie, *Cuba and the Platt Amendment* (New York: Foreign Policy Association, April 1929).

Buell, R. Leslie, *The Caribbean Situation* (New York: Foreign Policy Association, 21 June 1933).

Burns, Alan, *History of the British West Indies* (London: George Allen and Unwin, 1954).

Carmack, Robert M. (ed.), *Harvest of Violence: the Maya Indians and the Guatemalan Crisis* (Norman: University of Oklahoma Press, 1988).

Castro, Fidel, *In Defense of Socialism, Four Speeches on the 30th Anniversary of the Cuban Revolution* (New York: Pathfinder, 1989).

Castro, Fidel, *The World Crisis: Its Economic and Social Impact on the Underdeveloped Countries* (London: Zed Books, 1984).

Castro, Fidel, and Guevara, Ernesto Che, *To Speak the Truth* (New York: Pathfinder, 1992).

Columbus, Christopher, *Journal of the First Voyage (Diario del primer viaje), 1492*, edited and translated (with Introduction and Notes) by B. W. Ife (Warminster, England: Aris and Phillips, 1990).

Davis, John H., *The Kennedys: Dynasty and Disaster* (New York: SPI Books/Shapolsky, 1992).

Degler, Carl N., *Out of our Past: The Forces that Shaped Modern America* (New York: Harper and Row, 1970).

Detzer, David, *The Brink: The Cuban Missile Crisis of 1962* (London: Dent, 1972).

Diaz, Bernal, *The Conquest of New Spain*, translated and with an Introduction by J. M. Cohen (London: Penguin Books, 1963).

Dolgoff, Sam, *The Cuban Revolution: A Critical Perspective* (Montreal: Black Rose Books, 1976).

Domínguez, Jorge I., *Cuba: Order and Revolution* (Cambridge, Mass.: Belknap Press, Harvard University Press, 1978).

Dubois, Jules, *Fidel Castro – Rebel Liberator or Dictator* (New York, 1959).

Dugger, R., *On Reagan* (New York: McGraw Hill, 1983).

Eisenberg, Dennis, Dan, Uri and Landau, Eli, *Meyer Lansky, Mogul of the Mob* (London: Corgi, 1979).

Eisenhower, Dwight D., *Waging Peace: The White House Years 1956–61* (London: Heinemann, 1956).

Ettinger, Amos, *The Mission to Spain of Pierre Soulé, 1853–1855* (London, 1932).

Fernández-Arnesto, Felipe, *Columbus* (Oxford, England: Oxford University Press, 1992).

Fidel and Religion, Castro talks on revolution and religion with Frei Betto (New York: Simon and Schuster, 1987).

Fitzgibbon, Russel H., *Cuba and the United States: 1900–1935* (Menasha, Wisconsin, 1935).

Foner, Philip S., *A History of Cuba and its Relations with the United States,* vol. I, *1492–1845* (New York: International Publishers, 1962).

Foner, Philip S., *A History of Cuba and its Relations with the United States,* vol. II, *1845–1895* (New York: International Publishers, 1963).

Franklin, John Hope, *From Slavery to Freedom: A History of Negro Americans* (New York: Alfred A. Knopf, 1947).

Franklin, Jane, *The Cuban Revolution and the United States: A Chronological History* (Melbourne, Australia: Ocean Press, 1992).

Furiata, Claudia, *ZR Rifle: The Plot to Kill Kennedy and Castro* (Melbourne, Australia: Ocean Press, 1994).

George, Alexander (ed.), *Western State Terrorism* (Cambridge, England: Polity Press, 1991).

Geyer, Georgie Anne, *Guerrilla Prince: The Untold Story of Fidel Castro* (London: Little, Brown and Company, 1991).

Gosch, Martin A. and Hammer, Richard, *The Last Testament of Lucky Luciano* (Boston: Little, Brown and Company, 1975).

Green, Gil, *Cuba: The Continuing Revolution* (New York: International Publishers, 1993).

Griffiths, John and Griffiths, Peter, *Cuba: The Second Decade* (London: Writers and Readers Publishing Cooperative, 1979).

Guevara, Ernesto Che, *Bolivian Diary* (London: Jonathan Cape, 1968).

Guevara, Ernesto Che, *Reminiscences of the Cuban Revolutionary War* (London: George Allen and Unwin, 1968).

Gunson, Phil, *Panama: Made in the US* (London: Latin American Bureau, 1981).

Hagedorn, Herman, *Leonard Wood* (New York, 1931).

Haring, Clarence Henry, *The Spanish Empire in America* (New York: Oxford University Press, 1947).

Harrington, M. R., *Cuba Before Columbus* (New York: Museum of the American Indian, Heye Foundation, 1921).

Healy, David F., *The United States in Cuba, 1989–1902; Generals, Politicians and the Search for a Policy* (University of Wisconsin Press, 1963).

Hinckle, Warren and Turner, William W., *The Fish is Red: The Story of the Secret War against Castro* (New York: Harper and Row, 1981).

Hougan, Jim, *Spooks: The Private Use of Secret Agents* (London: W. H. Allen, 1979).

Howarth, Stephen, *To Shining Sea: A History of the United States Navy 1775–1991* (London: Weidenfeld and Nicolson, 1991).

Humboldt, Alexander, *The Island of Cuba*, translated by J. S. Thrasher (New York, 1856).

Isaacs, Harold R., *The New World of Negro Americans* (New York: Viking Press, 1963).

Jameson, Robert Francis, *Letters from the Havana during the Year 1820* (London: John Miller, 1821).

Jenks, Leland Hamilton, *Our Cuban Colony: A Study in Sugar* (New York: Arno Press and New York Times, 1970).

Johnson, Willis Fletcher, *The History of Cuba* (New York, 1920).

Josephson, Matthew, *The Robber Barons, the Great American Capitalists, 1861–1901* (London: Eyre and Spottiswoode, 1962).

Kahl, Joachim, *The Misery of Christianity* (London: Penguin Books, 1971).

Klein, Herber S., *Slavery in the Americas: A Comparative Study of Cuba and Virginia* (London: Oxford University Press, 1967).

Lacey, Robert, *Little Man: Meyer Lansky and the Gangster Life* (London: Century, 1991).

Lockwood, Lee, *Castro's Cuba, Cuba's Fidel* (New York, 1967).

Madden, R. R., *The Island of Cuba* (London, 1851).

Mañarch, Jorge, *Martí, Apostle of Freedom*, translated by Coley Taylor (New York, 1950).

Marchetti, Victor and Marks, John D., *The CIA and the Cult of Intelligence* (London: Jonathan Cape, 1974).

Matthews, Herbert L., *Castro: A Political Biography* (London: Allen Lane, 1969).

McCoy, Alfred W., *The Politics of Heroin: CIA Complicity in the Global Drug Trade* (New York: Lawrence Hill Books, 1991).

Milan, Michael, *The Squad: The US Government's Secret Alliance with Organised Crime* (London: Prio, Multimedia Books, 1989).

Molden, Dan E., *The Hoffa Wars: Teamsters, Rebels, Politicians and the Mob* (New York: Paddington Press, 1978).

Montejo, Esteban, *Autobiography of a Runaway Slave*, transcribed by Miguel Barnet (London, 1968).

Moore, Carlos, *Castro, the Blacks and Africa* (Los Angeles: Center for Afro-American Studies, University of California, 1988).

Morris, Edmund, *The Rise of Theodore Roosevelt* (London: Collins, 1979).

Munro, Dana, *Intervention and Dollar Diplomacy* (Princeton: 1964).

Murphy, Robert Daniel, *Diplomat among Warriors* (London: 1964).

Myers, Gustavus, *History of the Great American Fortunes* (New York: Random House, 1937).

Nearing, Scott and Freeman, Joseph, *Dollar Diplomacy: A Study in American Imperialism* (New York: Monthly Review Press, 1925).

Nevins, Allan and Commager, Henry Steele, *A Pocket History of the United States* (New York: Washington Square Press, 1962).

Nixon, Richard, *Memoirs* (London: Arrow Books, 1978).

O'Kelly J. J., *The Mambi-Land, or, Adventures of a Herald Correspondent in Cuba* (London and Philadelphia, 1874).

O'Toole, G. J. A., *The Spanish War: An American Epic, 1898* (New York: Norton, 1984).

Pérez, Louis A., *Cuba: Between Reform and Revolution* (New York: Oxford University Press, 1988).

Phillips, Ruby Hart, *Cuba: Island of Paradox* (New York: McDowell, Oblonsky, 1959).

Phillips, William D., *Slavery from Roman Times to the Early Transatlantic Trade* (Manchester, England: Manchester University Press, 1985).

Prescott, William H., *History of the Conquest of Mexico* (London: Routledge, 1898).

Pringle, H. F., *Theodore Roosevelt* (London, 1932).

Rae, John B. and Mahoney, H. D., *The United States in World History* (New York: McGraw Hill, 1964).

Ricardo, Roger, *Guantánamo: The Bay of Discord* (Melbourne, Australia: Ocean Press, 1994).

Rippy, J. F., *Rivalry of the United States and Great Britain over Latin America, 1808–1830* (Baltimore, 1929).

Rochester, Anne, *Rulers of America* (London: Lawrence and Wishart, 1936).

Rout, Leslie B., *The African Experience in Latin America* (London: Cambridge University Press, 1976).

Rubens, Horatio Seymour, *Liberty: The Story of Cuba* (New York: 1932).

Russell, Bertrand, *Unarmed Victory* (London: Penguin Books, 1963).

Sandford, Robin Rojas, *The Murder of Allende, and the End of the Chilean Way to Socialism* (New York: Harper and Row, 1976).

Sauer, Carl Ortwin, *The Early Spanish Main* (Berkeley, Los Angeles: University of California Press, 1966).

Scheer, Robert and Zeitlin, Maurice, *Cuba: An American Tragedy* (London: Penguin Books, 1964).

Scheim, David E., *The Mafia Killed President Kennedy* (London: W. H. Allen, 1988).

Schlesinger, Arthur M., Jr, *A Thousand Days: John F. Kennedy in the White House* (Boston: Houghton Mifflin, 1965).

Schlesinger, Arthur M., Jr, *The Imperial Presidency* (Boston: Houghton Mifflin, 1973).

Schlesinger, Stephen and Kinzer, Stephen, *Bitter Fruit: The Untold Story of the American Coup in Guatemala* (London: Sinclair Brown, 1982).

Sears, Louis Martin, *A History of American Foreign Relations* (London: Macmillan, 1928).

Severo, Richard and Milford, Lewis, *Wages of War: When America's Soldiers Came Home* (New York: Simon and Schuster, 1990).

Short, Martin, *Crime Inc.: The Story of Organised Crime* (London: Methuen, 1984).

Smith, Robert F., *The United States and Cuba: Business and Diplomacy, 1917–1960* (New Haven: 1960).

Stannard, David E., *American Holocaust: Columbus and the Conquest of the New World* (New York: Oxford University Press, 1992).

Stubbs, Jean, *Cuba: The Test of Time* (London: Latin American Bureau, 1989).

Szulc, Tad, *Fidel: A Critical Portrait* (London: Hutchinson, 1986).

Tablada, Carlos, *Che Guevara, Economics and Politics in the Transition to Socialism* (New York: Pathfinder, 1990).

The Voyage of Christopher Columbus: Columbus' Own Journal of Discovery Newly Restored and Translated, translated and with Introduction by John Cummins (London: Weidenfeld and Nicolson, 1992).

Thomas, Hugh, *Cuba, or The Pursuit of Freedom** (London: Eyre and Spottiswoode, 1971).

Thomas, Hugh, *The Cuban Revolution* (London: Weidenfeld and Nicolson, 1986).

Turnbull, David, *Travels in West Cuba: with Notices of Porto Rico, and the Slave Trade* (London, 1840).

Turton, Peter, *José Martí, Architect of Cuba's Freedom* (London: Zed Books, 1986).

Wald, Karen, *Children of Che: Childcare and Education in Cuba* (Palo Alto, California: Ramparts Press, 1978).

Walvin, James, *Black Ivory: A History of British Slavery* (London: HarperCollins, 1970).

Welles, Sumner, *The Time for Decision* (New York: Harper, 1944).

Westermarck, Edward, *Christianity and Morals* (London: Kegan Paul, French, Trubner & Co., 1939).

Weyl, Nathaniel, *Red Star Over Cuba: The Russian Assault on the Western Hemisphere* (New York: Devin-Adair, 1962).

Williams, Eric, *From Columbus to Castro: The History of the Caribbean 1492-1969* (London: André Deutsche, 1970).

Wisan, Joseph E., *The Cuban Crisis as Reflected in the New York Press 1895-1898* (New York: Octagon Books, 1977).

Wright, Irene Aloha, *The Early History of Cuba, 1492-1586* (New York: Macmillan, 1916).

Wurdemann, J. G. F., *Notes on Cuba* (Boston: James Monroe, 1844).

Wyden, Peter, *Bay of Pigs* (London: Jonathan Cape, 1979).

Zinn, Howard, *A People's History of the United States* (London: Longman, 1980).

---

* The second half of this epic history is reprinted as *The Cuban Revolution*. Since I used both editions, not least because the 1696-page *Cuba, or The Pursuit of Freedom* is very cumbersome, I have included both these titles in references and bibliography.

Index

ABC Organisation 245, 247–8, 249, 250
ABC Radical 248, 249
Aberdeen, Lord 124
abolition (of slavery), abolitionists 99, 102, 116, 118, 120, 121–2, 123–7, 137, 145–6, 150, 151, 154, 155, 171, 172, 178
Abourezk, James 10
Abrams, Elliot 330
Accardo, Tony 261
Adams, John (1735–1826) 168
Adams, John Quincy (1767–1848) 168
adelantado (border lord) 102, 103–104
Ad extirpanda (papal bull) 74
Adonis, Joe 261, 262
Afghanistan 317, 331
Africa 31, 50, 54, 74, 75, 289, 290, 317–19, 320–1
  see also individual countries
'Africanisation' (of Cuba) 125
Afro-Asian Peoples Solidarity Organisation (AAPSO) 320
Agadir 75
Agramonte, Aristídes 230
Agramonte, Ignacio 141, 143, 146, 147, 153
Agramonte, Roberto 271
Agricultural Production Cooperatives (CPAs) 23
agriculture 23, 43–4, 54–5, 66, 68, 94, 107, 108, 109, 111, 112, 161, 220–1, 326
  see also sugar; tobacco
Agrupación Comunista 242, 243
Agrupación Socialista of Havana 242
Aguero y Velazio, Francisco de 138, 139
Aguilera, Francisco Vicente 140
AIDS 31, 43
  see also disease

Alarcón, Ricardo 18
Alaska Purchase (1867) 182
Albania 58
Albert the Great 97
Aldama, Miguel 141
Alession, John 308
Alexander, Bill 11
Alexander VI (Pope) 74, 98
Alfa-Laval (Sweden) 18, 38
Alfonso VIII 72
Alger, Russell A. 196, 200–2
Algeria 54, 317, 318
Algiers 317, 318, 319
Allende, Salvador 328, 329, 335
Almeida, Juan 272–3, 289–90, 295
Almohads 72
Almoravids 72
Alonso de Ávila 88
Alphonsus (of Portugal) 75
Alvarado, Pedro de 88
Alvarez Chanca, Diego 68
Alvarez Tabío, Pedro 283
Amadeo, Don (King) 146
Amador de Lares 89
American and Foreign Anti-Slavery Society 150
American Civil Liberties Committee (ACLC) 12
American Electric Bond and Share Company 233, 253
American Molasses Company 246
American Public Health Association (APHA) 15–16, 27
American Society of Newspaper Editors (ASNE) 287
American Sugar Refining Company 177, 178, 188, 220, 226
Americas 74, 77, 80, 90, 102, 104, 105, 155, 184
  see also Caribbean; *and under individual countries*
Amistad funesta (novel) 156